REFLECTIONS/ REFRACTIONS

Self-Portraiture in the Twentieth Century

EDITED BY
WENDY WICK REAVES

WITH CONTRIBUTIONS BY
WENDY WICK REAVES
ANNE COLLINS GOODYEAR
ANN PRENTICE WAGNER
EMILY CAPLAN REED

Published in cooperation with

ROWMAN & LITTLEFIELD PUBLISHERS, INC.

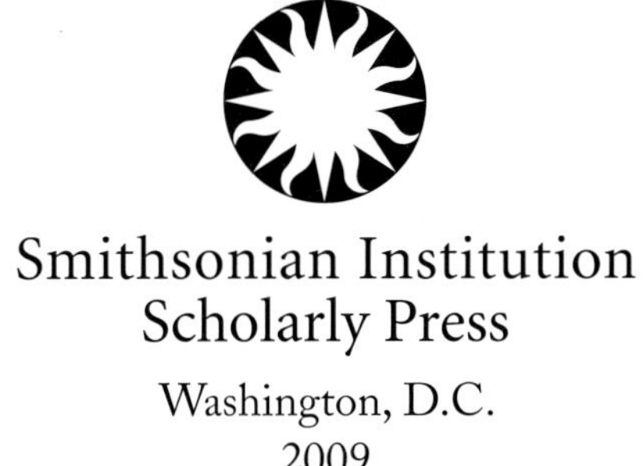

Smithsonian Institution
Scholarly Press
Washington, D.C.
2009

Published to accompany an exhibition at the
National Portrait Gallery, Smithsonian Institution
April 10–August 16, 2009

This exhibition is supported by the Marc Pachter Exhibition Fund.

Published by SMITHSONIAN INSTITUTION SCHOLARLY PRESS

P.O. Box 37012, MRC 957
Washington, D.C. 20013-7012
www.scholarlypress.si.edu

In cooperation with
ROWMAN & LITTLEFIELD PUBLISHERS, INC.

A wholly owned subsidiary of The Rowman & Littlefield Publishing Group, Inc.
4501 Forbes Boulevard, Suite 200, Lanham, Maryland 20706
www.rowmanlittlefield.com

Estover Road
Plymouth PL6 7PY
United Kingdom

Front cover: Alexander Calder self-portrait, ink on paper, c. 1960. National Portrait Gallery, Smithsonian Institution; the Ruth Bowman and Harry Kahn Twentieth-Century American Self-Portrait Collection (Cat. 38). © 2009 Calder Foundation/Artists Rights Society (ARS), New York/ADAGP Paris

Back cover: Louise Nevelson self-portrait, ink and watercolor on paper, c. 1938. National Portrait Gallery, Smithsonian Institution; the Ruth Bowman and Harry Kahn Twentieth-Century American Self-Portrait Collection (Cat. 28). © 2009 Estate of Louise Nevelson/Artists Rights Society (ARS), New York/ADAGP Paris

British Library Cataloguing in Publication Information Available

Library of Congress Cataloging-in-Publication Data:
Reflections/refractions : self-portraiture in the twentieth century / edited by Wendy Wick Reaves.
p. cm.
Includes bibliographical references and index.
ISBN-13: 978-0-9788460-2-2 (cloth : alk. paper)
ISBN-10: 0-9788460-2-8 (cloth : alk. paper)
1. Self-portraits, American—20th century. I. Reaves, Wendy Wick, 1950–
N7619.R44 2009
704.9'420904—dc22 2008042327

Printed in Canada

∞™ The paper used in this publication meets the minimum requirements of American National Standard for Information Sciences—Permanence of Paper for Printed Library Materials, ANSI/NISO Z39.48-1992.

CONTENTS

FOREWORD

SELF-PORTRAITS loom large in the National Portrait Gallery's collection. Even before the addition of the 187 twentieth-century self-portraits from the collection of Ruth Bowman and Harry Kahn, the museum possessed more than 300 self-portraits. This impressive figure does not rival the institution's presidential holdings: more than 1,350 paintings, sculptures, prints, drawings, and photographs capture the lives of those Americans who have occupied this prestigious position. Nevertheless, it reflects the commanding place self-portraits occupy in the Portrait Gallery's constellation of sitters, paying tribute to the role that artists have played in shaping our nation's culture.

As Wendy Wick Reaves, curator of prints and drawings at the National Portrait Gallery and curator of Reflections/Refractions, has noted in her illuminating essay, artists gravitate to self-portraits because the sitter is willing, constantly available, and—with rare exception—amiable about the process. One can see another benefit as well. Neither the sitter nor the patron—two other individuals usually involved in the making of a portrait—is going to be uncomfortable with artistic experimentation. For this reason, if for no other, it is often in self-portraits that one can find images that are the most stylistically advanced for their time.

The first self-portrait to enter the National Portrait Gallery collection was by George Fuller (1822–1884). No longer a household name, Fuller lived his adult life in Deerfield, Massachusetts, and was active and important in Boston and New York art circles. He was known primarily for his dreamy, tonalist landscapes. His portrait, created about 1860, came to the museum in 1965, three years after the institution was chartered by Congress and three years before it officially opened to the public. A modest image, its provenance tells a great deal about the early acquisition history of the Portrait Gallery, for it came to the museum as a transfer from the National Gallery of Art, where it had originally been donated by the widow of painter Augustus Vincent Tack. It was part of a group of approximately fifty portraits that National Gallery founder Andrew Mellon assembled with the intention of donating them to a National Portrait Gallery, should one be formed.

The earliest self-portrait in the Portrait Gallery's collection is that of the artist Matthew Pratt (1734–1805). Born in Philadelphia, Pratt perfected his trade while studying in London with the American expatriate Benjamin West. The museum acquired this portrait, made in London in 1764, in 1969. It thus predates by nearly two decades the self-portrait of John Singleton Copley, who likewise left America to study with the renowned Benjamin West. Although quite different in format—Pratt depicted himself as a half-length figure, Copley focused primarily on his head—both images convey the self-satisfaction and exuberance of a young artist who knows he is in the right place at the right time to further his career.

One could argue that the Portrait Gallery's most beloved self-portrait is the small watercolor by Mary Cassatt (1844–1926), done about 1880, just as this artist from Pennsylvania was becoming well ensconced in the Parisian art world. One could argue, too, that the prize for the most notorious self-portrait would go to Alice Neel (1900–1984) (see fig. 2-7). Depicting herself nude, she paints without apology all that time and gravity has done to her eighty-year-old figure.

In her preface to the catalog, Reaves pays homage to Ruth Bowman and Harry Kahn for the energy, intelligence, and enthusiasm that these two gave to the process of collecting, and acknowledges the importance of this collection to the National Portrait Gallery. I would like to add my thanks and admiration as well. In addition, I would like to acknowledge Reaves's own energy, intelligence, and enthusiasm in bringing this collection to the National Portrait Gallery and persuading our Commission—the ultimate arbiters of what the museum acquires—of the collection's significance and importance. Readers of this catalog have before them a treat as they read the essays of Reaves and Anne Collins Goodyear, assistant curator of prints and drawings, who have placed the history of this collection in the greater context of self-portraiture and in the art of the twentieth century. Of equal pleasure is a visit to the exhibition, where the treasures of the twentieth-century self-portrait collection of the National Portrait Gallery, mostly gifts of Ruth Bowman and Harry Kahn, are on view.

Carolyn Kinder Carr
Deputy Director and Chief Curator
National Portrait Gallery

PREFACE

THE ARTIST Leonard Baskin, fond of acquiring rare books and prints, once called collecting "the only activity I know of that involves every one of the seven deadly sins, even sloth."[1] For those of us who collect, acknowledging the grain of truth in this statement seems an unnecessary distraction from the envying, lusting, and so on so crucial for pursuing our quest. We can, of course, see our habit in a kinder light—indeed justify that addiction—if we acquire for a museum or plan to deposit our private collection in a public institution for all to share. This book on twentieth-century self-portraiture developed through the intersection of private and institutional collecting. Along with the exhibition it documents, it also celebrates two donors, Ruth Bowman and Harry Kahn, who were always proud of the enrichment their gifts bestowed on a museum's holdings. Their generosity reminds us that pride of this sort directly contrasts with the sinful one of the deadly seven.

If a private collection truly syncs with a public one, the dynamic engagement between them can result in a new focus and expanded scholarship. Aesthetic connections are made, gaps filled, fresh areas of inquiry brought to the fore. It is this larger contribution, even more than the works themselves, that really advances a museum and benefits its audiences. The Smithsonian's National Portrait Gallery was established in 1962 without any collections, and the task of assembling the images of those "who have made significant contributions to the history, development, and culture of the people of the United States," as our congressional legislation defined it, began immediately. Although we were charged with collecting portraits of subjects from all fields of endeavor, self-portraiture was an obvious category from the beginning, and portraits of artists were, predictably, often easier to find than images of others. A decade after we opened our doors in 1968, we had already acquired significant works by John Singleton Copley, George Catlin, Alexander Calder, Mary Cassatt, Robert Rauschenberg, and many others. We had even assembled self-portrayals made by amateur artists known for other accomplishments: George Gershwin, E. E. Cummings, and John Barrymore, for example. When we started collecting photography in the 1970s, we moved rapidly toward acquiring self-portraits of leading American photographers, including Edward Steichen, Imogen Cunningham, Man Ray, Walker Evans, and Richard Avedon, among many. But although we could boast great masterpieces of self-portraiture and considered it vital to our mission, we had not had the luxury of representing this genre as thoroughly as we might. We were especially delighted, therefore, when our piece-by-piece assemblage was greatly outpaced by the single acquisition in 2002 of 187 self-portraits representing 146 artists. It started with my visit in November 1998 to a remarkable leader in the visual arts, a scholar, activist, lecturer, advisor, board member, and collector, Ruth Bowman.

Walking through the front door of Bowman's New York apartment, one was confronted by a wall of faces—including one's own. A gold-framed mirror hung mischievously in the middle of a group of artists' images, introducing the theme of self-portraiture that preoccupied this insightful collector. Over the course of about fifteen years, Bowman had assembled the collection collaboratively with her companion, the late Harry Kahn, filling her entire Upper East Side apartment with eye-catching works on paper by American artists of the twentieth century.

Born in Denver, Colorado, raised in Washington, D.C., and educated at Bryn Mawr College, Bowman had been an art educator all her life. "Talking about art," she has often said in our conversations, "is as exciting an activity as I can think of." Starting in the 1960s, this dynamic single mother of three took courses at the Institute of Fine Arts at New York University and juggled jobs at museums and galleries. She got her master's degree in 1971 and worked in various institutions, including the Jewish Museum, World House Galleries, and the New York University Art Collection. Passionate about art and skilled at sharing her insights with others, she taught art history at New York University's School of Education and became a lecturer at the Museum of Modern Art and elsewhere. After a guest appearance on WQXR radio in 1963, she started conducting regular interviews of artists for WNYC radio, including several years on their "Views on Art" radio program.

Bowman's work on radio eventually led to television. Will Barnet's 1967 portrait of her gives us a keen understanding of the captivating, telegenic personality that led to her success (fig. 1–1). From 1968 to 1974, she did artist interviews for WNYC's weekly *One to One* art program. She then taught forty-six weekly sessions of art history for CBS television's *Sunrise Semester* in 1972–1973. Before she moved to California in 1974 with her husband, R. Wallace Bowman, Ruth helped found the Grey Gallery and Art Center at NYU. In the Los Angeles area, Bowman continued her energetic schedule, working as director of education for the Los Angeles County Museum of Art, serving on advisory boards, and hosting a weekly art commentary and interview program at KUSC radio. With bicoastal dexterity, she held a Rockefeller Foundation Senior Fellowship at the Metropolitan Museum of Art. Also during this time, she spearheaded the recovery of two lost Arshile Gorky murals at the Newark airport, which resulted in the traveling exhibition "Murals without Walls: Arshile Gorky's Aviation Murals Rediscovered." Bowman contributed to the catalog for the show and produced a film. After her husband was institutionalized in 1981, following a tragic, debilitating stroke, Bowman began spending more time in New York. She has served ever since on numerous boards and advisory committees, including the Craft and Folk Art Museum in Los Angeles,

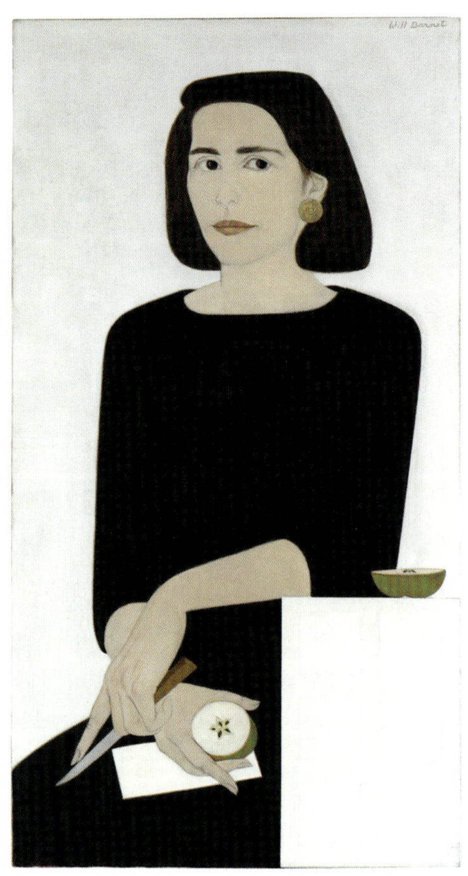

FIG. 1–1.
Ruth Bowman by Will Barnet, oil and pencil on canvas, 1967. Metropolitan Museum of Art, New York City; gift of Ruth and R. Wallace Bowman

the American Federation of the Arts, the Drawing Society, the Textile Museum, MIT List Visual Art Center, and the Archives of American Art.

Starting in 1987, Bowman and her companion, Harry Kahn, whose own spouse was felled by Alzheimer's, began collecting American self-portraits on paper. Kahn was an economist and retired investment advisor (fig. 1–2). He had earned an undergraduate degree from Harvard as well as a master's degree in public administration. After World War II, he served on the staff of the Marshall Plan Administration in Washington before going to Wall Street. Retiring in 1990 from the brokerage firm Neuberger & Berman, he became a collector, philanthropist, board member for a variety of institutions, and a long-term supporter of the Brooklyn Museum of Art. Kahn's principal interest was Asian art; the colorful contemporary works on Bowman's walls didn't intrigue him. But he did admire the wry, wiry self-portrait drawing by Alexander Calder that she owned (cat. 39).

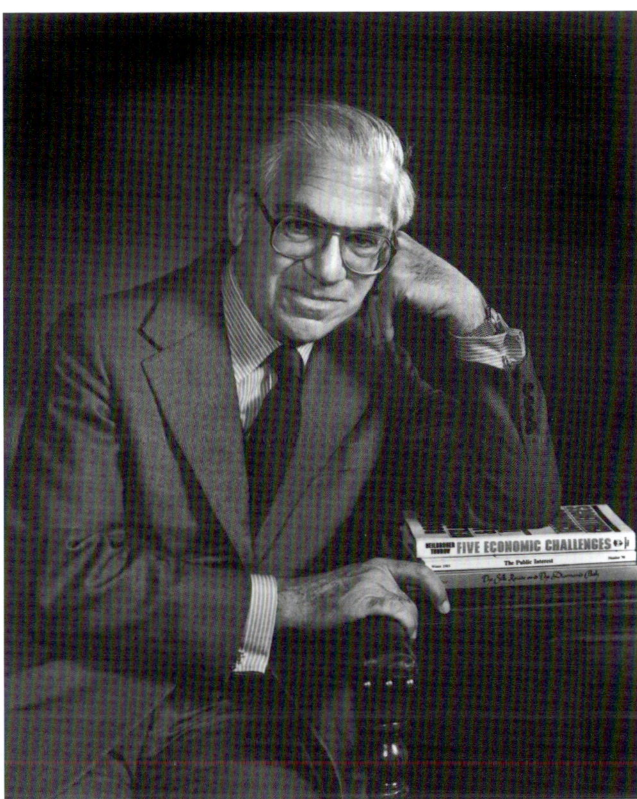

FIG. 1–2.
Harry Kahn by an unidentified photographer, 1983. Ruth Bowman

The question of how and why an artist might depict him- or herself so intrigued Bowman and Kahn that they launched a joint collecting adventure (fig. 1–3). Since Bowman was especially interested in graphic techniques and printmaking, and Kahn wanted to learn more, they focused primarily on prints and drawings and confined their search to American artists from the twentieth century. Although the collection they assembled together is diverse, unifying themes emerge. Their shared vision included an exacting aesthetic standard, an emotional intensity, and a serious commitment to technique. They bypassed intimate, informal sketches and fleeting whimsies in favor of works of rigorous self-expression and technical excellence. Many pieces might be described as monumental in size or conception.

Bowman and Kahn, both generous, civic-minded patrons of the arts, began to consider the Portrait Gallery as an appropriate repository for their thoughtfully assembled collection. Although our friendship blossomed, our plans stalled due to the sad occasion of Harry Kahn's death on August 20, 1999. But Ruth remained a delightful companion for me to join on museum visits whenever I went to New York. Not only did I learn from her deep knowledge of the art world, I always found her zest for life inspiring. We continued to talk about her collection coming to the Smithsonian, and, ultimately, in 2002, the Portrait Gallery acquired the Ruth Bowman and Harry Kahn Twentieth-Century American Self-Portrait Collection through a generous donative sale arrangement.

Since that acquisition, we have drawn upon the Bowman-Kahn collection in many ways, frequently using it as a teaching tool and incorporating individual pieces into a variety of exhibitions. But since the collection deepened and broadened our holdings in an area that has always been of vital interest to us, it seemed a good time for a closer look at the genre of self-portraiture, focusing particularly on how it was reconceptualized in the twentieth century. For the exhibition and catalog, we made a selection from the Bowman-Kahn collection. Searching for balance, diversity, and a chronological spread, we faced tough choices and regretfully had to leave out some of Bowman and Kahn's prized possessions. We also incorporated a few additional pieces from the Portrait Gallery's collection to illustrate themes or directions we wanted to represent. Although primarily works of art on paper, reflecting the nature of Bowman and Kahn's collecting interests, the group was a microcosm of self-portraiture in all the visual arts. Including such renowned names as Edward Hopper, George Grosz, Louise Bourgeois, Alexander Calder, Louise Nevelson, Hans Hofmann, Jacob Lawrence, Jim Dine, Chuck Close, David Hockney, Philip Pearlstein, Larry Rivers, and Andy Warhol, the collection represented a broad scope of twentieth-century artistic endeavor and expressed a wide range of themes and motivations for self-portraiture. In our essays, we have also illustrated paintings and photographs from the Portrait Gallery and other institutions as we assessed larger questions of self-representation during the time period.

In completing this project, we are keenly aware that one can never have the last word in a discussion of self-portraiture, which is of interest to so many, but it has been a stimulating pleasure to take part in the conversation. We hope that it inspires others to continue the focus on this very specific genre, correcting our inevitable mistakes and pushing our investigations in new directions.

This project was a team effort from the start, and we are indebted to all who contributed their time and talents. I was especially dependent on my

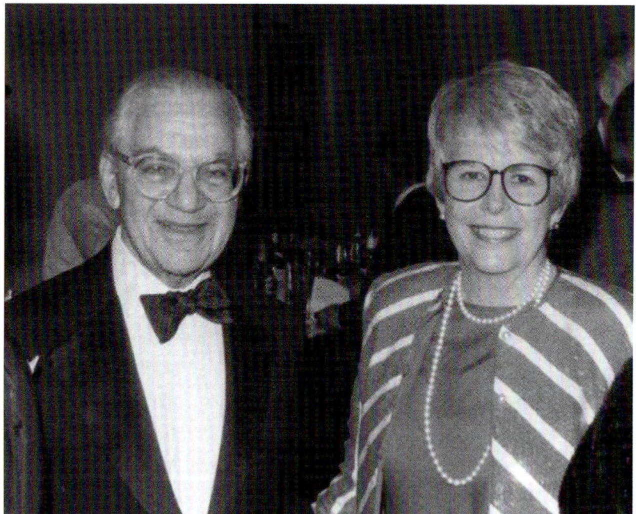

FIG. 1–3.
Harry Kahn and Ruth Bowman by Jeanne Trudeau, 1990. Ruth Bowman

cocurator, Anne Collins Goodyear, friend, colleague, and organizer supreme, who also wrote an essay and entries for this volume, as well as our extraordinary curatorial assistant, Amy Baskette, who played an invaluable role in all aspects of the undertaking, and, as always, made it more fun. Rosemary Fallon, another prized collaborator, spearheaded the conservation efforts and consulted on media questions. Working with our other catalog authors, Ann Prentice Wagner and Emily Caplan Reed, has also been a joy. Our team is indebted to many others on the Portrait Gallery staff, including our fellow curators and historians—Ellen Miles, Brandon Fortune, Ann Shumard, Frank Goodyear, Fred Voss, Sid Hart, David Ward, Amy Henderson, and Jim Barber—as well as Martin Sullivan, Carolyn Carr, Marc Pachter, Alan Fern, Beverly Cox, Nello Marconi, Al Elkins, Kristin Smith, Jennifer Robertson, Ed Myers, Lizanne Garrett, Mark Gulezian, Yvette Stickell, Marianne Gurley, and Dale Hunt. John McMahon has guided us through the logistics of collection moves with his unfailing wisdom and calm. We give a special nod to Todd Gardner, Mark Planisek, and Ann Wagner for lending their eyes and expertise in enlightening sessions of serious looking and discussions of craftsmanship. Dru Dowdy, our indefatigable head of publications, deserves our endless thanks for pulling off her usual miracles. We are also grateful to the Smithsonian Institution Scholarly Press and its partner, Rowman & Littlefield.

In the lengthy business of processing, cataloging, researching, and conserving the collection, we were launched by two crucial and much-appreciated conservation grants from the Smithsonian Women's Committee and were aided by a talented group of temporary assistants working on internships and short-term contracts, including Michelle Kung, Morgan Zinsmeister, Minah Song, Aurora Stokowski, Breanne Robertson, Molly Sciaretta, Hannah Wong, Beth Isaacson, Caroline Dickson, Emily Caplan Reed, and Maya Foo. The staffs of the Portrait Gallery library and the Archives of American Art have been extraordinarily generous and patient in assisting our research efforts. In addition we owe special thanks to June Wayne, Ruth Weisberg, Philip Pearlstein, Jackie Serwer, Betsy Anderson, Carter Foster, and Deborah Kiley Weyhe for their help with individual works of art. To other colleagues, unnamed here but enormously helpful during the long research phase of this project, please know how much we have gained from your generous contributions of time, information, and expertise. Personally, I owe unending gratitude to John Daniel Reaves for his unflagging support in this and every other effort of mine.

Caroline Tavelli, Joe Goddu, Sylvia Wolf, George Bookman, and, of course, Harry Kahn have been extraordinarily kind to us in the process of transferring the Bowman-Kahn collection into our hands. Ruth Bowman, above all, has been firmly established right at the heart of this project. She has inspired our thinking, stoked our enthusiasm, aided our research, and delighted us with her art world anecdotes. We have been blessed by her generosity, her guiding spirit, and her friendship. This book is dedicated to her.

Wendy Wick Reaves
Curator of Prints and Drawings
National Portrait Gallery

NOTE

1 Leonard Baskin, *Life,* January 24, 1964, 41.

REFLECTIONS/ REFRACTIONS

Self-Portraiture in the Twentieth Century

WENDY WICK REAVES

"ALL SELF-PORTRAITS," Ivan Albright once noted with wry humor, "have the advantage of having an available model when and where you want him. Both model and artist can rest at the same time. Conversation can be held to a minimum" (cat. 33).[1] Convenience: what a simple conceit he proposes for our understanding of self-portrayal. If you have a mirror, you have a willing model from which to practice. Many artists profess to agree with that notion. "The only sitter I could find with time for endless posing," Elaine de Kooning mentioned, "was myself."[2] Both Albright's and de Kooning's pictures, of course, convey far more than simple practice from a model. Albright, in his 1947 lithograph and related self-portrait paintings, placed himself in the center of a complex drama of mortality that addressed issues of motion, growth, decay, and the passage of time. And the twenty-eight-year-old de Kooning, in her 1946 oil (fig. 2-1), depicts herself in her artist's smock surrounded with carefully considered domestic objects. With her direct, forceful glance, she quietly challenges the masculine trope of the painter in an undomesticated studio space,[3] integrating her personal and professional selves with wary assurance.

Despite the evidence, we are tempted to think that the self-portrait should be a relatively simple form to understand; after all, we do not have to

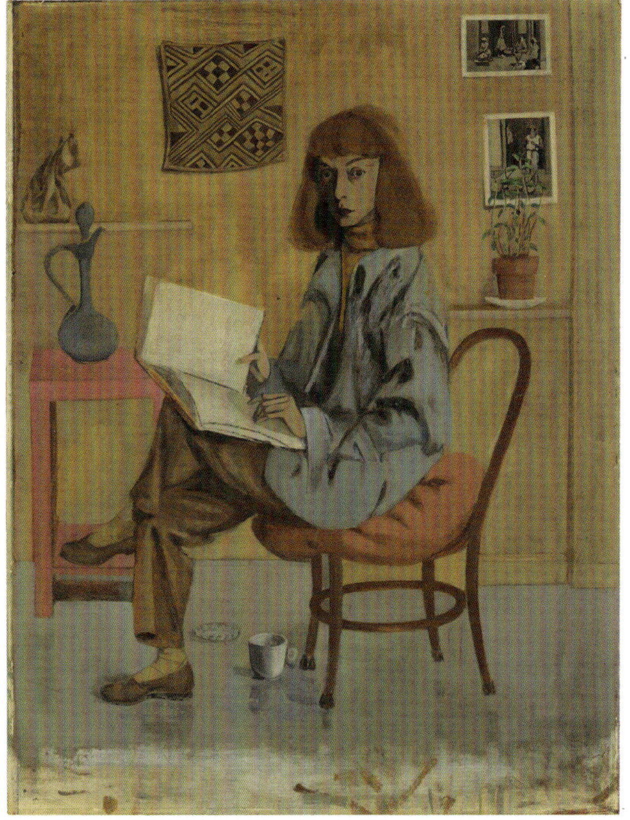

FIG. 2–1.
Elaine de Kooning (1918–1989), self-portrait, oil on Masonite, 1946. National Portrait Gallery, Smithsonian Institution

consider the intersection between artist and sitter that often raises unanswerable questions for the third-party viewer. But the self-portrait carries freighted expectations that images made of others do not, and twentieth-century artists grappled with newly evolved concepts about the individual that their predecessors could not imagine. Given the quantity and variety of self-representation in the twentieth century, how do we equip ourselves to understand it? A linear historical narrative lacks a coherent forward progression, and the confines of the century are very crude temporal contours for encompassing change. More useful, perhaps, is to introduce here a few commonalties—prominent themes, attitudes, and approaches—that signal a gradual shift into new territory and establish self-portraiture as a genre different from other forms of picture making. Since twentieth-century self-portraits are rarely commissioned, it is valuable to probe for the artist's motivation, asking biographical questions, searching aesthetic choices for hints, and ferreting out themes, historical precedents, and self-referential clues.

Self-portraiture brings us face-to-face, as it were, with an autobiographical urge that is a shared human trait. To some degree, we all want to reveal ourselves in a tangible way. As letters, diaries, and journals go out of fashion, they are replaced by e-mails, text messaging, Facebook pages, and blogs. Slides are gone but not snapshots; our own faces are just an arm's length away from the cell phone camera. We feel driven to document events, chart our journeys, tell our story. Sometimes this impulse is a subtle element of self-portraiture. Why, for instance, does Minerva Chapman inscribe the date July 5, 1906, on her forthright self-appraisal (cat. 4) and habitually date other self-portraits with the same specificity? For her, that self-portrait was a diary entry, particular to its time and place. For others, marking life's passages is more overt. Thomas Hart Benton's self-portrait at the beach with his wife, Rita, painted in 1922, the year they married, is not a marriage portrait in a traditional sense (fig. 2–2). But the painting throbs with sexuality and the newlyweds' interconnectedness. His virility as he stands with his hands framing her body, her sensual curves as she leans slightly toward him, and the landscape that echoes their seminude forms, all mark their moment of being passionately alive and together.

The special expectations observers bring to the genre also distinguish it from depictions of others. In most portraiture, we "meet" the subject through

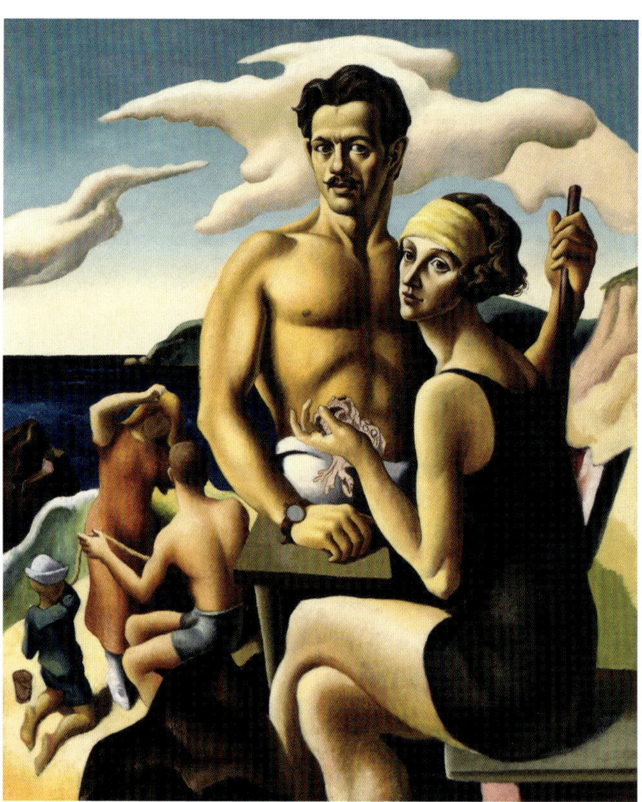

FIG. 2–2.
Thomas Hart Benton (1889–1975) and wife Rita, self-portrait, oil on canvas, 1922. National Portrait Gallery, Smithsonian Institution; gift of Mr. and Mrs. Jack H. Mooney

an intermediary—the artist—so our experience of that person is indirect. In self-portraiture, it is just the two of us. Our instinctive longing for connection with other human beings results in an unconscious desire to see the picture plane as transparent. With the same confidence that our forebears brought to the "science" of physiognomy, we trust our ability to read a face in order to discern character and personality. To see the handsome young man in John Wilson's 1944 self-portrait (cat. 31) is to feel we have met him, despite his inscrutable expression. This is especially true when the artist confronts us with the direct, outward-looking gaze that we see in Brian O'Doherty's riveting 1957 self-depiction (fig. 2–3) as well as the de Kooning, Benton, and Wilson portraits. As E. Luanne McKinnon has observed, the artist who has used the "undeviating gaze expects the viewer to engage with the sitter/subject/stranger in a visual and real manner."[4] And while her point holds for all direct gazes in the history of portraiture, it is especially acute for self-portraiture when that implied engagement is not mediated through a third person. Joseph

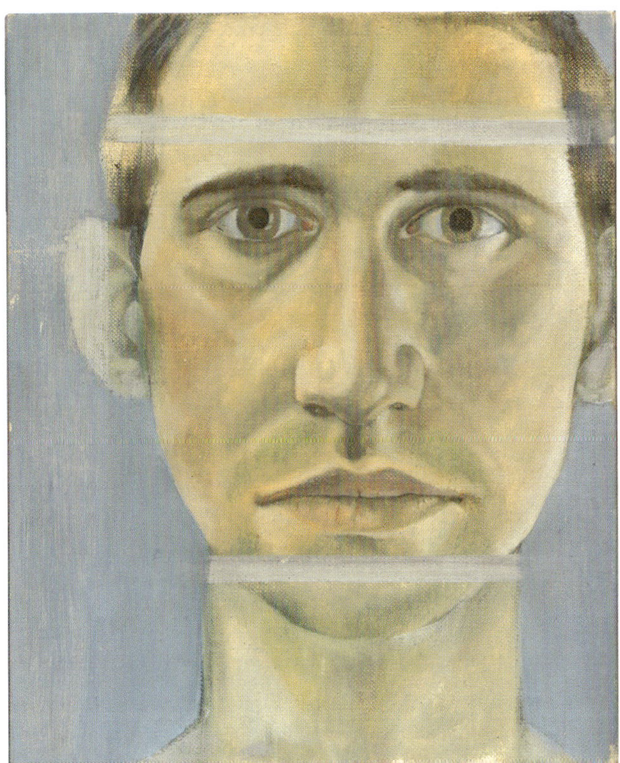

FIG. 2–3.
Brian O'Doherty (born 1928), self-portrait, oil on canvas, 1957. National Portrait Gallery, Smithsonian Institution; gift of Barbara Novak in honor of Marc Pachter

Koerner acknowledges the self-portraitist's unique understanding of that mirrored gaze in describing the artist's eyes in "a restless struggle simultaneously to see and to submit themselves to sight."[5]

The mirrored reflection, the basis of so much self-portraiture, has a long history weighted with symbolic implications, including two common tropes for the visual arts, the "mirror of virtue," leading to moral self-examination, and the "mirror of vanity," tempting one toward narcissism and self-deception.[6] By the twentieth century, symbolic significance has generally given way to perceptual games and optical concerns. The artist usually hides evidence of the mirror but in doing so is surely conscious of inviting the viewer's gaze in substitution for his or her own. "No one could spend that much time in front of a mirror," Jonathan Miller points out, "without occasionally asking himself who was looking at who."[7] Despite our intuitive acceptance of its role, the mirror itself can be an unsettling intrusion. The presence of a mirror frame in George Bellows's self-portrait destroys any pretense of transparency (cat. 11). If Bellows sits on both sides of the picture plane, where are we? Our privileged face-to-face encounter has been compromised; we are shoved aside. Robert Julius Brawley confounds us with a similarly challenging multilayered reality (cat. 65). His face, his hand, and the tools of his craft are all before us. But we don't *see* him as we might wish. We see the easel in his studio and the mirror propped up on it. Unable to replace the artist himself as we stand in front of the picture, we struggle with *three* concepts of Brawley: the drawn image, the mirrored image, and the unseen artist thus reflected.

Twentieth-century self-portraiture builds upon other long-standing traditions. Ever since the Renaissance era's emphasis on the individual brought self-portraiture into more common practice, artists have used it to commemorate events, bear witness, "sign" their work, examine their craft, establish social status, or impersonate mythic others in a redefinition of the self. The Greek myth of the youthful Narcissus falling in love with his own reflection has haunted the history of self-portraiture,[8] pointing toward vanity, self-consciousness, and the complex game of seeing. These historical themes of self-portraiture resonate strongly in the twentieth century. Few seemingly contemporary effects are entirely without precedent in self-portraiture's long, convention-breaking history.

But during this period, the notion of fixed, externally evident identity dissolved in the wake of new discoveries. From the mid- to late-nineteenth century, advancements in sociology, psychology, genetics, philosophy, and other fields complicated ideas about individual character. Since identity no longer seemed singular, God-given, or controllable, understanding it became paramount. By the dawn of the twentieth century we can recognize a heightened anxiety that came from these profound shifts; for artists, establishing the self within an increasingly complex world became a pivotal concern.[9] As if refracted through a prism, self-reflection was thus bent in new directions. John Yau described this break with tradition in his discussion of the self-portraits of Mexican artist Frida Kahlo, which "quite explicitly announce the impingements of both social and personal dynamics on a fixed stable identity."[10] Self-portraiture became a struggle to integrate changing or multiple identities, bridging the ruptures between competing selves or the real versus the imagined ideal.

Increased introspection—what one writer called "the twentieth-century project of self-scrutiny"[11]—

prompted a steady increase in self-portraiture. For many artists, self-study became a regular endeavor or even their principal subject. Painters such as Vincent Van Gogh, Frida Kahlo, Pablo Picasso, and Max Beckman, all intensely involved in self-portraiture, set influential precedents for American artists. By the beginning of the century, there was a broad breaking down of traditional conventions of pose and comportment. Self-portraitists have always updated figurative traditions with new stylistic approaches and added meaning or emotional effects through composition, color, landscapes, interior settings, or biographically suggestive objects. But art movements that emphasized abstraction and nonrepresentational picture making—seemingly unfriendly contexts for traditional figural depiction—provided the means to convey personality in newly expressive forms. Stanton MacDonald-Wright, for example, applied his color theories to *Self-Portrait with Squash* (fig. 2–4) referencing the abstract Synchromist movement with which he is identified.[12] Twentieth-century self-portraitists consciously evoked the symbolic weight of compositional mood, self-referential words, numbers, objects, colors, and other pictorial effects. Pure abstraction—or the symbolic substitutes of Robert Arneson's brick or Jim Dine's bathrobe (cats. 54, 55, and 39)—eliminated the figure altogether, stretching the boundaries of the genre farther than ever.

Increasing latitude to express previously taboo sensibilities added to boundary-breaking innovations.[13] In pondering the eternal question "Who am I?" interiority became a critical concern. Previous generations had tried to transcend restrictions related to gender, class, ethnicity, sexuality, disability, and almost any social or physical difference that led to a sense of exclusion from the mainstream. Instead, self-portraitists began to address such issues or express an affiliation with like others. Artists felt unprecedented freedom to choose unnatural poses or nudity; express sexual inclinations or uncomfortable emotions; study the effects of pain, childbirth, and disease; or masquerade with humor or enigmatic obfuscation. In depicting himself with Pablo Picasso in his print *Artist and Model*, David Hockney followed a long tradition of using self-portraiture to parallel or pay homage to another admired artist (cat. 49). But by humorously portraying himself as the younger, sexually desirable nude and incorporating an exploding phallic symbol directly behind him, he is inverting and transgressing centuries-old conventions. With new attitudes to both interior identity and the body, artists have updated or entirely revised traditions of portrayal.

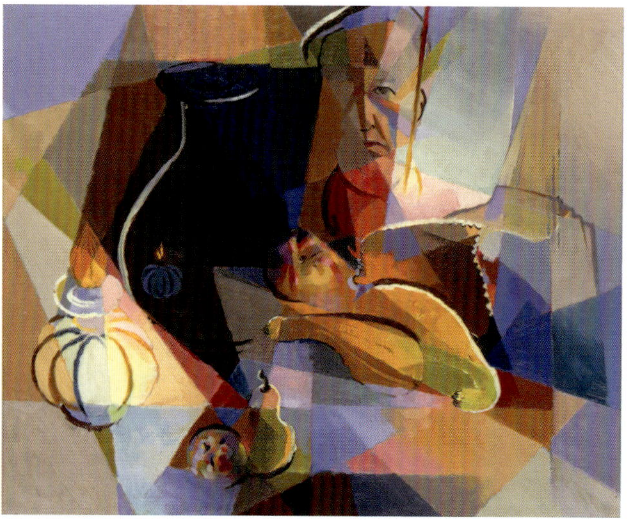

FIG. 2–4.
Self-Portrait with Squash by Stanton MacDonald-Wright (1890–1973), oil on wood, 1951. National Portrait Gallery, Smithsonian Institution

Grappling with issues of racial identity created a consciousness of otherness for black artists in America. In his study of African American self-portraiture, James Smalls notes the difficulty of locating a black self that had been fragmented by slavery, transplantation, and discrimination, and addresses the challenges of using the self-portrait "as a therapeutic and theatrical gesture for bonding the public racial self with the private inner self."[14] This notion explains some of the impact of John Wilson's self-portraits (cats. 31 and 32). "I felt like a foreigner in my own country," Wilson has said. "The thing that was always uppermost in my mind was this reality of being black in this impossible world."[15] His beautifully drafted portraits express an interior essence rather than a political or emotional confrontation. But the boldness of the dark media, the forceful gazes, and the positioning of the heads on the closely cropped sheets manifest a clear awareness of the challenge of presenting a black face in white America.

For women artists, the exploration of gendered and familial identity and the integration of a multiplicity of selves have been strong themes throughout the twentieth century. As Marsha Meskimmon has explored, being a woman and an artist in the early twentieth century was already "going against the grain." The notion of the artist as a genius was constructed in exclusively masculine terms, and "women's works parodied, challenged and rewrote masculine norms in self-portraiture."[16] The unabashed direct staring in images by Minerva Chapman, Isabel Bishop, and Pele de Lappe (cats. 4, 14, 15, and 26), defying any pretense of feminine modesty, seems more confrontational in this light. By holding our gaze, these artists challenge the objectification so frequently inherent in male depictions of women. Nonetheless, female artists often appear quite self-conscious about grooming and apparel, as if their choices of hats, clothes, jewelry, and hairstyles will have weighted significance in the eyes of their viewers. Minna Citron's vibrant personality is conveyed with a quickly rendered, animated expression, while the striped dress, curled hair, and stylish hat seem delineated with laborious care (cat. 22). Pele de Lappe's 1991 self-portrait (cat. 27) juxtaposes the young nude body with the aging self, accompanied by glasses, necklace, earrings, and mask, suggesting that disrobing, adornment, and role-playing are all part of a woman's desire to please and need for conscious presentation.

The beginning of the twentieth century, John Yau has observed, is marked by a broad acceptance of the Freudian notion that "the public self is a conditioned construct of the inner psychological self."[17] Self-portraiture reflects this preoccupation, but within a single artist's career, works often vacillate between revealing and concealing the inner self. Isabel Bishop ignores psychological probing in a 1929 etching, a study of modeling form and describing gesture (cat. 14). "Does painting a self portrait imply a desire to know oneself?" she once protested. "One's motive may be just to provide oneself a model, especially handy for a young artist as a means for studying picture problems."[18] How profoundly different is the portrayal of her older self in a powerful drawing from the mid-1980s, as she reveals distraught frustration over her diminished capacity to work (cat. 15). A delicate, introspective drawing by Berlin-born artist George Grosz (cat. 8), in startling contrast to his work as an angry Dada satirist, also presents self-portraiture in a raw, revealing guise. The drawing was made in 1916 at a moment when the artist's wartime experiences and subsequent breakdowns left him deeply scarred. The delicate charcoal suggests the acute sensitivity that nurtured his searing fury. Downcast eyes and soft charcoal shading, manipulated almost like a watercolor wash, convey an introspective expression and an anguished psyche.

Raphael Soyer's many self-portraits, direct and unemotive, seem to have an opposite effect, but their impact is cumulative. "How autobiographical my art is," he once claimed about his lifelong exploration of ethnic, religious, familial, and artistic identity. For Soyer, who described himself as "the shyest, the most inward, non-communicative character," self-portraiture was an alternate form of expression, a way of confirming his value and understanding the narrative of his own life.[19] As Samantha Baskind has argued, Soyer, who was embarrassed by his Russian accent, may have been drawn toward self-portraiture to counteract his feelings of exclusion as an immigrant.[20] Later in his career, Soyer may also have felt left out of new trends in art as he pursued his figurative style. A certain lonely melancholy pervades his self-portraits (cats. 9 and 10), and he frequently depicted himself looking older and wearier than he actually was.[21] For him, Baskind has concluded, self-portraiture was not just a convenience, but a "serious business . . . employed as an exploration of Soyer's limits and his liabilities, his strengths and his weaknesses, and . . . a challenge to his detractors."[22]

All serial self-portraitists inevitably confront the process of aging. Intimately familiar with the image in the mirror, they can observe acutely the changes of flesh and figure over the passing years. One might simply use self-portraiture, Jerome Myers once noted, "to let the brush portray the care and thoughtfulness that the observant eye sees in the mirror's record of the changes Time has wrought."[23] Raphael Soyer and Joseph Stella confront with unflinching lack of vanity the sagging or thickening contours of old age (cats. 10 and 3) in contrast to their younger selves. Even Chuck Close, who chooses to reveal little about himself, has not escaped noticing the aging process. As he good-naturedly puts it: "I watch my hair disappear."[24]

Most frequent self-portraitists acknowledge Rembrandt for probing investigations of the aging process.[25] But new interests in science and medicine are incorporated into traditional investigations of aging in the twentieth century. Ivan Albright's experience as a medical draftsman during World War I, for example, inflected his notion of bloated, wrinkled, corpse-like figuration (cat. 33). And while the image is grotesque, the giddy profusion of detailed materialism tempers the morbidity with something close to humor. The result suggests a scientific interest in the natural evolution of growth rather than a moral or psychological thanatopsis.

Albright's implications of decay also imply the inexorable advance of time. And the explicit depiction of temporal experience intrigued many artists. David Hockney first considered painting or drawing preferable to photography because the "hand moving through time reflects the eye moving through time (and life moving through time)." Photography was all right, he noted, "if you don't mind looking at the world from the point of view of a paralysed Cyclops—for a split second." He solved the problem of that frozen moment with the cubist effects of his photo collages (cat. 50), visualizing the shifting views of real experience over time.[26] Both Albright and Hockney invited the viewer into their pictures to move around and experience the imagery from different perspectives. Self-portraitists have often referenced the past to illuminate the present, evoking revered older artists, symbols of childhood, or previous accomplishments. That theme of memory is powerfully updated by new approaches to expressing time.

If scientific empiricism intrigued some artists, dramatic posturing asserts itself just as often. The bohemian "genius," given to hilarious high jinks on the one hand and moody suffering on the other, became a common stereotype of the artist by the early twentieth century. At a moment when having "personality" meant living life to the fullest with an audience-grabbing flair, everyone wanted to assume a dramatic role.[27] Everett Shinn cast himself as the cliché of a tempestuous artist with melancholy downcast eyes (fig. 2–5) in a 1901 pastel. Playing his role with keen self-consciousness, he inscribed the drawing to his idol, the actress Julia Marlowe. "Great fun," he wrote on a mocking self-caricature sent to his friend John Sloan a few years later, "being an artist, with temperament."[28]

The costumes, poses, defiant gestures, and wide-eyed confrontation of twentieth-century self-portraiture frequently reveal this sensibility of dramatic engagement. The bold frontal stare proliferates, suggesting the immodest, unabashed drama of a new age. As already noted, this obvious result of mirror gazing is not unique to the twentieth century; Albrecht Dürer's Christlike self-portrait from 1500 is a particularly famous example, and precedents abound.[29] Nonetheless, there is a significant increase in this confrontational pose. What McKinnon calls "the interplay of the reciprocal gaze" adds a heightened experience not found in other types of portraiture.[30] Complete frontality, Michael Quick has pointed out, "gives the impression of total exposure and frankness" and probably for that reason is rare in conventional nineteenth-century portraiture. That "enforced intimacy," he notes, "is almost startling."[31] While that outward-directed frontal gaze was common in the more intimate form of photographic portraiture, its translation to other artistic formats still seemed bold. In the Myers and Soyer self-portraits (cats. 16, 9, and 10), as well as in those of John Storrs, Pele de Lappe, and Brian O'Doherty (cats. 6 and 26; fig. 2–3), that unflinching eye contact compels us.

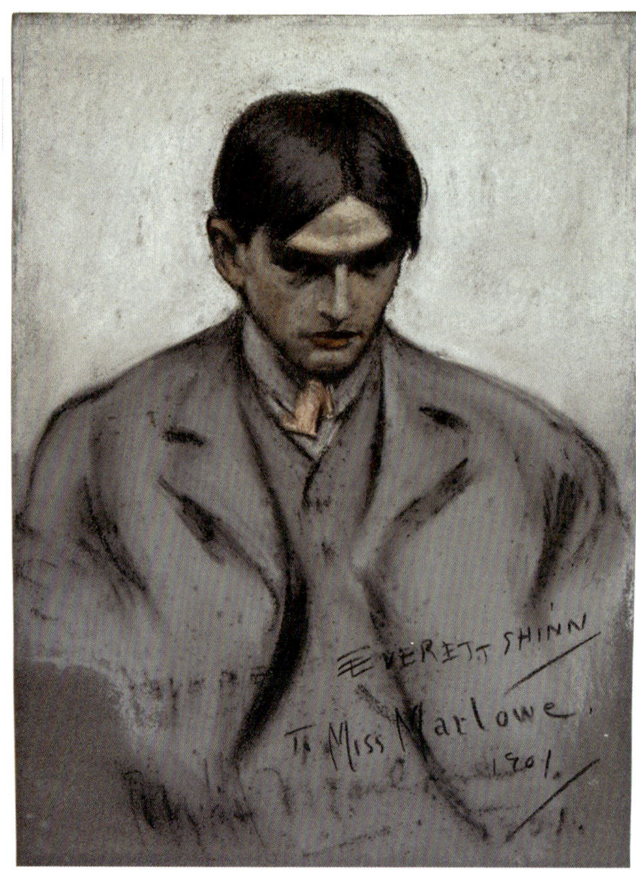

FIG. 2–5.
Everett Shinn (1876–1953) self-portrait, pastel on blue paper, 1901. National Portrait Gallery, Smithsonian Institution

Self-portraiture requires a considerable amount of inherently theatrical decision-making. Rather than negotiated with a sitter, the selection of costume, stance, gesture, expression, setting, and scenery is the artist's own, and fewer restrictive conventions of posing existed in the twentieth century than ever before. Childe Hassam depicted his beachwear—knickers, brimmed hat, and loose jacket—as well as the flowers and grasses of his outdoor setting with great specificity in his 1933 drawing (cat. 20). On the stagelike narrow boardwalk, he acted out his "plein air" sketching while letting his own facial features dissolve in the shadows. To a certain extent, of course, self-fashioning has long been a feature of self-portraiture. But as traditional approaches to posing and comportment gave way, the artists' choices were often more overtly theatrical.

Jerome Myers impersonates a Rembrandt-like figure in his 1929 self-portrait drawing, which sports a peculiar cloth headdress in the spirit of the latter's various caps and turbans (cat. 16). Myers, a regular self-portraitist, expressed the various uses of the genre: "In the mirror the artist comes face to face with himself in the many moods that life impresses on him. It may be in self-revelation, or a gay defiance to laugh with life or at it, to seize the fleeting moment of joy, to capture the symbol of happiness."[32] That laughing defiance in the face of life's challenges was a theatrical construct common to the age. Role-playing takes a far darker turn in Louis Lozowick's horrifying *Lynch Law (Lynching)* of 1936, where he imagines himself as a victim (cat. 18). The Supreme Court cases of the Scottsboro Boys in the mid-1930s introduced many white Americans to egregious racial injustices; Lozowick bears witness to such atrocities by projecting himself in the midst of them.

In the more detached portraiture of the midcentury avant-garde, which consciously spurned psychological probing, one still detects a certain dramatic self-projection. For all his nonnarrative intentions, Chuck Close, with his unruly hair and dangling cigarette, hits a note of rebellious defiance in a 1967–1968 self-portrait (fig. 2–6) that he later admitted had "a certain theatricality": "I chose to portray myself as the angry young man, the James Dean period of my life, with the cigarette hanging out of my mouth."[33] Likewise, William Beckman, in his bare-chested, sagging-jeans portrait of 1974, swaggers with classic youthful arrogance (cat. 52).

Artists of the midcentury had new reasons for self-consciousness in their depiction of the self. After the rise of abstract expressionism, portraiture declined as a progressive form of art making, and using the head as subject matter was a transgressive decision. "The dumbest, most moribund, out-of-date, and shopworn of possible things you could do," Chuck Close remembered, "was to make a portrait."[34] Nonetheless, he was intrigued, aware of the work of contemporaries Alex Katz, Philip Pearlstein, and Andy Warhol, artists, who, in his words, "kicked the door open for an intelligent, forward-looking kind of figuration."[35] For these artists, as well as Alice Neel,

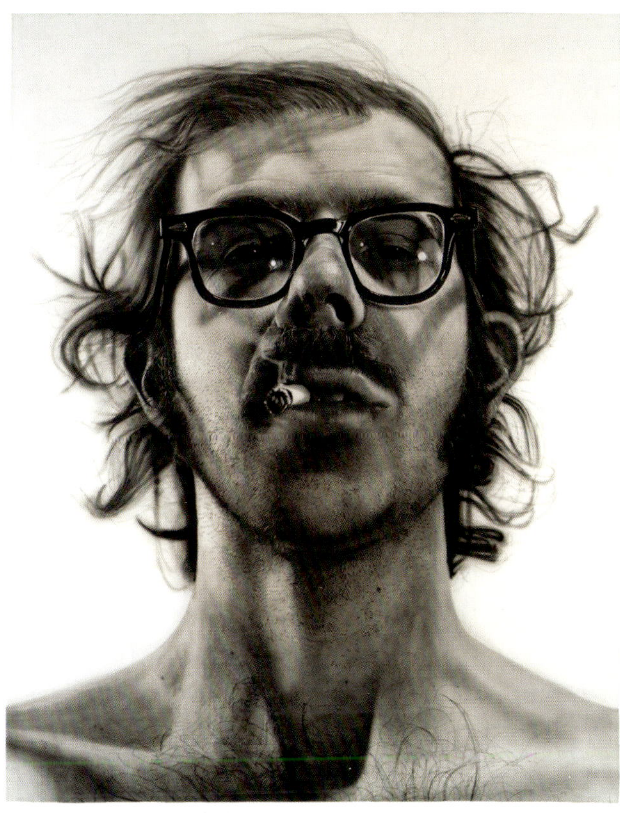

FIG. 2–6.
Big Self-Portrait by Chuck Close (born 1940), acrylic on canvas, 1967–1968. Walker Art Center, Minneapolis; Art Center Acquisition Fund, 1969

Elaine de Kooning, Fairfield Porter, and others, it was time to reinvent stale portrait traditions. The scathing regard of critics and art world cognoscenti for any figuration presented itself as a challenge to a generation of rebellious young artists.

Alex Katz determined to focus on representational art with the intention of making "something fresh and post-abstract."[36] His bright colors and smooth, flat surfaces signaled a new look for figuration, devoid of psychological or biographical narrative. "I'd like to have style take the place of content, or the style be the content," Katz noted. "I prefer it to be emptied of meaning, emptied of content."[37] The large scale, odd cropping, and billboard blandness of his heads and figures added to that sense of emotional distancing. Katz sought the same neutrality in his frequent self-portraits. "I wanted to see if I could paint [a self-portrait] that was not narcissistic, that was not soulful or sentimental, not maudlin."[38] Of course, anonymity and impersonal distancing is harder to achieve in a self-portrait, which, by definition, identifies the subject that we now know through his art.

Furthermore, Katz realized the inherently performative nature of even this distanced presentation. In his early portraits, John Coffey has observed, Katz "introduced his now-classic persona: the Stranger—aloof, austere, the strong, silent type." By the 1960s, he was more aware of that artifice, and when he painted himself, Coffey acknowledged, he "turns to the mirror and discovers the comedy, even the absurdity, of self-portrayal. He abandons the . . . Stranger and begins to improvise new roles—new personas—that spin out of whim and fantasy."[39] In Katz's smiling self-portrait drawing (cat. 64), we see even facial expression as a form of disguise. The smile, while common for face-the-camera affability in snapshots, signals a rare mood for formal portraiture. The familiar expression becomes oddly enigmatic.

When Chuck Close started painting large heads of his friends, he too intended their anonymity to distance the spectator from any psychological interpretation. He added to that detachment by using a photograph for his model because it represented "a frozen, poemlike moment in time."[40] Self-portraiture has been a consistent theme in his work ever since *Big Self-Portrait*, his giant disheveled head painted in 1967–1968, shocked the art world and established his iconography of enormous, close-up, frontal posing (fig. 2–6). Ultimately, as Close explored self-portraiture throughout his whole career, his posing became less artificial (cat. 61): "I think what's happened is, as I've gotten older and mellowed, I've become more at peace with who I am as a person. I have a greater awareness of and insight as to what makes me tick. I don't feel I need to pose in a certain way as much as I have posed myself and tried to pose other people."[41] But it is his emphasis on experimentation and process, often deriving numerous images from a single self-portrait photograph, that exposes his essence as an artist and a person. "Tenacity of technique equals tenacity of spirit," Madeleine Grynsztejn has noted. "More than any mimetic approximation, it is Close's aesthetic *practice* that points to a personality, an ethos even, in concordance with the ideas and activities of the mid-1960s avant-garde scene."[42]

Elaine de Kooning and Alice Neel took a different approach to portraiture's reinvention. No one tackled the struggle of female identity more forcefully than Alice Neel in her naked self-portrait at the age of eighty (fig. 2–7). After a lifetime of rebelling against conventions—challenging established mores of sexuality, marriage, and progressive art—Neel attacked traditional notions of the nude and female beauty with humor and unflinching honesty.[43] As Meskimmon has pointed out, female nudes in art are often meant to be "universal metaphors for masculine desire, creativity and culture."[44] But Neel, wearing only her glasses, paints herself with breasts and stomach sagging, pockets of cellulite bulging, shoulders stooped. Her expression seems more resigned than defiant; she has earned her wrinkles and drooping flesh. "My portraits—people used to be horrified," she admitted to critic Gerrit Henry in 1975. "I've had to have frightful endurance—to paint and not to have any destination for it."[45] Nonetheless, there is no trace of self-pity in her painting. She presents herself as an artist—glasses on and brush in hand—achieving an image of stunning vitality. "I want it to be one super figure of a person," she explained to Henry about her approach to portraiture, "and at the same time good art."[46]

While the familial group portrait has long been a natural extension of self-portrayal, women artists more frequently attempt to integrate their maternal and artistic selves. Ruth Weisberg has often woven spiritual and familial themes into her work. Her 1975 lithograph, *The Gift* (cat. 56), based on a performance piece where she danced in front of a projected film of her own toddler with other children, addresses not only the mutual gifts between mother and child but also the challenges of true generational connection. Louise Bourgeois explores that parent-child relationship symbolically in a diagrammatic representation of her young self between her father and mother (cat. 71).

The last quarter of the twentieth century, some have argued, has introduced a new era of self-scrutiny.[47] Of course, the reemergence of all figurative art as progressive and groundbreaking during this time encouraged the trend.[48] Nonetheless, as Dean Sobel has noted, the ongoing struggle with questions of personal and cultural identity in America encouraged artists toward self-portrayal in unprecedented numbers. Performance art, body art, video art, photographic manipulation and appropriation, along with other innovations, rejected the impersonality of pop and minimalist aesthetics, encouraged the return to figuration, and offered new ways to explore the self. Although the issues Sobel describes as paramount, including sexuality, gender, age, ethnicity, religion, and artistic and cultural identity, have precedence in earlier examples from the twentieth century, these themes intensified and

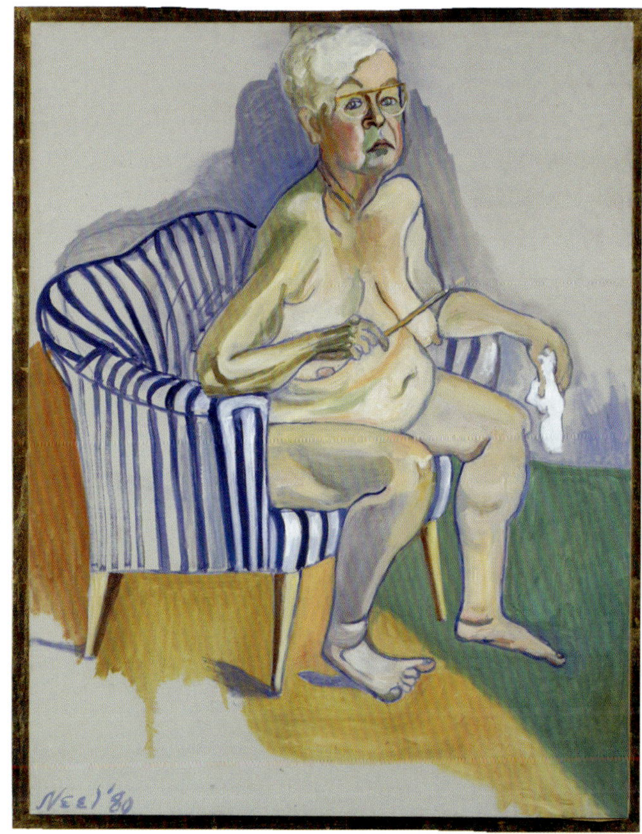

FIG. 2–7.
Alice Neel (1900–1984), self-portrait, oil on canvas, 1980. National Portrait Gallery, Smithsonian Institution

inspired different artistic approaches.[49] In Susan Hauptman's imposing 2001 charcoal portrait (cat. 77), the artifice of her mid-twentieth-century clothing references the questioning of feminine stereotypes by various photographers—most famously Cindy Sherman—who don costumes and adopt new personas (see fig. 3–8).[50] Hauptman's meticulously rendered ruffles and flowers, in contrast to her short, masculine haircut, hint at prevalent issues of gender and sexuality while remaining tantalizingly ambiguous. Her work approaches Sobel's notion of "nonidentity."[51] The contemporary artist can use disguise, abstraction, or substitutions for the self to obliterate personal reality and facilitate reinvention. Hauptman's gaze, Terrie Sultan has pointed out, "is both a confrontation and an entreaty, as she invites us into a scrutiny that is equal parts confession and theater."[52]

Reaction against the media emphasis on youth, fashion, cosmetic surgery, and celebrity culture has caused many artists to focus anew on the biological body. Robert Rauschenberg incorporated an X-ray of his skeleton in his self-portrait *Autobiography* (cat. 45). Genetic "portraiture," the use of blood or body fluids, images of body parts as symbolic substitutes, and photographs of the progression of disease are other approaches that investigate the biological self. Frances Borzello has studied the effects of feminism on a new wave of female self-portraiture, which often challenges stereotypes of beauty, health, ethnicity, and age.[53] Kiki Smith inventively focuses on her own body and its functions to address issues related to women's identity and body image. In her 1994 *Free Fall* (cat. 73) she depicts herself curled into a fetal position, removing the female nude from its sexual connotations and grounding it instead in its natal origins and own progenitive potential. A metaphor of artistic creativity, it highlights both a personal and a universal narrative.

To some degree, the elusive nature of self-understanding that we have been reviewing is an inherent quality in self-portrait practices that became common in the Renaissance. Barbara Rose has argued that the Renaissance artist's "consciousness of himself as a creator, with all the joy and misery that role implies, and of his art as deliberate illusion," can be seen as an early manifestation of the modern mind.[54] As understanding about the individual evolved, that heightened search for identity increased, as did the theatricality of illusory self-presentation. Both became defining aspects of twentieth-century self-portrayal.

As connected as it is to other forms of portraiture, the self-portrait has unique characteristics. "At once the icon and the index of their creator," Joseph Koerner has noted, "self-portraits attach what, in other artefacts, seems radically distinct." And while all pictures index their creator, "not all products of human making can indicate their maker in such an explicit way."[55] Our sense of this special quality is intuitive. The artist appears to confront us, to initiate a conversation, to ask us to understand what has been expressed of the interior self. Of course, that promise of intimacy is only an illusion. In self-portraiture, it could all be a teasing masquerade, a simultaneous revealing and concealing. In the end, it may not be personal insights we receive or even seek. As with all great art, it might be something much larger. For all our attempts to grasp the particular, it may be something more universal that moves us: the mysteries of human expression, connection, and understanding.

NOTES

1 Ann Van Devanter and Alfred V. Frankenstein, *American Self-Portraits, 1670–1973* (Washington, DC: International Exhibitions Foundation, 1974), 158.
2 Ibid., 180.
3 When male self-portraits were set in the studio, Marsha Meskimmon has noted, "that space was almost always conceived as beyond ordinary domestic routines." Marsha Meskimmon, *The Art of Reflection: Women Artists' Self-Portraiture in the Twentieth Century* (New York: Columbia University Press, 1996), 24.
4 E. Luanne McKinnon, "Notes on the Gaze," in *Eye to Eye* (Winter Park, FL: The George D. and Harriet W. Cornell Fine Arts Museum, Rollins College, 2006), 1.
5 Joseph Leo Koerner, "Self-Portraiture Direct and Oblique," in *Self Portrait: Renaissance to Contemporary*, ed. Anthony Bond and Joanna Woodall (London: National Portrait Gallery, 2005), 67.
6 Joanna Woodall, "Every Painter Paints Himself: Self-Portraiture and Creativity," in *Self Portrait: Renaissance to Contemporary* (see n. 5), 20.
7 Jonathan Miller, *On Reflection* (London: National Gallery Publications, 1998), 200.
8 John Welchman, *Narcissism: Artists Reflect Themselves* (Escondido, CA: California Center for the Arts Museum, 1996), 16.
9 This was also a concern for writers of the time. See Wendy Steiner, *Exact Resemblance to Exact Resemblance: The Literary Portraiture of Gertrude Stein* (New Haven, CT: Yale University Press, 1978), 2.
10 John Yau, "The Phoenix of the Self," *Artforum* 27 (April 1989): 147.
11 Frances Borzello, *Seeing Ourselves: Women's Self-Portraits* (New York: Harry N. Abrams, 1998), 139. An intriguing number of nonartists took up the challenge of visual self-depiction. For some examples, see Stanley Marcus, "Turbulent Indigo: Self-Portraits by 'Nonpainters,'" *American Artist* 61 (September 1997): 55–59.
12 Van Devanter and Frankenstein, *American Self-Portraits*, 188.
13 As Borzello puts it, "there is an exhilarating sense of breaking taboos in much self-portraiture as the century begins." Borzello, *Seeing Ourselves*, 125.
14 James Smalls, "The African-American Self-Portrait: A Crisis in Identity and Modernity," *Art Criticism* 15 (2000): 22, 24.
15 Interviews with the artist, July 12, 1994, transcript, p. 346, and April 6, 1993, transcript, p. 71, Archives of American Art, Smithsonian Institution.
16 Meskimmon, *Art of Reflection*, 8, 20, 16; in addition to Meskimmon's and Borzello's studies of women's self-portraiture, see also Liz Rideal et al., *Mirror, Mirror: Self-Portraits by Women Artists* (London: National Portrait Gallery, 2001).
17 Yau, "The Phoenix of the Self," 145–46.
18 Van Devanter and Frankenstein, *American Self-Portraits*, 140.
19 Raphael Soyer, *Self-Revealment: A Memoir* (New York: Maecenas Press, Random House, 1967, 1969), 117, 3.
20 Samantha Baskind, *Raphael Soyer and the Search for Modern Jewish Art* (Chapel Hill and London: University of North Carolina Press, 2004), 2.
21 Avis Berman, "Raphael Soyer at 80: Not Painting Would Be Like Not Breathing," *ARTnews* 78 (December 1979): 41.
22 Baskind, *Raphael Soyer and the Search for Modern Jewish Art*, 52.
23 Jerome Myers, *Artist in Manhattan* (New York: American Artists Group, 1940), 117.
24 Robert Storr, with essays by Kirk Varnedoe and Deborah Wye, *Chuck Close* (New York: Museum of Modern Art, 1998), 79.
25 For further investigation, see Christopher White and Quentin Buvelot, eds., *Rembrandt by Himself* (London: National Gallery, 1999).
26 Anne Hoy, "Hockney's Photocollages," in *David Hockney: A Retrospective*, ed. Maurice Tuckman and Stephanie Barron (Los Angeles: Los Angeles County Museum of Art, 1988), 55–57.
27 "This was the most theatrical generation in American annals," Ann Douglas has noted about the early twentieth century. Ann Douglas, *Terrible Honesty: Mongrel Manhattan in the 1920s* (New York: Farrar, Straus and Giroux, 1995), 55.
28 Wendy Wick Reaves, *Celebrity Caricature in America* (New Haven, CT: Yale University Press, 1998), 75.
29 For many dramatic examples, see Bond and Woodall, eds., *Self Portrait: Renaissance to Contemporary*.
30 McKinnon, "Notes on the Gaze," 1.
31 Michael Quick, "Introduction," *Artists by Themselves: Artists' Portraits from the National Gallery of Design* (New York: National Academy of Design, 1983), 20.
32 Myers, *Artist in Manhattan*, 117.
33 Lisa Lyons and Robert Storr, *Chuck Close* (New York: Rizzoli, 1987), 39.

34 Siri Engberg, "The Paper Mirror: Chuck Close's Self-Reflection in Drawings and Prints," in *Chuck Close: Self-Portraits, 1967–2005*, ed. Siri Engberg and Madeleine Grynsztejn (San Francisco and Minneapolis: San Francisco Museum of Modern Art and Walker Art Center, 2005), 137.

35 Storr, Varnedoe, and Wye, *Chuck Close*, 86.

36 Alex Katz, "Starting Out," *New Criterion* 21 (December 2002): 5.

37 Mark Strand, ed., *Art of the Real: Nine American Figurative Painters* (New York: Clarkson N. Potter, 1983), 124, 129.

38 John W. Coffey, *Making Faces: Self-Portraits by Alex Katz* (Raleigh: North Carolina Museum of Art, 1990), 7.

39 Ibid., 7, 9.

40 Lyons and Storr, *Chuck Close*, 30.

41 Ibid., 39.

42 Engberg and Grynsztejn, *Chuck Close: Self-Portraits,1967–2005*, 110.

43 As Carolyn Carr has explored, Neel painted numerous female nudes from life, including several images of pregnant women. Carolyn Carr, *Alice Neel: Women* (New York: Rizzoli, 2002), 136–56.

44 Meskimmon, *Art of Reflection*, 2.

45 Gerrit Henry, "The Artist and the Face: A Modern American Sampling," *Art in America* 63 (January–February 1975): 40.

46 Ibid.

47 Dean Sobel, *Identity Crisis: Self-Portraiture at the End of the Century* (Milwaukee, WI: Milwaukee Art Museum, 1997); Nina Sundell et al., *The Sense of Self: From Self-Portrait to Autobiography* (Washington, DC, and New York: Independent Curators, Inc., 1978); Sally Yard and Irving Sandler, *Images of the Self* (Amherst, MA: Hampshire College, 1979); Amy Goldin, "The Post-Perceptual Portrait" *Art in America* 63 (January–February 1975): 79–82; *Self Evidence: Identity in Contemporary Art* (Lincoln, MA: DeCordova Museum and Sculpture Park, 2004), 6. Studies of the return of portraiture at the end of the century generally include a large number of self-portraitists. See, for example, Donna de Salvo et al., *Face Value: American Portraits* (Southampton, NY: The Parrish Art Museum, 1995).

48 During this period contemporary self-portraiture became a popular topic for exhibitions in commercial galleries and museums. See, for example, Sobel, *Identity Crisis*; Sundell et al., *Sense of Self*; Yard and Sandler, *Images of the Self*; Rideal et al., *Mirror, Mirror*; Sean Kelly and Edward Lucie-Smith, *The Self Portrait: A Modern View* (London: Sarema Press, 1987); Joann Moser, *Face to Face: Self-Portraits in the Museum Collection* (Iowa City: University of Iowa Museum of Art, 1979); Katherine Lochridge, *As We See Ourselves: Artists Self Portraits* (Huntington, NY: Heckscher Museum, 1979); Richard Cox, *American Self-Portraits: An Exhibition of Original Prints* (New Orleans, LA: Tahir Gallery, 1981); James Goode, *Contemporary Self-Portraits from the James Goode Collection* (Washington, DC: National Portrait Gallery, 1993); *Selected 20th-Century American Self-Portraits* (New York: Harold Reed Gallery, 1980).

49 Sobel, *Identity Crisis*, 9. Edward Lucie-Smith observed in 1987 that in Great Britain as well, "the making of self-portraits is in the throes of a vigorous revival." Kelly and Lucie-Smith, *The Self Portrait*, 24.

50 In assembling an anthology of women's photographic self-portraits, Joyce Tenneson Cohen noted the recurring leitmotif of personal transformation: "Different identities are continually explored and old roles exorcised through the use of masks, costumes, make-up, montage, or combination printing." Joyce Tenneson Cohen and Patricia Meyer Spacks, *In/Sights Self-Portraits by Women* (Boston: David R. Godine, 1978), vii.

51 Sobel, *Identity Crisis*, 9–12.

52 Terrie Sultan, "Contemporary Portraiture's Split Reference," *Art on Paper* 3 (March–April 1999): 41.

53 Borzello, *Seeing Ourselves*, 159–91. At the end of the century, female self-portraiture has been a popular topic for exhibitions in commercial galleries and museums.

54 Barbara Rose, "Self-Portraiture: Theme with a Thousand Faces," *Art in America* 63 (January–February 1975): 73.

55 Koerner, "Self-Portraiture Direct and Oblique," 68.

REPETITION AS REPUTATION

Repositioning the Self-Portrait in the 1960s and Beyond

ANNE COLLINS GOODYEAR

To an ever greater degree the work of art reproduced becomes the work of art designed for reproducibility.
—Walter Benjamin[1]

Repetition adds up to reputation. —Andy Warhol[2]

FOR MORE than a quarter century, art historians and other cultural theorists have sought to come to terms with a phenomenon that has alternately been described as "postmodern" portraiture, "post-perceptual" portraiture, an "identity crisis," and "the portrait's dispersal."[3] While each of these monikers testifies to the perception of a break in portraiture's history, roughly locatable in the 1960s, each also attests to the persistence of this long-standing genre and its reconstitution along new lines. This essay seeks to come to terms with the sources of the crisis in portraiture that simultaneously inspired its renewal. At the epicenter of this transformation is the special category of the self-portrait, a site for the overlapping demands of process and persona, a space where the distance between maker and subject collapses.

Focusing on American art, this study turns to a defining moment in the history of the genre of self-portraiture, as the hegemony of the unique work of art—the autograph painting or drawing—gave way to the new model of the readily reproducible multiple in a new era of mass reproduction. This development, in turn, raised thorny questions not only about the threatened status of the original but also the very authority of the artist. These are the problems that paved the way to the revolutionary approach to self-portrayal practiced by the artists discussed here—Marcel Duchamp, Jasper Johns, Andy Warhol, Roy Lichtenstein, Jim Dine, Chuck Close, Robert Arneson, Lucas Samaras, Cindy Sherman, and Bruce Nauman—each of whom, with the exception of Duchamp and Sherman, is represented in the accompanying exhibition.

As a point of departure, it is worth reflecting upon the emergence of self-portraiture as a new category of representation during the course of the fifteenth century. This new class of images implies, of course, the development of attendant social, political, economic, and intellectual structures that enabled artists to recognize and assert their independent identity through the device of the autograph image.[4] If the birth of self-portraiture indeed conferred upon the artist a privileged status as "creator"—a form of social distinction that made an impression upon a young Jasper Johns—this recognition was tied in large part to the production of unique objects.[5] As Anthony Bond has observed, it was precisely evidence of the artist's hand—in the form of recognizable mark making—that differentiated Renaissance "art" from Medieval icons.[6] Implicitly, then, the autograph self-portrait seemed to imply a special relationship between artist and audience, a connection forged by the act of looking: our eyes absorb the same image consumed by the artist at work, contemplating his or her own features reflected by a mirror. In accepting this vision of self-portrayal, points out T. J. Clark, "We have acquiesced in an equation of seeing with knowing and visa-versa, one that is built deep into our accounts of the world: Paul de Man calls it 'the fundamental metaphor of understanding as seeing.'"[7]

The justification for such intense engagement is only present, however, as long as the conceit of the artist/subject's own engagement with ocular and intellectual absorption holds. Implicit in the relationship is also the assumption that one is experiencing and deciphering a unique, autograph object, endowed with the artist's presence both pictorially and indexically—that is, through his or her physical mark. But such assumptions are threatened by the advent of the mechanically reproducible image and its acceleration, particularly with the development of new techniques to reproduce the photograph in the early years of the twentieth century.[8]

Although written in the mid-1930s, the 1968 republication, in English translation, of "The Work of Art in the Age of Mechanical Reproduction"—Walter Benjamin's seminal account of the transformation of art brought about by techniques of mass reproduction, particularly the proliferation of film—testifies to the essay's relevance for a new generation.[9] Using a metaphor particularly apt for a study of self-portraiture, Benjamin describes the sensation of a film actor, deprived of a human audience, contemplating the camera. "The feeling of strangeness that overcomes the actor before the camera," observes Benjamin, "is basically the same kind as the estrangement felt before one's own image in the mirror. And the reflected image has become separable, transportable."[10] The change is a critical one.

By the second half of the twentieth century, the unique painting or drawing no longer functioned as the model for the creation and consumption of images—even fine art. Yet, given the long historical hold of painting and drawing as modes of figuring the self, much of the literature describing the development of (self-) portrayal is predicated upon the production of the singular autograph image.[11] Perhaps partly for this reason, art of the pop era is frequently assumed not to include portraiture.[12] And yet, despite accounts to the contrary, the figure—and the self-portrait in particular—does not disappear during the 1960s and 1970s; rather, the very meaning of portrayal was reformulated as the concept of the self and personal agency shifted during this period, leading to fundamentally new approaches to portraiture and self-portrayal.

With the inherent reproducibility of the work of art affecting its manufacture as well as its dissemination, the artist's relationship to the public was irrevocably transformed. Roland Barthes characterized the shift in 1968 as "The Death of the Author." Ultimately, the transformation that Barthes marked does not concern so much the production of texts (of which an artwork may be seen as an example) as their reception:

> [A] text is made of multiple writings, drawn from many cultures and entering into mutual relations of dialogue, parody, contestation, but there is one place where this multiplicity is focused and that place is the reader, not, as was hitherto said, the author. The reader is the space on which all the quotations that make up the writing are inscribed without any of them being lost; a text's unity lies not in its origin but in its destination. . . . [T]he birth of the reader must be at the cost of the death of the Author.[13]

Perhaps most important, Barthes's dramatic account of the simultaneous "death of the author" and "birth of the reader" demonstrated his recognition that meaning of the work had become unfixed. No longer could the author, or artist, rely upon his or her intentions being regarded as paramount. Instead, the authority for the interpretation of a work's significance moved to the audience.

In identifying this transition, Barthes's essay reflects an intriguing similarity to a statement voiced a decade earlier by Marcel Duchamp, whose deeply conceptual approach to art and self-representation would exercise enormous influence on American artists from the late 1950s onward. In "The Creative Act," Duchamp, like Barthes, explored the audience's input into the "completion" of the artwork, asserting:

> the creative act is not performed by the artist alone; the spectator brings the work in contact with the external world by deciphering and interpreting its inner qualifications and thus adds his contribution to the creative act. This becomes even more obvious when

posterity gives its final verdict and sometimes rehabilitates forgotten artists.[14]

If Duchamp in the mid-1950s had himself in mind as a "forgotten" artist who might be "rehabilitated" by the actions of posterity, he quite deliberately took advantage of the very tools that might seem to threaten artistic autonomy—namely those associated with mass reproduction—and turned them to his advantage, much as a poker player might stack the cards in his favor. Perhaps most famously, Duchamp played the gambit with his *Wanted: $2,000 Reward* of 1923 (fig. 3–1), a rectified readymade (a term for a found object manipulated by Duchamp) portraying the artist as a fugitive wanted for impersonation and operating "a bucket shop," or illegal betting operation.[15] Modeled specifically after a poster designed for mass dissemination, Duchamp would reproduce the work himself, first in 1938 for inclusion in his *Boîte-en-Valise*—a boxed collection of highlights of his oeuvre, with large works reproduced in miniature—and again, in 1963, for the exhibition poster for his first retrospective at the Pasadena Museum of Art.[16] In each context, the work took on new inflections, and—as the artist successfully gambled—changing audiences interpreted it anew. Its influence took hold and spread like wildfire. In addition to nearly instantaneous responses to the *Wanted* poster by the artists Sturtevant and Richard Pettibone in the mid-1960s, evidence of its conceptual sway and that of Duchamp's career also emerges quite forcefully in the work of others, including Jasper Johns, Andy Warhol, Roy Lichtenstein, Jim Dine, and Chuck Close.[17]

Although the career of Jasper Johns is not generally associated with self-portraiture, Johns's *Souvenir* series provides an important engagement with and challenge to the genre, and has, in fact, been widely discussed in this context.[18] What is perhaps most intriguing about this group of works is not only how it comes to define Johns's own practice at key moments in his career, but also its implicit conversation with Duchamp. Johns absorbed Duchamp's lessons, and, like him, deliberately constructed a self-representation without a single fixed meaning.

The conceptual significance of *Souvenir* in Johns's oeuvre is evident from the numerous variations on the theme he executed between 1964 and 1970.[19] Originally developed as a pair of assemblages of identical dimensions, *Souvenir* and *Souvenir 2* (figs.

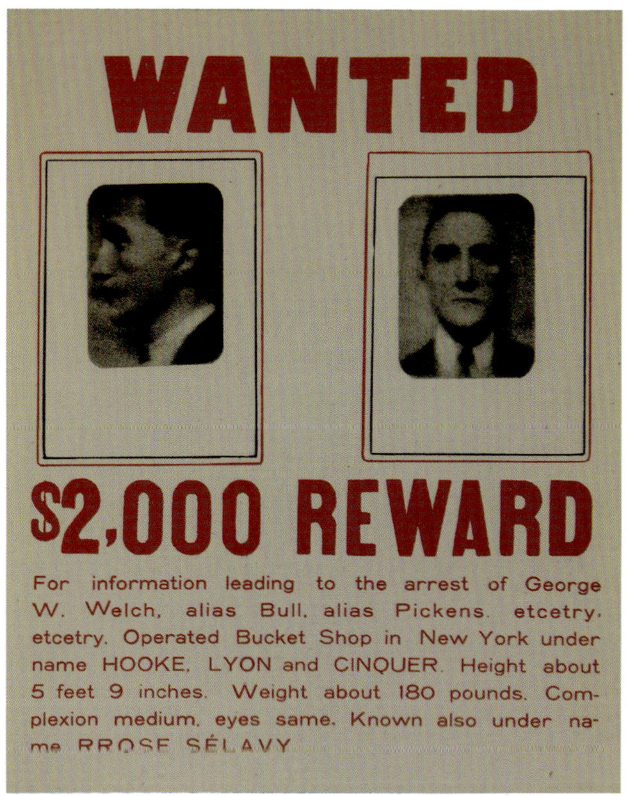

FIG. 3–1.
Wanted: $2,000 Reward (from *Boîte*—Series D) by Marcel Duchamp (1887–1968), lithograph, 1961 after 1923 original. Frances Beatty and Allen Adler

3–2 and 3–3) were made in the wake of his first retrospective exhibition.[20] Both canvases feature working flashlights along the right side of the canvas; a rearview bicycle mirror at upper right; and a plate, with a picture of the artist, resting on a small ledge in the lower left.[21] However, there are notable distinctions. *Souvenir* depicts a dark environment where little is visible. A portrait of the artist, housed on a shelf in the lower left corner of the composition, appears in grisaille, as do the words describing color. In *Souvenir 2*, one discerns colors in Johns's self-depiction, as well as the back of a previously unseen canvas, suggesting that the flashlight included along the left edge of the canvas has been illuminated.[22] If the illumination of the canvas draws attention to its theme of memory through its revelation of the word "souvenir," it also throws attention back on the flashlight itself.[23] It was perhaps in a playful reference to this imagery that Duchamp referred to Johns as one of the "lights" of his generation in 1965.[24] Although Duchamp's remark was made after Johns had finished his compositions, his perceptiveness may reveal yet another hidden association implicit

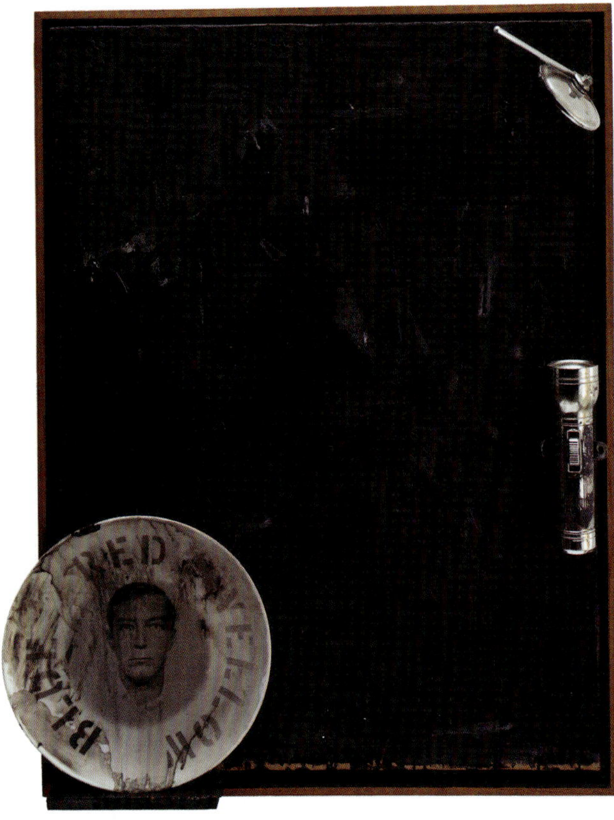

FIG. 3–2.
Souvenir by Jasper Johns (born 1930), encaustic on canvas with objects, 1964. Collection of the artist

in the canvas: a reference back to "Les Phares" (The Beacons)—artistic giants—so designated in a poem by the French poet and critic Charles Baudelaire.[25] Might Johns, well acquainted with Baudelaire's art criticism and deeply cognizant of the powerful imagery created by many generations of his artistic predecessors, seek, through his complex autobiographical *Souvenir*, to find his place among other "beacons" who lit the way for him?[26]

In a 1959 statement, Johns acknowledged the important example provided for him by a number of predecessors. Perhaps most suggestive in this context was Johns's recollection of "Marcel Duchamp's suggestion 'to reach the impossibility of sufficient visual memory to transfer from one like object to another the memory imprint.'"[27] If Johns's own composition clearly resonates with Duchamp's allusion to memory and its transfer, other Duchampian traces abound in his work. Particularly relevant is the hidden picture within a picture. Shortly after the completion of *Souvenir 2*, Johns would include a hidden portrait of Duchamp on a hinged canvas in *According to What*.[28] Even the dark canvas of *Souvenir* seems to bear a reference to this portrait, prominently displaying a dripping "shot" of paint, which would also appear with the hidden image of Duchamp. The memory of Duchamp is also suggested in Johns's deadpan self-depiction from a photo booth, which conjures up similar self-portraits by Duchamp, particularly his *Wanted* poster.[29]

Yet if Johns implicitly acknowledges the presence of other artists in the formation of his own artistic identity, it is his own likeness that provides the measure against which the composition as a whole functions. In a 1964 note that describes the composition of *Souvenir*, Johns directs himself to "Determine the size of [painting] from plate size."[30] Likewise, as Richard Field observed when Johns created the related lithograph (cat. 46), "the plate was the determining module [in its scale]." Arriving at Universal Limited Art Editions (ULAE), the artist came bearing a photo silk screen of the plate, which was not subject to manipulation.[31]

"Anything could perhaps be something else," wrote Johns about 1970. Including a direct reference to Duchamp, the commentary also relates to the *Souvenir* lithograph, in which Johns reminds himself to "Use silkscreen of dish from Souvenir as image." In the same group of notations, Johns also ponders the possibility that "There may be the question of resemblance or substitution," calling to mind the close compositional relationship between the placement of his likeness in the lower left corner of *Souvenir* and that of Marcel Duchamp's image in *According to What*. The following year, in a print project elaborating on aspects of *According to What*, Johns would allow his signature to appear with a cross through it, opposite Duchamp's initials, in a composition revealing Johns's interpretation of the elder artist's self-portrait: "I have deliberately taken Duchamp's own work and slightly changed it, and thought to make a kind of play on whose work it is, whether mine or his."[32] In raising the problem of authorship, Johns reveals the tangled patterns of influence and discourse that ultimately define identity. Later in his career, Johns would adopt a shadow reminiscent of both Duchamp and Pablo Picasso to convey his own likeness in the Seasons series.[33]

"I am concerned with a thing's not being what it was," Johns has said, "with its becoming something other than what it was."[34] Given his acute sensitivity to the new nuances introduced with each iteration of a composition, with its travel across media and time, Johns certainly recognized the new autobiographical

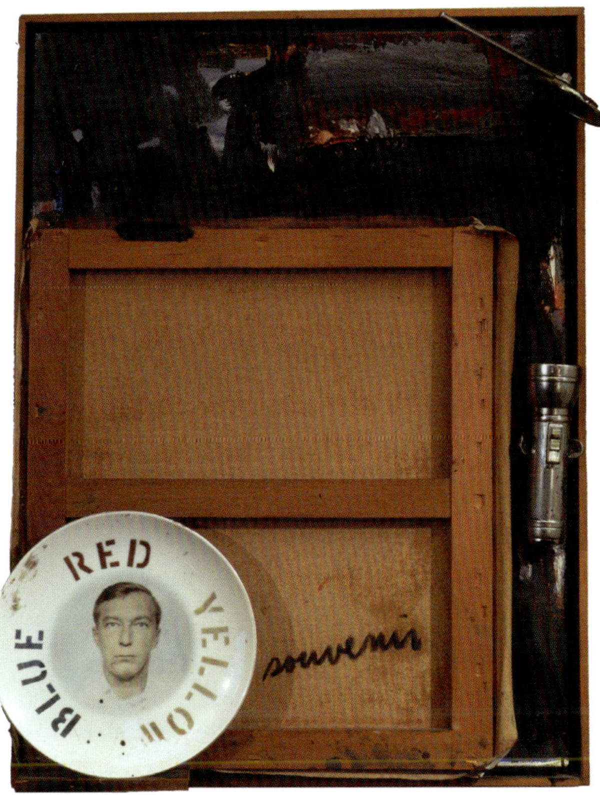

FIG. 3–3.
Souvenir 2 by Jasper Johns (born 1930), oil on canvas with objects, 1964. Private collection

focus *Souvenir* took on with its subsequent translation into a lithograph that would also serve as the basis for the poster advertising his 1970 print retrospective at the Philadelphia Museum of Art. On this occasion Johns may well have recalled the precedent provided by Marcel Duchamp's use of his *Wanted: $2,000 Reward* for the poster for his 1963 retrospective at the Pasadena Art Museum as well as a silk-screened version of his self-portrait in profile to promote the release of Robert Lebel's 1959 monograph and related exhibitions.[35] Yet, just as a mirror reflected back upon itself produces an illusion of infinity, so Johns's decision to face one canvas off against another produces a proliferation of readings, which allows autobiography to take on other associations. Perhaps it was just such a transformation the artist had in mind in 1966: "Thinking anything could be a souvenir of something else, not specifically a self-portrait. Ego was not clear. Maybe just another way of dishing up a Johns."[36]

If Jasper Johns teasingly collapses "Johnsian" style with his self-depiction, Andy Warhol, perhaps more than any other artist of his era, integrated his mechanical style with his image, creating a persona that was virtually indecipherable from the very technique and consumption of mass media. Describing his use of silk screens to produce paintings, Warhol declared in an early interview: "The reason I'm painting this way is that I want to be a machine, and I feel whatever I do and do machine-like is what I want to do."[37] As though anticipating, and perhaps partly inspiring, literary theorists such as Roland Barthes and Michel Foucault, who described the dissolution of the independent authority of the writer/artist in the late twentieth century, Warhol mounted his own challenge to traditional systems of ascribing meaning—and hence value—to works of art based upon their assignment to a particular author. In this spirit, Warhol asserted: "I think somebody should be able to do all my paintings for me. . . . I think it would be great if more people took up silkscreens so that no one would know whether my picture was mine or somebody else's."[38] Accepting the consequences of such a declaration, Warhol postulated himself as a nonexistent agent, constructed precisely—and exclusively—for consumers. Assessing Warhol's stance in 1971, Harold Rosenberg noted: "His mass production of paintings and his dramatization of himself are a radical reflection of the values that came to the fore in the art world toward the end of the 1950s. . . . Warhol has been the personification of [the public's] experience of art."[39]

Fascinated by Duchamp, Warhol appears to have fully absorbed the implications of Duchamp's description of the audience's input into the realization of the artist's creative act.[40] Famously turning to others to provide ideas, even the production of his self-portraits was generated by the suggestion of friends. Warhol's first self-portrait—based on photographs of himself captured in a photo booth and clearly indebted to the example of Duchamp's *Wanted: $2,000 Reward*—was done on commission for Florence Barron.[41] Warhol later credited art dealer Ivan Karp with the inspiration to create a likeness of himself.[42]

Created as a "giveaway" for an exhibition at which he announced his supposed retirement from painting, Warhol's 1966 self-portrait (cat. 43) became the basis for a remarkable series of silk-screen paintings (fig. 3–4), each repeating the same picture in different hues. The first group appeared only months later, at a popular exhibition of the artist's work organized by the Boston Institute of

Contemporary Art. The same image would go on to represent Warhol's contribution to the 1967 World's Fair in Montreal. While Warhol's proliferation of pictures representing himself in a signature pose might be interpreted as a mechanism to trumpet his fame, it also provided a means by which the artist could hide, as the public reveled in a sense of false familiarity based simply on a certain appearance. Not long after Warhol's self-portrait was exhibited in an international venue, the artist permitted a double to replace him at lectures, drawing the ire of the public once the ruse was discovered, but making the artist's point: "If you want to know all about Andy Warhol, just look at the surface of my paintings and films and me, and there I am. There's nothing behind it."[43] In 1971, at the opening of a retrospective exhibition at the Whitney, Warhol would legally change his name to "John Doe," the epitome of every man and no one special.[44]

If Warhol allowed himself to be absorbed and refracted through the idiom of popular culture, consciously permitting the public to construct him in its own image, the implications of this self-erasure seem to be the subject of Roy Lichtenstein's humorous 1978 *Self-Portrait* (fig. 3–5), in which the artist figures himself as an empty T-shirt above which a picture of a mirror hovers in place of the artist's own face.[45] The work raises a host of poignant questions. It reflects the historical role of the mirror in self-portraiture and simultaneously suggests the absence of authorial agency, as though the artist's own presence will be perpetually eclipsed by that of the viewer who stands before the work. The object also invites a comparison between mass reproduction and the autograph object. As Michel Lobel has observed, the mirror is an "image duplicator" par excellence, and the benday dots Lichtenstein employs refer back to images reproduced in the popular press—indeed, the very T-shirt Lichtenstein pictures was copied from a newspaper advertisement.[46] But the object itself is a painting that suggests—but does not replicate—the action of the mirror, thus firmly identifying the work with Lichtenstein rather than an indeterminate public.[47]

Lichtenstein's self-stylization as an unoccupied garment immediately calls to mind the famous bathrobes of Jim Dine, which functioned for more than a decade as a stand-in for the artist. Dine's appropriation of the emblem of the bathrobe (cat. 39), which he discovered in a 1964 newspaper advertisement, enabled him to define himself in terms of public culture.[48] As Dine explained:

FIG. 3–4.
Double Self-Portrait by Andy Warhol (1928–1987), silk-screen ink on synthetic polymer paint on canvas, 1967. The Detroit Institute of Arts; Founders Society Purchase, Friends of Modern Art Fund

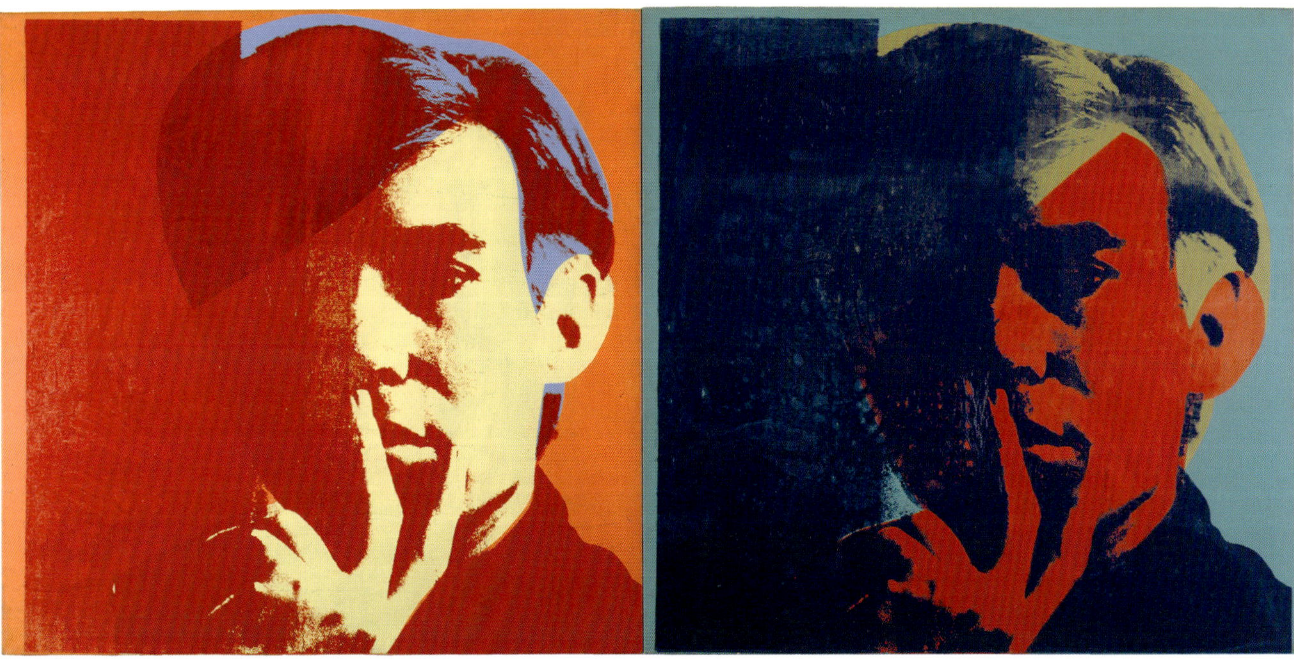

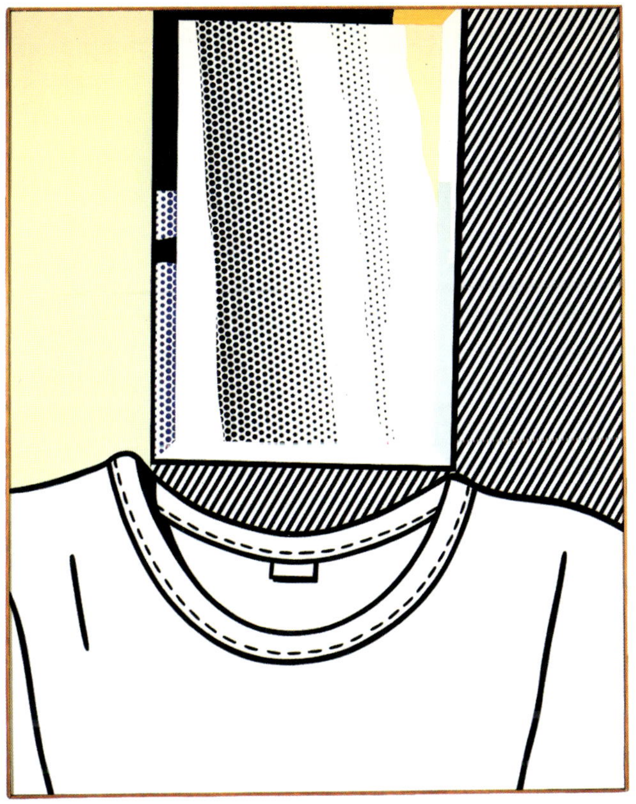

FIG. 3–5.
Self-Portrait by Roy Lichtenstein (1923–1997), oil and magna on canvas, 1978. Private collection

"There was nobody in the bathrobe, but when I saw it, it looked like me."[49] Ultimately, however, the representation ceased to be satisfying for an artist whose use of imagery in fact relied upon intensely personal associations.[50] By the late 1970s, Dine had begun to create figurative self-representations depicting his own features (cat. 40) and had come to claim that "Now bathrobes are bathrobes. They can truly be what they are."[51] He would reiterate in a later interview: "My attitude to the image *has* changed. In the beginning I did it as a stand-in for the self. But as I became more familiar with it, it became like everything else, more neutral. It started out being a bathrobe, and it ended up being a bathrobe: just that."[52]

Dine's use of the bathrobe in the mid-1960s points to a fundamental reexamination of the very nature of the historic enterprise of self-portrayal. Among the artists most deeply involved with recasting the meaning and practice of portraiture—and self-portraiture—was Chuck Close. Unlike Warhol, Johns, Dine, and Lichtenstein, Close has made the human face the exclusive focus of his career. But in so doing, Close deliberately wrested from his "heads" any conventional associations with portraiture. Indeed, Close's approach to portrayal may be described as rebellious on at least two fronts. First was his very decision to depict the face in an environment that continued to favor abstraction.[53] Second was his stubborn resistance to having his works identified as portraits, particularly early in his career.[54] In his determination to upend the genre's conventions, Close, deliberately or not, emulated Duchamp, whose own self-transformations playfully courted the absurd with his use of makeup, unconventional haircuts, and other accoutrements that enabled him to change his gender, his age, and his very identity as he repeatedly pictured himself in a wide range of guises. As with Duchamp, Close's affront to the tradition of portraiture reflected methodical thinking and, like Duchamp's practice, had the effect of opening up the field in new ways.

Close's defiant approach to portraiture resounds in the first of his "big heads," a giant self-portrait measuring approximately nine by seven feet (see fig. 2–6). The artist's expression, most easily readable in reproductions of the painting, mirrors his intentions. As Close put it: "Initially I wanted to make big, aggressive, confrontational images. I chose to portray myself as the angry young man. . . . I think there was a kind of theatricality there."[55] Such "theatricality" is accentuated by the artist's decision to enhance his towering presence (at the time Close stood at six feet three inches tall) by depicting himself from below, forcing the viewer to look up at him and confront a surly expression intensified by unkempt hair, an unshaven face, and a half-smoked cigarette.[56] Amplifying the confrontational sentiment was the work's gigantic scale, a calculated move on the artist's part, "forcing the viewer to focus on one area at a time," as Close explained, and thereby exposing those aspects of the pictorial "landscape" normally overlooked—the blurred field of peripheral vision—or the "little surface details" on a face.[57] Only by backing up several feet can the spectator take in the picture as a whole, which puts the process at odds with traditional portrayal.

In this manner, the painting—quite deliberately—did all the wrong things. Working from a photograph—one he shot himself with great awkwardness—Close did not suppress evidence of the photo-mechanical

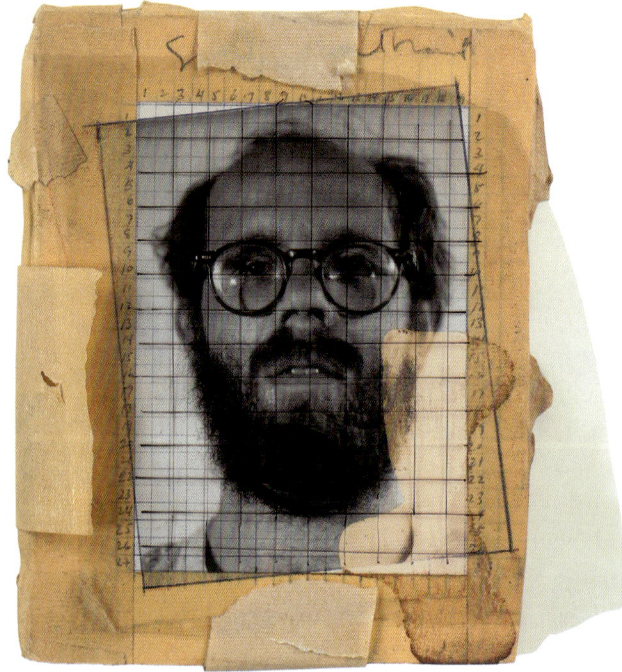

FIG. 3–6.
Self-Portrait Maquette by Chuck Close (born 1940), black and white Polaroid photograph scored with pencil and masking tape with plastic overlay, 1975. Private collection

origin of his work, but instead exploited it.[58] Even the painting surface, made using only "a couple tablespoons of black paint," airbrushed on, emulated that of a giant photograph.[59] The gesture was a defiant one. "It's hard to remember now," recounts Close, "but I was considered the Antichrist in the sixties by representational painters because my paintings looked like photographs, and were made from photographs, and because I suppressed virtuoso flourishes that were a sign of the painter's touch."[60]

Close's own face has frequently served as a site for the artist's exploration and experimentation, and he has made more self-portraits than any other subject in his oeuvre, creating at least one for every exhibition.[61] Like Duchamp, Johns, Warhol, Dine, and Lichtenstein, Close has frequently transferred a single image to different media to watch its transformation. Of the pictures he has selected, none has been used more than a 1975 photograph of the bearded artist wearing round spectacles, his teeth visible through slightly parted lips (fig. 3–6).[62] But interestingly enough, the photograph has never been made into a painting. Instead, it has inspired numerous paper-based works, including pencil and pastel drawings, an etching, and a pair of paper-pulp works, such as the manipulated paper-pulp piece in this exhibition (cat. 61). To a significant degree, Close has treated his own self-portrait as a yardstick, once musing: "I almost wish I had decided that, say, all prints were going to be self-portraits, or something like that. Just so that for that entire body of work, one constant would always be there."[63]

Yet while using his face, and photographs of it, as a physical barometer for new techniques, Close resists attempts to read his repeated returns to his own likeness as an attempt at psychological portrayal.[64] Indeed, his own countenance remains self-consciously inscrutable, even as it ages. However, in the sheer number and variety of self-portraits, Close seems to defeat the notion that one can possibly identify the "quintessential Close," suggesting instead the proliferation of individual selves over space and time and through the various media in which his image appears. Just as Barthes suggests that "the modern scriptor is born simultaneously with the text," so Close recasts and refigures himself with each iteration he produces of a portrait head. In portraying himself so multifariously, Close produces a powerful metaphor for the reconceptualization of the self in the era of mass production, the self as a multiplicity, rather than an essential unity.[65] As Maurice Blanchot writes, providing a gloss on Foucault's analysis of the "author-function":

> [I]t is accepted as a certainty that Foucault . . . got rid of, purely and simply, the notion of the subject: no more oeuvre, no more author, no more creative unity. But things are not that simple. The subject does not disappear; rather its excessively determined unity is put in question. What arouses interest and inquiry is its disappearance (that is, the new manner of being which disappearance is), or rather its dispersal, which does not annihilate it but offers us, out of it, no more than a plurality of positions and a discontinuity of functions.[66]

If Close's work points toward this reconceptualization of the self as a multiplicity, such an explosion of a solitary "essence" into myriad competing identities becomes explicit in the self-portrayals of artists such as Robert Arneson, Lucas Samaras, and Cindy Sherman during the 1970s and later. Indeed, through such works as Arneson's *Kiln Man* of 1971 (fig. 3–7), Samaras's *Photo-Transformation* series of 1976, and Cindy Sherman's *Untitled Film Stills* (fig. 3–8), made between 1977 and 1980, each artist vividly presents him- or herself via the simultaneous presentation of numerous distinct likenesses. Arneson, playing with the motif of the brick highlighted in *Kiln Man*, would later distill this self-representation into the very unit of the brick itself—the very emblem of the repeatable, and perhaps unknowable, entity (cat. 54). Indeed, although self-representation would proliferate in the careers of Arneson, Samaras, and Sherman (Arneson made eighteen self-portraits during the year he executed *Kiln Man*[67]), such repetition did not invite, or imply, increasing familiarity on the part of viewers with the artist, but instead emphasized the artist's very estrangement and distance. As Arneson would comment in 1989: "I never did a self-portrait. I always use a self-portrait as a mask."[68] Along similar lines, Sherman resists describing her *Untitled Film Stills* as self-portraiture, commenting: "I really don't think that [the pictures] are about me. It's maybe about me not wanting to be me and wanting to be all these other characters. Or at least try them on."[69] This sentiment becomes even more palpable in the work of Bruce Nauman, who has commented about his print-multiples (cat. 68): "Not knowing what you're supposed to look at keeps you at a distance from the art while the art keeps you at a distance from me. . . . I think that's a very strong part of my work—giving you some information about myself by giving you a piece of art, but also not letting you get any closer to me."[70]

Reproduction, then, contributes to the collapse not only of the autograph original but also of the notion of the artist as an individual whose personality can be easily imbibed through the activity of looking. "Suppose the stitching that normally holds seeing and understanding together in our view of things were to come undone. Where would that leave the look of self-portraiture?" asks T. J. Clark. "It might be possible as a result to pose the question of identity in a new way—to rescue it from the one mode of cognition (the privileged 'visual') and have it be

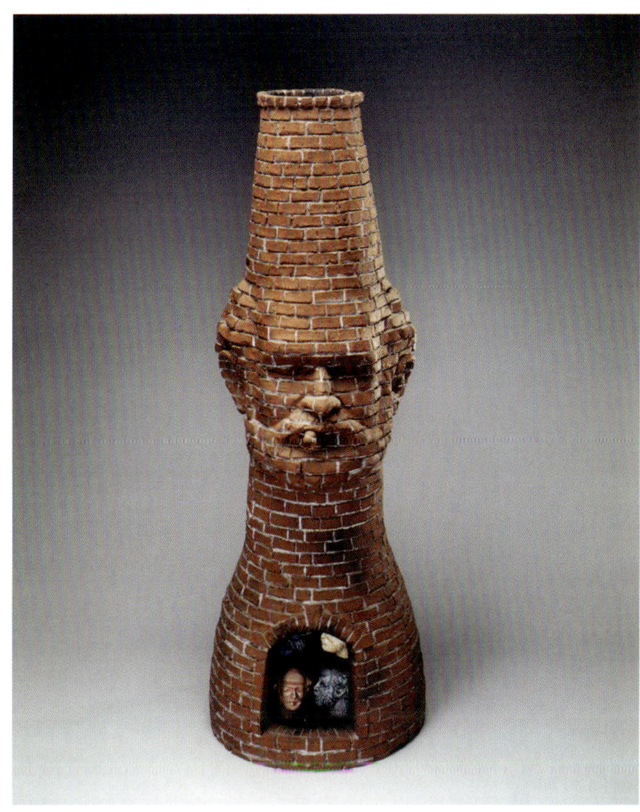

FIG. 3–7.
Kiln Man by Robert Arneson (1930–1992), glazed ceramic, 1971. Hirshhorn Musuem and Sculpture Garden, Smithsonian Institution, Washington, D.C.; Joseph H. Hirshhorn Bequest Fund, 1998

scattered among the modes of mask, place, sign, name, lineage, affiliation, performance, language-game. Under this rubric all forms of self-knowledge, looking included, would be 'insufficient.'"[71] In the wake of the proliferation of the mass-reproduced image, the very question of the category of the visual itself as a center of insight has come into question.

As suggested at the outset of this essay, a paradigm shift, initiated during the 1960s, transformed the field of self-portraiture as artworks became multiples by default and the authority of the artist was eclipsed by that of the audience. Each of the artists discussed here has employed overlapping strategies to reinvent portraiture—to dislodge it from the model of the unique original and to address the insistent questions about the status of individual identity. Rather than asserting the privileged perspective of the artist-creator-subject, these self-portraits seem to open the way to reexamine points of origin—exploring our models' influences. In the

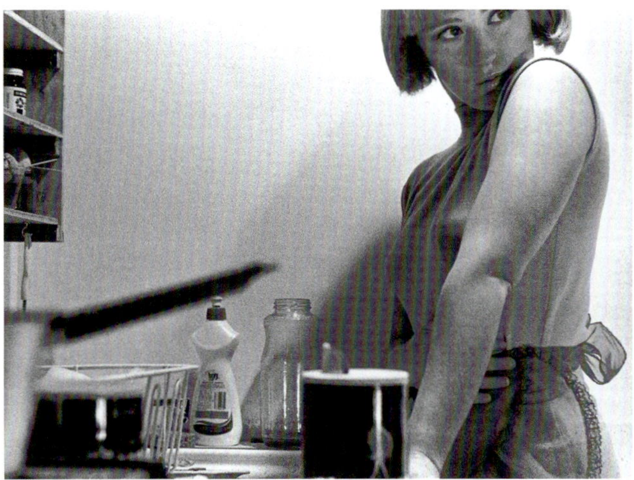

FIG. 3–8.
Untitled Film Still #3 by Cindy Sherman (born 1954), black-and-white photograph, 1977. Museum of Modern Art, New York City; courtesy of the artist and Metro Pictures

wake of the revolution in self-portrayal of the 1960s, the self-portrait has been repositioned not as a site of self-knowledge, but as a locus for uncertainty and the questioning of long-held assumptions. Far from destructive, this renegotiation has proved powerfully productive, as self-portraiture has proven capable of sustaining infinite reproducibility and the very instability of the self. In this reformulated state, self-depiction poses—and will continue to pose—provocative questions about personal identity in the late twentieth and early twenty-first centuries—and beyond.

NOTES

I thank Wendy Wick Reaves and Jennifer E. Quick for their feedback on this essay and Emily Caplan Reed for her assistance with research queries connected with it.

1 Walter Benjamin, "The Work of Art in the Age of Mechanical Reproduction," in *Illuminations: Essays and Reflections*, ed. Hannah Arendt (New York: Schocken Books, 1968), 224; essay originally published in *Zeitschrift für Sozialforschung* 5, no. 1 (1936).

2 Quoted in Christopher Finch, *Pop Art: Object and Image* (London: Studio Vista, 1968), 150; quoted by Wendy Steiner, "Postmodern Portraits," *Art Journal* 46 (Fall 1987): 174.

3 Publications treating recent portraiture, made from the mid-1960s forward, include (exclusive of catalogs on individual artists): Amy Goldin, "The Post-Perceptual Portrait," *Art in America* 63 (January–February 1975): 79–82; Carla Gottlieb, "Self-Portraiture in Modern Art," *Sonderdruck aus dem Wallraf-Richartz-Jahrbuch* (Cologne: Dumant Buchverlag, 1981), 267–302; Steiner, "Postmodern Portraits," 173–77; Ernst van Alphen, "The Portrait's Dispersal: Concepts of Representation and Subjectivity in Contemporary Portraiture," in *Portraiture: Facing the Subject*, ed. Joanna Woodall (Manchester: Manchester University Press, 1997), 239–56; Dean Sobel, *Identity Crisis: Self-Portraiture at the End of the Century*. (Milwaukee, WI: Milwaukee Art Museum, 1997); Melissa E. Feldman, *Face-Off: The Portrait in Recent Art*. (Philadelphia: Institute of Contemporary Art, University of Pennsylvania, 1994); B. H. Buchloh, "Residual Resemblance: Three Notes on the Ends of Portraiture," in Feldman, *Face-Off*, 53–69; Paul Moorhouse, *Pop Art Portraits* (New Haven, CT: Yale University Press, 2007); Wendy Wick Reaves et al., *Eye Contact: Modern American Portrait Drawings from the National Portrait Gallery* (Seattle and Washington, DC: University of Washington Press for the National Portrait Gallery, 2002); Monique Yaari, "Who/What Is the Subject? Representations of Self in Late Twentieth-Century French Art," *Word and Image* 16 (October–December 2000): 363–77.

4 In his excellent study of Albrecht Dürer, Joseph Leo Koerner explores the intellectual and interpretative implications of the emergence of the concept of the self in Dürer's art; see Joseph Leo Koerner, *The Moment of Self-Portraiture* (Chicago: University of Chicago Press, 1993).

5 According to Jasper Johns: "I'd wanted to be an artist from age 5. No one in my immediate family was involved in art (I had a grandmother who painted, though I never knew her) but somehow the idea must have been conveyed to me that an artist is someone of interest in society." Jasper Johns, quoted in Grace Glueck, "'Once Established,' Says Jasper Johns, 'Ideas Can Be Discarded,'" *New York Times*, October 16, 1977, sec. 2, pp. 1, 31; reprinted in Kirk Varnedoe, ed., *Jasper Johns: Writings, Sketchbook Notes, Interviews* (New York: Museum of Modern Art, 1996), 162; also quoted by Riva Castleman, *Jasper Johns: A Print Retrospective* (New York: Museum of Modern Art, 1986), 11.

6 Anthony Bond, "Performing the Self?" in *Self-Portrait: Renaissance to Contemporary*, ed. Anthony Bond and Joanna Woodall (London: National Portrait Gallery, 2005), 37.

7 T. J. Clark, "The Look of Self-Portraiture," in *Self-Portrait: Renaissance to Contemporary*, 59.

8 William Ivins offers an informative account of the development of the halftone reproduction process and its implications in *Prints and Visual Communication* (1953; New York: Da Capo Press, 1969), 126–29.

9 Arguably, film was to Benjamin what television was to artists maturing during the 1960s. As Jonathan Fineberg and others have noted, in the decade from 1947 to 1957 alone, the consumption of television sets rose dramatically, increasing from a mere 10,000 in American homes to 40 million; see Jonathan Fineberg, *Art Since 1940: Strategies of Being*, 2nd ed. (Englewood Cliffs, NJ: Prentice Hall, 2000), 244. For Warhol and Close, the television served as a constant source of accompaniment; see Andy Warhol, *The Philosophy of Andy Warhol* (New York: Harcourt Brace and Company, 1975); for information concerning the presence of the television in Close's studio, I thank Richard Shiff.

10 Benjamin, "The Work of Art in the Age of Mechanical Reproduction," 230–31.

11 See, for example, Bond and Woodall, *Self-Portrait: Renaissance to Contemporary*.

12 Buchloh, for example, describes the "refusal of the genre" among artists of the pop era (Buchloh, "Residual Resemblance," 60); redressing this misperception is the goal of Moorhouse, *Pop Art Portraits*.

13 Roland Barthes, "The Death of the Author," in *Image, Music, Text*, ed. and trans. Stephen Heath (New York: Hill and

Wang, 1977), 148; essay originally published as "La mort de l'auteur," *Mantéia* 5 (1968).

14 Marcel Duchamp, "The Creative Act," in *The Writings of Marcel Duchamp*, ed. Michel Sanouillet and Elmer Peterson (New York: Da Capo Press, 1973), 140. Talk originally delivered by Duchamp in Houston at the American Federation of the Arts, April 1957; first published in *ARTnews* 56 (Summer 1957); also reprinted in Robert Lebel, *Marcel Duchamp*, trans. George Heard Hamilton (1959; New York: Paragraphic Books, 1967), 77–78.

15 Keith Hartley, "Andy Warhol: The Photomat Self-Portraits," in *Andy Warhol Self-Portraits* (Ostfildern-Ruit: Hatje Cantz Verlag, 2004), 50.

16 These works are discussed at length in the context of Duchamp's self-portrayal in Anne Collins Goodyear and James W. McManus, eds., *Inventing Marcel Duchamp: The Dynamics of Portraiture* (Washington, DC: National Portrait Gallery, distributed by MIT Press, 2009), on Duchamp's *Wanted: $2,000 Reward* and his *Poster within a Poster*, see cats. 25 and 65, respectively.

17 On Sturtevant's *Duchamp Wanted* and Richard Pettibone's *Ferus Poster*, see ibid., cats. 93 and 72. The power of this image continues to manifest itself. In 2006, Gavin Turk created his own interpretation of the work (see ibid., cat. 101). Sturtevant and Pettibone continue to shape their response to *Wanted: $2,000 Reward*—Sturtevant's *Duchamp Wanted* is published as an open edition. Pettibone recently completed *Marcel Duchamp, "Wanted, #2* (2007), a painted appropriation of Duchamp's *Wanted: $2,000 Reward*, in which Pettibone has substituted the name "Lee en Rose"—a reference to a pseudonym listed in his 1966 *Ferus Poster*—for Rrose Sélavy, Duchamp's famous female persona.

18 See, for example, Barbara Rose, "Self-Portraiture: Theme with a Thousand Faces," *Art in America* 63 (January–February 1975): 71, 73; Ann C. Van Devanter and Alfred V. Frankenstein, *American Self-Portraits, 1670–1973* (Washington, DC: International Exhibitions Foundation, 1974), 224–25; Gottlieb, "Self-Portraiture in Modern Art," 277–80.

19 A number of the variations are published in Richard S. Field, "Souvenir: Theme and Execution," in *Jasper Johns: Prints, 1960–1970* (Philadelphia: Philadelphia Museum of Art, 1970), unpaginated. For a detailed discussion of related drawings, see Nan Rosenthal and Ruth E. Fine, *The Drawings of Jasper Johns* (Washington, DC: National Gallery of Art, 1990), cat. 51, *Souvenir*, and cat. 52, *Souvenir 2*, 192–94. Several sketchbook notes made by Johns also refer to this series of works. See for example, Jasper Johns, Book A, pp. 49, 51, and 53, 1964; and Book C, c. 1970–1971 reprinted in Varnedoe, *Jasper Johns*, 56–58, and 73 respectively.

20 *Souvenir* and *Souvenir 2* are part of a tightly interrelated group of four compositions, made in close succession, which also includes *Watchman* and *According to What*. The close conceptual links between the pieces are revealed by interrelated notes for the pieces that suggest elements of the compositions were working together in Johns's mind. On the conceptual connections between these pieces, see Field, "Souvenir"; Michael Crichton, *Jasper Johns* (New York: Whitney Museum of American Art, 1977), 51–53; Francis M. Naumann, *Jasper Johns: According to What and Watchman* (New York: Gagosian Gallery, 1992); Roberta Bernstein, *Jasper Johns' Paintings and Sculptures, 1954–1974: "The Changing Focus of the Eye"* (1975; Ann Arbor: UMI Research Press, 1985), 113–23.

21 Rosenthal and Fine clarify that the flashlights did in fact function (Rosenthal and Fine, *Drawings of Jasper Johns*, 192).

22 Crichton notes that the flashlight system did not work, when executed, as well as Johns had hoped. (Crichton, *Jasper Johns*, 50).

23 Field also suggests that, in the lithograph, "the 2 on the back of the 'canvas' alludes to the insufficiency of memory to transfer an image from reality to memory and back to reality" (Field, "Souvenir").

24 Naumann, *Jasper Johns*, 18, quoting "Pop's Dada," *Time*, February 5, 1965, 85.

25 In his 1855 poem "Les Phares" ("The Beacons"), published as part of his collection *Les fleurs du mal* (*The Flowers of Evil*), Baudelaire meditates on the work of artists he considers to be the greatest. These include (in the order introduced by Baudelaire): Rubens, Leonardo, Rembrandt, Michelangelo, Watteau, Goya, and Delacroix. Johns's familiarity with Baudelaire is suggested by a 1967 note, "Have made a silkscreen of Baudelaire's description of sculpture as an inferior art" (Johns, Book B, c. 1967, reprinted in Varnedoe, *Jasper Johns*, 63).

26 In a 1959 artist's statement, Johns specifically acknowledged the importance of the examples provided by Leonardo, Cézanne, and Duchamp for him (Jasper Johns, artist's statement, in *Sixteen Americans*, ed. Dorothy Miller [New York: Museum of Modern Art, 1959], 22; reprinted in Varnedoe, *Jasper Johns*, 19–20). Throughout his career, Johns's work has included meditations on the work of numerous other historic models,

including Grünwald, Munch, and Picasso.

27 Johns specifically mentions his interest in this note from Duchamp's *Green Box*, "to reach the Impossibility of/sufficient visual memory/ to transfer/ from one/ like object to another/ the *memory* imprint" in his artist's statement for *Sixteen Americans* (ibid.); Johns's familiarity with *The Green Box* was such that he published a review of the English translation; see Jasper Johns, "Duchamp," *Scrap* no. 2 (December 23, 1960): 4; reprinted in Varnedoe, *Jasper Johns*, 20–21. Roberta Bernstein, like Field, notes the relationship between *Souvenir* and Johns's professed admiration for Duchamp's note; see Bernstein, *Jasper Johns' Paintings and Sculptures, 1954–1974*, 59 and 116–17; and Field, "Souvenir."

28 For an extensive discussion of this work, see Naumann, *Jasper Johns*; on Johns's portrayal of Duchamp, see also Anne Collins Goodyear, "Reflections on 'A Made-Up History': Documenting Duchamp's Impact on Recent Portraiture," in Goodyear and McManus, *Inventing Marcel Duchamp*.

29 In a note related to *According to What*, Johns described the system he puts into play in *Souvenir*: "In WHAT use a light and a mirror. The mirror will throw the light to some other part of the painting." Johns, Book A, p. 51, 1964, in Varnedoe, *Jasper Johns*, 57.

30 Johns, Book A, p. 53, 1964, ibid., 58.

31 Field, "Souvenir."

32 Johns, Book C, c. 1970–71, in Varnedoe, *Jasper Johns*, 73. Johns, quoted in John Coplans, "Fragments according to Johns: An Interview with Jasper Johns," *The Print Collector's Newsletter* 3 (May–June 1972): 29–32; reprinted in Varnedoe, *Jasper Johns*, 141.

33 A detailed discussion of the Seasons is included in Rosenthal and Fine, *Drawings of Jasper Johns*, 312–39. A profile collage of Marcel Duchamp, based on Duchamp's *Self-Portrait in Profile*, is included in the *Fall* panel; I thank Ruth Fine for first bringing this profile to my attention. This work is discussed in Goodyear, "Reflections on 'A Made-Up History.'"

34 Quoted in Gene R. Swenson, "What Is Pop Art?" (part 2), *ARTnews* 62 (February 1964): 43, 66–67; reprinted in Varnedoe, *Jasper Johns*, 93; quoted in Castleman, *Jasper Johns Print Retrospective*, 16.

35 Bernstein notes that Johns owns a copy of this poster, as well as other versions of Duchamp's *Self-Portrait in Profile*, specifically one of the editions reproduced with "25 numbered copies of Ulf Linde's *Marcel Duchamp* (1963)" and in Arturo Schwarz's *Marcel Duchamp: Ready-Mades, Etc.* (1964), both of which Johns owns (Bernstein, *Jasper Johns' Paintings and Sculptures, 1954–1974*, 119).

36 Ibid., 117. Also quoted in Charlotte Willard, "Eye to Eye," *Art in America* 54 (March–April 1966): 57; and reprinted in Varnedoe, *Jasper Johns*, 129.

37 Andy Warhol, interview with Gene Swenson, in *Art in Theory, 1900–1990*, ed. Charles Harrison and Paul Wood (Oxford: Blackwell, 1992), 732; originally published in Gene Swenson, "What Is Pop Art?: Interviews with Eight Painters" (part 1), *ARTnews* 62 (November 1963).

38 Ibid. When queried by Swenson about whether Warhol's proposition "would turn art history upside down," Warhol simply replied "yes."

39 Harold Rosenberg, "Art's Other Self," *New Yorker*, June 12, 1971, 101–3.

40 On Warhol's fascination with Duchamp see Hartley, "Andy Warhol," 50; and on Warhol's 1964 *Screen Test* of Duchamp, Goodyear and McManus, *Inventing Marcel Duchamp*, cat. 70.

41 Hartley, "Andy Warhol," 50; and Dietmar Elger, "'The Best American Invention—To Be Able to Disappear,'" in *Andy Warhol: Self-Portraits*, 122.

42 Andy Warhol and Pat Hackett, *Popism: The Warhol '60s* (New York: Harcourt Brace Jovanovich, 1980), 17; quoted in Elger, "'The Best American Invention,'" 122.

43 Quoted by Dietmar Elger, "The Best American Invention—To Be Able to Disappear," in *Andy Warhol: Self-Portraits* (Ostfildern-Ruit: Hatje Cantz Verlag, 2004), 127.

44 Barbara Rose, "In Andy Warhol's Aluminum Foil, We Have All Been Reflected," *New York*, May 31, 1971, 54.

45 For an insightful discussion of the trope of portraiture in the art of Roy Lichtenstein, see Buchloh, "Residual Resemblance," 63–65.

46 Michael Lobel, *Image Duplicator: Roy Lichtenstein and the Emergence of Pop Art* (New Haven, CT: Yale University Press, 2002), 72.

47 Michael Lobel makes a similar point. See ibid., 72–73.

48 Note that Dine has acknowledged his debt to Duchamp in using a "readymade" robe in this fashion; see Marco Livingstone, *Jim Dine: The Alchemy of Images* (New York: Monacelli Press, 1998), 191. Paul Moorhouse persuasively argues that Dine's *Green Suit* (1959) also functions as a "metaphorical self-portrait," created at a time of anguish. See Moorhouse, "Overt, Covert and Imaginary: The Iconography of the Pop Art Portrait," in Moorhouse, *Pop Art Portraits*, 82–84.

49 "Poet of the Personal," *Time*, March 9, 1970, 50.

50 Dine felt intensely personal associations in tools that he used (see Jean E. Feinberg, *Jim Dine* [New York: Abbeville Press, 1995], 24). Indeed, Dine moved away from using found objects precisely "because they have too much of other's people's mystery about them" (Jim Dine, quoted in "Jim Dine" entry, *Current Biography*, ed. Charles Moritz [New York: H. W. Wilson, 1969], 125.).

51 Quoted in Livingstone, *Jim Dine*, 198; from interview with Constance W. Glenn, January and April 1979, in Glenn, *Jim Dine Figure Drawings, 1975–1979* (New York: Harper and Row, 1979), 17.

52 Quoted in Livingstone, *Jim Dine*, 198; from interview with Livingstone, July 22 and 23, 1986.

53 On Close's rejection of what he perceived as Clement Greenberg's interdiction of the portrait, see Robert Storr, "Interview with Chuck Close," in Storr, *Chuck Close* (New York: Museum of Modern Art and Harry N. Abrams, 1998), 92.

54 On Close's refusal to identify his work as portraiture see, for example, "A Progression by Chuck Close: Who's Afraid of Photography," artist's statement distilled from conversation between Chuck Close, Amy Baker Sandback, and Ingrid Sischy, *Artforum* 22 (May 1984): 50; and Storr, *Chuck Close*, 86.

55 Quoted in Lisa Lyons, "Expanding the Limits of Portraiture," in Lisa Lyons and Robert Storr, *Chuck Close* (New York: Rizzoli, 1987), 39; quoted in Madeleine Grynsztejn, "A Constant-in-Progress," in *Chuck Close: Self-Portraits, 1967–2005*, ed. Siri Engberg and Madeleine Grynsztejn (San Francisco and Minneapolis: San Francisco Museum of Modern Art and Walker Art Center, 2005), 108.

56 In December 1988, Chuck Close experienced a medical event leading to partial paralysis that requires him to use a wheelchair. This episode and his recovery are described in detail by John Guare, *Chuck Close: Life and Work, 1988–1995* (New York: Thames and Hudson, 1995).

57 Quoted in Cindy Nemser, "An Interview with Chuck Close," *Artforum* 8 (January 1970): 53.

58 Douglas R. Nickel, "Chuck Close's Glass Eye," in *Chuck Close: Self-Portraits*, 132.

59 Close describes the small amount of paint he uses in Nemser, "An Interview with Chuck Close," 53; on the comparison of the surface to a photograph, see Grynsztejn, "A Constant-in-Progress," 109.

60 Chuck Close, in Michael Kimmelman, *Portraits: Talking with Artists at the Met, the Modern, the Louvre, and Elsewhere* (New York: Random House, 1998), 246; quoted by Nickel, "Chuck Close's Glass Eye," 131.

61 Siri Engberg, "The Paper Mirror: Chuck Close's Self-Reflection in Drawings and Prints," in *Chuck Close: Self-Portraits,* 123 and 121 n. 7.

62 Grynsztejn, "A Constant-in-Progress," 114.

63 From a 1997 interview with Deborah Wye, quoted in Wye, "Changing Expressions: Printmaking," in Storr, *Chuck Close*, 79.

64 Ibid., 79.

65 Barthes, "The Death of the Author," 145.

66 Maurice Blanchot, "Michel Foucault as I Imagine Him," trans. Jeffrey Mehlman, in *Foucault/Blanchot* (New York: Zone Books, 1987), 76–77; cited by Buchloh, "Residual Resemblance," 53.

67 Robert Arneson, from an interview with Maddie Jones, 1978; quoted by Neal Benezra, *Robert Arneson: A Retrospective* (Des Moines, IA: Des Moines Art Center, 1985), 30.

68 Robert Arneson, "Alice Street and After," faculty research lecture, University of California at Davis, quoted by Jonathan Fineberg, "Humor at the Frontier of the Self," in *Robert Arneson: Self-Reflections* (San Francisco: San Francisco Museum of Modern Art, 1997), 14.

69 Cindy Sherman, in Mark Stevens, "How I Made It: Cindy Sherman on Her 'Untitled Film Stills,'" *New York*, April 7, 2008, available at www.nymag.com/anniversary/40th/culture/45773, p. 3. In the same interview, Sherman tells Stevens it is a mistake to identify the *Untitled Film Stills* as self-portraits. But, in another context, Sherman told an interviewer: "I divide myself up into many different parts. One part is myself in the country, when I go upstate. My professional self is another part, and my work self in the studio is another." (Cindy Sherman in Noriko Fuku, "A Woman of Parts—Artist Cindy Sherman—Interview," *Art in America* 85 [June 1997]: 79).

70 Christopher Cordes, "Talking with Bruce Nauman," in *Bruce Nauman Prints, 1970–89* (New York: Castelli Graphics and the Lorence-Monk Gallery, and Chicago: Donald Young Gallery, 1989), 24.

71 Clark, "The Look of Self-Portraiture," 65.

CATALOG

Contributors

WENDY WICK REAVES	**WWR**
ANNE COLLINS GOODYEAR	**ACG**
ANN PRENTICE WAGNER	**APW**
EMILY CAPLAN REED	**ECR**

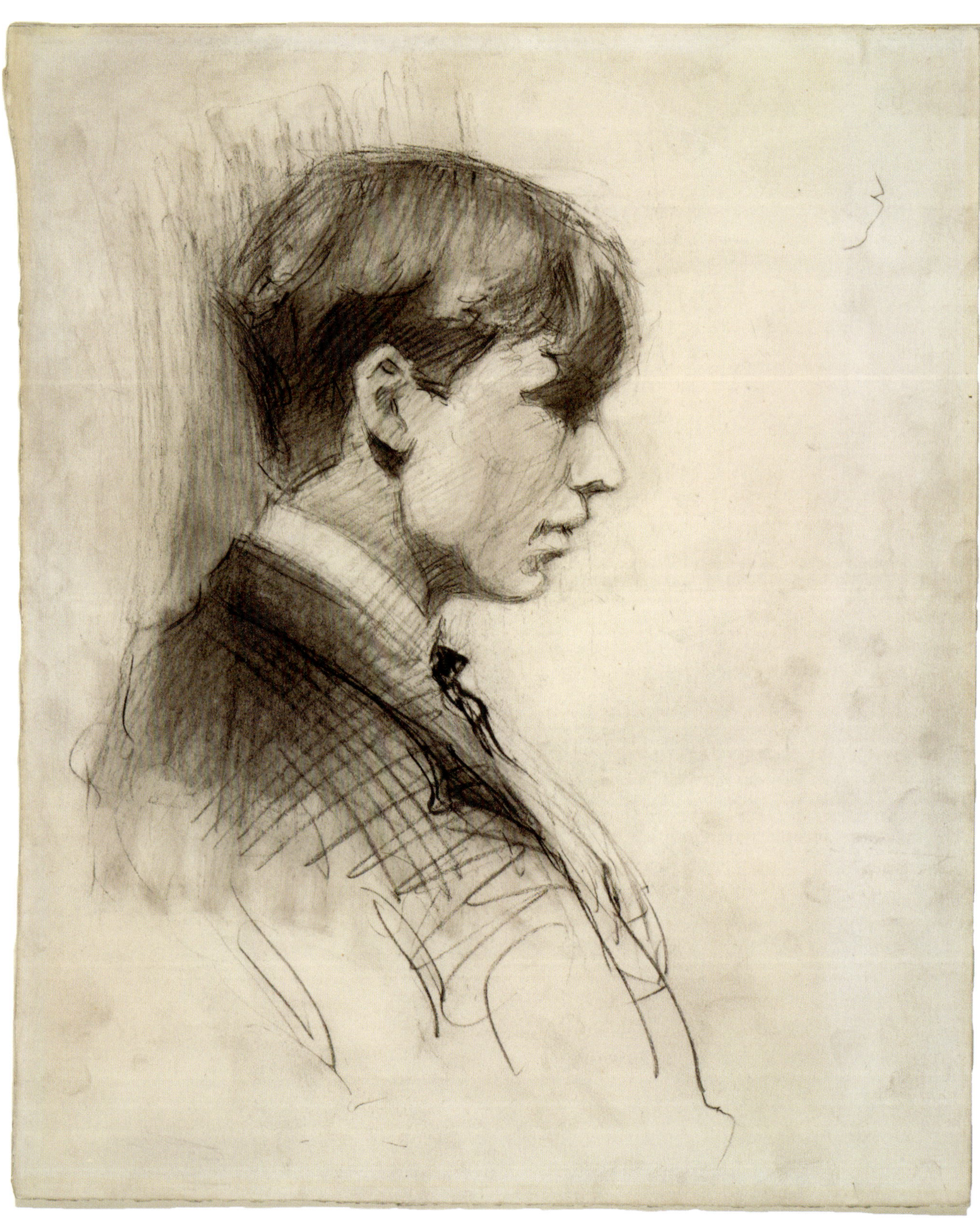

1.

Edward Hopper (1882–1967)

Charcoal on paper, 27 x 22.5 cm
(10 5/8 x 8 7/8 in.), c. 1900–1905
The Ruth Bowman and Harry Kahn Twentieth-Century American Self-Portrait Collection
NPG.2002.276

EDWARD HOPPER'S fellow student at the New York School of Art, Rockwell Kent, recalled Hopper's reliably producing "brilliant" drawings with impressive speed.[1] This self-portrait demonstrates that Kent's confidence was well founded. Despite the challenging profile view, the young Hopper worked with striking mastery of his medium. He laid down the basic shapes with swift marks, then erased and rubbed the charcoal to capture the play of light on top of his glossy dark hair and the midrange shadows on his jacket. He finished the drawing by deftly adding black strokes to strengthen the darkest shadows and sharpen the outlines of his collar, hair, ear, and profile.

As Hopper was crafting such student works he was also laying the foundation for his artistic career. He had started his training with the practical goal of becoming an illustrator. In 1899 he enrolled at the New York School of Illustrating; the following year he transferred to the more distinguished New York School of Art, although he continued to study illustration.[2] Under the tutelage of Kenneth Hayes Miller and other teachers, Hopper's skills soon eclipsed the naive literalism of the drawings he had made in 1900. This drawing has a new polish and sophistication that suggests the influence of William Merritt Chase, with whom Hopper began to study painting in 1901, and Robert Henri, who arrived at the school in 1902.[3] In these early years of the twentieth century, Hopper's growing confidence as a painter and draftsman helped him to make rapid progress toward his new ambition to become a professional painter.[4] This portrait, however, demonstrates the young man's lingering shyness as he hid his eyes under a thick lock of hair.

APW

Notes

1 Rockwell Kent, *It's Me O Lord: The Autobiography of Rockwell Kent* (New York: Dodd, Mead, & Co., 1955), 84.

2 Gail Levin, *Edward Hopper: An Intimate Biography* (New York: Alfred A. Knopf, 1996), 27–35.

3 Ibid., 35, 39. For illustrations of student drawings by Hopper dated 1900 see Gail Levin, *Edward Hopper: The Art and the Artist* (New York and London: W. W. Norton, in association with the Whitney Museum of American Art, 1980), plates 1 and 2.

4 For awards for art that Hopper won beginning in 1903 and his rise from student to teacher at the New York School, see Levin, *Intimate Biography*, 45.

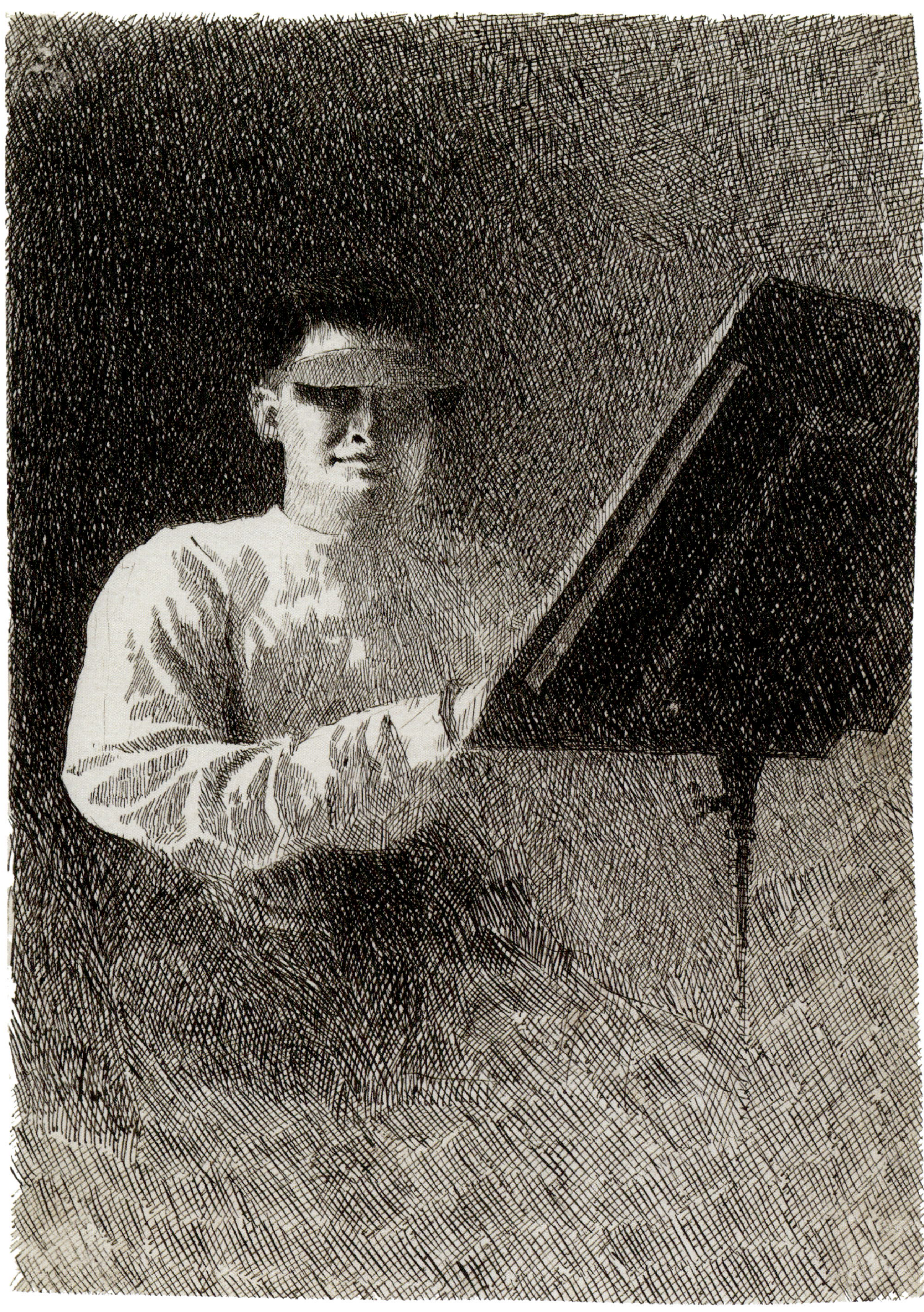

2.

Joseph Stella (1877–1946)

Ink on paper, 17.7 x 12.6 cm (6 15/16 x 4 15/16 in.), c. 1900
The Ruth Bowman and Harry Kahn Twentieth-Century American Self-Portrait Collection
NPG.2002.345

CREATED NEARLY four decades apart, these self-portrait drawings of Joseph Stella, executed at the turn of the twentieth century and in 1937, reflect both ongoing trends and evolution in Stella's work. As an Italian immigrant to the United States who became a citizen in 1923, Stella fluctuated between the "old world" of his native country and the modern sensibility of his adopted home. Merging the classic with the contemporary, Stella's drawing technique and style demonstrates a strong interest in the work of the old masters as well as a commitment to modern symbolism and, in his maturity, an aesthetic of flatness and linearity.

Stella's early ink self-portrait reflects the young artist's commitment to his craft. Depicting himself at his easel with a visor to sharpen his focus, Stella demonstrates a skillful use of cross-hatching and a nuanced handling of modeling from dark to light, reminiscent of the example of Rembrandt. Although Stella had intended to follow his older brother—who had come earlier to the United States—into medicine, he soon enrolled in art school, studying at the Art Students League and at the New York School of Art with William Merritt Chase. The confidence that Stella exudes in his self-portrait may well have resulted from the admiration his teacher and classmates expressed for his draftsmanship. In 1901, Chase praised one of Stella's portrait studies with the assertion: "Manet couldn't have done it better!" His fellow students applauded his accomplishment.[1]

Although Stella became enamored of the bright colors and abstraction associated with Futurism during the 1910s, particularly during a trip to Paris in 1911, he did not lose his interest in more classical representation. The technique of silver- and goldpoint, demanding a specially prepared ground and permitting no erasure, both demonstrated Stella's interest in tradition and his own extraordinary facility. Describing his allegiance to metalpoint drawing, Stella expressed his "ardent wish to draw with all precision possible, using the inflexible media of silver- and goldpoint that reveal instantly the clearest graphic eloquence."[2]

In adhering to the demands of a history-laden technique in the early twentieth century, Stella compared himself to a tree, digging its "roots obstinately, stubbornly" into the medium.[3] Intriguingly, this very imagery played a key role in Stella's 1937 self-portrait, executed in metalpoint.[4] The strong presence of a thick tree trunk, which occupies the left half of the composition, with a protruding branch that frames the artist's head, reflects Stella's mystical interest in the natural world

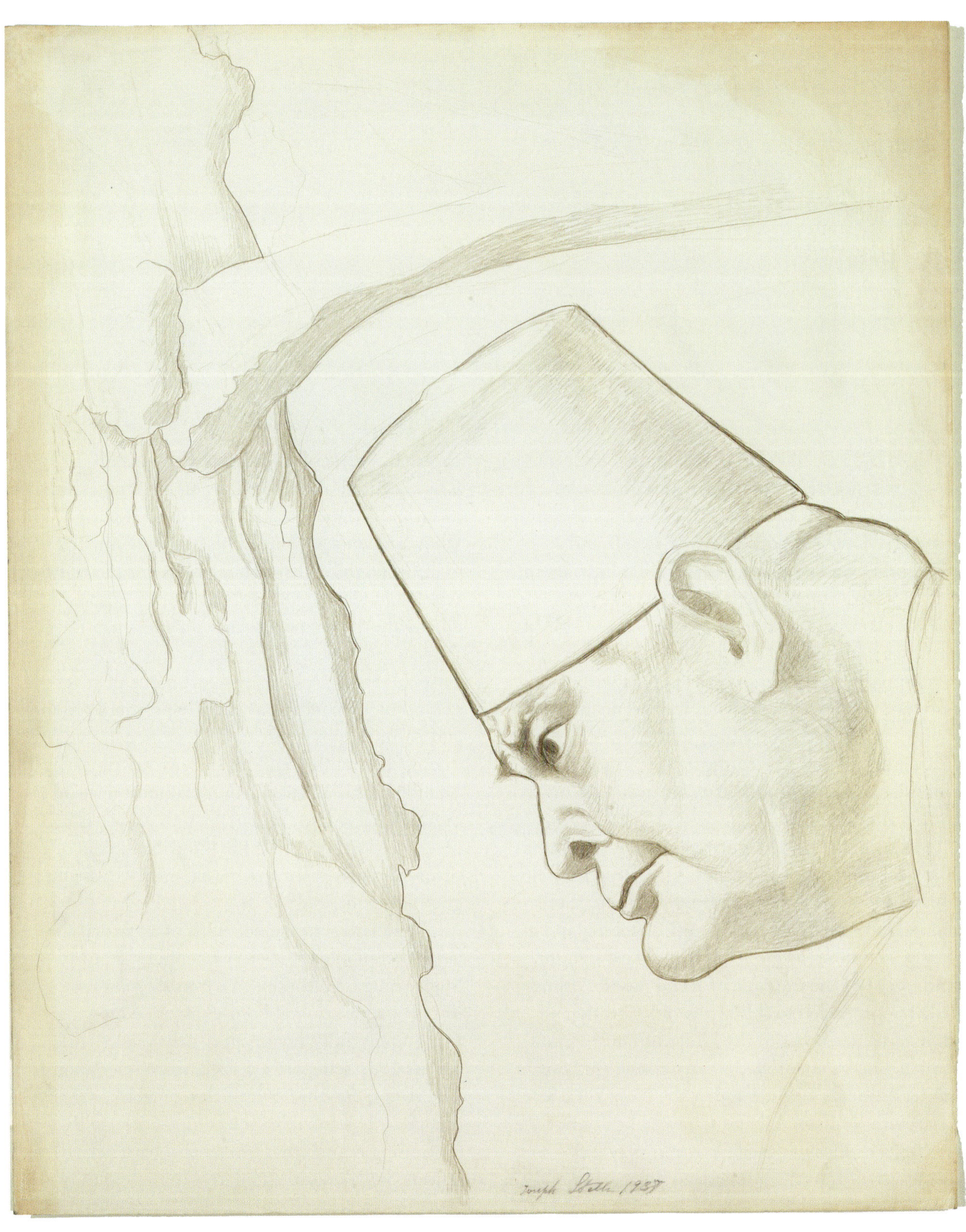

3.

Joseph Stella (1877–1946)

Metalpoint on paper, 73.6 x 58.5 cm
(29 x 23 1/16 in.), 1937
The Ruth Bowman and Harry Kahn Twentieth-Century American Self-Portrait Collection
NPG.2002.346

and, more specifically, his long-standing interest in the symbolic power of the tree. "The artist is like a tree," Stella wrote a friend in 1928, "growing older, bent under the weight of its fruit, it presses always closer to the maternal womb that gave it birth."[5] The artist's use of this natural imagery may have been stimulated in part by his travels to Barbados in 1937 with his sick wife, Mary French Stella. The trip invigorated the aging artist, who seems to construct a counterpart for himself in the gnarled bark of the thick trunk at which he gazes intently.

Stella's adoption of the fez in his late self-portrait may have many different associations. It may signal in part his fierce Italian pride in Benito Mussolini, whose elite Blackshirts incorporated the fez, and whom Stella considered a "savior" in the years before World War II.[6] It could also refer to the region of North Africa where Stella had traveled, or perhaps more broadly to the exotic mysticism with which the artist wished to associate himself.

Stella's self-portraiture reflects the confidence and deliberation of an artist able to merge the modern with the traditional; the mystical with the observed; and the symbolic power of medium, technique, and image. "The greatest effort of the artist is to catch and render permanent (materialize) that blissful moment (inspiration) of his when he sees things out of normal proportion, elevated and spiritualized, appearing new, *as seen for the first time*," wrote Stella in the early 1920s.[7] As reflected in this pair of drawings, which frame Stella's career, the freshness of his vision, his capacity to reimagine and recast himself through the act of drawing, evident in his youth, continues undiminished, and more nuanced, at the conclusion of his career.

ACG

Notes

1 Joann Moser, *Visual Poetry: The Drawings of Joseph Stella* (Washington and London: Smithsonian Institution Press, 1990), 4. Moser is citing Joseph Stella, "Notes about Joseph Stella," Joseph Stella Papers, Archives of American Art, roll 346, frame 1278.

2 Quoted in Barbara Haskell, *Joseph Stella* (New York: Whitney Museum of American Art; distributed by Harry N. Abrams), 120, from Joseph Stella, "Confession," n.d., reprinted in Haskell, 220.

3 Ibid.

4 As Joann Moser points out, it is virtually impossible to distinguish between silverpoint and goldpoint, which Stella was also known to have used, see Moser, *Visual Poetry*, 150 n. 92.

5 Joseph Stella, letter to Ferdinando Santoro, quoted in *Italiani pel Mondo*, August 1928, quoted by Irma B. Jaffe, *Joseph Stella* (1970; New York: Fordham University Press, 1988), 109.

6 Haskell, *Joseph Stella*, 163.

7 Stella, "Notes" (c. 1921–1925), printed in ibid., 205.

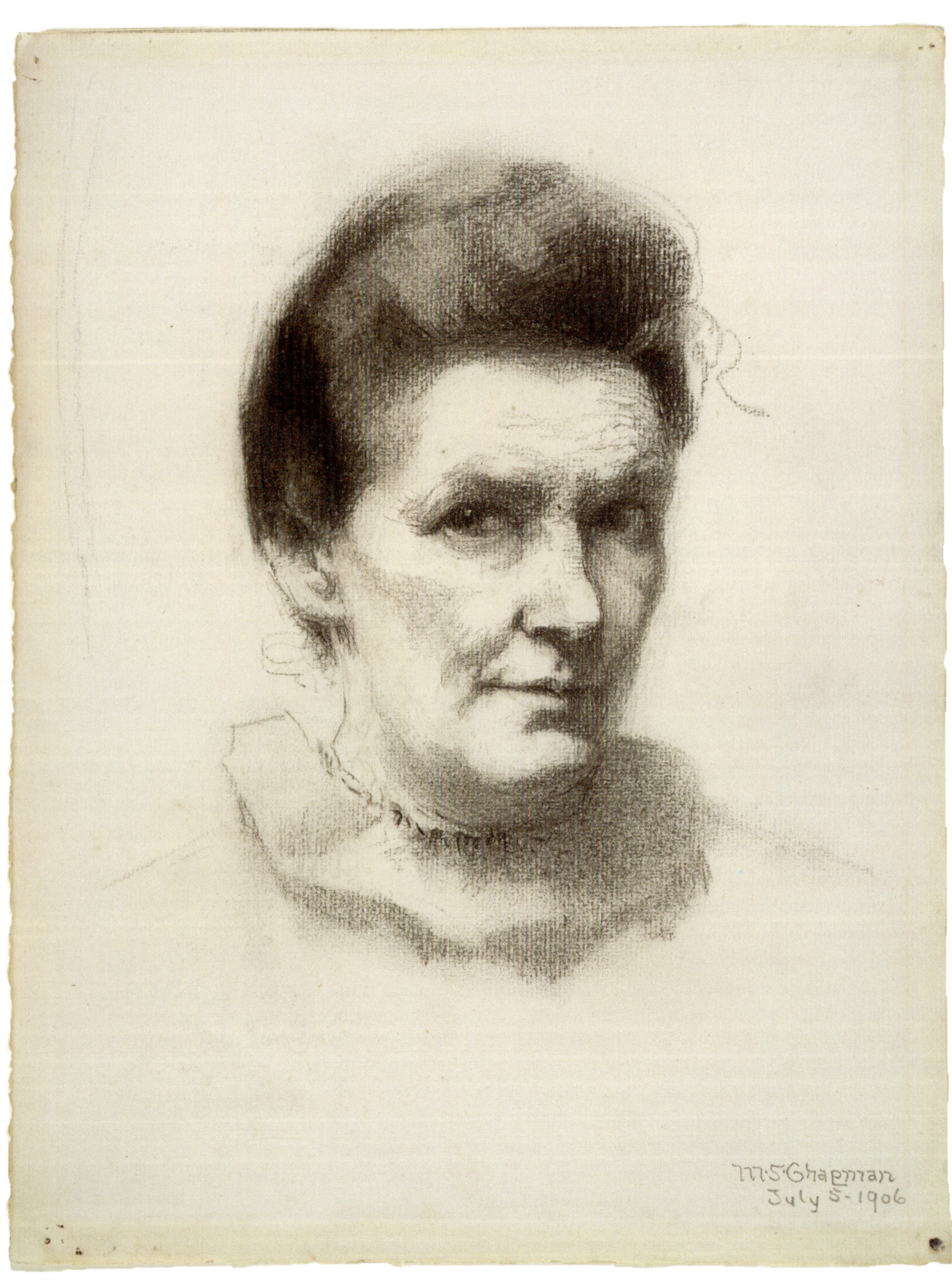
M.S. Chapman
July 5-1906

4.

Minerva Chapman (1858–1947)

Charcoal on paper, 31.6 x 24 cm
(12 7/16 x 9 7/16 in.), 1906
The Ruth Bowman and Harry Kahn Twentieth-Century American Self-Portrait Collection
S/NPG.2002.226

IN 1906, THE YEAR she created this portrait, Minerva Chapman became one of the first women to be elected to France's Salon of the Société Nationale des Beaux Arts (The National Society of Fine Arts).[1] Raised in Chicago, Chapman began her formal training at the Art Institute of Chicago before leaving for Europe in 1886. The artist ultimately settled in Paris, where she studied at the Académie Julian and with Charles Lasar, an important supporter of female artists, with whom she developed an enduring friendship.[2] A successful painter and a miniaturist, Chapman exhibited her work internationally, receiving numerous awards.[3]

This sensitive three-quarter portrait, one of numerous self-depictions Chapman created during the course of her career, suggests an air of animated reserve consistent with advice she received from Lasar: "Power is never seen, only suspected."[4] Committed to her craft, Chapman firmly asserts her identity as a professional artist, rather than talented amateur, testifying to her work ethic with a furrowed brow, stray hairs above her brow and at the nape of her neck, and slight shadows beneath her eyes. Chapman's seriousness is evident not only in her mastery of modeling in charcoal and her facility with drawing techniques, but also in a series of words—amounting to a mantra—that she recorded in her notebook early in her career: "Work. Ambition. Perseverance. Determination."[5] Although the artist's self-portrait modestly captures only her head, the ruffle of her collar, and her shoulders, the glint in her eyes and her upturned lips—hinting at a smile—suggest that her penetrating gaze took in far more. "When you draw the ankle, look at the neck," Chapman urged. "In drawing look up and down—way above, way below."[6]

ACG

Notes

1 As Peter Hastings Falk points out, Mary Cassatt and Elizabeth Nourse were also elected members of this body. See Peter Hastings Falk, "Biography," in Paul J. Staiti and P. Hastings Falk, *Minerva Chapman* (South Hadley, MA: Mount Holyoke College Art Museum, 1986), 9.

2 Chapman studied officially with Lasar—who also taught Cecilia Beaux and Violet Oakley—from 1889 to 1897; their lasting friendship is suggested by two miniatures she created of her teacher in 1907 (Falk, *Minerva Chapman*, 10–12).

3 On Chapman's work as a miniaturist, see ibid., 12–14.

4 From Chapman's Studio Diary, maintained when she studied with Lasar, quoted in ibid., 11.

5 Chapman's Studio Diary, quoted in ibid., 10.

6 Chapman's journal, quoted in Theodore A. Cooper, *Minerva J. Chapman* (Washington, DC: Adams, Davidson Galleries, 1971), 8.

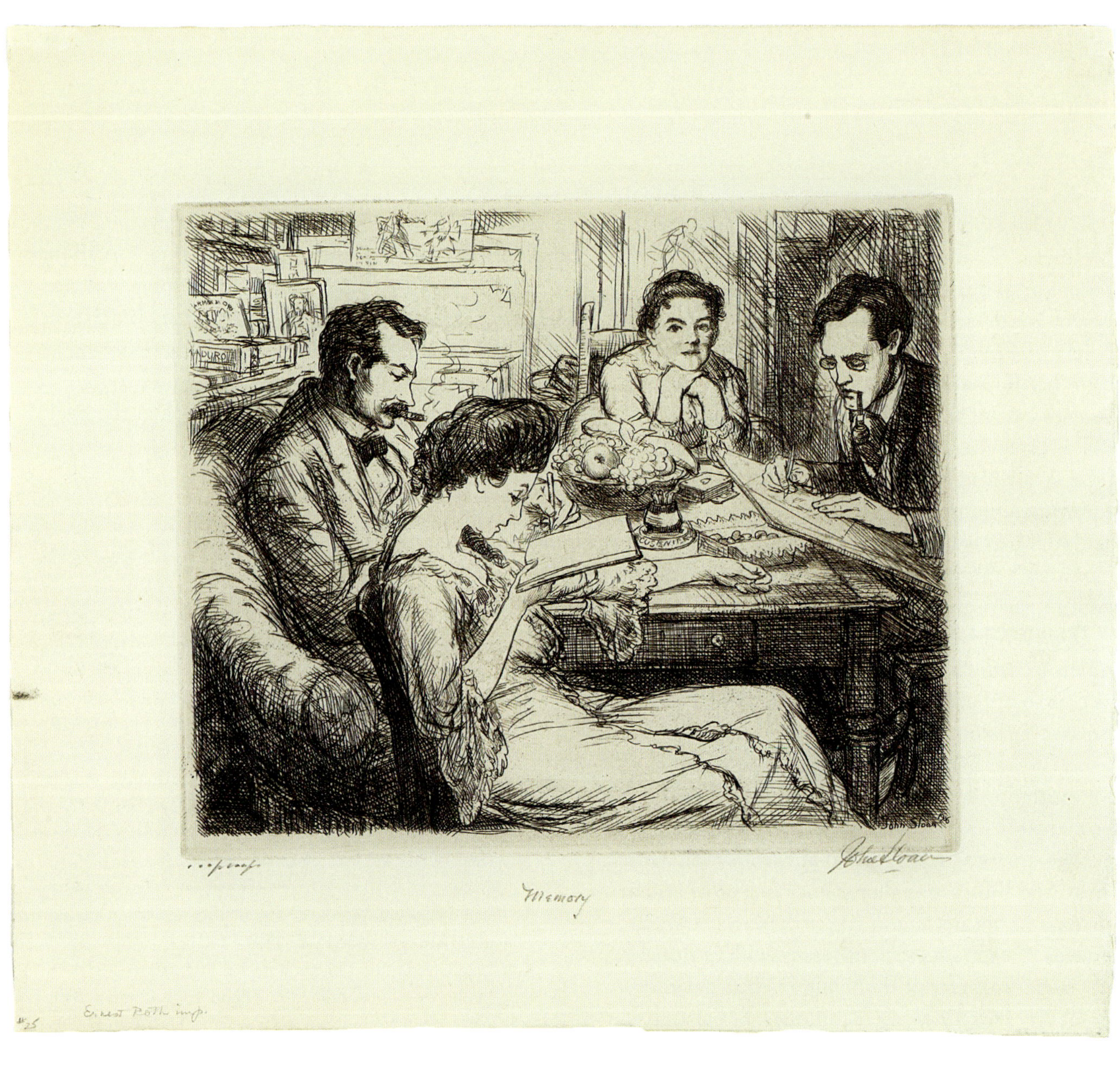

5.

John Sloan (1871–1951)

Memory
With Robert Henri (1865–1929), Linda Craige Henri (c. 1875–1905), and Dolly Sloan (1876–1943)
Etching, 29.1 x 39.1 cm (11 7/16 x 15 3/8 in.), 1906
The Ruth Bowman and Harry Kahn Twentieth-Century American Self-Portrait Collection
NPG.2002.332

MEMORY IS AN apt title for this serene image of warmly recalled friendship. John Sloan depicted himself smoking a pipe and drawing while his wife, Dolly, sits nearby; in the foreground Robert Henri draws while his wife, Linda, reads aloud. The etching memorializes the many evenings in 1905 when the four gathered in Henri's New York apartment. By January 1906, when Sloan made this etching, the scene was only a memory.[1] Linda Henri had died in December 1905.[2]

In 1892 the young illustrator Sloan had met Henri, just returned from Paris, at a Christmas party given by their fellow Philadelphia artist Charles Grafly.[3] Sloan and Henri warmed to each other immediately. Sloan recalled, "It was Robert Henri who set me to painting seriously."[4] In the 1890s illustrators gathered around Henri in Philadelphia; many took up painting and moved to New York City. In 1898 Henri married one of his art students, Linda Craige, who came from a wealthy Philadelphia family.[5] In the same year Sloan met his future wife, the vivacious Dolly Wall, a struggling bookkeeper. After an extended European honeymoon, the Henris joined the other Philadelphians in New York; when the Sloans followed in 1904, the foursome of *Memory* was complete.[6]

The happy time recalled in *Memory* was all too brief; the details remained vivid in Sloan's mind in January 1906 as he made this etching. Sloan used swift, incisive lines to describe his friends and their surroundings: the pile of art behind the couples; the cigar in Henri's mouth and the box it came from; the unconscious gestures of Linda's left hand as she read.[7] While her three companions stare down in concentration, Dolly looks up to hear Linda's voice and the soft scratching of pencils. Returning her gaze, we can almost hear the sounds of *Memory*.

APW

Notes

1 Sloan also referred to the print by the equally fitting title *Family Group*, which reflects the great closeness between these two couples. Peter Morse, *John Sloan's Prints: A Catalogue Raisonné of the Etchings, Lithographs, and Posters* (New Haven, CT, and London: Yale University Press, 1969), 146–47.

2 Linda Henri died of gastritis on December 8, 1905. Bennard B. Perlman, *Robert Henri: His Life and Art* (New York: Dover Publications, 1991), 66.

3 John Loughery, *John Sloan: Painter and Rebel* (New York: Henry Holt and Company, 1995), 23.

4 John Sloan, *Gist of Art: Principles and Practice Expounded in the Classroom and Studio* (New York: Dover Publications, 1977), 3. For more on the relationship between Sloan and Henri, see Bruce St. John, ed., *John Sloan's New York Scene: From the Diaries, Notes and Correspondence, 1906–1913* (New York: Harper & Row, 1965) and Bennard B. Perlman, ed., *Revolutionaries of Realism: The Letters of John Sloan and Robert Henri* (Princeton, NJ: Princeton University Press, 1997).

5 Perlman, *Robert Henri*, 38–39, 45.

6 Anna "Dolly" Wall was plagued by alcoholism and associated problems that John Sloan hid from many friends, but not from the Henris. Loughery mentions that Linda Henri was particularly supportive of Dolly. Loughery, *John Sloan*, 49–52, 72, 79.

7 In a manuscript of 1945 Sloan noted "Henri was always amazed that I had remembered her gesture: her hand rolling her fingers as she read aloud. It was made purely from memory." Morse, *John Sloan's Prints*, 147.

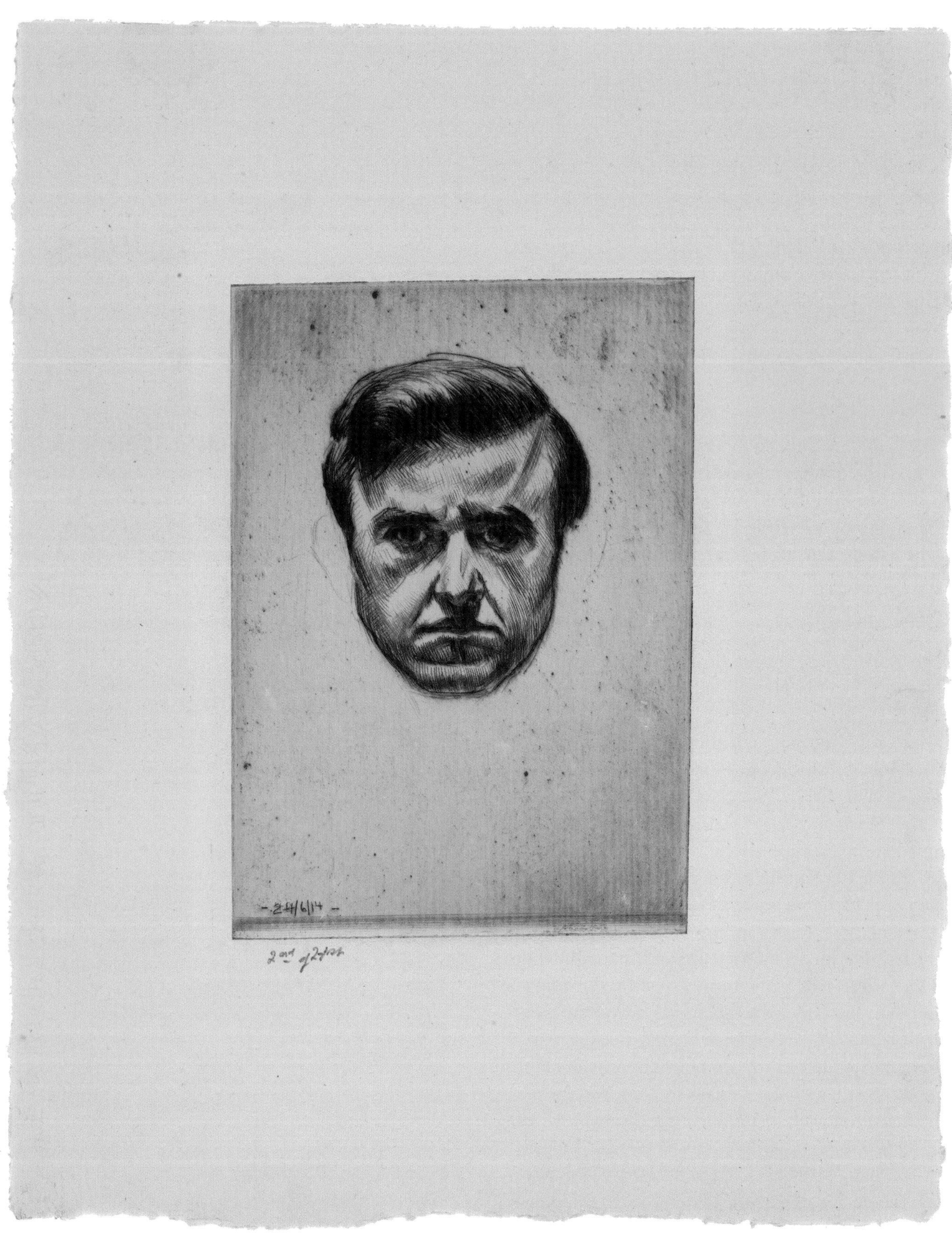

6.

John H. B. Storrs (1885–1956)

Etching, 32.9 x 25.7 cm (12 15/16 x 10 1/8 in.), 1914
The Ruth Bowman and Harry Kahn Twentieth-Century American Self-Portrait Collection
S/NPG.2002.350

JOHN STORRS is most celebrated for his sleekly abstracted metal sculptures derived from skyscrapers, yet human faces played a major role in his sculpted and graphic oeuvre. Storrs etched this haunting self-portrait in June 1914, while the Chicago-born artist was studying with the great French sculptor Auguste Rodin (1840–1917). The moment would prove to be a pivotal one.

When Storrs began working with Rodin in 1912, he had already studied at a variety of art academies in France and the United States.[1] Storrs's sketches made in the 1910s, like this etching, display a mastery of academic drawing and anatomy.[2] But Storrs looked beyond this comfortable academic style. The young American's interest was piqued by the cubist and futurist works of Alexander Archipenko (1887–1964), Fernand Léger (1881–1955), and others he saw at the spring 1912 Salon des Indépendants.[3] Even while he was still studying with Rodin, cubist sculptor Jacques Lipchitz (1891–1973) spurred Storrs to look seriously at such radical new art.[4]

While Storrs rendered his 1914 self-portrait in a traditional style, modeling the forms of the face with careful layers of hatching, he surely had more than this in mind. The rigidly frontal image, isolated from the body and drawn with a heavy outline under the chin, suggests that he was studying his own form to explore the underlying structural symmetry. By 1917 and 1918, Storrs would be making prints and then sculptures of geometrically stylized human faces and bodies. When he made this print on June 24, 1914, he gazed into the mirror, seeking insights to advance his art. Storrs could not have known that only four days later an event would occur that would transform the future of far more than his art. On June 28, Austro-Hungarian Archduke Franz Ferdinand was assassinated, sparking World War I.[5]

APW

Notes

1 These schools included the Académies de la Grand Chaumière, Franklin, and Colarossi, all in Paris; as well as the school of the Art Institute of Chicago, and the Pennsylvania Academy of the Fine Arts. Noel Frackman, *John Storrs* (New York: Whitney Museum of American Art, 1986), 11–13.

2 See the drawings microfilmed in the John Henry Bradley Storrs Papers, 1847–1987, reel 1555, Archives of American Art, Smithsonian Institution, Washington, DC.

3 Frackman, *Storrs*, 14.

4 Noel Stern Frackman, *The Art of Johns Storrs* (Ann Arbor, MI: UMI, 1987), 37–39.

5 Robin Prior and Trevor Wilson, *The First World War*, Smithsonian History of Warfare, series ed. John Keegan (Washington, DC: Smithsonian Books, 2004), 10.

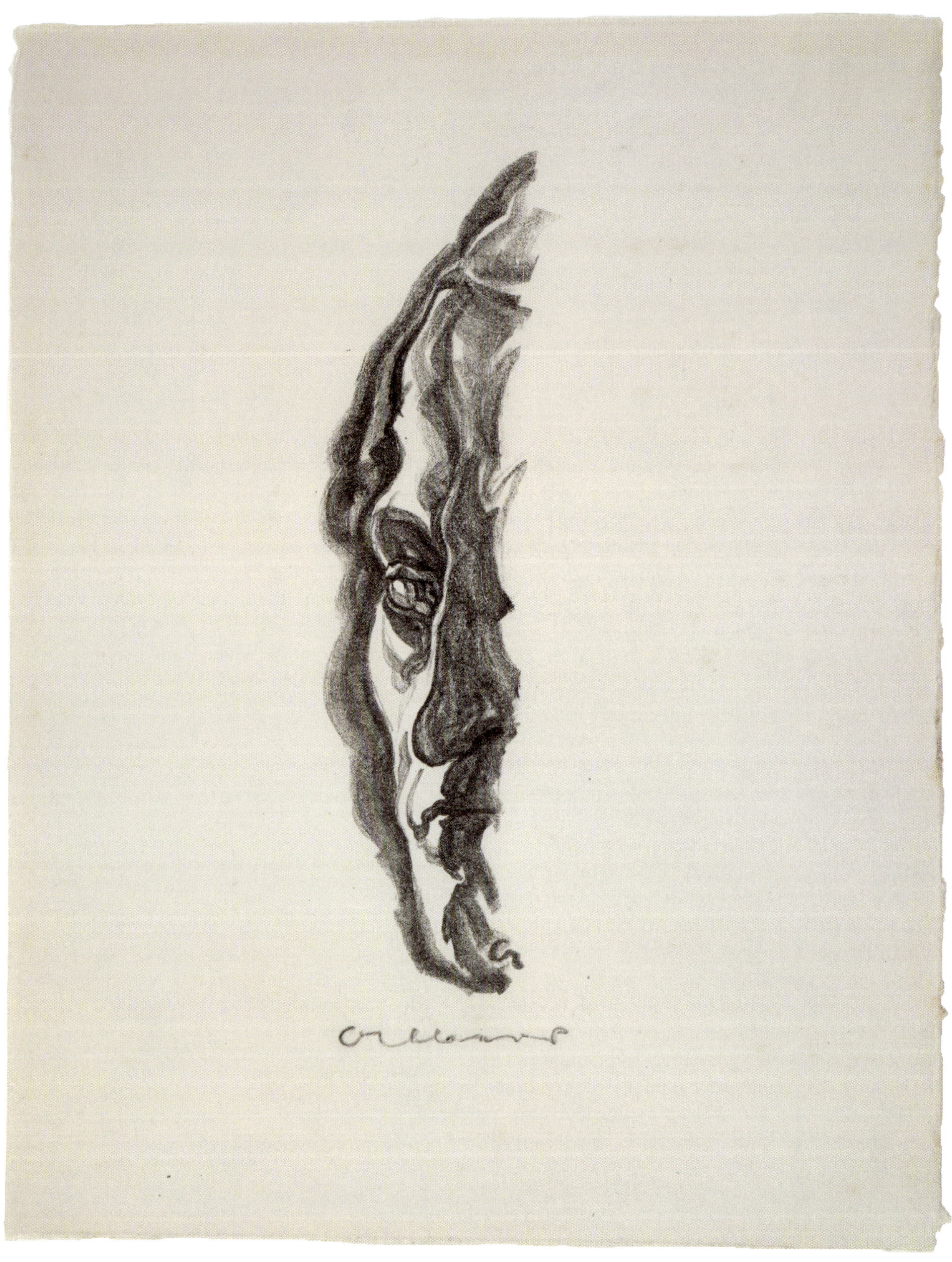

7.

Josef Albers (1888–1976)

Lithograph, 30.3 x 23 cm ($11\frac{15}{16}$ x $9\frac{1}{16}$ in.), 1916
The Ruth Bowman and Harry Kahn Twentieth-Century American Self-Portraiture Collection
NPG.2002.188

CREATED EARLY in his career, shortly after completing studies at the Royal Art School in Berlin, Josef Albers's boldly experimental 1916 self-portrait lithograph reflects the young artist's interest in new artistic currents, particularly expressionism and cubism, as well as his willingness to experiment with new media. Indeed, for Albers, self-portraiture, as indicated by works made between 1916 and 1918, provided critical terrain for artistic experimentation.[1]

This print serves more as an exercise in the articulation of plastic form than a psychological study, although the intensity of the subject's expression is palpable. The subject's only visible eye turns away from the viewer, shutting off a sense of personal connection. Only a portion of the artist's face is visible, its features compressed by Albers's strange rotation of the profile into a more spatially complex three-quarter view. This intriguing turn provides an opportunity to explore the implications of contrasting zones of light and dark and prefigures the artist's future abstraction and concern with tonality.

In addition to formal experimentation, one can read in the artist's fragmented self-representation something of the strains of World War I. Although exempted from service due to his high school teaching post, the privations and destruction of the war cannot have escaped Albers's notice. Even as gas masks and bandages transformed faces at the front, the mutilated bodies of returning veterans demonstrated the lasting physical toll of the war.[2] Indeed, Albers's striking self-portrayal, with its powerful sense of motion arrested on the page, anticipates the experiments in portrayal through paint, sculpture, photography, and collage of many of his contemporaries, including Hans Richter, Sophie Tauber, Marcel Janco, Hanah Höch, Raoul Hausmann, and El Lissitsky.[3] With this self-portrait, Albers not only suggests his mastery of modern art of the recent past, but his focus on the future and his capacity to lead in the development of new artistic idioms.

ACG

Notes

1 On Albers's use of self-portraiture, see Nicholas Fox Weber, *The Drawings of Josef Albers* (New Haven, CT, and London: Yale University Press, 1984), 17–20.

2 On the impact of World War I on visual art of the period, see Leah Dickerman, "Introduction," in *Dada*, ed. Leah Dickerman (Washington, DC: National Gallery of Art, in association with Distributed Art Publishers, 2006), 2–7.

3 A number of such works appear in ibid., passim.

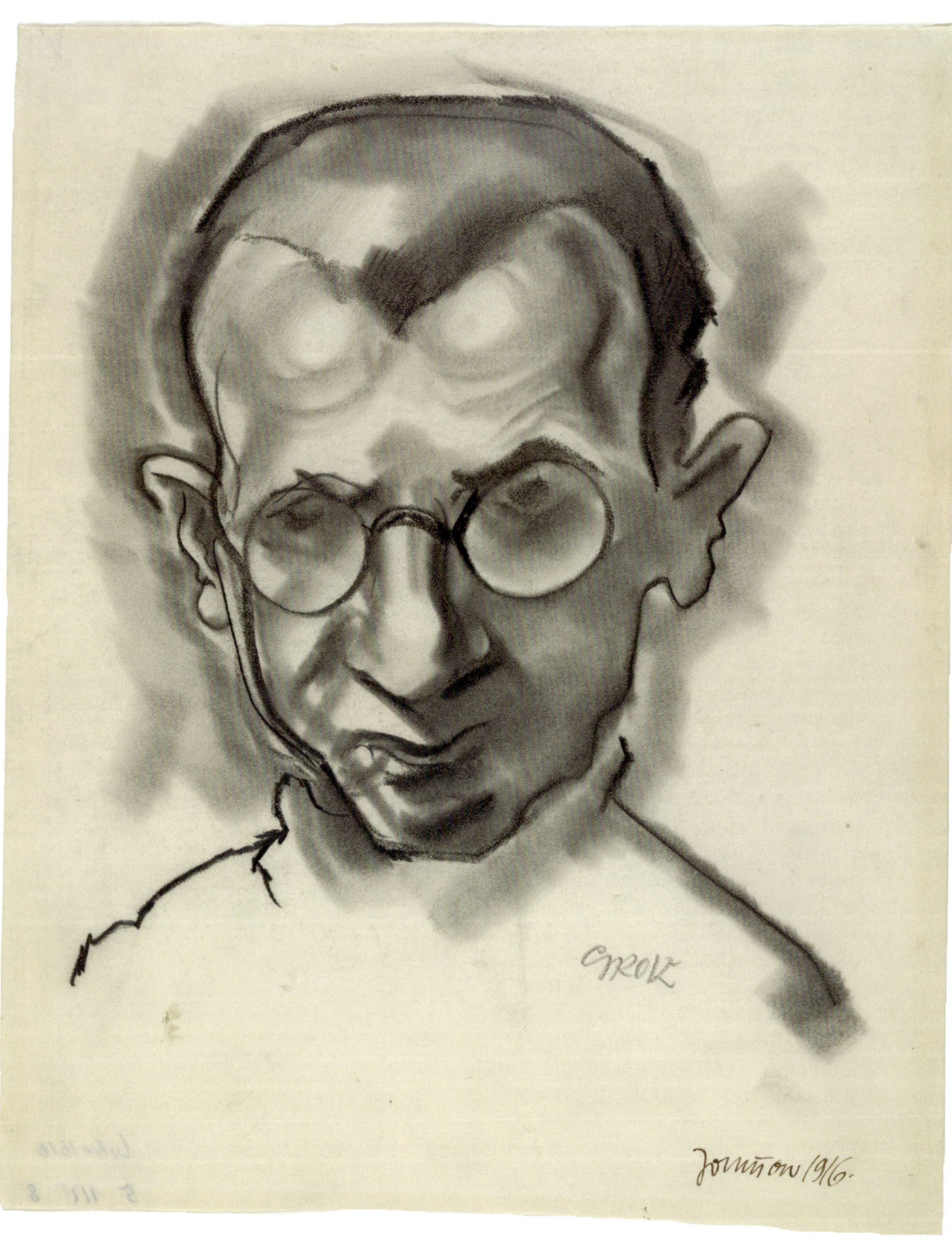

8.

George Grosz (1893–1959)

Charcoal and graphite on paper, 26.9 x 21.1 cm (10 9/16 x 8 5/16 in.), 1916
The Ruth Bowman and Harry Kahn Twentieth-Century American Self-Portrait Collection
NPG.2002.260

BERLIN-BORN artist George Grosz drew this 1916 self-portrait at a moment of intense psychic turmoil that would affect his art for years to come. Grosz had enlisted in the German army in November 1914. Although his service was brief, by the time he was discharged in March 1915, he was psychologically scarred by his experience. War, he concluded, "meant horror, mutilation, annihilation."[1] Grosz channeled his disgust into political satire and apocalyptic imagery, extrapolating from his wartime sketchbooks hideously maimed soldiers, hardened prostitutes, bloated profiteers, grotesque generals, and debauched officials. His reputation grew as his trenchant drawings were published in portfolios.

The assessment of Grosz by his friend Wieland Herzfelde, who wrote that his "eyes were those of a marksman taking aim, and his mouth had a bitterness about it," might almost describe this self-portrait.[2] The delicacy of the charcoal and the introspective expression, however, reveal a painful vulnerability that one friend felt explained his ferocity rather than contradicted it. Grosz had "an excessively sensitive nature," arts patron Count Harry Kessler noted, "which turns outrageously brutal by reason of its sensibility, and he has the talent for delineating this brutality creatively."[3] Circular highlights on his forehead echo the eyeglasses and further emphasize the psychological.

But Grosz aimed his graphic skills most frequently toward polemical ends. That aggressive engagement with the breakdown of contemporary culture was characteristic of the emerging Dada movement, and Grosz became a leading figure of the Berlin Dadaists. The bitter irony so typical of his work permeated that branch of Dada expression.[4] Grosz eventually moved to America in 1933 and became a citizen in 1938. Although he never felt appreciated by the art establishment, he received admiring attention in America, garnering honors, prizes, commissions, and exhibitions. Admiration for Grosz's work has never waned; his unflinching diatribes against war and corruption mark him as a visionary witness to his era.

WWR

Notes

1 George Grosz, *George Grosz: An Autobiography*, trans. Nora Hodges (1946; New York: Macmillan, 1983), 97–98.

2 Frank Whitford, *The Berlin of George Grosz: Drawings, Watercolours and Prints, 1912–1930* (New Haven, CT: Yale University Press and London: Royal Academy of Art, 1997), 28, 31.

3 Ibid., 31.

4 Leah Dickerman, *Dada* (Washington, DC: National Gallery of Art, 2006), 7–11; 87–112; M. Kay Flavell, *George Grosz: A Biography* (New Haven, CT: Yale University Press, 1988), 286.

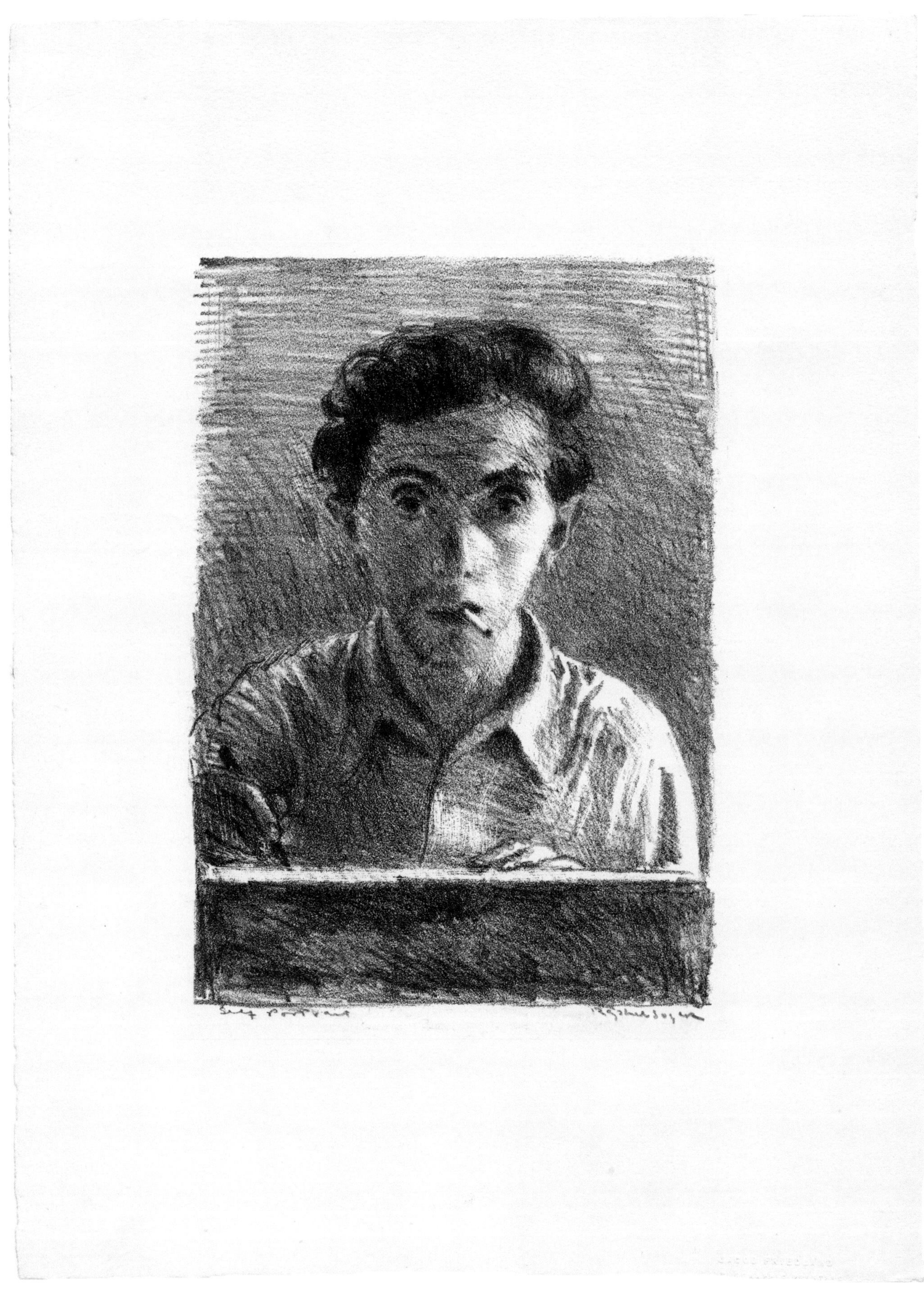

9.

Raphael Soyer (1899–1987)

Lithograph, 37.7 x 27.2 cm (14 13/16 x 10 11/16 in.), c. 1920
The Ruth Bowman and Harry Kahn Twentieth-Century American Self-Portrait Collection
NPG.2002.336

IN BOTH OF these self-portraits, Raphael Soyer shows himself as a slight man looking straight out at the viewer from hooded eyes under arched eyebrows that rise self-appraisingly. The multiplying wrinkles on the artist's brow and his receding hair show the passage of more than half a century between the lithograph, made in about 1920, and the drawing from 1972. The two images also demonstrate a subtle evolution, not only in what Soyer saw, but also in how he saw as he gazed into mirrors over the decades.[1]

When Raphael Soyer and his twin brother, Moses, immigrated to the United States from Russia with their family in 1912, the two boys were already enthusiastic artists. However, as a teenager, Raphael was cripplingly shy, afraid of revealing his Russian accent to his New York neighbors. He later admitted that as a young man, "I had lots of problems, and for a long time I wouldn't talk, I wouldn't go out."[2] It was only through art that he was able to face the world.

Soyer found a comforting emotional home at the Metropolitan Museum of Art, where he and his brothers learned the galleries by heart. Artists like Rembrandt became heroes and models for the young men. In his first self-portrait, a 1917 etching, Soyer described his own features with lines unabashedly inspired by Rembrandt's youthful self-portrait etchings.[3] In this lithograph, made about three years later, Soyer was bold in sketching his wavy hair and wrinkled shirt, but still warily camouflaged himself. Moving past historical examples, Soyer looked to his New York contemporaries as exemplars. As he recalled, "In those days everybody smoked. It was the fashion for an artist to draw or paint with a cigarette in his mouth."[4]

With these early works Soyer began a decades-long process of constructing a self-image. Although he was a relatively successful artist in the hard times of the 1930s and he continued to prosper in succeeding decades, he habitually portrayed himself looking as down-and-out as the unemployed men he hired to pose for him.[5] Soyer's self-portraits became more hollow-eyed and haunted as he passed from middle age to old age. One author noted that those who met Soyer might be relieved to see how much healthier the artist looked in person than in his art.[6]

Indeed, Soyer was aware that his self-portraits were far from photographic, but he did not feel that he was constructing a false surface. Rather, in self-portraits like this 1972 drawing, Soyer asserted that he was probing beneath what the world saw. From a network of swiftly drawn, silvery lines the familiar face emerges: now wise and gray, his head resting wearily on his hand. Soyer often used this thoughtful pose in self-portraits,[7] as if to ally touch to vision; the lean cheek the artist felt with his left hand informed the features he drew with his right. As his art and understanding grew over the years, Soyer came to understand how not only his self-portraiture but all of his art reflected such intimate knowledge and subjective perceptions:

> Your work is what you are. You look at the world through yourself. Just as the aloofness of Degas and Cézanne is reflected in their work,

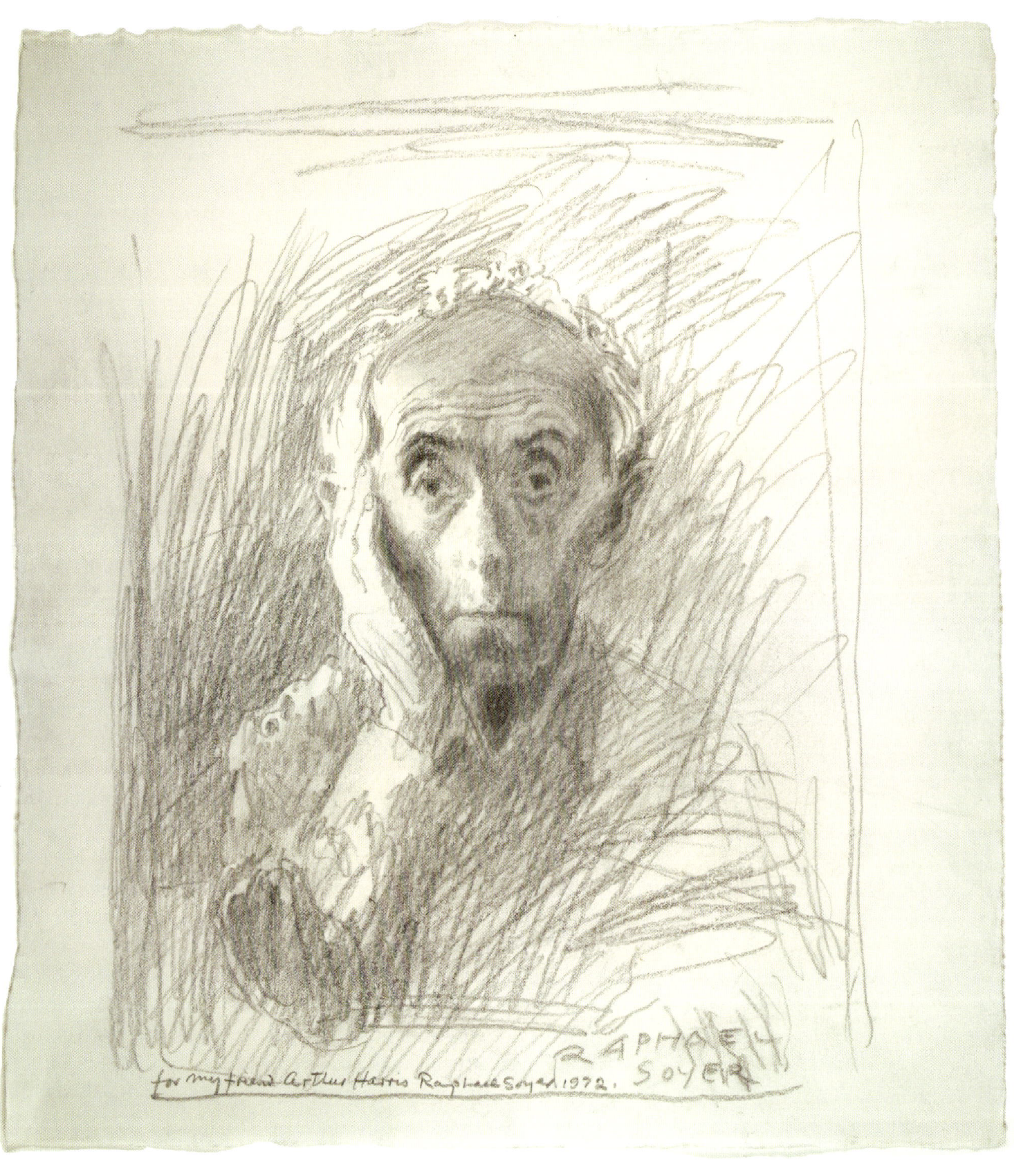
RAPHAEL SOYER
for my friend Arthur Harris Raphael Soyer 1972.

10.

Raphael Soyer (1899–1987)

Lithographic crayon on paper, 42.5 x 38 cm (16¾ x 14$^{15}/_{16}$ in.), 1972
The Ruth Bowman and Harry Kahn Twentieth-Century American Self-Portrait Collection
NPG.2002.338

my people are introverted people, dissociated from one another even when they're painted together.

I always paint myself appearing introverted. Painting myself is like talking about myself, but I never make myself entirely like myself. I always appear older-looking, or unshaven, or all alone. It's the result of looking a little bit more deeply.[8]

APW

Notes

1 For a survey of Soyer's career see Lloyd Goodrich, *Raphael Soyer* (New York: Harry N. Abrams, 1972).
2 Quoted in Israel Shenker, "Raphael Soyer: 'I Consider Myself a Contemporary Artist Who Describes Contemporary Life," *ARTnews* 72 (November 1973): 55.
3 Quoted in Frank Gettings, *Raphael Soyer: Sixty-Five Years of Printmaking* (Washington, DC: Smithsonian Institution Press, 1982), 18.
4 Quoted in ibid., 20.
5 Samantha Baskind, *Raphael Soyer and the Search for Modern Jewish Art* (Chapel Hill and London: University of North Carolina Press, 2004), 94.
6 Avis Berman, "Raphael Soyer at 80: Not Painting Would Be Like Not Breathing," *ARTnews* 78 (December 1979): 41.
7 Soyer recalled "In the fifties I painted in quick succession a number of small self-portraits all in the same pose, my face resting in the palm of my hand. Once, alone in the studio as I usually was when painting myself, I began to think of the self-portraits of some of my favorite artists, and it suddenly occurred to me to paint myself in this pensive pose alongside self-portraits of Rembrandt, Corot and Degas which I had copied from reproductions. Placing myself in their company was not a delusion of grandeur, but an expression of esteem and of love for their work." Raphael Soyer, *Self-Revealment: A Memoir* (New York: Maecenas Press, Random House, 1967, 1969), 103.
8 Quoted in Shenker, "Raphael Soyer." 55.

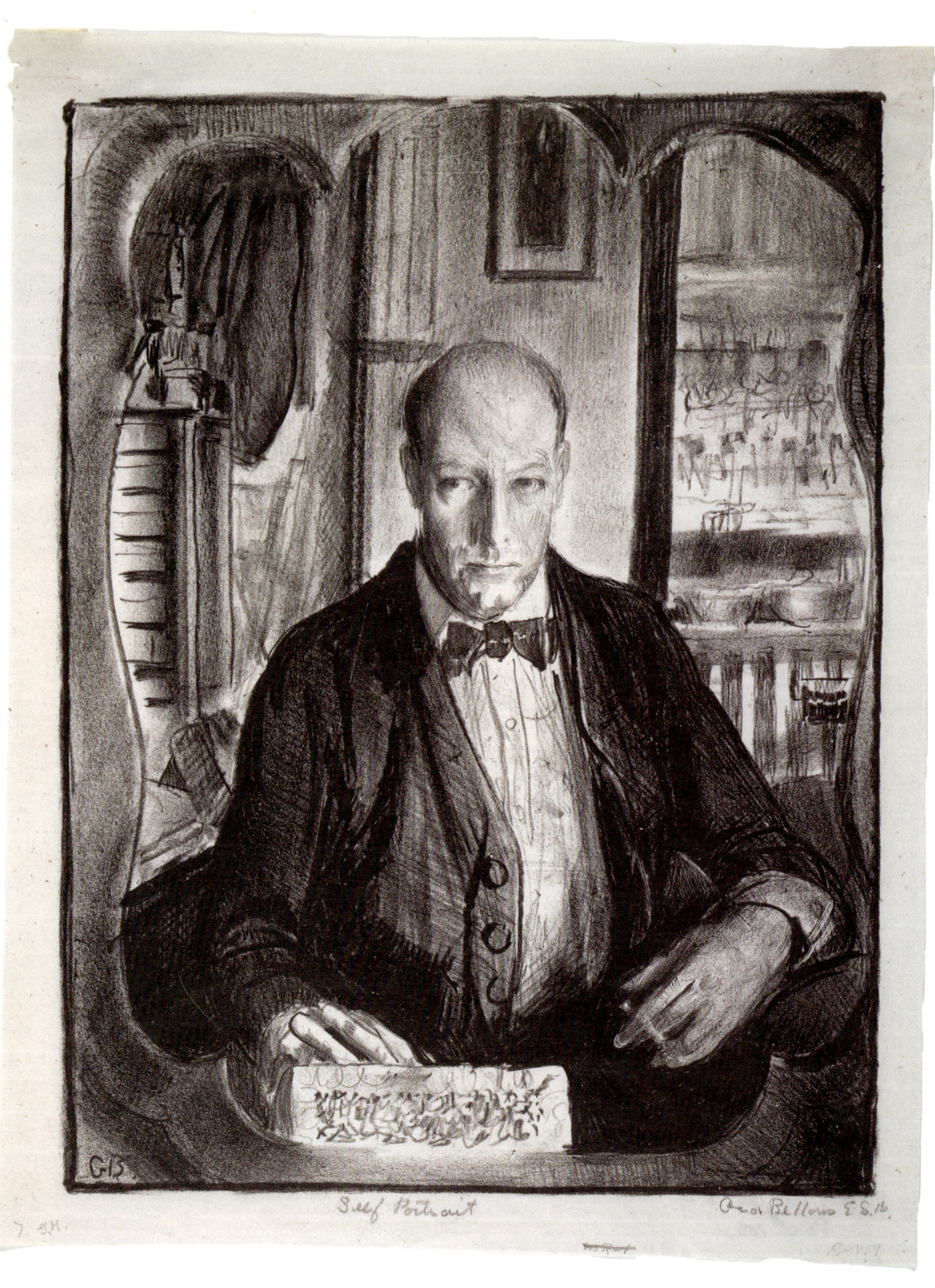
Self Portrait

11.

George Bellows (1882–1925)

Lithograph, 29.4 x 22.3 cm ($11^{9}/_{16}$ x $8^{3}/_{4}$ in.), 1921
The Ruth Bowman and Harry Kahn Twentieth-Century American Self-Portrait Collection
NPG.2002.204

THE LITHOGRAPHS of George Bellows "strike you like quick expletives," Frank Weitenkampf wrote in the *Print Connoisseur* in 1924: "the intrusion of a somewhat angular set of leg or arm, or a largish hand . . . a gesture born of the fear that there might be a little too much grace, too much unbroken beauty of line. A touch of self-assertiveness?"[1] In this 1921 self-portrait, Bellows does assert what the writer called his "vigorous personality."[2] And slight distortions, spatial ambiguities, and the contrast between obscured and carefully delineated passages give the work that unexpected, curiously effective quality Weitenkampf noticed.

Inspired by his friend, the artist and printmaker Albert Sterner, Bellows had purchased a lithographic press in 1916. Although also renowned for his paintings of urban and sporting scenes, Bellows devoted much of his short career to printmaking, producing 197 images on stone.[3] In this self-portrait, he appears to revel in the rich range of tones from velvety darkness in the shadows to delicate grays for the window's distant view. The sparkling clarity of the atmosphere, the bold black and white contrasts, as well as his pose actually drawing on the stone, all speak to Bellows's love affair with lithography.

This seemingly straightforward depiction of the artist working at his craft is actually quite a complex approach to self-portrayal. Behind the figure is a complicated grid of horizontal and vertical elements. We know from descriptions that this space probably describes a tall cabinet for holding prints and a window through which we see a balcony railing and a city view, but it also suggests Bellows's keen interest in geometric spatial composition.[4] The scalloped frame of what we read as a mirror, however, contrasts sharply with the vertical and horizontal geometry in the interior of the picture while giving the viewer an ambiguous sense of displacement.

WWR

Notes

1 Frank Weitenkampf, "George W. Bellows, Lithographer," *Print Connoisseur* 4 (July 1924): 225.

2 Ibid.; Lauris Mason and Joan Ludman, *The Lithographs of George Bellows: A Catalogue Raisonné, Revised Edition* (San Francisco: Alan Wofsy Fine Arts, 1992), 182.

3 Ibid., 17.

4 Jean Bellows Booth recalled that her father made most of his lithographs on a "balcony." Described as the size of a good-sized room overlooking over the studio, it included series of tall shelves "to store all his lithographic prints." Jane Myers and Linda Ayres, eds., *George Bellows, the Artist and His Lithographs* (Fort Worth, TX: Amon Carter Museum, 1988), 1, 102. Bellows was very intrigued by Jay Hambridge's theory of dynamic symmetry; see Mason and Ludman, *Lithographs of George Bellows*, 20.

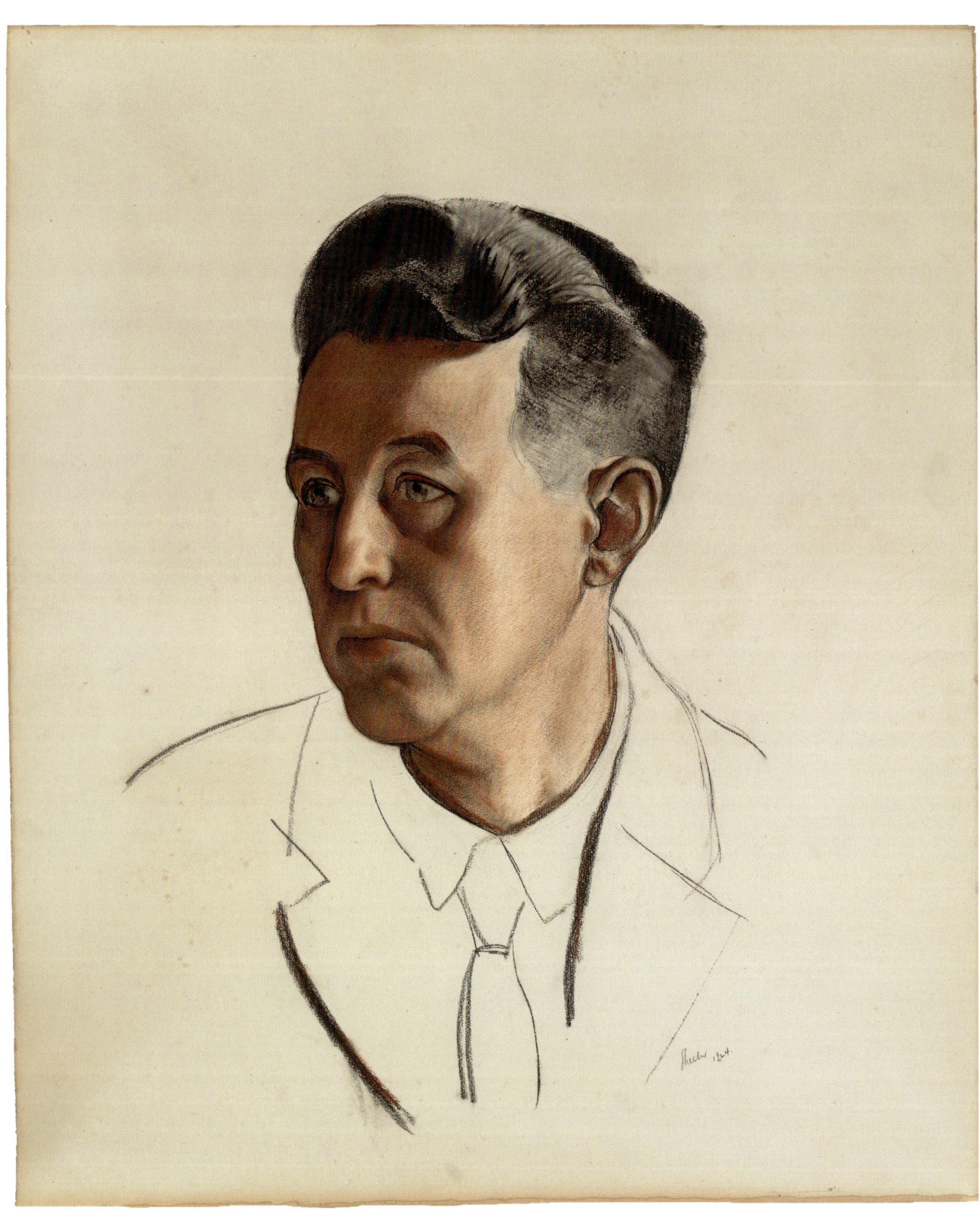

12.

Charles Sheeler (1883–1965)

Pastel on paper, 58.4 x 48.2 cm (23 x 19 in.), 1924
NPG.73.15

CHARLES SHEELER composed this pastel—a rare venture into self-portraiture—with a modernist's sensibility and a photographer's eye.[1] Although it seems more conventional than the still lifes and architectural and industrial landscapes he preferred, it shares some of their characteristics. By 1924, when he drew this image, Sheeler was working variously as a commercial artist, fine art photographer, avant-garde filmmaker, and painter with close ties to Walter and Louise Arensberg's circle of Dada artists and writers. He had shown six paintings at the 1913 Armory show, produced the groundbreaking film *Manhatta* with Paul Strand in 1920, and had a number of one-man exhibitions of his paintings, drawings, and photographs. Sheeler's portrait, like his analytically observed, meticulously rendered barns, skyscrapers, and interiors, reveals what he called "the absolute beauty we are accustomed to associate with objects suspended in a vacuum."[2]

Although his photographs at different points in his career were exhibited separately from his paintings and drawings, his work in all media was cross-referential.[3] In 1924, an exhibition at the Whitney Studio Club was drawing attention to his enigmatic realism. Critics admired what his friend the poet William Carlos Williams later called the "bewildering directness of his vision, without blur."[4] The pastel parallels his approach to photography specifically, particularly in the strong, artificial lighting that throws the head into sharp relief, casting abstract patterns of light and shadow. Sheeler understood, Williams wrote, that through the camera "his subject [could] be intensified, carved out, illuminated."[5] A similar heightened reality enhances his self-portrayal with its intensely focused, mysteriously melancholy gaze. Although straightforward in comparison to his symbolic "self-portrait" of 1923, featuring a meticulously drawn telephone with the artist's headless torso subtly reflected in the window behind it,[6] Sheeler's 1924 pastel, strongly resonant of his integrated artistic vision across media, adds a startling new clarity to realist portraiture.

WWR

Notes

1 Sheeler made another pastel self-portrait at approximately the same time in a similar style but with the face turned forward rather than to the side; see *Bulletin of the Whitney Museum of American Art, 1982–83* (New York: Whitney Museum of American Art, 1983), 49.

2 Carol Troyen and Erica E. Hirshler, *Charles Sheeler: Paintings and Drawings* (Boston: Little, Brown, 1987), 16.

3 For a detailed study of this theme, see Charles Brock, *Charles Sheeler Across Media* (Berkeley: University of California Press, 2006).

4 William Carlos Williams, "Introduction," in *Charles Sheeler: Paintings, Drawings, Photographs* (New York: Museum of Modern Art, 1939), 6. See also Troyen and Hirshler, *Charles Sheeler*, 15.

5 Williams, "Introduction," 9. This quality of sharp-edged clarity would later be understood as a precisionist sensibility that Sheeler shared with such artists as Charles Demuth, Ralston Crawford, and Louis Lozowick.

6 Troyen and Hirshler, *Charles Sheeler*, 96–97; Brock, *Charles Sheeler Across Media*, 122; Constance Rourke, *Charles Sheeler: Artist in the American Tradition* (New York: Da Capo Press, 1939), 56, 94–96.

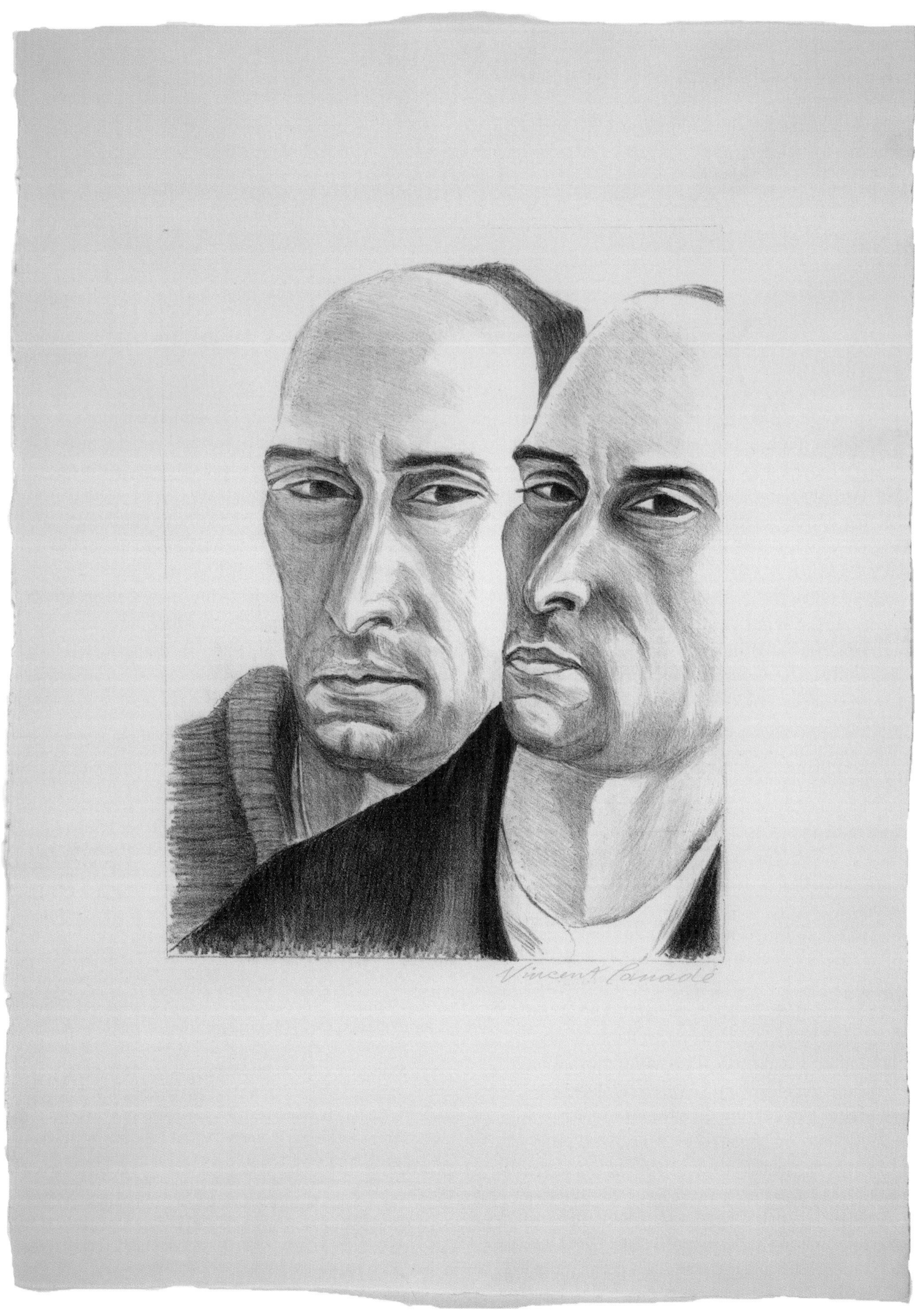
Vincent Canadé

13.

Vincent Canadè (1879–1961)

Double Self-Portrait
Lithograph, 40.8 x 29 cm (16 1/16 x 11 7/16 in.), 1927
The Ruth Bowman and Harry Kahn Twentieth-Century American Self-Portrait Collection
S/NPG.2002.222

WHY DO TWO nearly identical faces gaze at us from this print? Those who saw Vincent Canadè's paintings in New York galleries in the 1920s and 1930s were intrigued by this self-taught artist who obsessively depicted himself with such intensity. He showed groups of self-portraits together, or, as here, Canadè might constitute a group within a single work, with four eyes lining up to form a disconcerting row of gazes.[1] The artist freely distorted perspective and anatomy as he compulsively depicted and reiterated his staring eyes, hooked nose, and clinched lips. This print is based upon the 1923 painting of which critic Guy Eglinton said, "His self-portraits reveal most clearly the increasing turmoil of his mind, for, since the conflict is primarily within himself, it is against himself that his bitterest hatred is directed. . . . In the famous *Double Self-Portrait* (*Sunday and Monday)* he is the complete degenerate."[2]

The artist led a difficult life, giving him ample reasons for bitterness and regret. He had been born into a wealthy Italian family, but his father and brother lost all of their money gambling. Young Vincent immigrated to America, where he struggled to support himself and then a growing family. He shifted from job to job, working sporadically as a jewelry designer or house painter until artist Joseph Stella found the poverty-stricken man and pointed him toward fine art.[3]

Canadè posed and answered his own question, "Why do I paint? Because I like it. And I like it because painting transports me into another world where I dream and fancy myself different and sometimes forget my sorrows."[4] But ironically, desiring escape, he chose to look at himself rather than away. The center of his troubles fascinated and haunted the artist. Tantalized by hopes of self-transformation, Canadè told Eglinton that he painted "himself . . . as he is and as he would like to be."[5]

APW

Notes

1 Jeffrey R. Hayes, *Vincent Canadè: Pastel Still Lifes* (Milwaukee, WI: UWM Art Museum, Vogel Hall Galleries, University of Wisconsin, 1986), unpaginated.

2 Guy Eglinton, "Vincent Canadé," *Creative Art* 3 (July 1928): xxxiii. The direction of the accent on the artist's name varies from publication to publication, or it may be excluded entirely. The oil painting on which this print is based is illustrated in "Double Self-Portrait by Vincent Canade," *ARTnews* 33 (December 15, 1934): 14. The small canvas *Double Self-Portrait* is now in the collection of the Weyhe Gallery, Mount Desert, Maine. The lithograph was published by Weyhe Gallery in 1927 and printed by George Miller in an edition of ninety-seven. Carl Zigrosser, "The Lithographs of Vincent Canadè," *Artist Proofs* 5 (1963): 32.

3 Carl Zigrosser, *My Own Shall Come to Me: A Personal Memoir and Picture Chronicle* (Haarlem, Netherlands: J. Enschedé en Zonen, 1971), 207–8. Zigrosser, cofounder of Weyhe Gallery, married the artist's daughter Laura in 1946. Lee Sorensen, ed., "Zigrosser, Carl," *Dictionary of Art Historians* (website) available at www.dictionaryofarthistorians.org/zigrosserc.htm.

4 Vincent Canadé, "Self-Portrait," *Creative Art* 3 (July 1928): xxix.

5 Eglinton, "Vincent Canadé," xxxiii.

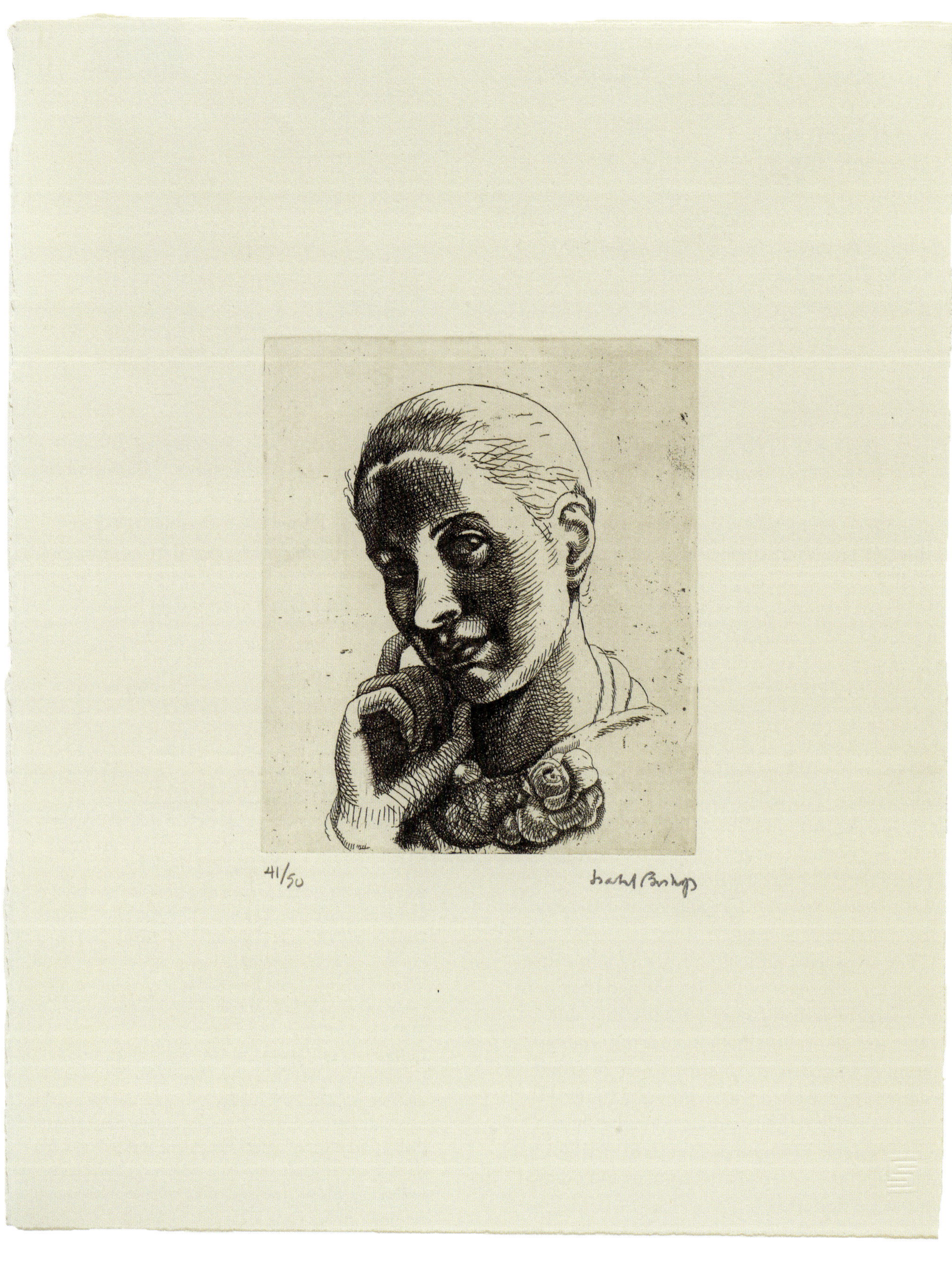

14.

Isabel Bishop (1902–1988)

Etching, 39.2 x 30.5 cm ($15\frac{7}{16}$ x 12 in.), 1929; printed c. 1988–1989
The Ruth Bowman and Harry Kahn Twentieth-Century American Self-Portrait Collection
NPG.2002.211

NEW YORK ARTIST Isabel Bishop chose her subject matter from the urban street life that flowed through Union Square, beneath her studio window. Bishop had studied at the Art Students League, where her teachers Kenneth Hayes Miller and Guy Pène du Bois and her friend Reginald Marsh transmitted a tradition of urban realism inspired by the Ashcan school. Although she moved to the Bronx after her marriage, Bishop continued to travel almost daily to her downtown studio to sketch laborers, shop girls, children, and unemployed men. "I'd feel afresh," she claimed, "the miracle of this movement, the incredible richness of this coming and going of these multitudes of people." She called the process of observing the local street life "nourishment."[1]

There were two moments—in Bishop's youth and in old age—when self-portraiture played an important role. As a young woman in the late 1920s, she found herself a convenient subject: "Then for myself, I did heads, of myself, because I was there."[2] In several of this series of images she is glancing out of the corner of her eye as if at a mirror. In this etching, made in 1929 and printed in a later edition, her concerns are formal. The detachment, unreadable expression, and elegant geometry of the head all disguise personality. She used her reflected image to work out fundamental problems: structure, form, gesture, and the play of light on a tilted, slightly turned face. Even the hand, resting too lightly to support her head, seems merely a pose she wished to explore. "To understand form plastically," she reminded herself, "is to comprehend its inner character and its position in nature."[3] In exhibitions at the Midtown Galleries, such critics as Margaret Breuning noted her "discipline and research in form" and her "rare combination of precision and delicacy"; Henry McBride called her a "careful and scholarly draftsman."[4]

Bishop had a long, successful career and worked into her eighties, although she did not need to support herself. Her paintings, prints, and drawings were exhibited regularly and collected by leading museums. She received awards and honorary degrees and was elected to the National Academy of Design and the National Institute of Arts and Letters. When asked why artists don't retire, she responded, "Because you're always looking for a breakthrough."[5] But in the mid-1980s, failing health forced her to give up the beloved Union Square studio. Deprived of her usual models, she turned again to self-portraiture in a haunting series of images, including this ink wash. Once again she gazes out from the corner of her eyes. But formal problems of light, form, and movement through space are solved with a minimum of confident brushstrokes; her concern here is psychological. These unsparing self-appraisals convey the anguish of her physical limitations. The nurse who tended her in her later years recalled her intense frustration at her failing abilities. "She was in agony. Not physical pain, but emotional agony. . . . Art was her life."[6] Nonetheless, in these remarkable images, she was working out new challenges. "About ten years ago," she recalled about a year before this drawing was made, "I began to be preoccupied with movement. Before, I was preoccupied with mobility, the *potential* for movement. . . . When I

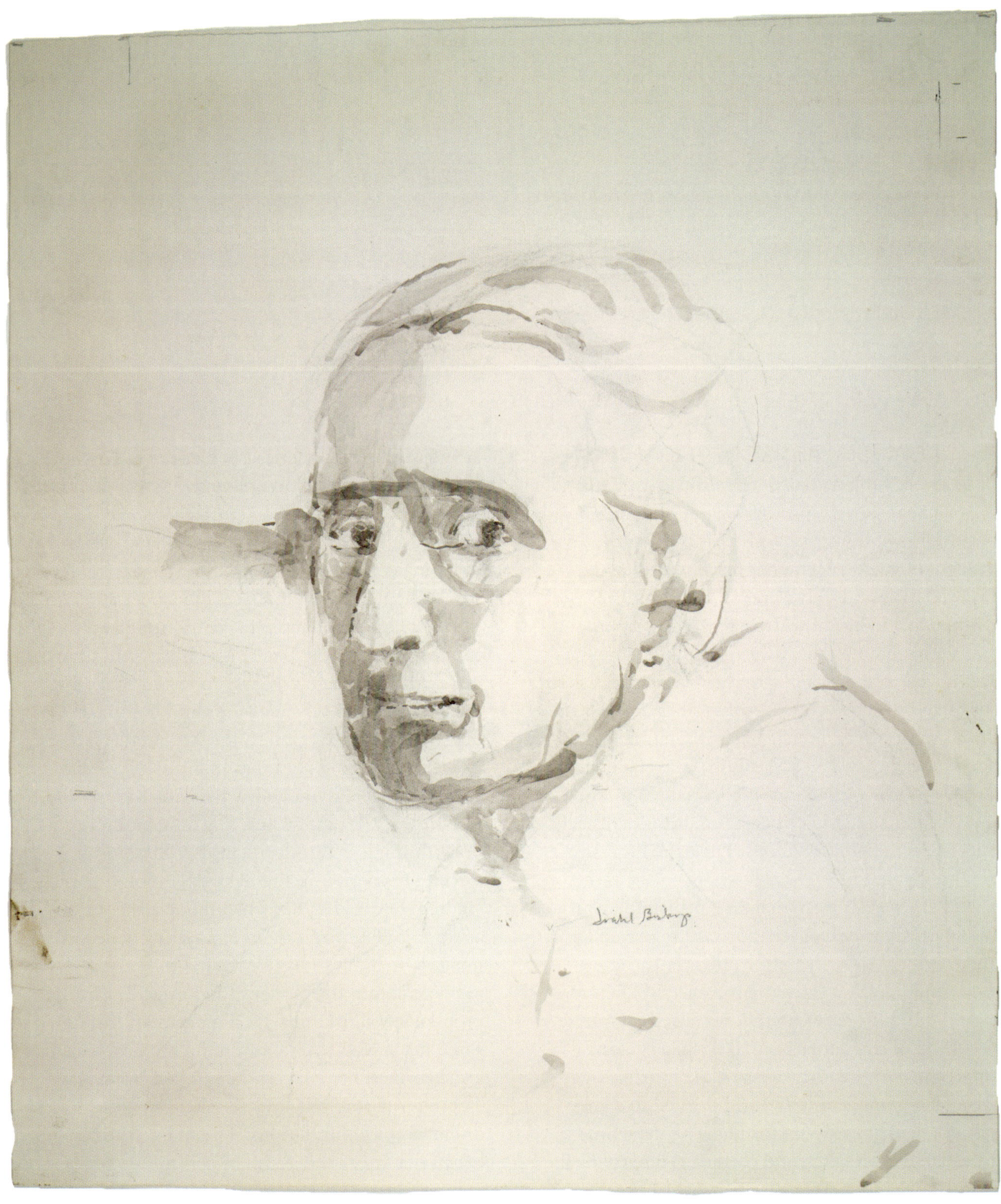

15.

Isabel Bishop (1902–1988)

Ink wash on paper, 43.7 x 36.9 cm
(17 3/16 x 14 1/2 in.), c. 1984–1985
The Ruth Bowman and Harry Kahn Twentieth-Century American Self-Portrait Collection
NPG.2002.212

went from mobility to motion, I found I was much less interested in the genre aspect of the picture, in particularity."[7] In this drawing, one senses the turning head the very moment after its rotation. That immediacy, ironically, does not impart a particular individual and precise moment but the sense of a timeless, universal truth.

WWR

Notes

1 Helen Yglesias, *Isabel Bishop* (New York: Rizzoli, 1989), 16.
2 Ibid., 14.
3 Catherine Barnett, "A Woman of Substance: Remembering Isabel Bishop," *Arts and Antiques* 11 (December 1988): 69.
4 Margaret Breuning, "At the Midtown Galleries," *New York Post*, March 16, 1935, and Henry McBride, "Attractions in the Galleries," *New York Sun*, May 6, 1949, cited in Karl Lunde, *Isabel Bishop* (New York: Harry N. Abrams, 1975), 164, 166. Margaret Breuning found Bishop's etchings "technically sound" but "less fluent and spontaneous" than her drawings. But Bishop liked that austerity. For her, etching was a way to find out whether there was a valid "visual idea in her sketch." Barbaralee Diamonstein, *Inside New York's Art World* (New York: Rizzoli, 1979), 53.
5 Avis Berman, "When Artists Grow Old," *ARTnews* 82 (December 1983): 77.
6 Barnett, "A Woman of Substance," 70.
7 Berman, "When Artists Grow Old," 82.

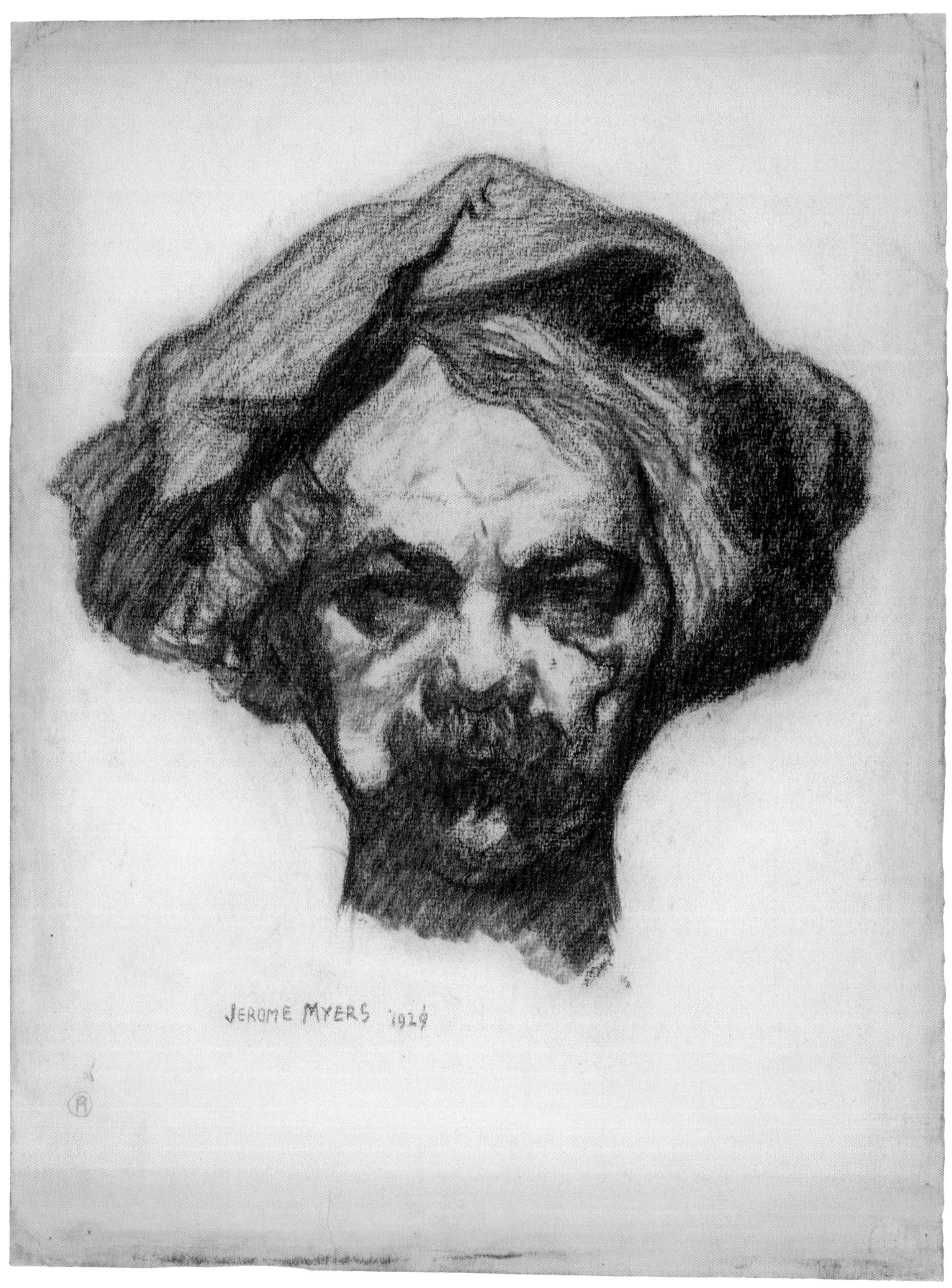
JEROME MYERS 1920

16.

Jerome Myers (1867–1940)

Charcoal on paper, 40.8 x 30.4 cm
(16 1/16 x 11 15/16 in.), 1929
The Ruth Bowman and Harry Kahn Twentieth-Century American Self-Portrait Collection
S/NPG.2002.305

IN THIS DRAWING Jerome Myers fiercely meets the viewer's gaze. Could such a formidable man portray children sympathetically? In fact, Myers made many paintings of children at play in the poverty-stricken ghettos of New York's Lower East Side. Myers was best known for these gentle genre groupings and for his self-portraits.[1] In both aspects of his art, he consciously borrowed from the seventeenth-century artist Rembrandt van Rijn.[2]

In his autobiography Myers delightedly noted:

> Taking my resemblance to the Dutch master as a starting point . . . as he went to live in the Dutch ghetto, so I too went to study in the ghetto—that of our own East Side. Again like Rembrandt, I too have made many self-portraits. . . . It may be that Rembrandt's Dutch courage has sustained me, even as his art has inspired me.[3]

Myers painted several playful self-portraits in which he likened his bulbous nose and mane of gray hair to Rembrandt's, donning black tams and gold chains like those the Dutch artist depicted himself wearing. As *ARTnews* said of such a painting, "It DOES Look Like Rembrandt!"[4]

This drawing exemplifies a more serious vein of Myers's self-portraits that moved away from the literal example of Rembrandt while taking lessons from his work. Myers departed from his Dutch model in his precisely frontal view and balanced lighting, contrasting with the angled view and illumination Rembrandt preferred. The light cloth binding Myers's hair evokes the white linen caps in several of Rembrandt's late self-portraits,[5] but more important connections emerge in Myers's rich charcoal shadows and his thoughtful study of character and mood. Myers's gaze, too, is distinctive in its forceful challenge to the viewer. Although Myers idealized his paintings of East Side immigrants, he did not flinch from confronting himself in the mirror and on paper.

APW

Notes

1 Grant Holcomb, "The Forgotten Legacy of Jerome Myers (1867–1940): Painter of New York's Lower East Side," *American Art Journal* 9 (May 1977): 78–91.

2 Myers had easy access to Rembrandt paintings at the Metropolitan Museum of Art and public and private collections of the master's etchings.

3 Jerome Myers, *Artist in Manhattan* (New York: American Artists Group, 1940), 74–75.

4 "It DOES Look Like Rembrandt!" *ARTnews* 22 (October 27, 1923): 1.

5 Edwin Buijsen, Peter Schatborn, and Ben Broos, "Catalogue," in *Rembrandt by Himself*, ed. Christopher White and Quentin Buvelot (London and the Hague: National Gallery Publications Limited and Royal Cabinet of Paintings Mauritshuis, 1999), 211.

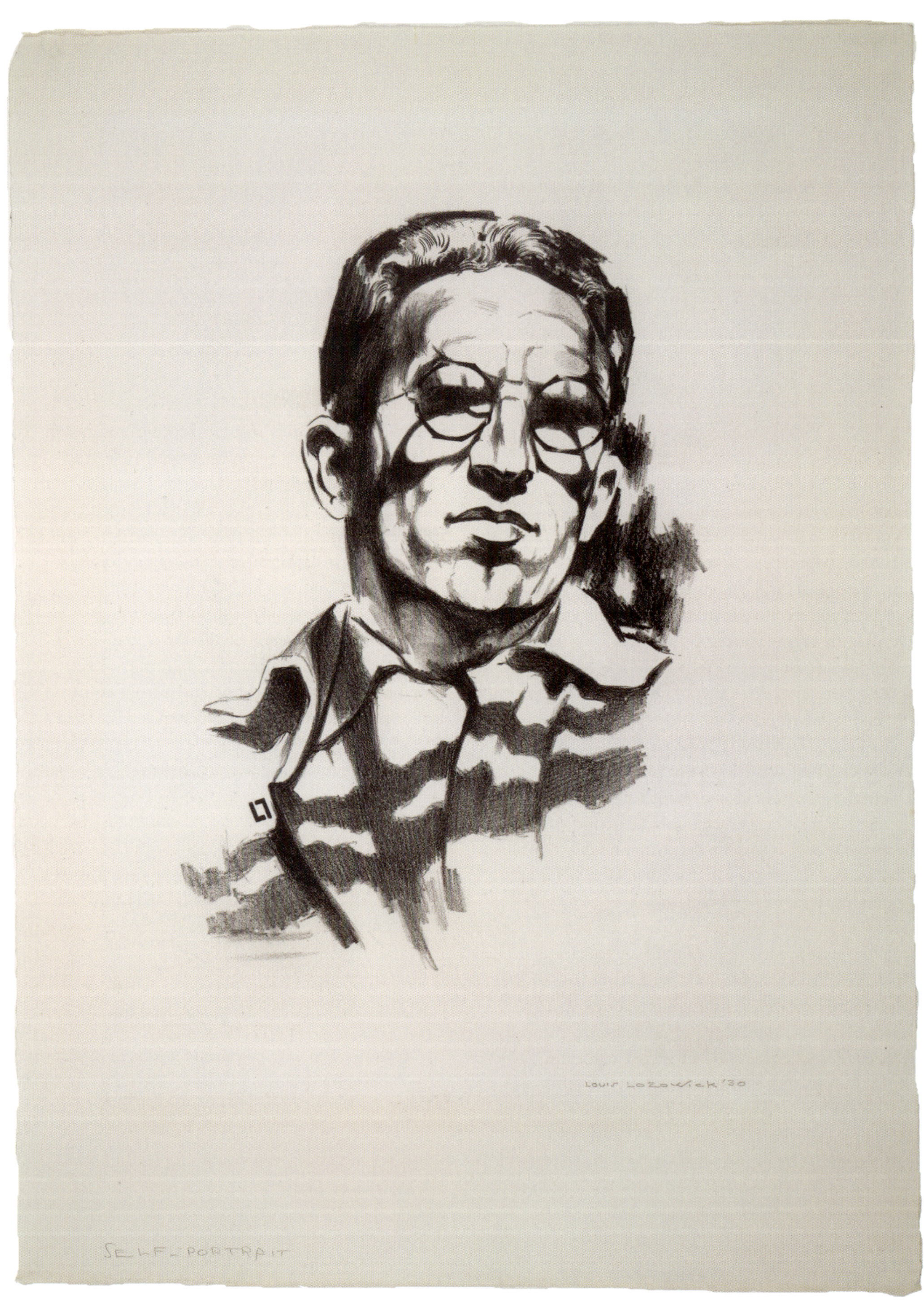
LOUIS LOZOWICK '30
SELF-PORTRAIT

17.

Louis Lozowick (1892–1973)

Lithograph, 40.3 x 28.9 cm (15⅞ x 11⅜ in.), 1930
The Ruth Bowman and Harry Kahn Twentieth-Century American Self-Portrait Collection
NPG.2002.295

THE HUMAN FACE appears with curious indirectness in Louis Lozowick's art. His best-known images center instead on colossal constructions: bridges, factories, and skyscrapers. People appear as industrial workers or urban dwellers whose faces are hidden or generalized into anonymity. Lozowick pictured himself obliquely, too; often he used self-portraiture to speak less for himself than for others.

Lozowick was born into a poor family in a Ukrainian village. His older brother helped him to attend an art school in Kiev that taught a precise academic approach to drawing. In 1906 Lozowick followed his brother to New York.[1] In the early 1920s Lozowick worked in Paris, Berlin, and Moscow, where he encountered constructivist artists full of enthusiasm about modern American engineering and architecture.[2] Under their influence, he combined the exacting draftsmanship he had learned in Kiev with constructivist concepts to create idealized geometric views of American cities.[3]

Beginning in the later 1920s, Lozowick's urban scenes took a less clean and idealized approach, allowing figures of workers to appear. In his 1930 self-portrait, a grid of shadow plays across the artist's chest, implying that he is gazing up at a bridge or a building under construction. Lozowick rendered his own face with the same crisp strokes and muscular symmetry he used to depict construction workers and the structures they erected. The artist looms above the viewer like some monumental but mysterious hero. Sunlight streams down on his brow while masklike darkness occludes his eyes. His glasses cast strange hollow shadows on his cheeks. Is Lozowick watching the construction workers sweating at their arduous tasks, or does the artist notice only the glorious structure rising?

During the thirties Lozowick's self-portraits reflected his political beliefs more clearly. He openly attacked social injustice in prints like *Tear Gas*, which depicted the artist himself as a protestor threatened by a mounted policeman.[4] Lozowick was one of the founders of the American Artists' Congress, an organization that stood for free expression and opposed fascism.[5] In 1935 the Congress mounted one of two highly publicized art exhibitions held in New York that year to attack the brutal lynching of African Americans by southern mobs and to champion antilynching legislation.[6] The following year Lozowick made his own antilynching image: a powerful self-portrait lithograph with his face shockingly depicted as the lynched man. The print was a very public statement that appeared in the book of 100 socially engaged prints, *America Today*, and in the associated exhibition that the Artists' Congress mounted in thirty-five cities.[7]

Most antilynching images of the 1930s showed the victim full-length, emphasizing his physical suffering and the brutality of the mob that whipped, burned, and hung him. Lozowick, however, isolated the victim's face and brought it to the extreme foreground, forcing the viewer to confront the man's humanity. Thus Lozowick accusingly put viewers in the place of the unseen lynch mob, facing the man they were murdering. *America Today* did not identify Lozowick's *Lynching* as a self-portrait, and the extreme contrast of firelight and night shadows

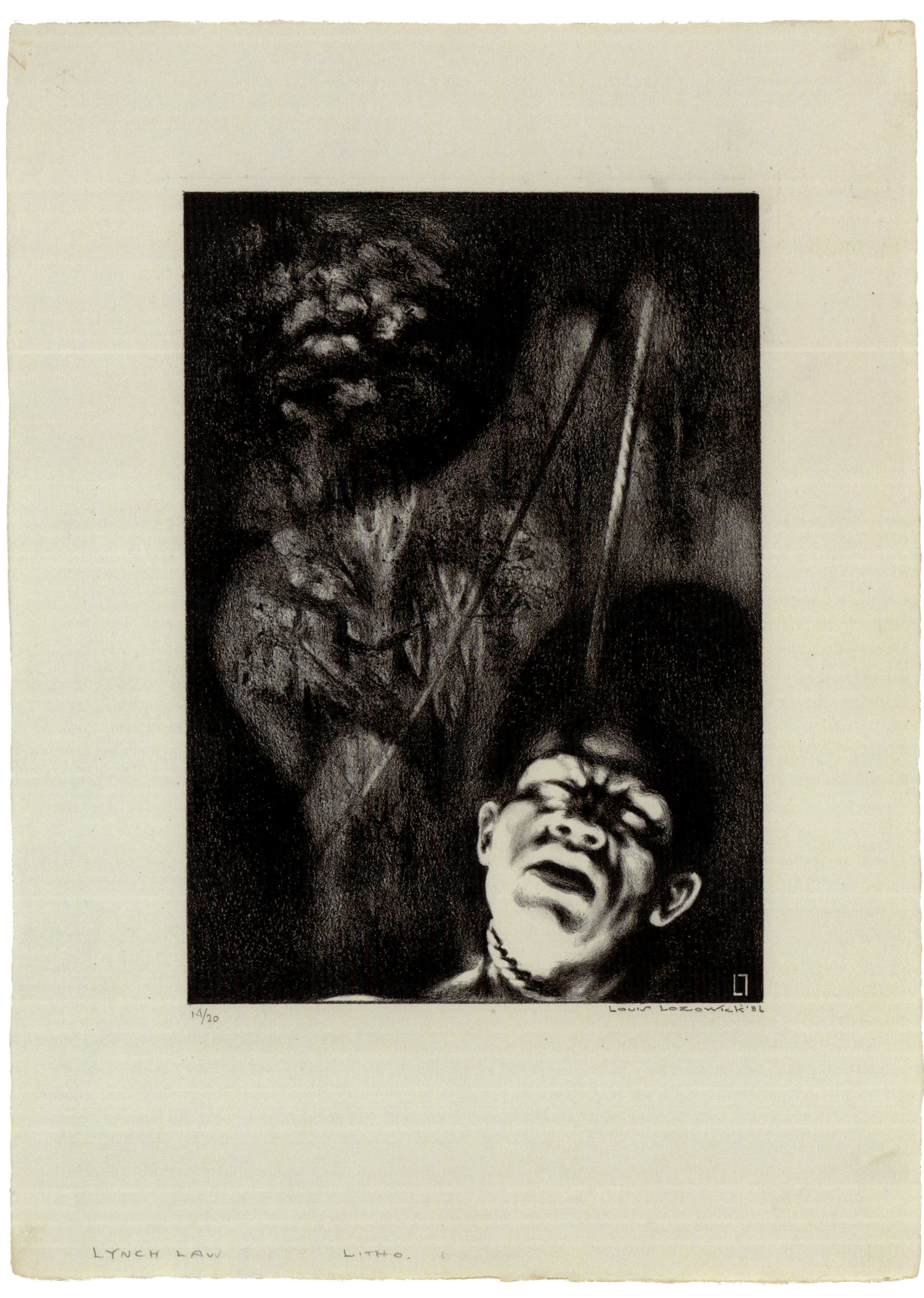
14/20
Louis Lozowick '36
LYNCH LAW
LITHO.

18.

Louis Lozowick (1892–1973)

Lynching (Lynch Law)
Lithograph, 40.6 x 29.5 cm (16 x 11⅝ in.), 1936
The Ruth Bowman and Harry Kahn Twentieth-Century American Self-Portrait Collection
NPG.2002.296

and the contortion of the features left the race of the victim uncertain. But for those who did know that the face was the artist's, the print held an additional grim message. By 1935 American Jews like Lozowick were hearing about Nazi oppression of German Jews, as well as Hitler's stance against blacks.[8] Lozowick's print terrifyingly suggested to American Jews, and to Americans of all faiths and races, that if Nazi fascism came to America, their own heads would be next in the noose.

APW

Notes

1 Louis Lozowick, *Survivor from a Dead Age: The Memoirs of Louis Lozowick* (Washington, DC, and London: Smithsonian Institution Press, 1997), 90–93, 140, 143.
2 Ibid., 160–249.
3 Barbara Wahl Kaufman, *Louis Lozowick, 1892–1973* (South Orange, NJ: Student Center Art Gallery, Seton Hall University, 1973), 2–3.
4 These included the 1934 lithographs *Strike Scene* and *Tear Gas*, and the 1937 lithograph *Demonstration*. Janet Flint, *The Prints of Louis Lozowick: A Catalogue Raisonné* (New York: Hudson Hills Press, 1982), 112–13, 124. For the identification of the figure as a self-portrait of Lozowick, see Virginia Hagelstein Marquardt, "Back in America," in Lozowick, *Survivor from a Dead Age*, 270.
5 On Lozowick's role in the American Artists' Congress, see Matthew Baigell and Julia Williams, introduction to *Artists against War and Fascism: Papers of the First American Artists' Congress* (New Brunswick, NJ: Rutgers University Press, 1986), 4–25. On Lozowick's membership in the John Reed Club and his role in founding the radical journal *The New Masses*, see Marquardt, "Back in America," 268–72.
6 The exhibitions, both shown in New York, were "An Art Commentary on Lynching," mounted by the NAACP and on view from February 15 to March 2, 1935, and "Struggle for Negro Rights," mounted by the American Artists' Union and several Communist-affiliated organizations, on view from March 3 to March 16, 1935. Marlene Park, "Lynching and Antilynching: Art and Politics in the 1930s," *Prospects* 18 (1993): 311–65; Helen Langa, "Two Antilynching Art Exhibitions: Politicized Viewpoints, Racial Perspectives, Gendered Constraints," *American Art* 13 (Spring 1999): 10–39.
7 American Artists' Congress, *America Today; a Book of 100 Prints Chosen and Exhibited by the American Artists' Congress* (New York: Equinox Cooperative Press, 1936), 14, plate 98. For details of the exhibition and book see Baigell and Williams, introduction to *Artists against War*, 24.
8 Milly Heyd, "Jews Mirroring African Americans on Lynching," in *Mutual Reflections: Jews and Blacks in American Art* (New Brunswick, NJ: Rutgers University Press, 1999), 86–116.

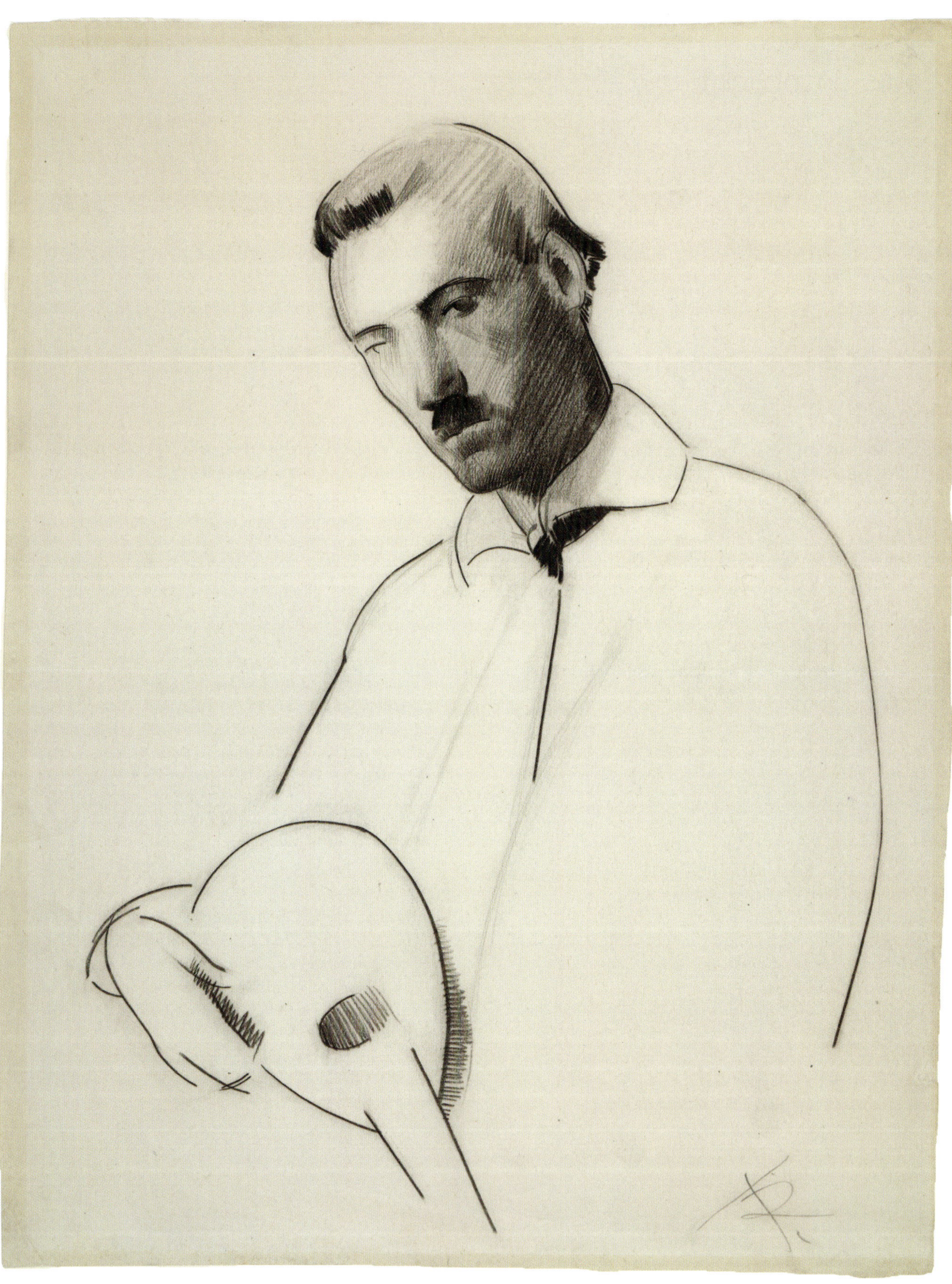

19.

Theodore Roszak (1907–1981)

Charcoal on paper, 30.5 x 23.1 cm
(12 x 9 1/8 in.), c. 1927–1929
The Ruth Bowman and Harry Kahn Twentieth-Century American Self-Portrait Collection
NPG.2002.317

IN THEODORE ROSZAK'S youthful self-portrait drawing, he depicts himself as a brooding romantic creative figure with his face half in darkness. The image evokes Roszak's duel artistry as both a visual artist and a trained musician.[1] Here the Polish-born artist holds a mandolin, which was commonly played in Polish folk music. Roszak described his dark hair and mustache and defined the planes of his classic features using layers of precisely controlled shading that clearly display his graphic mastery.

Yet this self-portrait is not the product of a strutting genius. Roszak's drawing is restrained, the careful modeling giving way to elegant outlines around his right eye, his hand, and the briefly indicated mandolin. His style suggests that the truth might lie with simplicity rather than detailed description. In earlier drawings, the young Roszak, who studied drawing at the Art Institute of Chicago and then taught the same subject, had indulged in fanciful linear patterning in the hair and clothing of figures out of folklore.[2] By the time he made this work in the late twenties, Roszak's line was becoming more sparse and forceful. He pared away surface detail to display such basic structures as the cylinder that forms his head and neck.

In 1929, perhaps soon after or just before he made this drawing, Roszak traveled to Europe, where he first saw the works of surrealism, cubism, and other forms of modern art that would inspire him to become a constructivist sculptor. Polished three-dimensional metallic forms became his characteristic vocabulary during the thirties.[3] But in the late twenties, before he saw European modern art, Roszak began discovering for himself the expressive force of abstraction. In this drawing he began to practice it on his own features.

APW

Notes

1 Interview of Theodore Roszak by James Elliott, February 13, 1956, Theodore Roszak Papers, Archives of American Art, Smithsonian Institution, Washington, DC. Indeed, Roszak originally tried to be both a musician and a visual artist. "Ultimately, he decided to pursue art rather than music, but his quandary is reflected in numerous paintings and drawings with musical themes or elements." Douglas Dreishpool, *Theodore Roszak: Paintings and Drawings from the Thirties* (New York: Hirschl & Adler Galleries, 1989), 12.

2 Douglas Scott Dreishpool, *Theodore J. Roszak (1907–1981): Painting and Sculpture* (Ann Arbor, MI: University Microfilms, 1993), 12, 16.

3 For early works by Roszak in drawing, painting, and sculpture see Dreishpool, *Theodore Roszak: Paintings and Drawings from the Thirties*; Howard E. Wooden, *Theodore Roszak: The Early Works, 1929–1943* (Wichita, KS: Wichita Art Museum, 1986); Joan Marter, *Theodore Roszak: The Drawings* (New York: Drawing Society and University of Washington Press, 1992); and Harold Ernst Gallery, Ltd., *Roszak: Early Paintings* (Boston: Harold Ernst Gallery, Ltd., 1973).

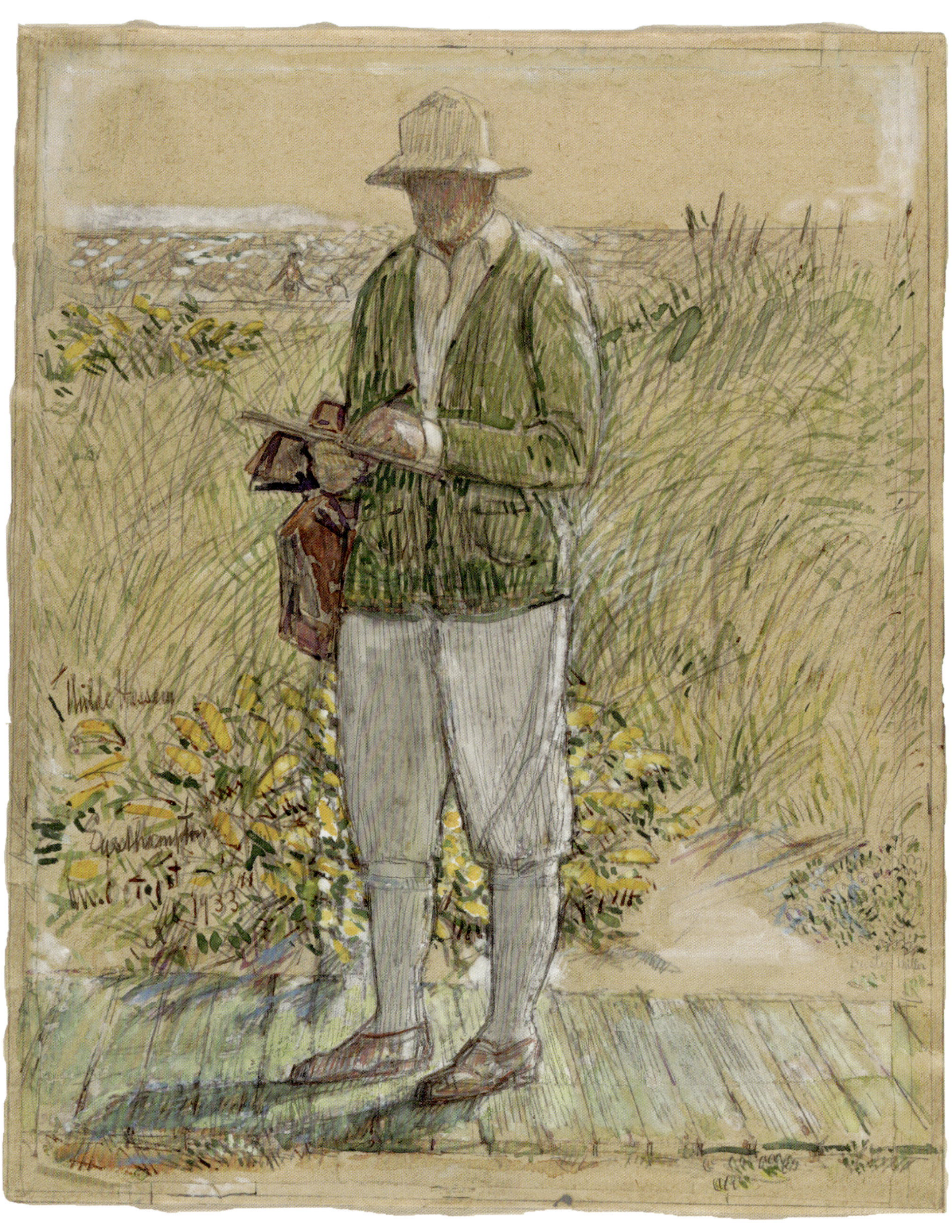

20.

Childe Hassam (1859–1935)

Watercolor, graphite, and gouache on paper,
24 x 9.1 cm (9 7/16 x 3 9/16 in.), 1933
The Ruth Bowman and Harry Kahn Twentieth-Century American Self-Portrait Collection
NPG.2002.267

CHILDE HASSAM'S self-portrait, picturing the artist on the boardwalk at the Maidstone Beach Club, combined his twin loves of art making and the landscape of East Hampton. "It has a character all its own," stated Hassam about the town in which he summered from 1919 forward, "may it never be changed."[1] His high regard for the setting is reflected in an inscription—almost hidden—that meticulously records the place, the date, and even the presence of the flower Dusty Miller. Less than two years later, the artist would choose to spend his final months in his coastal home.

The surf pictured behind Hassam held special significance for him. "My principal pleasure has always been, apart from painting and etching, to swim in the ocean," he reported.[2] Indeed, on October 17, 1933, only sixteen days after this drawing was completed, a local newspaper documented his daily swim, which culminated at the Maidstone Beach Club, in an article celebrating the artist's seventy-fourth birthday.[3]

One of several self-portraits in which the artist depicted himself at work, Hassam created the image with the help of a mirror located on a cabana. Often characterized as an "American impressionist," Hassam here demonstrates his artist's sensitivity to the interplay of light and landscape as well as his desire to capture an instant in time with sketches executed out of doors rather than belabored in the studio. Yet despite the work's spontaneous appearance, a related sketch, with its blocking out of forms and shapes, on the verso of the page reveals the artist's concern with composition. Shortly after its completion, the drawing would become the basis for a related etching. At this late stage in his career, Hassam, who began his career as an illustrator before training as a fine artist in Paris, noted the special significance of works on paper in his career, remarking: "I began my career in the graphic arts, and I am ending it in the graphic arts."[4]

ACG

Notes

1 Interview, *East Hampton Star*, August 31, 1923; quoted in John Esten, *Childe Hassam: East Hampton Summers* (East Hampton, NY: Guild Hall Museum, 1997), 12.
2 Childe Hassam Papers, Archives of American Art, Smithsonian Institution, quoted by Esten, *Childe Hassam*, 14.
3 The article was carried in the *East Hampton Star*, October 17, 1933; see ibid.
4 Quoted in Donelson F. Hoopes, *Childe Hassam* (New York: Watson-Guptill Publications, 1979), 18.

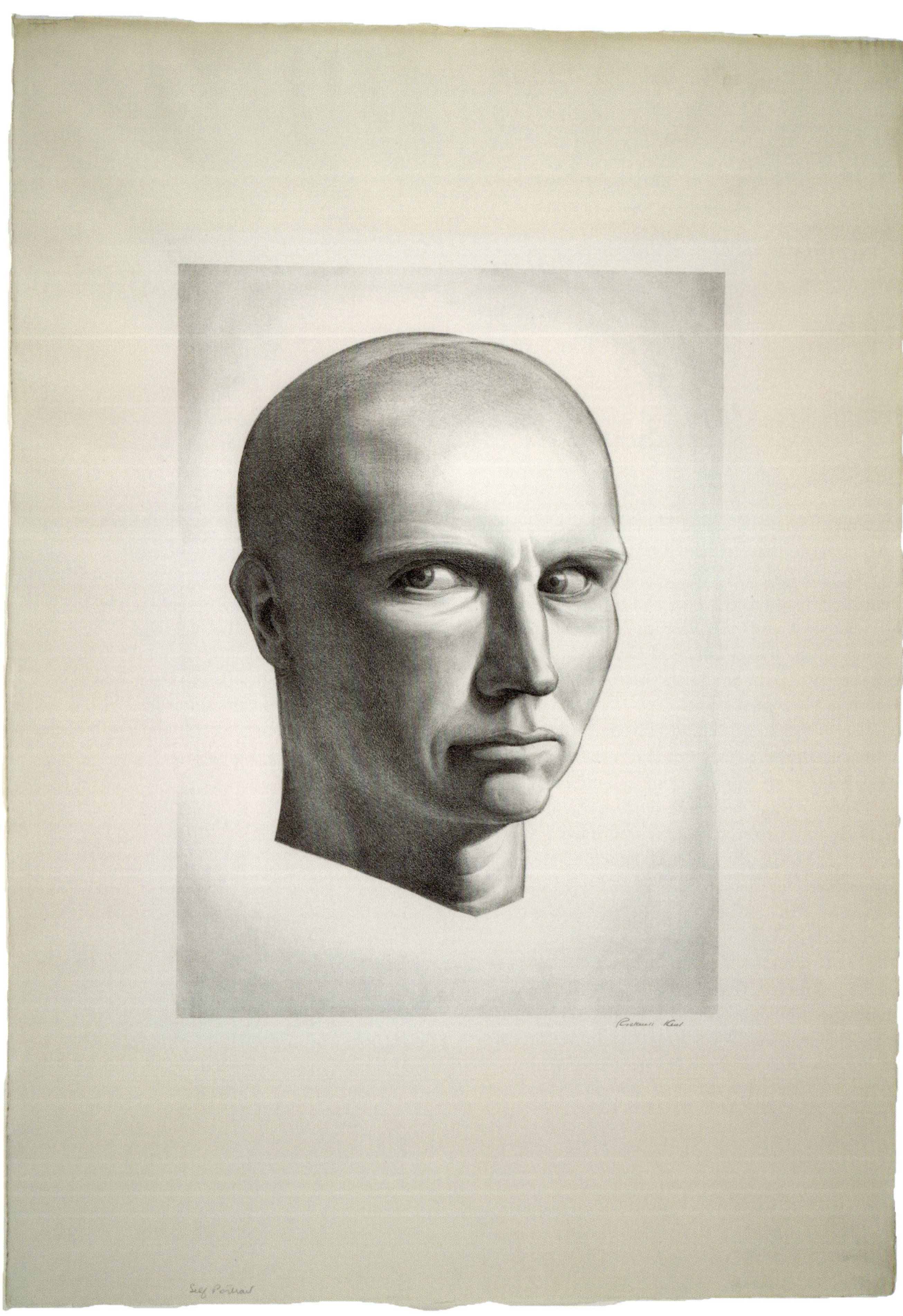

21.

Rockwell Kent (1882–1971)

Das Ding an Sich/It's Me O Lord
Lithograph, 58 x 40.7 cm ($22^{3}/_{16}$ x 16 in.), 1934
The Ruth Bowman and Harry Kahn Twentieth-Century American Self-Portrait Collection
NPG.2002.282

ROCKWELL KENT composed this self-portrait in Igdlorssuit, Greenland, one of his favorite locales and artistic subjects. At the time, he was in the midst of a summer-through-spring residence within a native community, producing landscapes and full-length ethnographic studies depicting native activities, physiognomy, and dress. He also wrote *Salamina*, one of several illustrated books he published about his adventures in Greenland and other rugged, isolated places he visited for extended periods.[1]

Das Ding an Sich means "the thing in itself," and refers to Immanuel Kant's postulation about the existence of two types of "things"—the impenetrable thing-in-itself, a noumenon, and the thing as it appears to an observer, a phenomenon. Kent was similarly concerned with human perception and reality, and explained in 1919, "It is the ultimate which concerns me, and all physical, all material things are but an expression of it."[2]

The penetrating gaze and startling disembodiment of Kent's self-portrait, which resembles a Roman marble as much as a human face, highlight his eccentric intellectualism. This quality was also inherent to his interest in and exploration of the wilderness, where he claimed he "sensed a fresh unfolding of the mystery of life."[3] By the time he composed this lithograph, his numerous prints, paintings, and writings about his revelatory adventures made him one of the United States' most popular artists and personalities.

The self-portrait's secondary title, which Kent also used for his 1955 autobiography, comes from the African American spiritual lyric, "It's me, it's me, it's me, O Lord,/Standin' in the need of prayer."[4] According to art historian Constance Martin, it "suggests a sense of humility rarely if ever evident in Kent's typically egocentric conduct and the grandiloquence of much of his published prose."[5] Although Kent's precise inspiration for this title remains a matter of speculation, it is a lasting testament to his quest to reconcile his self-expression with "the ultimate."

ECR

Notes

1 Kent visited Greenland on three occasions and wrote three books about his experiences: *N by E* (New York: Literary Guild, 1930; New York: Blue Ribbon Books, 1930); *Salamina* (New York: Harcourt, Brace and Company, 1935), and *Greenland Journal* (New York: Ivan Obolensky, 1962). See also Kent, *Salamina*, with a foreword by R. Scott Ferris (Middleton, CT: Wesleyan Press, 2003).

2 Rockwell Kent, "Alaska Drawings," *Arts and Decoration* (June 1919), quoted in Dan Burne Jones, introduction to *The Prints of Rockwell Kent, a Catalog Raisonné by Dan Burne Jones, Revised by Robert Rightmire* (San Francisco: Alan Wofsy Fine Arts, 2002), xxii. Kent defended his realist style for much of his career. In a 1931 article he argued, "It is wrong to take French art to be the expression of a special human quality, the Frenchman, and rash to look upon it as a better art or a more near approach to an ideal of sheer and absolute perfection." Instead, he insisted, "The highest merit and most moving quality that a work of art can have is its integrity, its integrity as the expression and embodiment of a human being and of those native influences that have civilized him." Rockwell Kent, "Apple Jack (1931)" in *Rockwellkentiana* (New York: Harcourt, Brace and Company, 1933), 39–40.

3 Kent, "Alaska Drawings," quoted in Jones, *Prints of Rockwell Kent*, xxii.

4 Rockwell Kent, *It's Me, O Lord, the Autobiography of Rockwell Kent* (1955; New York: Da Capo Press, 1977).

5 Constance Martin, "Rockwell Kent: The Odyssey," in *Distant Shores: The Rockwell Odyssey of Rockwell Kent* (Chesterfield, MA: Chameleon Books and the Norman Rockwell Museum at Stockbridge, 2000), 17.

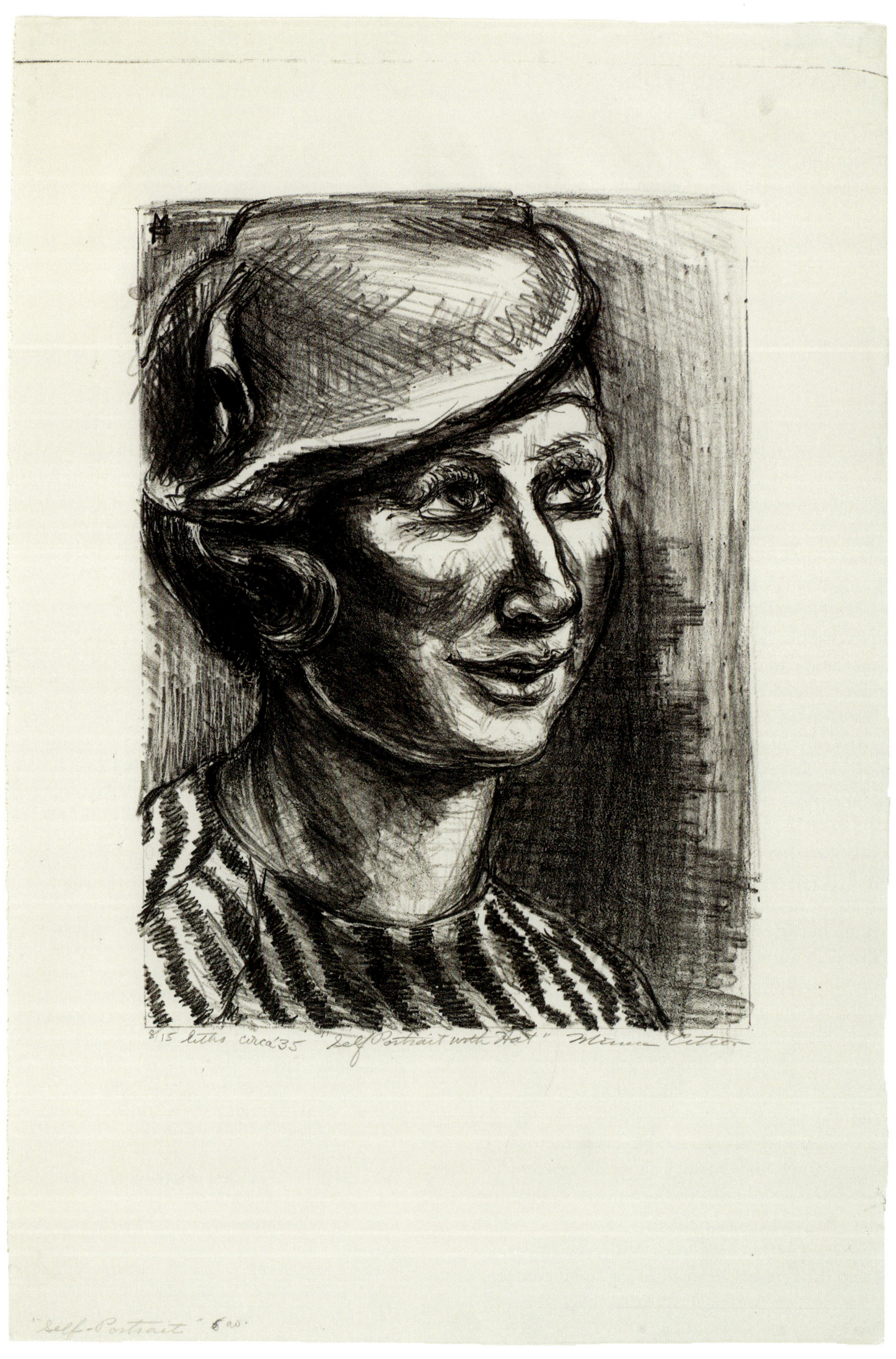
8/15 litho circa '35 "Self Portrait with Hat" Minna Citron
"Self-Portrait" 6.00

22.

Minna Citron (1896–1991)

Self-Portrait with Hat
Lithograph, 48.1 x 32 cm (18 15/16 x 12 5/8 in.),
c. 1935
The Ruth Bowman and Harry Kahn Twentieth-Century American Self-Portrait Collection
S/NPG.2002.228

MINNA CITRON is best known for the abstract prints and drawings she made from the mid-1940s on, but this self-portrait dates to an earlier era, when she realistically portrayed the people she saw around her Manhattan studio in Union Square. Like her fellow "Fourteenth Street school" artist, Isabel Bishop, Citron was a penetrating observer of urban women coping with the challenges of the Great Depression. Her works were often humorous satires of such women, including herself. Citron's 1935 solo exhibition "Feminanities" featured *Self-Expression*, a decidedly ungraceful painting of her working at her drafting table.[1]

In this self-portrait lithograph made in about 1935, Citron pictured herself as a fashionable young woman in a fetching hat and a striped dress rather than as a serious artist at work. She excluded the wider setting and additional characters she usually employed to give a plot to her works. But the tighter focus of this composition did not prevent the artist from telling a story. The gestural lines describing her features suggest a vivacious woman charming the people around her. She looks up and away from the viewer, her heavily drawn eyelashes apparently batting as she gazes into the eyes of a taller person. Perhaps she is flirting with a man?

Citron was just as dynamic and captivating in real life as she appears in this print. Having studied painting since the 1920s, in 1935 she boldly left her middle-class married life to become an artist and single mother.[2] Citron divorced her husband, paper box manufacturer Henry Citron, who was quoted in the *Chicago Daily Tribune* moaning, "I could not keep up with my wife's studies in sexual ethics, nudity, free love, golf, music, and psychiatry."[3] Few could keep pace with the lively Citron, who remained an active artist in New York until the end of her long life.[4]

APW

Notes

1 Judith Brodsky, "Minna Citron," *Women's Caucus for Art Honor Awards for Outstanding Achievement in the Visual Arts* (Philadelphia: Women's Caucus for Art and Moore College of Art, 1985), 1–2. Louis Weitzenkorn, *"Feminanities": Paintings by Minna Citron* (New York: Midtown Galleries, 1935). For Citron's abstract works, see Max Chapman, *From the 80 Years of Minna Citron* (New York and Newark, NJ: Tunnel Gallery, Ingber Gallery, and the Newark Public Library, 1976).

2 Brodsky, "Minna Citron," 1–2.

3 "Minna Citron Is Ordered Quizzed in Divorce Case," *Chicago Daily Tribune*, December 5, 1935, 3.

4 For biographical information on Citron's later years, see Susan Teller Gallery, *Minna Citron: A Survey of Paintings and Works on Paper, 1931–1989* (New York: Susan Teller Gallery, 1990) and Chapman, *From the 80 Years of Minna Citron.*

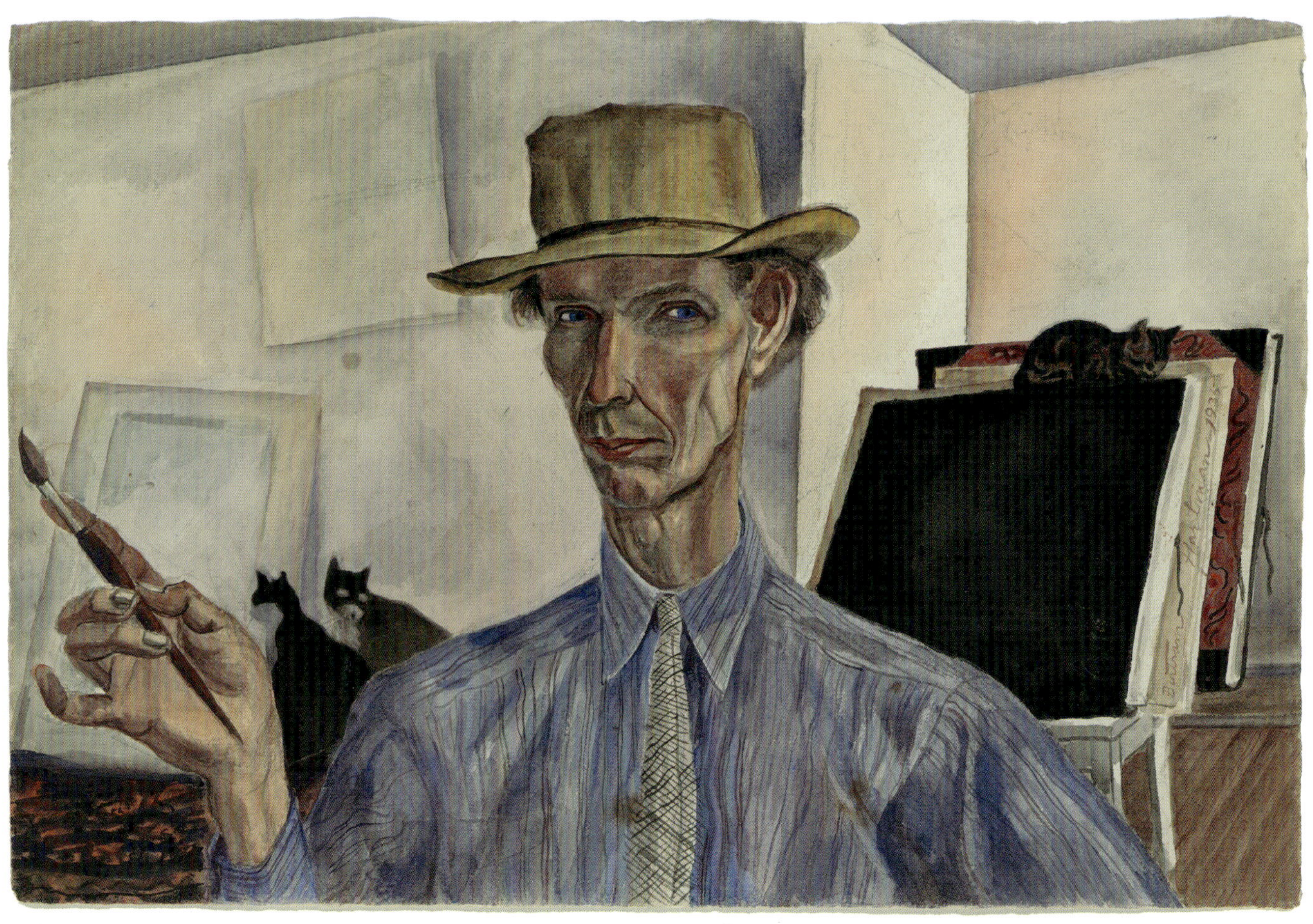

23.

Bertram Hartman (1882–1960)

Watercolor over graphite on paper, 39 x 56.9 cm (15 3/8 x 22 3/8 in.), 1935
Gift of Kurt Delbanco
S/NPG.91.203

KANSAS-BORN ARTIST Bertram Hartman, shown in his studio, was once well known in artistic circles of New York and Paris. While living in Greenwich Village with his wife, Augusta, in the 1910s, Hartman hosted what fellow artist Jerome Myers called "exhilarating" evenings.[1] Although he worked in magazine illustration, batik designs, and commercial art, he also exhibited his oils and watercolors alongside prominent American modernists and befriended John Marin, Gaston Lachaise, and William and Marguerite Zorach. When he went to Paris from late 1923 to 1925, he enjoyed the company of Ernest Hemingway and other prominent expatriates; the French press regularly noted the Hartmans' interesting costumes and their travels.[2] Returning to New York, Hartman resumed exhibiting in the galleries and was particularly admired for his watercolors. Critics liked the multiple perspectives and cubist patterning of his landscapes and skyscrapers, which, as Henry McBride noted, play "a rhythmic game."[3]

Hartman used the same playful repetitive geometric shapes to animate this wry, somewhat dandified self-portrait, rendered in the finished style of his exhibition watercolors. Although better known for his landscapes and cityscapes, he occasionally exhibited his figure paintings and periodically used self-portraiture to push himself toward a more angular rendering. "The little deer in the idyllic landscapes have marched right out of the picture, thank God," he responded to criticism about an unflattering full-length self-portrait exhibited at the Montross Gallery in 1929.[4] In 1936, he mounted a show of figurative watercolors at Another Place gallery. "Forms, light, and patterns of color interplay in sweeping rhythms," the *New York Times* reviewer noted. "Hartman's lyricism is uppermost in these watercolors and dash and freshness are explicit."[5]

Despite this recognition, Hartman's reputation was founded primarily on his batik textiles, book illustrations, stained glass, mosaics, and designs for rugs hooked by his wife, and it suffered when he abandoned his decorative designs to focus exclusively on mural and easel painting.

WWR

Notes

1 Jerome Myers, *Artist in Manhattan* (New York: American Artists Group, 1940), 100–101.
2 Full biographical information can be found in Martha Gage Elton, "Bertram Hartman (1882–1960), An Early Modernist from Kansas" (PhD diss., University of Kansas, 2004).
3 *New York Sun*, January 9, 1927.
4 *Art Digest* 3 (mid-January 1929): 5; see also *New York Times*, June 17, 1934, for another self-portrait.
5 "Figure Paintings," *New York Times*, December 13, 1936.

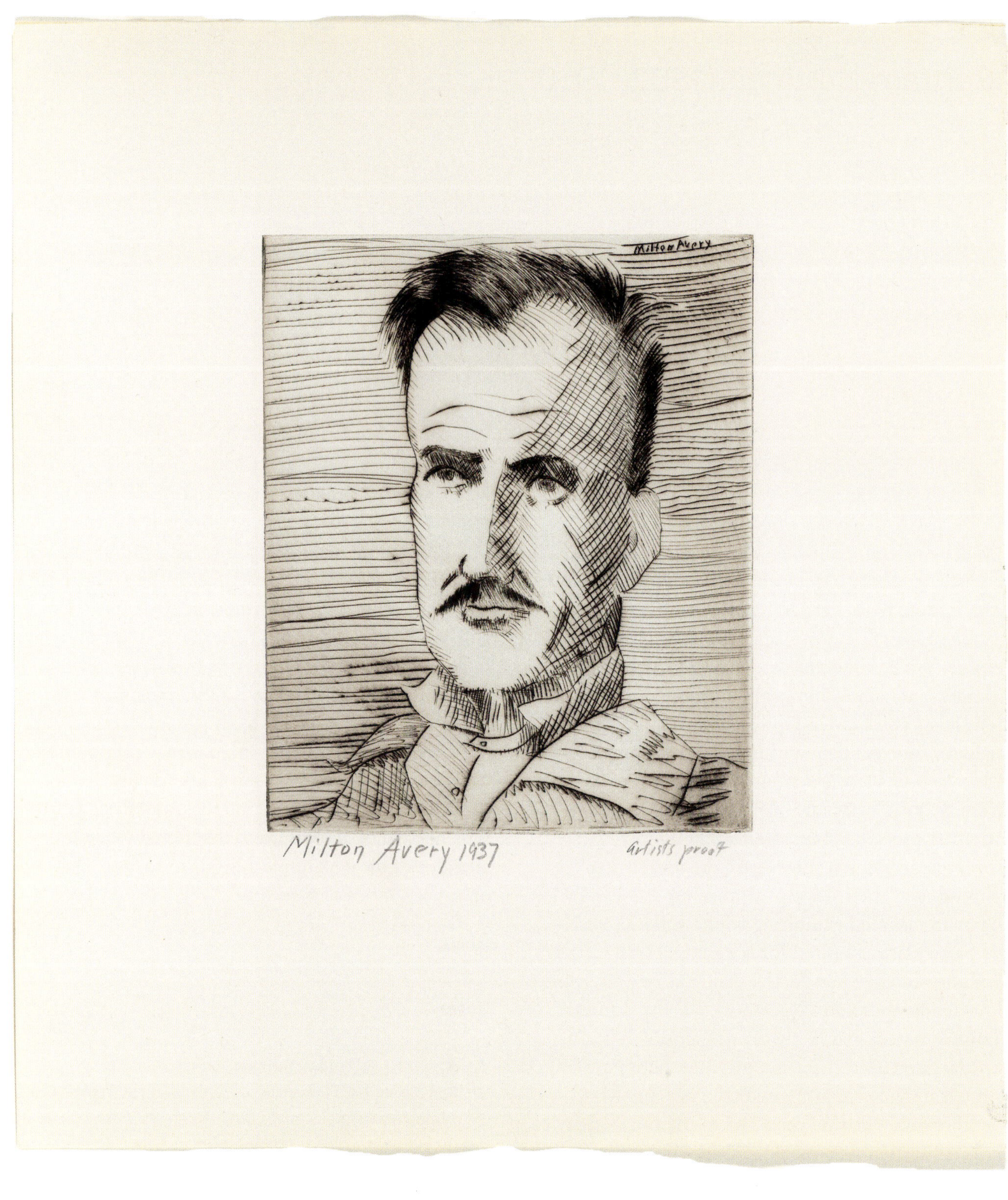
Milton Avery
Milton Avery 1937
artists proof

24.

Milton Avery (1885–1965)

Drypoint, 37.8 x 33.4 cm (14⅞ x 13⅛ in.), 1937
The Ruth Bowman and Harry Kahn Twentieth-Century American Self-Portrait Collection
NPG.2002.193

MILTON AVERY made this self-portrait print in 1937 as he explored new artistic territory. Having been trained in academic methods at the Connecticut League of Art Students, he was at first unaware of any art newer than impressionism. In 1925 he moved to New York City, where he suddenly and joyfully discovered the latest modern art.[1] During the next fifteen years, Avery gradually broke from his training. By the late thirties he was painting flattened forms in rich colors inspired by French modernist Henri Matisse. In black and white works like this one, Avery undertook a similar stylistic journey from realism to abstraction.

Avery and his wife, Sally, drew in their home and at the Art Students League, surrounded by friends.[2] Avery developed a playful graphic style in which linear patterning functioned much like the expressive color in his paintings. In 1933, when Avery's sister-in-law brought him some scrap zinc and copper printing plates from a commercial engraving shop, the artist applied his drawing style to printmaking.[3]

Avery seldom printed his plates,[4] but he was fascinated by the qualities of line he could achieve in drypoints like this self-portrait. He raked a sharp tool across the plate to draw dark furry lines of hair, while a lighter touch made more delicate lines. At times his tool caught in the metal, creating a saw-toothed effect. Horizontal strokes defined the background so aggressively that their sharp points appear to pierce Avery's skin. He based this print on an earlier softly modeled pencil drawing;[5] in the print he transformed the shading into heavy cross-hatching poised uneasily between modeling the face and flattening it. He also introduced an element of exaggeration, making his face very tall and rectangular in contrast to his small, fussy mustache. He effortlessly brought together this range of graphic approaches to create a masterful self-image.

APW

Notes

1 Barbara Haskell, *Milton Avery* (New York: Whitney Museum of American Art in association with Harper & Row, 1982), 16–26.
2 Ibid., 25–30.
3 Una Johnson, *Milton Avery: Prints and Drawings, 1930–1964*, American Graphic Artists of the Twentieth Century, no. 4 (Brooklyn, NY: Brooklyn Museum, 1966), 11.
4 Avery printed only a few proofs from his drypoint plates of the thirties. No editions were printed from them until 1947 and 1948. Further editions were printed in 1964 by Anderson and Lamb Photogravure Corporation. Avery signed and dated the prints, and this print was made at that time. Carlotta J. Owens, *Milton Avery: Works on Paper* (Washington, DC: National Gallery of Art, 1994), 18–20. On Avery's prints also see Harry Lunn Jr., comp. and ed., *Milton Avery: Prints, 1933–1955* (Washington, DC: Graphics International, 1973).
5 The drawing is illustrated in Linda Konheim Kramer, *Milton Avery in Black and White: Drawings, 1929–59* (Brooklyn, NY: Brooklyn Museum, 1990), 6.

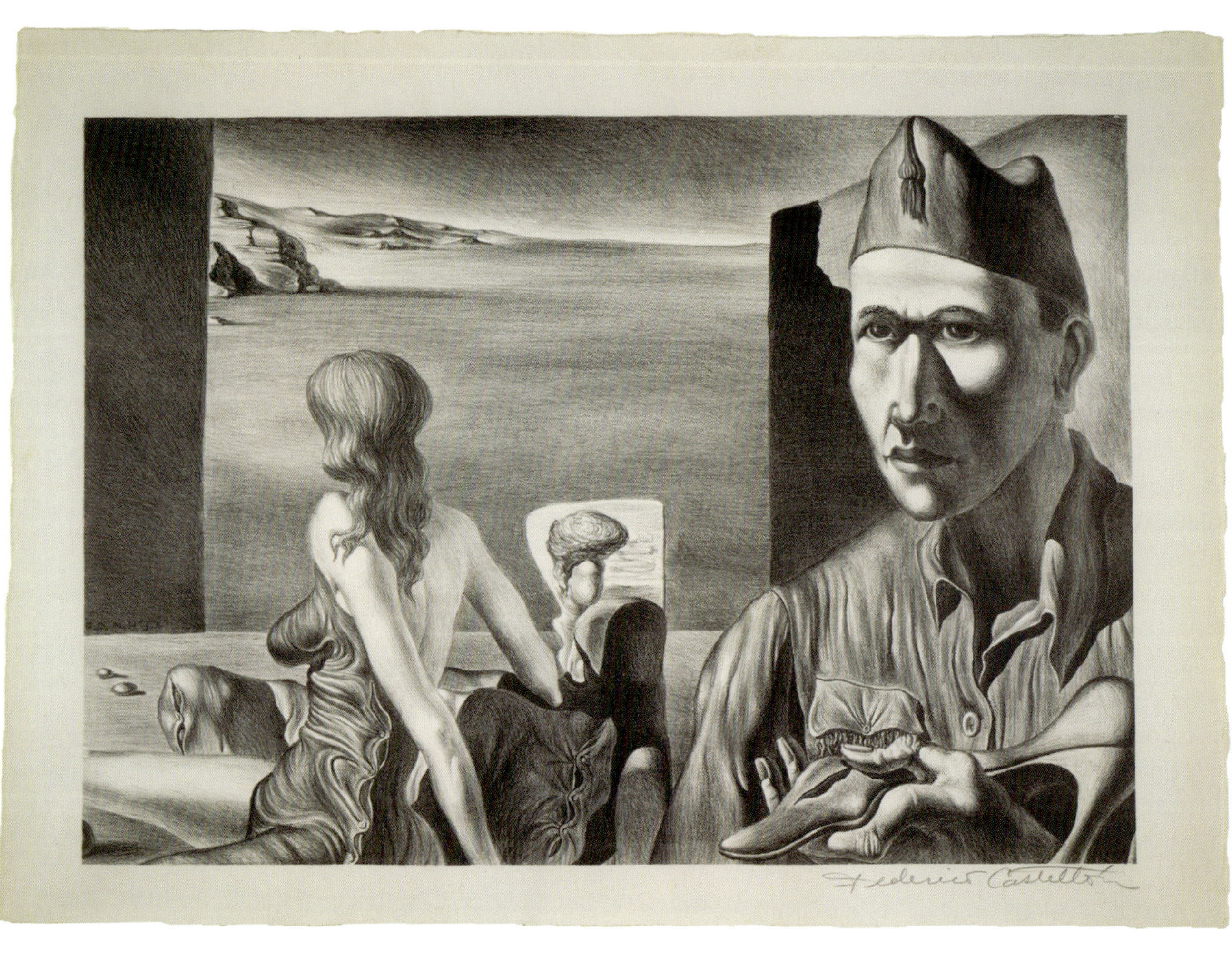

25.

Federico Castellon (1914–1971)

Self-Portrait with Spanish Cap
Lithograph, 29.8 x 40.5 cm (11¾ x 15¹⁵/16 in.), 1937
The Ruth Bowman and Harry Kahn Twentieth-Century American Self-Portrait Collection
NPG.2002.224

IN HIS SURREALIST lithograph *Self-Portrait with Spanish Cap*, Federico Castellon explored his conflicted identity as a Spanish-born artist living in America. He depicted himself against a coastal landscape reminiscent of his native southern Spain, which he had revisited in the early 1930s.[1] The recipient of a Spanish government fellowship to travel, study, and exhibit art in Spain and France, Castellon was visiting his native country for the first time since emigrating at age seven.[2] Although Castellon fled Spain to avoid mandatory military service before the outbreak of the Spanish Civil War, he portrayed himself in 1937 in what appears to be the hat of a Loyalist soldier.[3]

After an influential exposure to Europe's old masters and contemporary art, Castellon returned to the United States in 1936.[4] Upon his return, he had his second solo exhibition at the Weyhe Gallery in New York. He started to produce lithographs in 1937, the year of this self-portrait, and began to gain critical and financial success.[5]

Self-Portrait with Spanish Cap conveys a keen sense of longing, with its sensuous, yet averted and unavailable female figure; limp, fetishistic shoe; and sexually suggestive imagery. Castellon's self-depiction within, but oriented away from, his native landscape, reflects some of the isolation that characterized his childhood as, he recalled, a "rejected foreign child" whose art was "a way that I could assert myself as a human being."[6] Although Castellon preferred to describe his art as "poetic mysticism,"[7] he was identified with and clearly influenced by the surrealists Salvador Dalí and Joan Miró, with whom he exhibited his work in Paris in 1935. In the program for his 1936 solo show at Weyhe, he identified Edgar Allan Poe as a major inspiration, particularly the author's interest in "other worlds than this—other thoughts than the thoughts of the multitude." His self-portrait, characterized as it is by commingled longing and nostalgia, seems to be a portal into one of Castellon's own "other worlds."[8]

ECR

Notes

1 Castellon drew both barren plains and coastal landscapes of southern Spain in 1937. See August L. Freundlich, *Federico Castellon: His Graphic Works, 1936–1971* (Syracuse, NY: College of Visual and Performing Arts, Syracuse University, 1978).

2 The artist Diego Rivera helped Castellon to obtain the fellowship and introduced him to the critic and Weyhe Gallery director Carl Zigrosser. Zigrosser gave Castellon a solo exhibition at Weyhe, and it would remain his gallery for many years. See oral history interview conducted by Paul Cummings, April 7–15, 1971, Archives of American Art, Smithsonian Institution, Washington, DC.

3 A Spanish draft notice was mailed to Castellon's New York residence in 1935, while he was living in Paris. He was treated as a draft dodger and assigned to Spanish Morocco. Consequently, he fled Spain in the late spring of 1936, intending to "purchase [his] way out of military service" from the States, and eventually complete the last eighteen months of his four-year fellowship. The war, which broke out in July 1936, thwarted his plan. Castellon oral history interview.

4 Castellon considered paintings to be his teachers; public school art lessons were the extent of his formal training.

5 He was called in *Art Digest* "the young Spanish American surrealist whose work is finding increasing recognition in the art world." "Young Castellon, Who Recalls Poe and Redon," *Art Digest* 13 (May 1939): 25.

6 Castellon oral history interview; Freundlich, *Federico Castellon*, 14.

7 Castellon oral history interview.

8 *Federico Castellon* (New York: Weyhe Gallery, 1936), unpaginated.

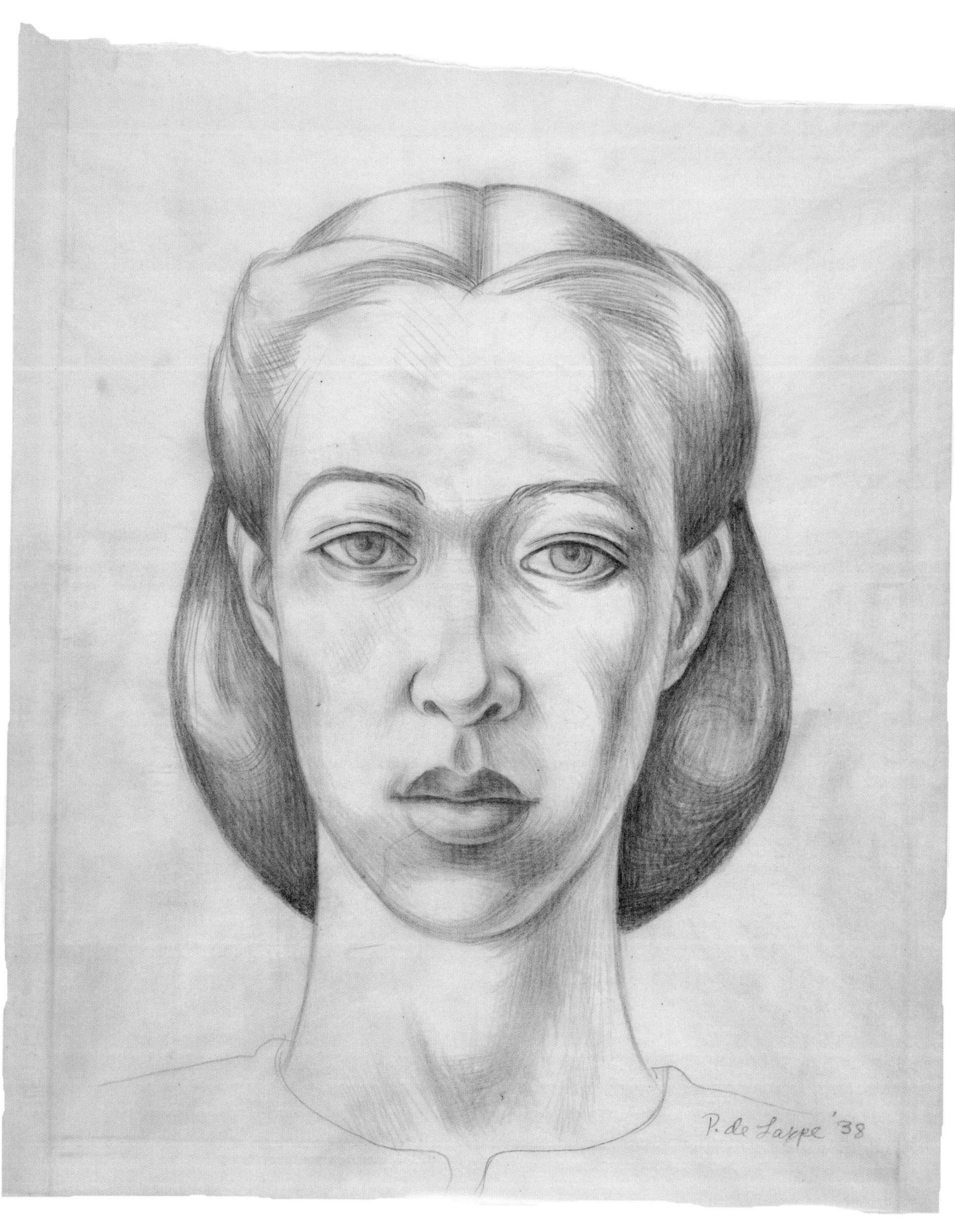
P. de Lappe '38

26.

Pele de Lappe (1916–2007)

Graphite on paper, 34.8 x 27.5 cm
(13 11/16 x 10 13/16 in.), 1938
The Ruth Bowman and Harry Kahn Twentieth-Century American Self-Portrait Collection
S/NPG.2002.290

PELE DE LAPPE'S two self-portraits, produced more than fifty years apart, encompass a long life in which she produced a relatively small body of work. De Lappe shared with many female artists of her generation the challenge of maintaining an artistic career while raising children and making a living. Her confident graphite drawing from 1938, however, which conveys both her extraordinary beauty and her solemn self-assurance, asserts an auspicious beginning. Born in San Francisco, de Lappe inherited drafting skills from her illustrator father and political radicalism from her activist mother. Starting at the California School of Fine Arts (now the San Francisco Art Institute) at age fourteen, she met artists Arnold and Louise Blanch and through them Diego Rivera and Frida Kahlo. She became a sketching companion to the two women.[1]

By 1931, de Lappe had moved to New York where she accompanied the Blanches to Woodstock and then entered the Art Students League. There she studied with Kenneth Hayes Miller, learned lithography, and befriended Reginald Marsh, with whom she sketched subjects from dance marathons, burlesque shows, and Coney Island. Recruited into the Communist Party, she joined the John Reed Club, contributed to the *Daily Worker*, and met William Gropper and Raphael Soyer.[2] An occasional cartoonist for the *New Masses*, she also worked on civil rights causes and discovered jazz in Harlem. By the time she returned to San Francisco in 1934, she had aligned her art with social realist themes and the depiction of the working class. Her style, however, differed from the quick sketch approach of many of her New York compatriots. Her figures reflected the sculptural forms of Kenneth Hayes Miller but also the Mexican muralists; in addition to Rivera, she was an intimate friend of David Alfaro Siqueiros. In her 1938 self-portrait, the monumental quality of the statically posed and sharply outlined face recalls Rivera's drawings of the 1930s. Many of her lithographs of the period have a muralist's sensibility, with simplified composition, broad planes, low viewpoint, and heroic figural forms.

The 1991 lithograph, entitled *On Being Female*, dates from a very different moment of de Lappe's life. Marriage, parenthood, relocations, and two divorces had all interfered with her career in art. For many years she was a cartoonist and editor for the San Francisco-based communist paper *The People's World*. To support her family, she took a low-paying job for nineteen years as a layout designer for Moore Business Forms. But in the 1980s and 1990s, New York gallery owner Susan Teller and de Lappe's late-in-life partner, Byron Randall, encouraged her return to art. In this self-portrait, she addresses the complexities of being female. As a white-haired older woman, de Lappe, who had had many lovers and admirers in her youth, remembers with seeming regret the voluptuous beauty she once was. By signing both the lithograph of her aging self and the drawing of the young nude tacked on the wall, she suggests that art was a crucial part of her identity at both of those moments of her life. And by turning away the face in one portrayal and holding a mask in the other, she implies that the female must hide her true self in order to play expected roles. In this context, both the nudity of the young woman and the jewelry of the older one could be choices designed to appeal, implying sexual availability or simply femininity. But

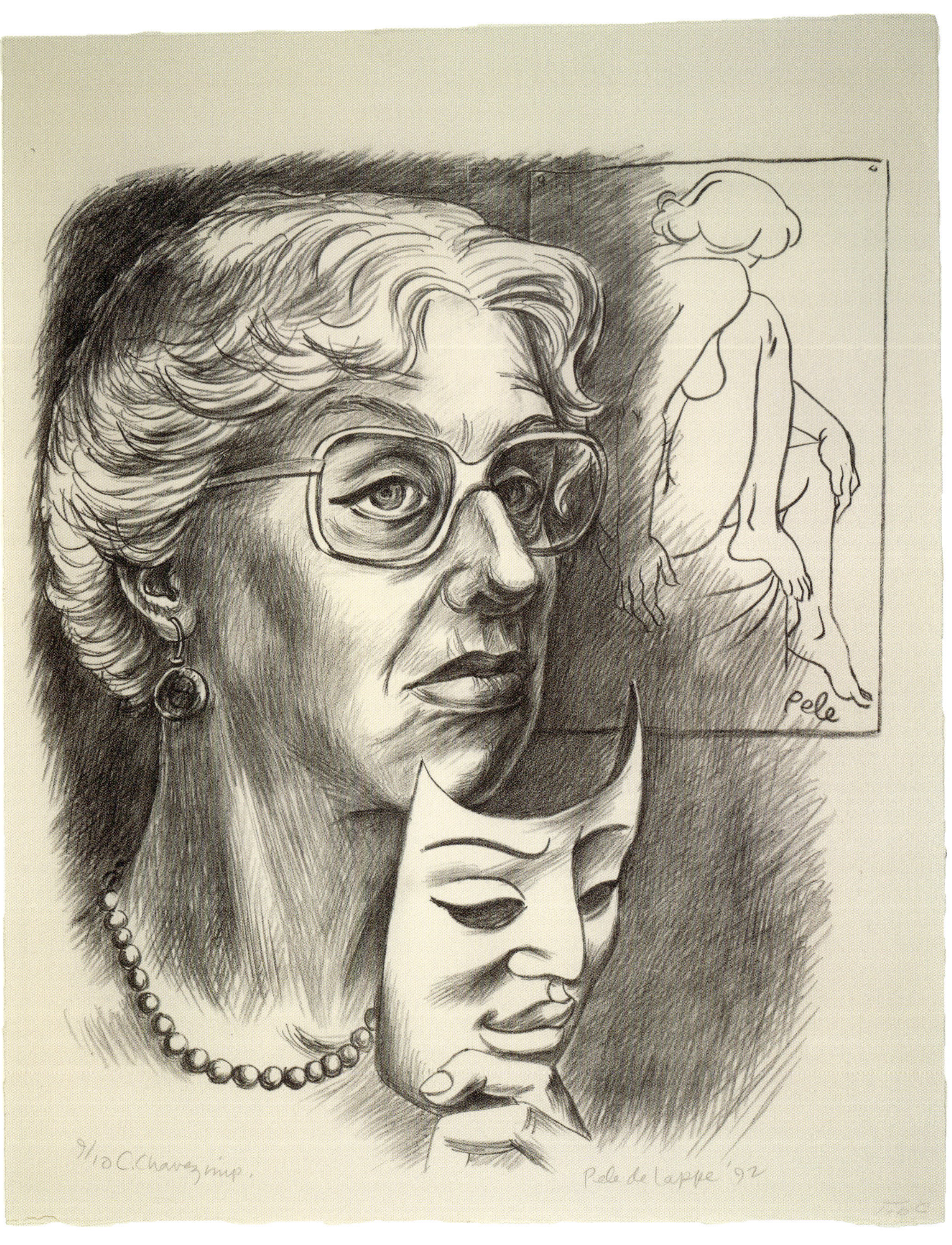
Pele
9/10 C. Chavez imp.
Pele de Lappe '92

27.

Pele de Lappe (1916–2007)

On Being Female
Lithograph, 42.3 x 33.2 cm (16⅝ x 13¹⁄₁₆ in.), 1991
The Ruth Bowman and Harry Kahn Twentieth-Century American Self-Portrait Collection
S/NPG.2002.291

while de Lappe's own life had been challenging, she emerges in her late work as defiantly engaged with art and those around her. "I'm still alive and still part of society," she told a reporter, "I can't stop functioning in relation to other people. And I refuse to take it lying down."[3]

WWR

Notes

1 Pele de Lappe, *Pele: A Passionate Journey Through Art & the Red Press* (self-published, c. 1999), 9.

2 Ibid., 15.

3 Gretchen Giles, "Love's Labor Won: Petaluma Artist Pele de Lappe's Passionate Journey," *North Bay Bohemian,* September 12–18, 2002. See also her 2007 obituary, Jonathan Curiel, "Pele de Lappe—artist, journalist, rights activist dead at 91," *San Francisco Chronicle*, October 5, 2007.

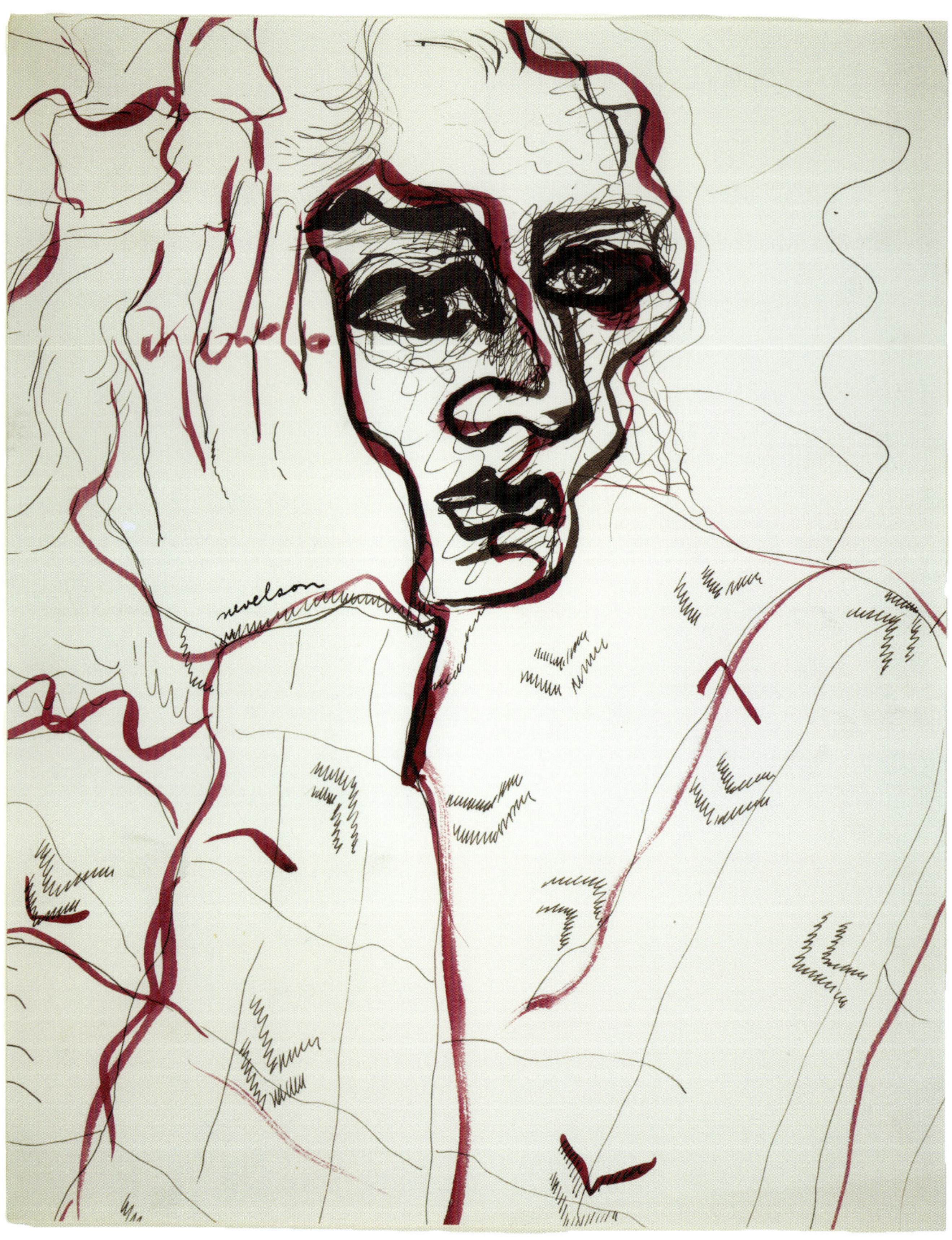
nevelson

28.

Louise Nevelson (1899–1988)

Ink and watercolor on paper, 40 x 30.9 cm
(15¾ x 12$^{3}/_{16}$ in.), c. 1938
The Ruth Bowman and Harry Kahn Twentieth-Century American Self-Portrait Collection
NPG.2002.307

"WHEN I USED a line, it was like a violin," sculptor Louise Nevelson claimed about her drawings.[1] The artist, a prolific draftsman, was passionate about expressing herself on paper. For Nevelson, drawings provided an outlet for ideas and emotions, and she frequently exhibited them along with her better-known sculptures. Although she often drew with an abbreviated outline style, reminiscent of Henri Matisse or Gaston Lachaise,[2] this self-portrait, probably made in the late 1930s,[3] is much more complex. Wiry scratches, squiggles, bold black contours, and a strong red overdrawing compete for attention. The drawing conveys her troubled transition to an artistic life and the influences she voraciously absorbed in that process. Raised in Maine, Nevelson had married and moved to New York at a young age. In the early 1930s, separated from her husband and infant son, she traveled in Europe and studied briefly with Hans Hofmann. Returning to New York, she struggled financially. But although periodically depressed and impoverished, she was determined to make a career of her art.

That determination is evident in her self-portrait. Dramatic distortions, agitated lines, and a look of troubled introspection reveal her admiration for expressionist art.[4] She also applies a cubist dislocation of the figure in space; her shoulder seems to lead the body around to our left, while the face seems to be turning toward our right. The double red contours suggest the profile as well as the side of the face, recalling experiments in double exposure photography designed to imply a rotation of the head.[5]

In the 1950s and 1960s, Nevelson's large sculptures—monumental, wall-sized assemblages made of boxes stacked into a grid and painted a single color—finally began to bring her fame and many honors. As an older woman, she maintained the theatrical persona (and heavily outlined eyes) seen in this early self-portrait. Of that period of her life, she has written, "the thirties and early forties were very important to me. More than any specific events standing out, it was a time of searching and finding myself as an artist."[6]

WWR

Notes

1 Diana MacKown, *Dawns + Dusks: Taped Conversations with Diana MacKown* (New York: Charles Scribner's Sons, 1970), 119, quoted in Laurie Lisle, *Louise Nevelson: A Passionate Life* (New York: Summit Books, 1990), 73.

2 For Nevelson's outline drawings, see Una Johnson, *Louise Nevelson: Prints and Drawings, 1953–1966* (New York: Brooklyn Museum, 1967).

3 This drawing relates stylistically to painted portraits that she made in the 1930s including a 1938 self-portrait and a 1932 portrait of Diego Rivera. See Arnold B. Glimcher, *Louise Nevelson* (New York: E. P. Dutton & Co., 1976), 55, 42.

4 "For me," Nevelson noted, "cubism and expressionism are the two great movements." John Gordon, *Louise Nevelson* (New York: Whitney Museum of American Art, 1967), 9.

5 See, for example, Jeffrey S. Weiss et al., *The Cubist Portraits of Fernande Olivier* (Washington, DC: National Gallery of Art, 2003), 33–34.

6 Glimcher, *Louise Nevelson*, 44.

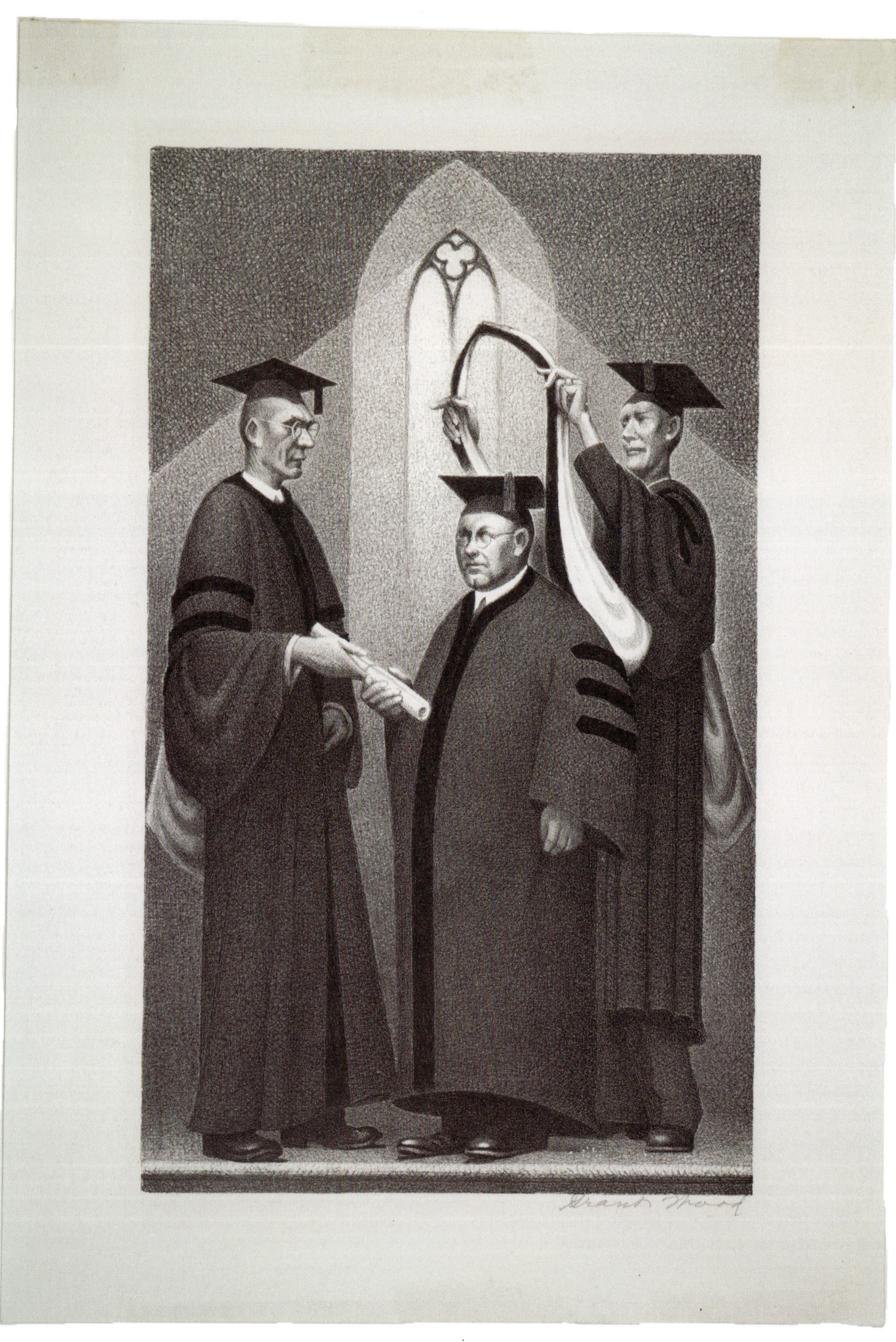

29.

Grant Wood (1892–1941)

Honorary Degree
Lithograph, 37.2 x 25.4 cm (14⅝ x 10 in.), 1938
The Ruth Bowman and Harry Kahn Twentieth-Century American Self-Portrait Collection
NPG.2002.368

BY THE TIME *Honorary Degree* appeared in 1938, the popularity of Wood's 1930 painting *American Gothic* had made him a celebrity. Much of the painting's prominence arose from debates in the local and national press over whether Wood's deadpan portrayal ridiculed or celebrated rural midwesterners like the pair he showed standing before a simple house with a Gothic window.[1] There is no doubt, however, that the artist had a dry wit that he exercised at the expense of the prim tea-drinking ladies in his 1932 painting *Daughters of Revolution* and at his own expense in *Honorary Degree*.[2]

In 1936 Wood received the first of several honorary degrees, offering him the excuse to deprecatingly play upon his celebrity.[3] In *Honorary Degree* Wood effectively winks at his devoted audience of ordinary Americans who bought this and his other prints for five dollars each through the Associated American Artists.[4] Wood was associate professor of fine arts at the University of Iowa, but he had never earned an academic degree; his rural subject matter and habit of painting in overalls gave him a far from academic public image.[5] Wood appears here in the unaccustomed pomp of doctoral robes. But the short, plump artist, his shoes conspicuous under his robes, keeps his feet firmly on the ground while the towering academics who confer his diploma and hood have their heads nearly in the clouds. Wood slyly points to the source of his acclaim by including a Gothic window in the background that bathes the trio in heavenly light while the artist's hood assumes the shape of a pointed Gothic arch.[6] He could also smile more privately about his honors bringing him more glory than his obscure academic superior at the University of Iowa, art historian Lester Longman, who attacked the popular artist for his supposedly fascist paintings.[7]

APW

Notes

1 For the initial success of *American Gothic* see Wanda M. Corn, *Grant Wood: The Regionalist Vision* (New Haven, CT, and London: Yale University Press for the Minneapolis Institute of Arts, 1983), 131. For Wood's continuing fame, see James M. Dennis, *Grant Wood: A Study in American Art and Culture* (Columbia: University of Missouri Press, 1986), 133–35. *American Gothic*, in the collection of the Art Institute of Chicago, is illustrated as plate 32 in Corn, *Grant Wood*.

2 See Corn, *Grant Wood*, 98–101. *Daughters of Revolution*, in the collection of the Cincinnati Art Museum, is illustrated as plate 19.

3 James M. Dennis, "Grant Wood Works on Paper: Cartooning One Way or the Other," in Jane C. Milosch, ed., *Grant Wood's Studio: Birthplace of* American Gothic (Cedar Rapids, IA: Cedar Rapids Museum of Art; New York: Prestel, 2005), 45. Wood "became a doctor of letters at the University of Wisconsin. Later, he was awarded a master of arts at Wesleyan University, a doctor of fine arts at Lawrence College, and a doctor of fine arts at Northwestern University." Hazel E. Brown, *Grant Wood and Marvin Cone: Artists of an Era* (Ames: Iowa State University Press, 1972), 95.

4 On the Associated American Artists and the marketing of this print and others by mail order, see Corn, *Grant Wood*, 49–50, and Clinton Adams, *American Lithographers, 1900–1960: The Artists and Their Printers* (Albuquerque: University of New Mexico Press, 1983), 139–41.

5 Corn, *Grant Wood*, 148. For Wood's use of overalls as painting garb see Jane C. Milosch, "Grant Wood's Studio: A Decorative Adventure," in Milosch, *Grant Wood's Studio*, 95.

6 Dennis makes this observation about the shape of the window and hood. He also notes that the academic figures are Dean Carl Seashore and Professor Norman Foerster of Iowa City. Dennis, "Grant Wood Works on Paper," 45.

7 Joni L. Kinsey, "Cultivating Iowa: An Introduction to Grant Wood," in Milosch, *Grant Wood's Studio*, 27–29.

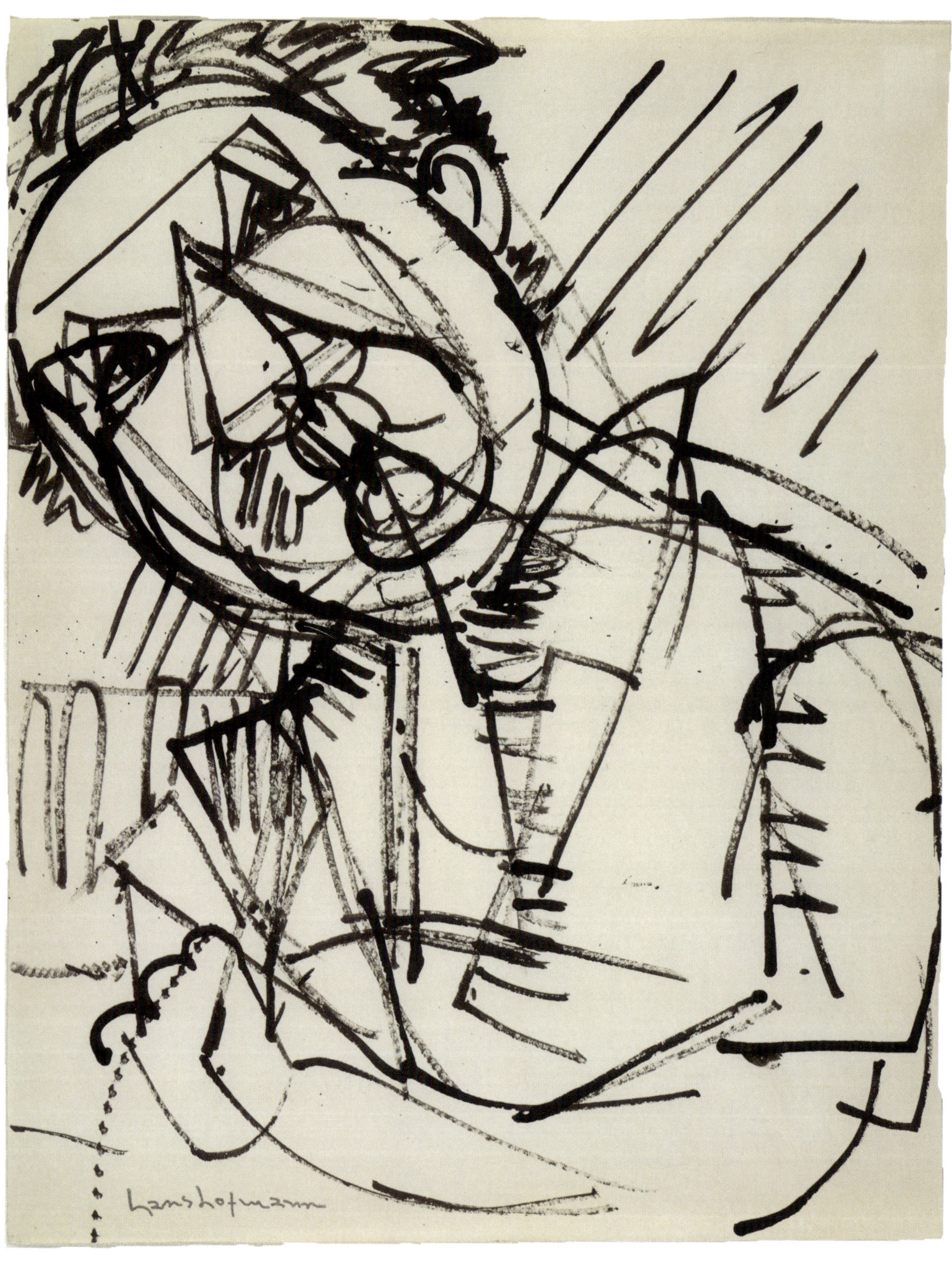

30.

Hans Hofmann (1880–1966)

Ink and pen on paper, 18.1 x 21.6 cm
(7 1/8 x 8 1/2 in.), c. 1942
The Ruth Bowman and Harry Kahn Twentieth-Century American Self-Portrait Collection
NPG.2002.274

AN INFLUENTIAL teacher and theorist, Hans Hofmann dedicated his career to the creation of plastic forms that captured the artist's physical and spiritual experience of the world. Although not a "realist," Hofmann nonetheless actively pursued what he described as the "real" in art, and it was the techniques for achieving an aesthetic in which human observation and metaphysical sensation were equivalent that underlay his approach to making images.[1] As he wrote late in his career, "A picture is . . . a universe—it holds its own life and mirrors a mind and a soul."[2] Drawing on the lessons of the cubists and fauvists—he was personally acquainted with Pablo Picasso and Henri Matisse—Hofmann sought to develop techniques to realize in two dimensions the three-dimensional character of the world. Resulting from this challenge was an analog for human struggles and triumphs. "Space sways and resounds," Hofmann remarked. "[It is] filled with tensions and functions . . . with life and rhythm and the disposition of sublime divinity. . . . Depth, in a pictorial, plastic sense, is not created by the arrangement of objects one after another toward a vanishing point, . . . but on the contrary . . . by the creation of forces in the sense of *push* and *pull*."[3]

While best known for his vibrant painterly abstractions, portraiture and self-portraiture played a critical role in Hofmann's intellectual and artistic development. This undated self-portrait drawing appears to be related to a series of paintings Hofmann made of himself in 1942.[4] In those compositions, as here, Hofmann conceives of his physiognomy as a vocabulary of shapes: triangles, squares, circles, and ovals.[5] Yet it was not simply his own form that concerned the artist, but also the integration of his body with the space that surrounded it, as indicated by the artist's activation of this area of the composition with energetic diagonal lines. Hofmann's decision to tilt his head to the left intensifies this interaction between planes. Hofmann's drawing thus reveals, in the artist's words, likeness in "a plastic sense, not in a photographic one," obtaining an independent reality of its own.[6]

ACG

Notes

1 Hofmann observed: "The *Real* in art never dies, because its nature is predominantly spiritual," see Hans Hofmann, "The Search for the *Real* in the Visual Arts," in *The Search for the Real and Other Essays*, ed. Bartlett H. Hayes Jr. and Sara T. Weeks (Cambridge, MA: MIT Press, 1967), 48; "Real" is capitalized and italicized by Hofmann.

2 Hans Hofmann, January 12, 1956, typescript, estate of the artist, published in *Hans Hofmann*, ed. Cynthia Goodman (Munich: Prestel, 1990), 176.

3 Quoted by Harold Rosenberg, "Hans Hofmann's 'Life' Class," *Portfolio and Art News Annual*, no. 6 (Autumn 1962): 112.

4 Cynthia Goodman notes that Hofmann tends to use a standard vocabulary of forms in describing himself; see Goodman, *Hans Hofmann* (New York: Abbeville Press, 1986), 33.

5 Hofmann's vocabulary of shapes grew out of his admiration for Cézanne. In his *Creation in Form and Color: A Textbook for Instruction in Art* (1931, 1933–1934), Hofmann quoted Cézanne's observation: "In nature you see everything that is in perspective in relation to the cylinder, the sphere, and the cone in such a way that each side—each surface of the object—moves into depth in relation to a central point." (See Goodman, *Hans Hofmann* [1986], 19).

6 Hofmann, 1938–1939 lecture series, lecture 1, estate of the artist, cited by Cynthia Goodman, "Hans Hofmann: A Master in Search of the 'Real,'" in Goodman, *Hans Hofmann* (1990), 22 and 75 n. 22.

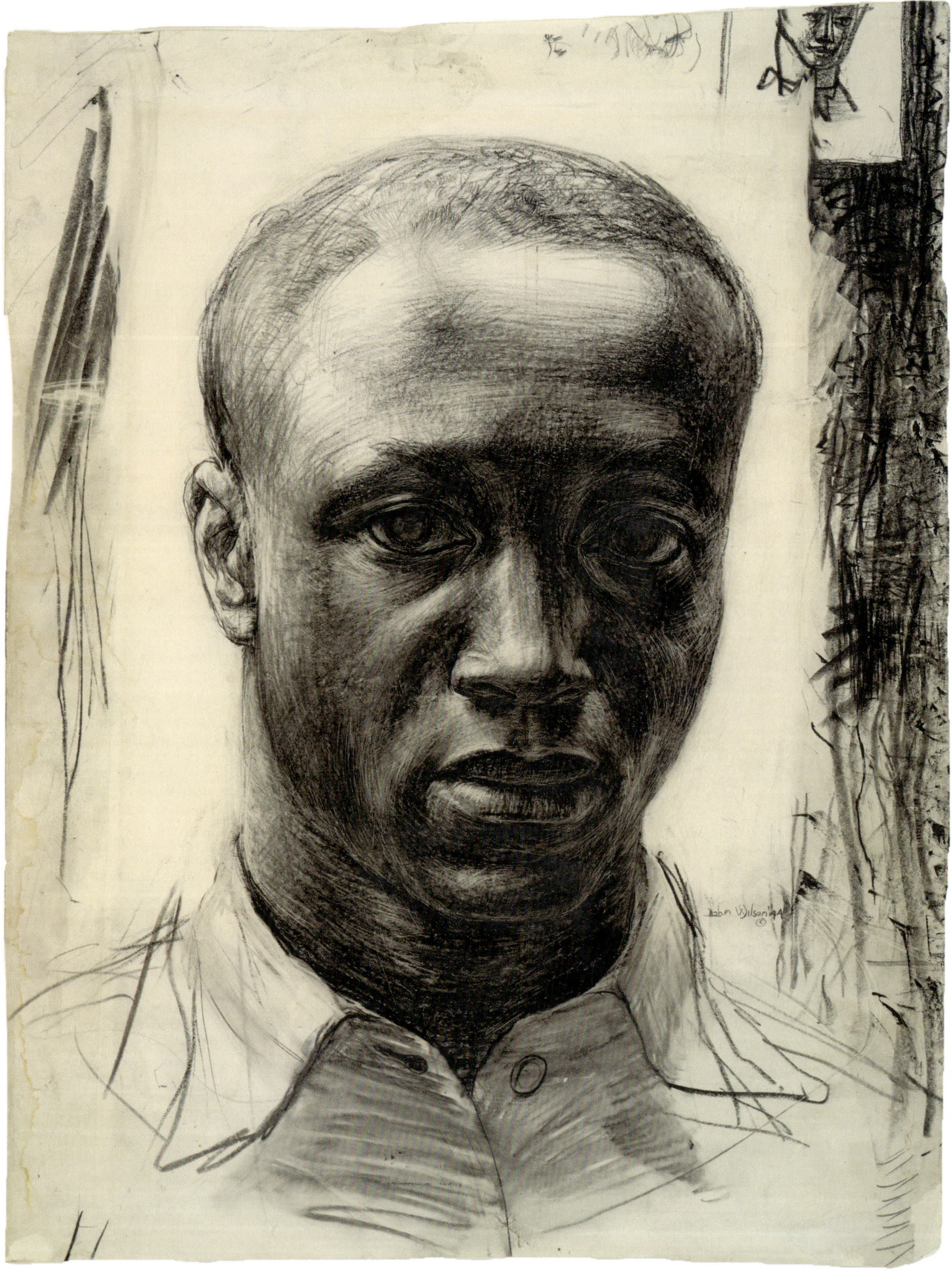

31.

John Wilson (born 1922)

Lithographic crayon on paper, 41.6 x 31.2 cm (16³/₈ x 12⁵/₁₆ in.), 1944
The Ruth Bowman and Harry Kahn Twentieth-Century American Self-Portrait Collection
S/NPG.2002.366

"THIS BUSINESS of looking at people I latched onto when I was very young," John Wilson once noted.[1] Wilson's 1944 self-portrait, drawn in lithographic crayon, reveals the twenty-two-year-old's assured draftsmanship and experience in modeling faces. The Roxbury, Massachusetts–born son of émigrés from the former British Guiana, Wilson was taught to draw at the Roxbury Boys' Club. The chances of a poor young black man succeeding in an artistic career seemed slim at the time. But with the advocacy of his Boys' Club teachers, he enrolled in 1939 in the school of Boston's Museum of Fine Arts, from which he graduated with highest honors. He graduated from Tufts University in 1947 and started to teach and exhibit his work. Receiving the museum school's prestigious travel grant, he spent 1947 to 1949 in Paris, studying modernism with Fernand Léger and learning about non-Western art forms.

Wilson would return to portraiture regularly in his career. As in his two self-portraits, he probed beyond momentary expressions and personality quirks to hint at an interior essence and universal human qualities. In the process of studying faces, he has stated, you discover "a kind of inner energy that all living and even inert things have."[2] He noticed that the Buddhas in the Boston Museum "are quiet, still, but they have a spiritual force, an inner energy." He used similar terminology in his admiration for paintings by Piero Della Francesca, whose subjects, he felt, "are still, almost statues, yet you feel the inner movement, the power in these people."[3]

Wilson's racial consciousness was a consistent theme of his art. "My experience as a black person has given me a special way of looking at the world," he has stated, "and a special identity with others who experience injustice. . . . I grew up in a world that said I could be killed if I stepped out of line."[4] Influenced by Harlem Renaissance writers and artists, and especially moved by Richard Wright's 1940 novel *Native Son*,[5] he was determined to express the African American experience. His 1944 portrait, with its forceful frontal confrontation and beautifully articulated dark skin tone, demands our awareness of both his blackness and his artistic skill.

From an early point in his artistic career, Wilson had also been attracted to the Mexican muralists, particularly David Alfaro Siqueiros and José Clemente Orozco, whose work, he felt, had a "kind of dense power."[6] He admired their social consciousness and commitment to public art. The boldness and scale of his heads echo their heroic portrayals and themes of universal humanity. In 1950, with the help of a succession of grants, he and his new wife traveled to Mexico City, where they stayed five years. He studied murals and worked at the famous printmaking studio Taller de Gráfica Popular. Wilson befriended other African American artists in Mexico, all of whom relished working in a less racist atmosphere. "I had to go into this foreign country to feel like a human being," he once noted.[7]

Ultimately Wilson and his family returned to the United States, where he worked in Chicago and New York before launching a successful twenty-three-year teaching career at Boston University. Wilson's second head, drawn with bold black pastel lines in 1963 just before his move to Boston, resonates with the empowerment of the 1960s civil rights movement.

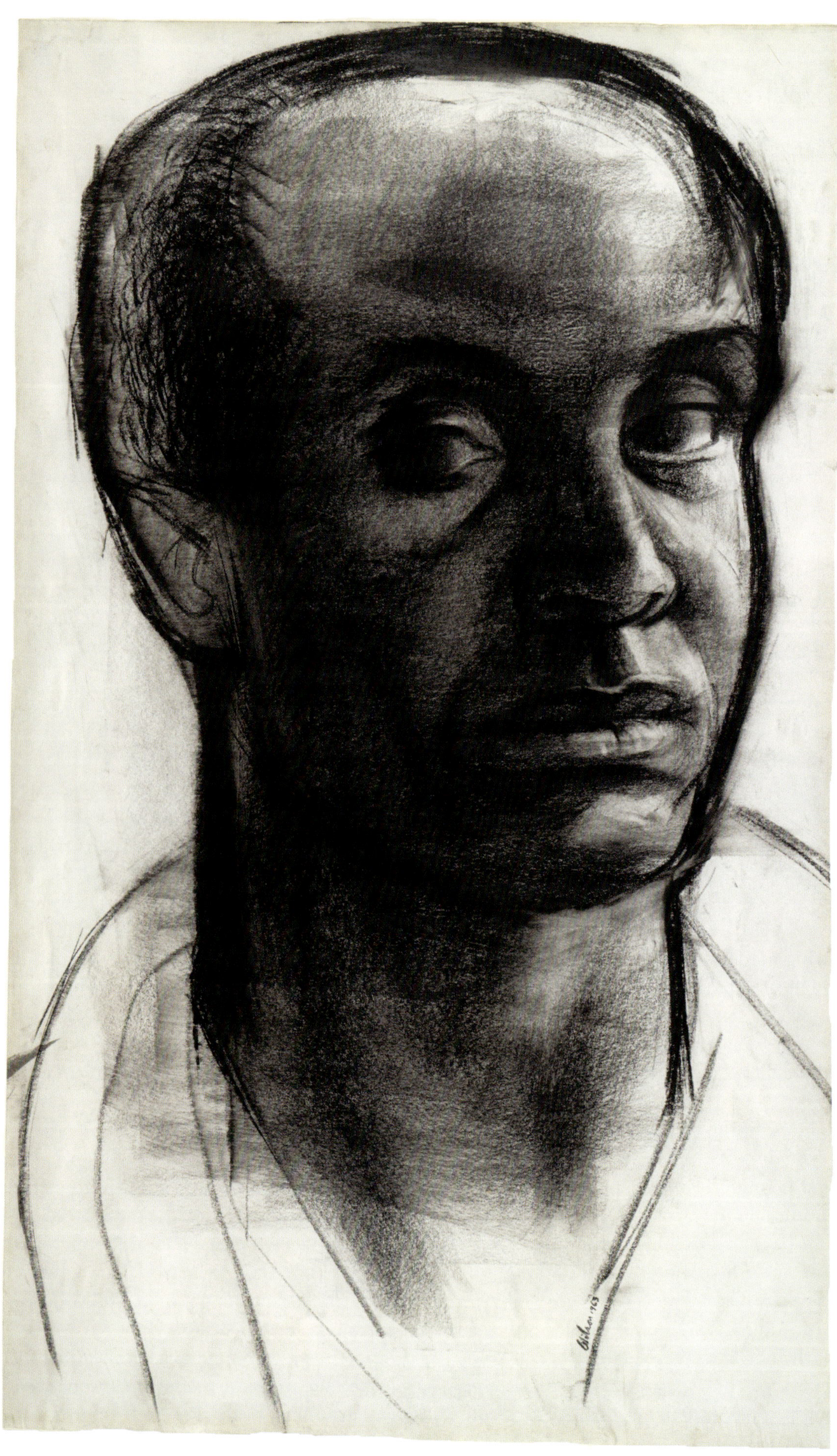

32.

John Wilson (born 1922)

Pastel on paper, 60.8 x 35.3 cm
($23^{15}/_{16}$ x $13^{7}/_{8}$ in.), 1963
The Ruth Bowman and Harry Kahn Twentieth-Century American Self-Portrait Collection
S/NPG.2002.367

Both of his self-portraits seem to access the "inner energy" he admired, which raised the individual into the realm of the universal. He brought these same qualities to the monumental heads that he sculpted later in his career, including a bust of Martin Luther King at the U.S. Capitol building.[8]

WWR

Notes

1 Patricia Wild, "Portrait, John Wilson: Artist, Teacher," *Arts Around Boston*, September/October 1999, 62.
2 Ibid.
3 Interview with Dave Williams, October 28, 2003, quoted in Williams, "John Wilson: Black Artist," in Kay Wilson Jenkins et al., *John Wilson: A Retrospective* (Grinnell, IA: Grinnell College, 2004), 27.
4 Interview with Sandy Coleman, *Boston Globe*, July 16, 1995, quoted in Williams, "John Wilson," 25.
5 Edmund Barry Gaither and Shelley R. Langdale, "John Wilson / Joseph Norman: An Introduction," in *Dialogue: John Wilson / Joseph Norman* (Boston: Museum of the National Center of Afro-American Artists and Museum of Fine Arts, Boston, 1995), 10.
6 Patricia Hills, "A Portrait of the Artist as an African-American: A Conversation with John Wilson," in ibid., 30.
7 John Wilson oral history interview by Robert F. Brown, July 12, 1994, Archives of American Art, Smithsonian Institution, Washington, DC, transcript page 346.
8 David Saltman, "King Sculpture for the Capitol," *Washington Post*, April 17, 1985; Gaither and Langdale, "John Wilson," 14.

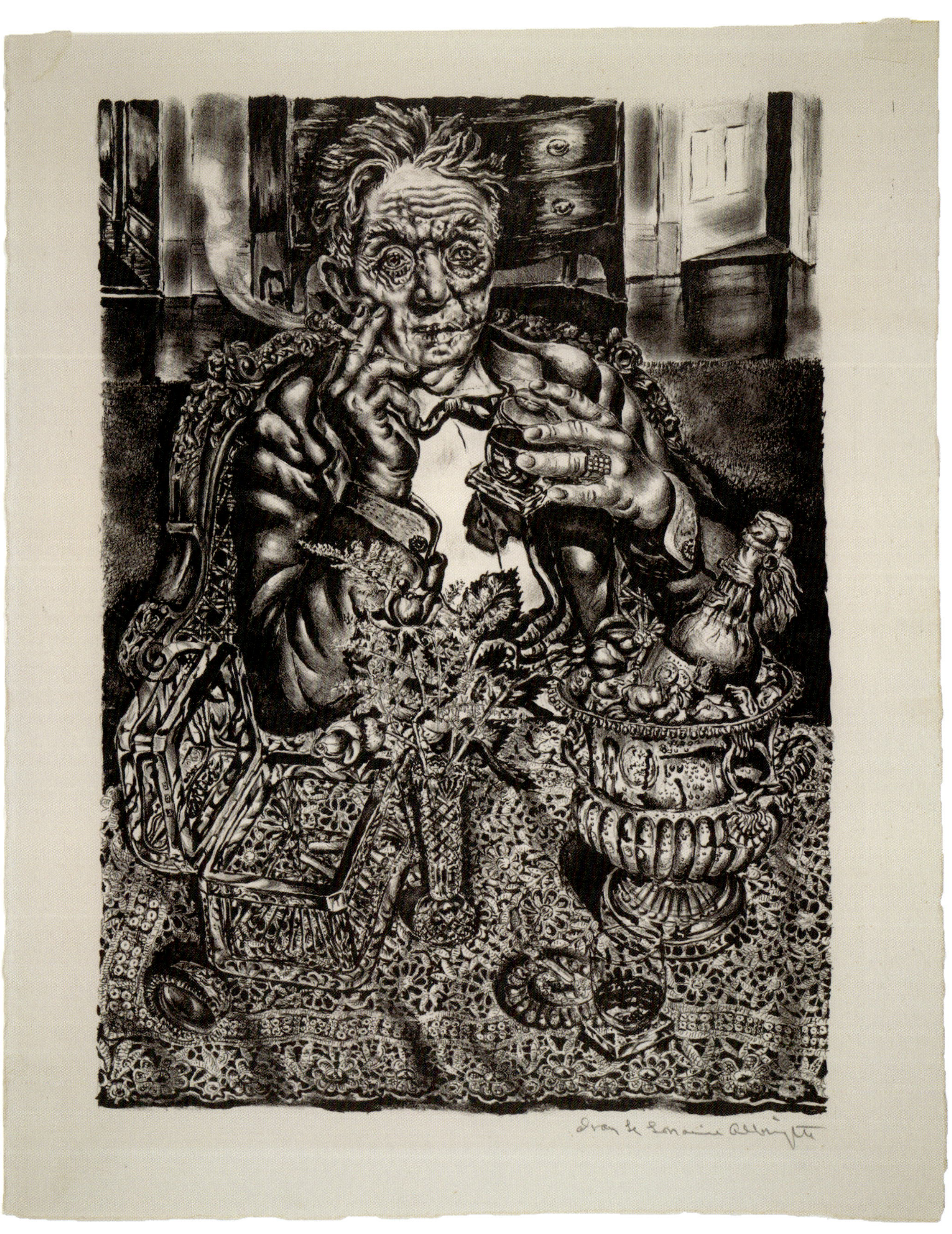

33.

Ivan Albright (1897–1983)

Self-Portrait at 55 East Division Street
Lithograph, 42.2 x 33.3 cm (16⁵/₈ x 13¹/₈ in.), 1947
The Ruth Bowman and Harry Kahn Twentieth-Century American Self-Portrait Collection
NPG.2002.189

"IT MATTERS LITTLE whether I paint a squash, a striped herring, or a man," Ivan Albright claimed. "The space, the light, the motion, the position have one thing in common—decay."[1] Although Albright denied the influence of his wartime service as a medical draftsman, it explains his strange obsession; he was only fifty when he made this lithograph and hardly the aged creature he depicted.[2] Here, the monstrous face, contrasted with the implied enjoyment of companionable drinking, suggests the theme of "vanitas," a reminder of the ephemeral nature of life's pleasures. But prematurely aging flesh addressed more than just mortality for Albright. He saw decomposition as a natural part of continual growth, a process with its own beauty, strength, and universality.[3] He envisioned the changing, evolving nature of life, always in motion, always affected by the passage of time.

Albright's admiration for northern European art, cubism, and German expressionism help explain the impact of his art. Minute rendering, shifting viewpoints, and human anguish are all embedded in his work. In his lithographic self-portrait and two related paintings, claustrophobic overabundance satirizes profligate materialism. Hyperrealistic details of furniture, glassware, lace, flowers, and silver, smother the figure. This minute technique, Albright claimed, knit together the discordant elements of his composition.[4] He also infuses his image with motion, experimenting with multiple viewpoints and perspectives. Looking for a way of "making the object more realistic by walking around it," he invited the viewer to circulate inside the picture, experiencing space from different angles.[5] He was not only a realist, he claimed, but also "an abstractionist in that I'm trying to have motion."[6]

In a haunting series of drawings done just before his death, Albright undertook a merciless self-examination, facing in the mirror the aging flesh and mortality that had long fascinated him.[7]

WWR

Notes

1 Ann Van Devanter and Alfred V. Frankenstein, *American Self-Portraits, 1670–1973* (Washington DC: International Exhibitions Foundation, 1974), 158

2 Gael Grayson, *Graven Images: The Prints of Ivan Albright, 1931–1977* (Lake Forest, IL: Lake Forest College, 1978), cat. 13.

3 Katharine Kuh, *The Artist's Voice* (New York: Harper and Row, 1960), 23–24; Susan F. Rossen, ed., *Ivan Albright* (Chicago: Art Institute of Chicago, 1997), 61–62.

4 Kuh, *Artist's Voice*, 25.

5 Paul Cummings, *Artists in Their Own Words: Interviews by Paul Cummings* (New York: St. Martin's Press, 1979), 61; Kuh, *Artist's Voice*, 25.

6 Cummings, *Artists in Their Own Words*, 63.

7 See Richard Brettell et al., *Ivan Albright: The Late Self-Portraits* (Hanover, NH: Dartmouth College, 1986).

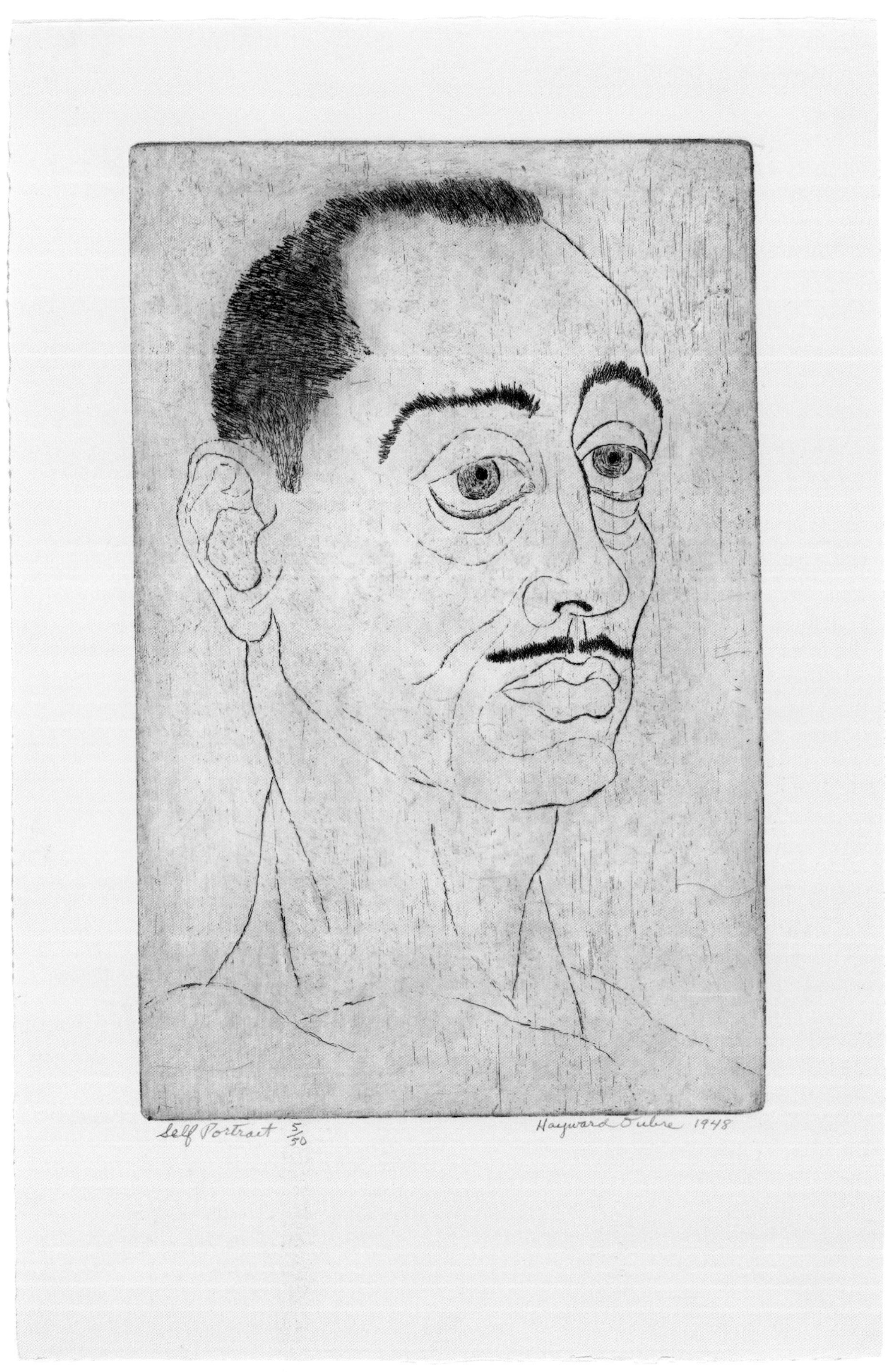
Self Portrait 5/50
Hayward Oubre 1948

34.

Hayward Oubré (1916–2006)

Etching, 56.5 x 36.4 cm (22¼ x 14 5/16 in.),
1948; printed 1993
The Ruth Bowman and Harry Kahn Twentieth-Century American Self-Portrait Collection
S/NPG.2002.309

ALTHOUGH THE elegantly drawn features in this print appear serene, Hayward Oubré perceived his own face as a battleground. He was born into a family of color in New Orleans, but his skin tone would have allowed him to "pass" for white. Oubré defiantly refused to do so, stating, "I am proud to be a black man."[1]

Oubré joined an African American army unit that was not allowed to fight in World War II; rather, the unit faced brutal weather to build the Alcan Highway linking Alaska to the rest of the United States.[2] After the war, he earned his MFA on the GI Bill, choosing the outstanding art department at Iowa University despite its segregated dormitories. Even in the printmaking class where he made this self-portrait, Oubré faced prejudice.[3] When a student made a racist remark, Oubré responded with a print of a black man attacking a snake representing the white race. He asserted "I fought racism with my art."[4]

In his self-portrait Oubré resisted racism by subtly refusing to "pass." He stressed the tan tone of his skin by using buff paper and leaving a heavy plate tone.[5] He shaded the inner edges of his upper and lower eyelids to contrast his skin with the whites of his eyes. Oubré exaggerated the size of his eyes, but avoided the gaze of the viewer, suggesting his sense of alienation. Below the eyes are premature sags, evoking the stress under which he and his wife lived, not daring to go out at night.[6]

Oubré proudly showed outstanding African American art to his students at Florida A&M University, Alabama State College, and Winston-Salem State University.[7] But his own face haunted him; in his last years he confessed "I stay at home now. . . . I am tired of being mistaken for white."[8]

APW

Notes

1 Quoted in Jerry Langley, "Overlooked, but Unbowed: Hayward L. Oubre," *International Review of African American Art* 17 (2001): 20.

2 Ibid., 18. See E. Valerie Smith, "The Black Corps of Engineers and the Construction of the Alaska Highway," *Negro History Bulletin* 51–57 (December 1993): 22–37.

3 Oubré studied at Iowa University with master printmaker Mauricio Lasansky. For Lasansky's powerful influence on American printmaking of the postwar era, see William M. Friedman, *A New Direction in Intaglio: The Work of Mauricio Lasansky and His Students* (Minneapolis: Walker Art Center, 1949). Oubré's self-portrait etching was included in this exhibition.

4 Quoted in Langley, "Overlooked," 18.

5 The National Portrait Gallery's impression of this print was made many years after Oubré printed the original edition. The Clark Atlanta University Art Galleries own an impression from the original edition. In a telephone call to the author on June 26, 2008, Erikka J. Searles, curatorial assistant at the Clark Atlanta University Art Galleries, confirmed the buff color of the paper on which her institution's impression is printed.

6 Langley, "Overlooked," 18.

7 Jerry Langley, *Remembering the Atlanta University Art Annuals: Hayward Oubré* (Atlanta: Clark Atlanta University Art Galleries, 2003), 5; Floyd Coleman, "African American Art Then and Now: Some Personal Reflections," *American Art* 17 (Spring 2003): 23; Amalia K. Amaki, *The Magnificent 7: Hayward Oubré's Students: Works from the Paul R. Jones Collection* (Newark: University of Delaware, 2003).

8 Langley, "Overlooked," 20.

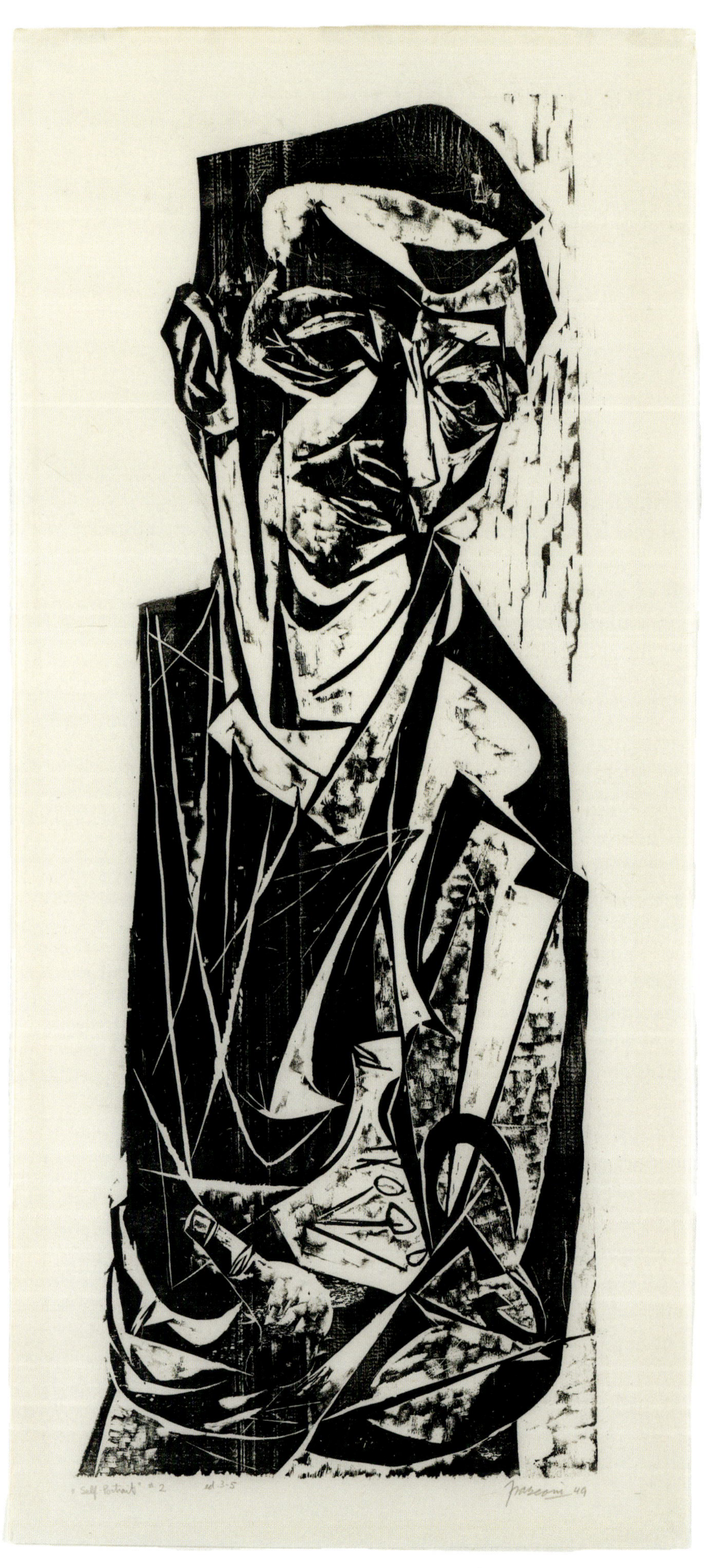

35.

Antonio Frasconi (born 1919)

Woodcut, 90.8 x 40.8 cm (35 3/4 x 16 1/16 in.), 1949
The Ruth Bowman and Harry Kahn Twentieth-Century American Self-Portrait Collection
NPG.2002.248

THIS PRINT IS a monumental but challenging self-portrait of Antonio Frasconi; the shifting, elusive forms reflect the immigrant artist's struggle with his evolving art and identity. Frasconi was born in Buenos Aires two weeks before his Italian-born parents moved to Montevideo, Uruguay.[1] He began his professional art career drawing political cartoons attacking abuses in Uruguay and Europe,[2] but he shifted toward fine artwork after transformative experiences seeing exhibitions of European graphic art. He recalled, "When I saw the first Gauguin woodblock I was just shaking. . . . At the same time I saw the German Expressionists. Well, that's what really changed my life completely from the drawings to this personal medium [woodcut]."[3] The expressionists' visceral, unrefined prints encouraged Frasconi to freely employ rough shapes and aggressive textures in works like this one.

Frasconi remained committed both to woodcut and political causes after his 1945 immigration to the United States to study at the Art Students League in New York.[4] In 1948 and 1949 Frasconi used a freely distorted, convoluted cubist style in a series of paintings and woodcuts that he stated represented the "people of Spain [suffering under the Franco regime] . . . through the heroic presence of Don Quixote."[5] The idealistic knight on his steed originally appeared at the left of this print. The agony of the Spanish struggle is reflected in the artist's face with its distracted, hooded eyes, and his pose hugging his elbows tightly to his body.[6] Frasconi later cut away the section of the block picturing Don Quixote. The artist thus simplified a complex and specific image into a more flexible representation. He detached his identity from specifically European concerns, leaving himself free to take on the new subjects he would find in the United States.

APW

Notes

1 Nat Hentoff, introduction to Nat Hentoff and Charles Parkhurst, *Frasconi: Against the Grain, the Woodcuts of Antonio Frasconi* (New York: MacMillan and London: Collier MacMillan, 1974), 13.

2 Edith A. Tonelli, "Frasconi's Art of Involvement," in Edith A. Tonelli, ed., *Involvement: The Graphic Art of Antonio Frasconi* (Los Angeles: Wight Art Gallery, University of California, 1987), 17.

3 Transcript of recorded interview with Antonio Frasconi by Paul Cummings, June 9, 1971, Archives of American Art, Smithsonian Institution, Washington, DC, 8.

4 Tonelli, "Frasconi's Art of Involvement," 20.

5 Spanish author Miguel de Cervantes Saavedra (1547–1616) first published his classic book *El Engenioso Hidalgo Don Quixote de la Mancha* in 1605. Antonio Frasconi, "Statement written about his Don Quijote series," Exhibition Statement, E. Weyhe Gallery, New York, March 1949, quoted in Tonelli, "Frasconi's Art of Involvement," 21.

6 The complete version of the print is listed as *Self-Portrait with Don Quijoté*, number 130, while the cut-down version is listed as self-portrait number 128 in Leona E. Prasse, Elaine A. Evans, and Louise Richards, *The Work of Antonio Frasconi: Catalogue of an Exhibition Sponsored by the Print Club of Cleveland and the Cleveland Museum of Art* (Cleveland, OH: Cleveland Museum of Art, 1952), 18. Both prints are dated 1949. An impression of the original version of the print is in the collection of the Library of Congress under the title *Self-Portrait*, accession number FP-XX-F837, no. 31.

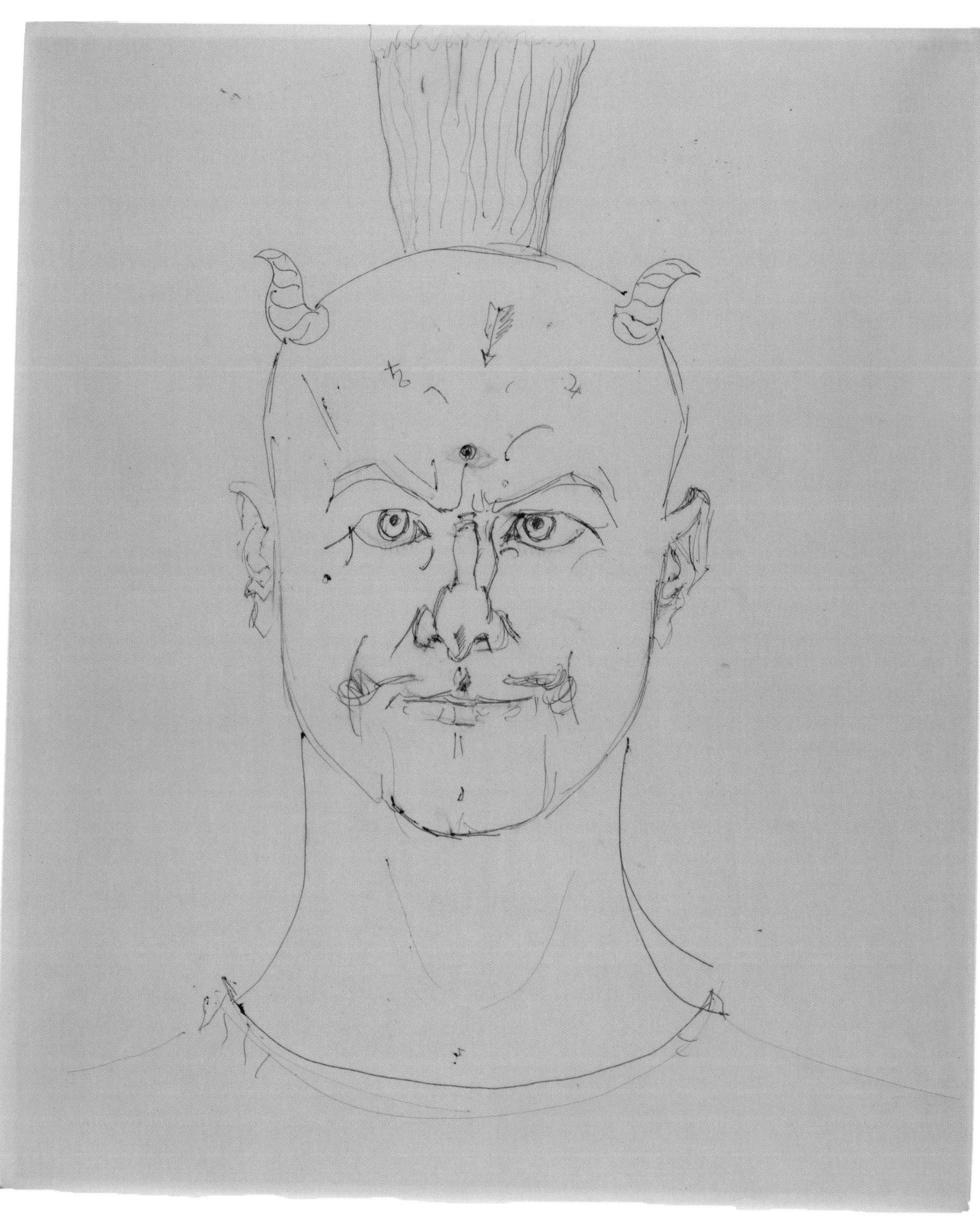

36.

John Graham (1886–1961)

Self-Portrait as Fallen Angel
Ballpoint pen on paper, 42.9 x 35.1 cm
(16 7/8 x 13 13/16 in.), c. 1955
The Ruth Bowman and Harry Kahn Twentieth-Century American Self-Portrait Collection
NPG.2002.258

"THE GREATNESS OF *a living man can be judged only by juxtaposing his work against his personality*," stressed John Graham in his *System and Dialectics of Art*.[1] During the course of his career, Graham, who rechristened himself upon his immigration to the United States, fashioned an elaborate and mystical persona, often using the vehicle of self-portraiture.[2]

The multivalent imagery of Graham's *Self-Portrait as Fallen Angel* reflects a great deal about the artist's self-construction. The drawing's title, as well as the horns and flame-like emanation with which Graham embellishes his likeness, resonates with Graham's characterization of genius as being "of Satan" in its rivalry of "the first creator."[3] In likening himself to a "fallen angel," Graham referenced the divine origins he claimed, asserting in his posthumously published "Autoportrait" that he was "the son of Jupiter and a mortal woman," sent by his father "to live with the human beings though I was not altogether human."[4] The implied role of prophet suggests yet another nuance to his inclusion of horns: an allusion to Moses, who was depicted with horns during the Renaissance due to a faulty translation of Hebrew. "*Sum qui sum*, I am who I am," declared Graham in his literary self-portrait, borrowing the words of the Biblical prophet.[5]

The work's mystical underpinnings are accentuated through technique. Using both the front and back of the paper, Graham's drawing invites the viewer to peer through the surface to an "inner eye," a Buddhist symbol for the state of spiritual enlightenment, positioned in the center of his forehead. The image may have been refined over time, as the artist took pride in working on some paintings "layer after layer, scraping, retracing them and painting again."[6]

With its dynamic interchange between recto and verso, figuration and abstraction, Graham's portrait overtly asserts the artist's self-characterization as shaman. The bold and nonconventional self-portrayal anticipates the increasingly conceptual approach to self-portraiture taken by American artists from 1960s forward, offering a powerful legacy on which to build.

ACG

Notes

1 John Graham, *John Graham's System and Dialectics of Art*, annotated by Marcia Epstein Allentuck (1937; Baltimore: Johns Hopkins University Press, 1971), 178; emphasis is Graham's.

2 An engaging account of Graham's career and self-construction is provided by Eleanor Green, *John Graham: Artist and Avatar* (Washington, DC: Phillips Collection, 1987). Born in Kiev, Ivan Gratianovitch Dombrowski renamed himself John Graham upon arriving in the United States.

3 Graham, *System and Dialectics of Art*, 98; in her commentary on Graham's text, Marcia Allentuck points out that in notes Graham also refers to the artist as a "demiurge," linking the positive and destructive aspects of creation, ibid.

4 John Graham, "Autoportrait," *Mulch* 2, no. 1 (Spring 1972): 2. The undated manuscript, not published in Graham's lifetime, is part of the Papers of John Graham, Archives of American Art.

5 Exodus 3:14. The phrase also appears as the title for a pictorial self-portrait made in the early 1950s.

6 Graham, "Autoportrait," 3.

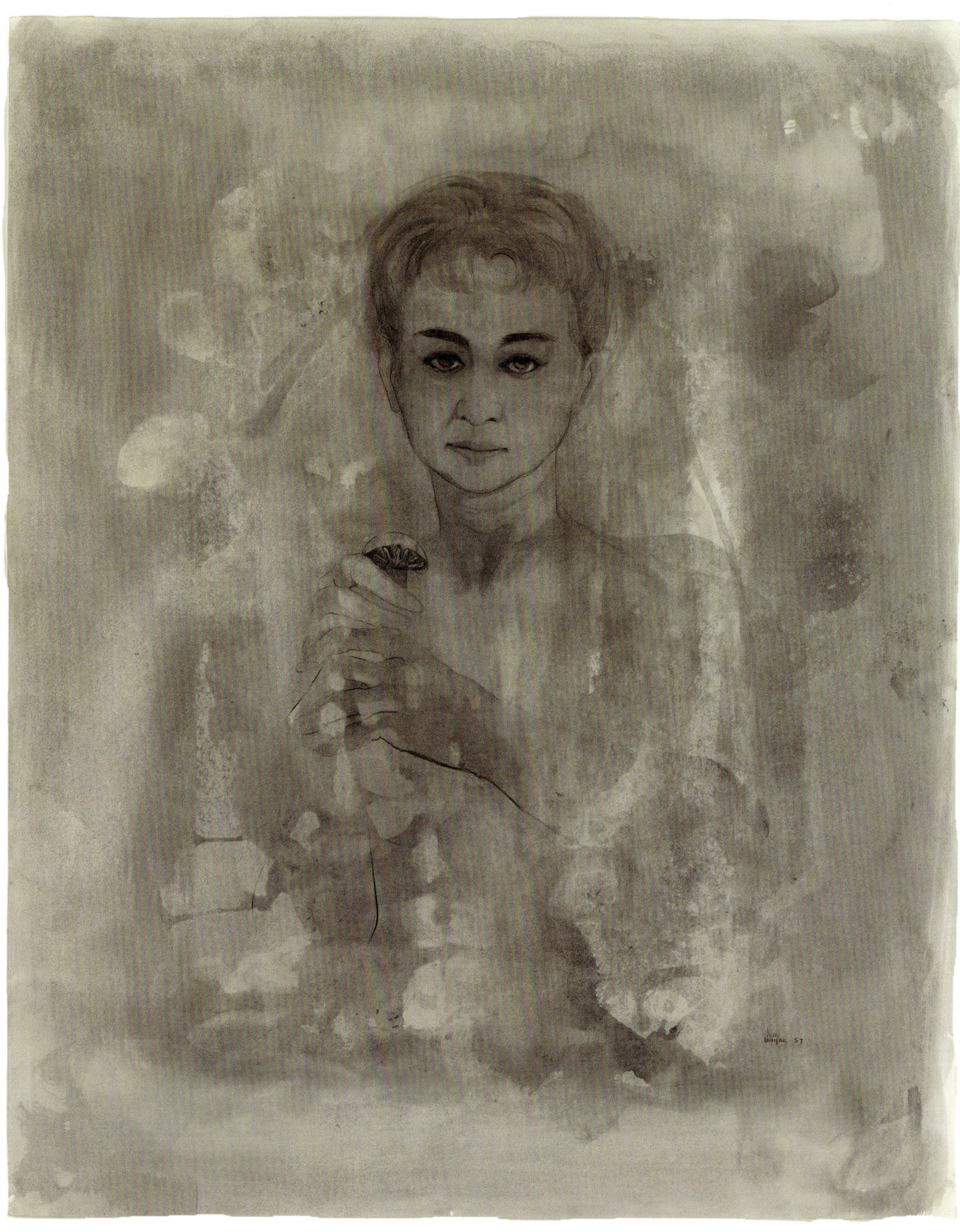

37.

June Wayne (born 1918)

Ink, ink wash, graphite, colored pencil, lithographic tusche, and gum arabic on paper, 73.7 x 58.5 cm (29 x 23 1/16 in.), 1957
The Ruth Bowman and Harry Kahn Twentieth-Century American Self-Portrait Collection
S/NPG.2002.362

IN 1960 June Wayne put aside her own art to labor on behalf of the larger world of art when she established the Tamarind lithography workshop in Hollywood, California. As Wayne had hoped, Tamarind revitalized lithography in the United States. Before she began this venture for which she is best known, Wayne created a rich artistic oeuvre.[1] In this self-portrait the artist presented a vision of herself and her art as they existed before she started Tamarind.

Wayne made her first lithographs in 1948, working in Los Angeles with printer Lynton Kistler.[2] In 1956 Wayne began a series of technically daring, emotionally powerful lithographs inspired by the ecstatic love poetry of seventeenth-century English poet John Donne.[3] This drawing, made in Los Angeles, explores the imagery and techniques of this series, which she would continue in Paris.[4] Wayne shows herself holding the phallic form of a mushroom, a symbol she had taken as her emblem since 1948, when mushrooms figured importantly in her series of prints and paintings made in reaction to the writings of Czech author Franz Kafka.[5] In Wayne's Donne series, the figures of lovers appear vulnerably nude, like the artist herself here. Many of them wear mushroom-cap–shaped headdresses like larger versions of Wayne's short, rounded hairstyle. Wayne thus freed her figures from the prosaic specificity of dated clothing and hairstyles, giving her subjects—and here the artist herself—timeless universality.

Wayne appears in a cloudy atmosphere that she achieved on paper with media normally reserved for lithographic stones or plates. The artist often, as in this instance, examines the subjects or technical approaches to her prints through drawings made not as studies but as independent creations.[6] Here, Wayne applied ink washes, then repeatedly dropped small amounts of greasy lithographic tusche and gum Arabic into the wet pools. The tusche and gum separated into intricate networks of irregular dots. The resulting airy, delicate textures envelop the artist in the same shadowy dreamscape in which she set Donne's lovers to wander.[7]

APW

Notes

1 Arthur C. Danto, "June Wayne: A Life in Work," in Robert P. Conway, *June Wayne: The Art of Everything: A Catalogue Raisonné, 1936–2006* (New Brunswick, NJ: Rutgers University Press, 2007), 17. On Tamarind lithography studio, see Clinton Adams, *American Lithographers: The Artists and Their Printers* (Albuquerque: University of New Mexico Press, 1983), 193–203, 205–6, and Marjorie Devon, ed., *Tamarind: 40 Years* (Albuquerque: University of New Mexico Press, 2000).

2 Robert P. Conway, "June Wayne en Collage," in *June Wayne: The Art of Everything*, 4.

3 Conway, *June Wayne: The Art of Everything*, 118–155.

4 June Wayne telephone conversation with the author, August 1, 2008. Wayne made this drawing in the early months of 1957, just before she left for Paris to work with French lithographer Marcel Durassier. June Wayne telephone conversation with the author, August 1, 2008.

5 On Wayne's use of the mushroom in her art and as the chop mark on her lithographs, see Mary Baskett, *The Art of June Wayne* (New York: Harry N. Abrams; Berlin: Gebr. Mann Verlag, n.d.), 9–22, and Arlene Raven, *June Wayne: A Retrospective* (Purchase, NY: Neuberger Museum of Art, Purchase College, State University of New York, 1997), 8–9.

6 For examples from the 1950s see Conway, *June Wayne: The Art of Everything*, 117, 122, 135–36, 148–49, 152, 155, 159.

7 Wayne described this technique to the author in two telephone calls, August 1, 2008.

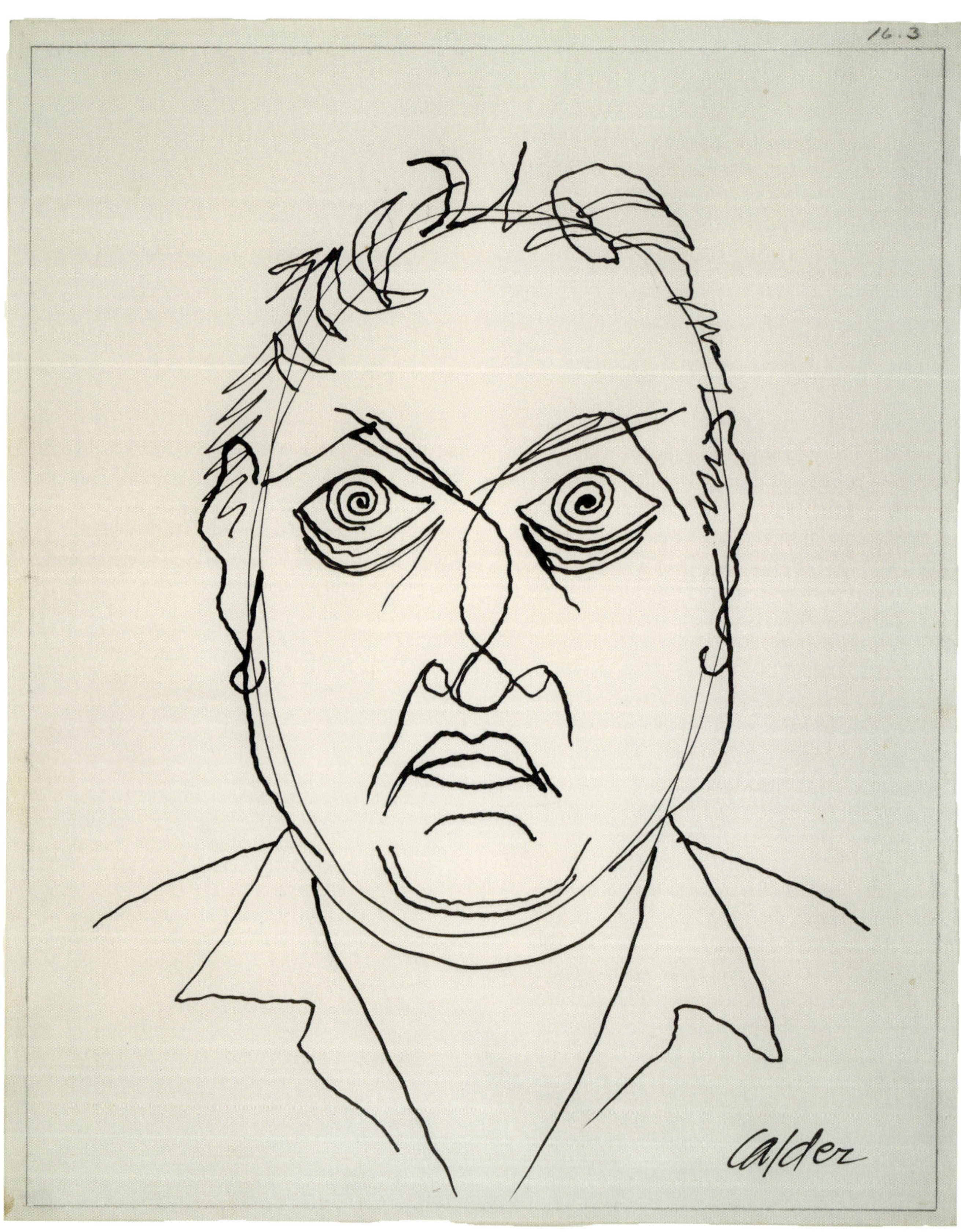
16.3
Calder

38.

Alexander Calder (1898–1976)

Ink on paper, 36.8 x 31.8 cm (14½ x 12½ in.), c. 1960
The Ruth Bowman and Harry Kahn Twentieth-Century American Self-Portrait Collection
NPG.2002.221

BY THE 1960s, when Alexander Calder probably made this drawing, he was already celebrated for his painting, drawing, stage sets, toys, tapestry designs, jewelry, and book illustrations; and his wire portraits, miniature circus, mobiles, and monumental stabiles had firmly established his influence on twentieth-century sculpture. His ink self-portrait reveals the intersection of drawing, caricature, and wire sculpture that propelled him to the first stage of his international renown. Calder had trained as a mechanical engineer but enrolled at the Art Students League in 1923. He easily mastered techniques of drawing and could even complete a picture without lifting his pen. "I seemed to have a knack," he noted after sketching people on the subway, "for doing it with a single line."[1] Calder acknowledged that his reductive linear approach had an affinity to caricature. In his 1926 book, *Animal Sketching*, he defined caricature as "emphasiz[ing] the characteristic features, whatever they may be."[2] The vogue for lighthearted, abbreviated celebrity caricature that pervaded the press in the 1920s could only have encouraged his predilections.[3]

Calder's own wit, interest in caricature, economical line, and ability to capture a defining essence helped inspire the wire sculptures that established his fame in the mid-1920s in Paris. With a passion since childhood for constructing things, Calder wielded pliers like an artist's tool, bending wire into stylized portraits or circus animals. The ink lines of this drawing have a brittle stiffness, sticking out and bending back much like brass wire. And the image relates to a wire self-portrait that Calder made slightly later, in 1968.[4] Both capture Calder's still effervescent personality.[5] Critic John Canaday concluded that a serious analysis of Calder's innovations missed three-quarters of the point; more important was the "quality of fun, along with elegance and vigor, [that] is captured in everything he does."[6]

WWR

Notes

1 Alexander Calder, *Calder: An Autobiography with Pictures* (New York: Pantheon Books, 1966), 61.

2 Alexander Calder, *Animal Sketching* (1926; New York: Dover Publications, 1973), 43.

3 Wendy Wick Reaves, *Celebrity Caricature in America* (New Haven, CT: Yale University Press, 1998), 122; see Calder's own caricature of artist Aline Fruhauf, 162.

4 Elizabeth Hutton Turner, *Americans in Paris (1921–1931)* (Washington, DC: Counterpoint, in association with the Phillips Collection, 1996), 141. The author is grateful to Barbara Zabel for sharing the photograph, taken in January 1968, of Calder making a wire self-portrait.

5 Calder probably made this drawing for architect Frederick Kiesler, whom he had befriended in Paris in 1930. See Marla Prather et al., *Alexander Calder, 1898–1976* (Washington, DC: National Gallery of Art, 1998), 19. Ruth Bowman purchased the drawing at a benefit auction for New York's Channel 13 in 1966. Kiesler's widow, Lillian, had given it to dealer Harold Diamond to sell after Kiesler's 1965 death. Lillian, who had married Kiesler the previous year, thought that Calder had given it to Kiesler in the late 1930s or early 1940s. When Calder himself was asked about the date of the drawing in 1968, he could not recall when he drew it but speculated that it must have been "quite a number of years ago, long before Kiesler died" (see correspondence in NPG curatorial files). Since the shape of the face and jowls are closer to Calder's features later in life, the c. 1960 date seems a better guess than the 1940s. Alexander Rower of the Calder Foundation and Barbara Zabel confirm the date, noting that the slightly wavering line suggests that Calder was already suffering from Parkinson's Disease.

6 Jean Lipman, *Calder's Universe* (New York: Viking Press and Whitney Museum of Art, 1976), 30.

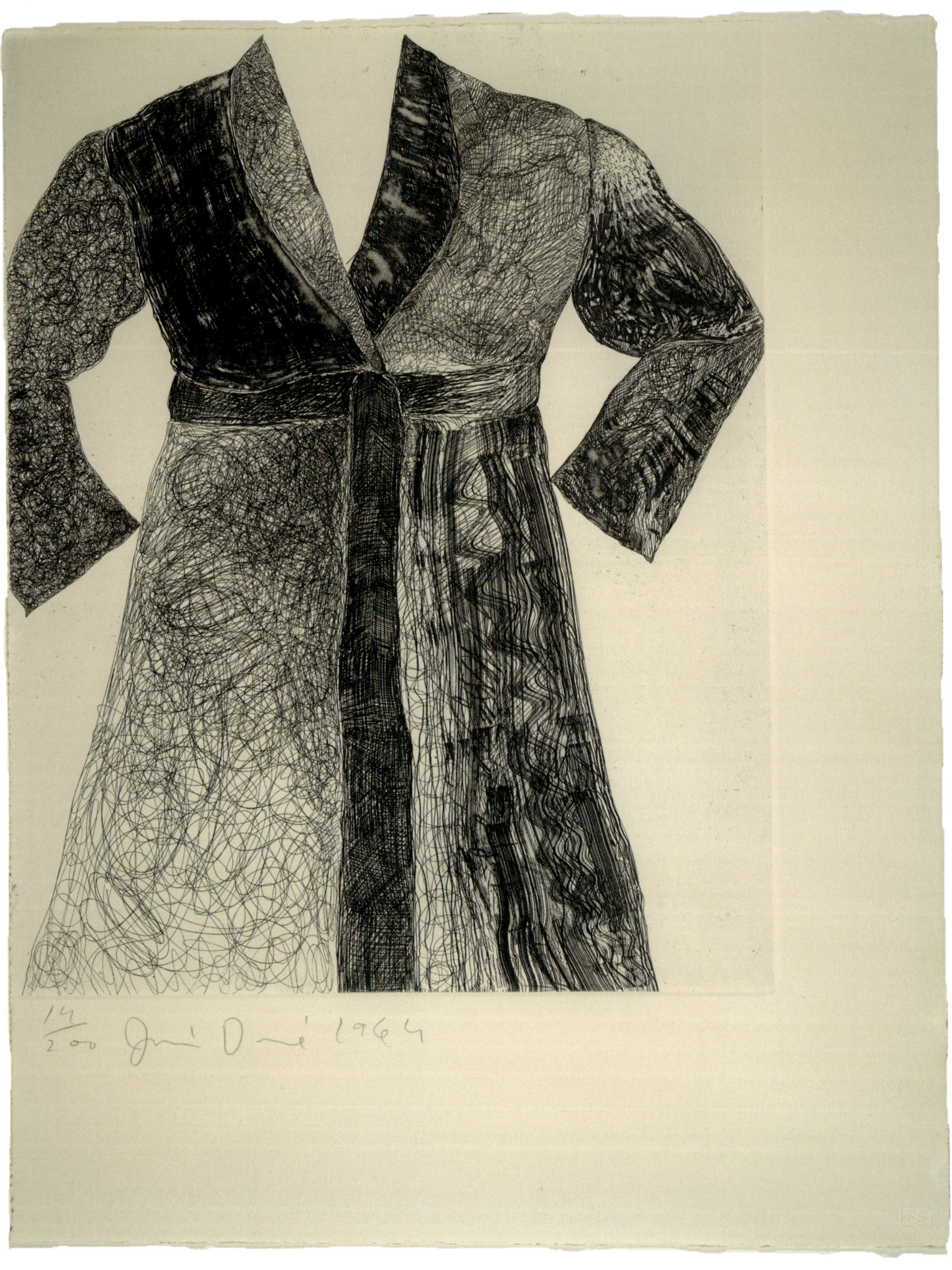

39.

Jim Dine (born 1935)

Bathrobe
Etching, 56.1 x 43 cm (22 1/16 x 16 15/16 in.), 1964
Published in *New York Ten* portfolio, 1965
The Ruth Bowman and Harry Kahn Twentieth-Century American Self-Portrait Collection
NPG.2002.235

CREATED NEARLY a decade and a half apart from one another, Jim Dine's *Bathrobe* (1964) and *Self-Portrait on J.D. Paper* (1978) both reflect the ongoing concern with autobiographical expression that has characterized Dine's career.[1] "In some way or another, it's all about my landscape," Dine reported in 1970. "I'm really only interested in being a biographer of myself."[2] Together, the works shed light upon the artist's transition from the use of inanimate objects as surrogates for the self to his increasing focus on figuration to depict the self in the late 1970s.

Dine, whose work often depicts objects—particularly tools—with which he feels a personal association, adopted the motif of the bathrobe as a self-portrait after seeing an advertisement in the *New York Times* in 1964.[3] For Dine, the image was more than just a found object, as he explained: "There was nobody in the bathrobe, but when I saw it, it looked like me."[4] Shortly thereafter, the robe became the basis for an exhibition of paintings at the Sidney Janis Gallery.[5] The robe, as Marco Livingstone has observed, also served as the motif for the artist's first foray into etching, a medium that has come to have particularly strong personal associations for Dine.[6]

The etched robe of 1964 reflects explosive energy. Densely packed lines, sometimes layered over one another, evoke a richly textured surface. In the dark passages at upper left and along the right lapel, Dine has worked the plate so hard that it ceases to hold ink, leading to brighter passages that give a sense of the nap of the fabric.[7] The printed impression runs off the upper left portion of the page, heightening one's sense of the robe as object, rather than illusion. Yet even the seeming "accident" may have autobiographical significance for the artist, who has remarked about printmaking, "My biggest problem, as is my biggest problem in life, is staying within the borders."[8] As though reflecting his pride in his early command of a medium that he would describe as "drawing with acid," the bent elbows of the robe—conveying the invisible gesture of an artist with his hands on his hips—seem to signal youthful satisfaction.[9]

Dine's experimentation with etching would contribute to a sea change in his approach to portraiture and self-representation. As the artist later observed: "Making prints was the first place my interest in figurative art raised its head."[10] The artist's transition to figuration reflected increased personal and professional confidence.[11] Dine's 1978 *Self-Portrait on J.D. Paper* demonstrates the artist's new pleasure in depicting his own features. With an intense gaze, the artist confronts the viewer. As in *Bathrobe*, Dine has worked the plate to the point that it no longer holds ink, creating highlights over his left eye and over the left lens of his glasses (on the right side of the image). A profusion of expressive lines runs throughout the image, capturing the thickness of his beard, the hair around his temples, and conveying the aging of his skin. Professing his interest in "what life has done to the face," Dine has remarked that "I love people's tracks. . . . I want all that history."[12] Taking advantage of the capacity of etching to register such expressive marks, Dine invests this self-portrait with yet another layer of autobiographical significance, printing it on paper watermarked with his initials: J.D.[13]

Drawing attention to this detail—invisible unless the print is held up to light—through his title, Dine insists upon the importance of the materiality of his work, endowing process and medium with

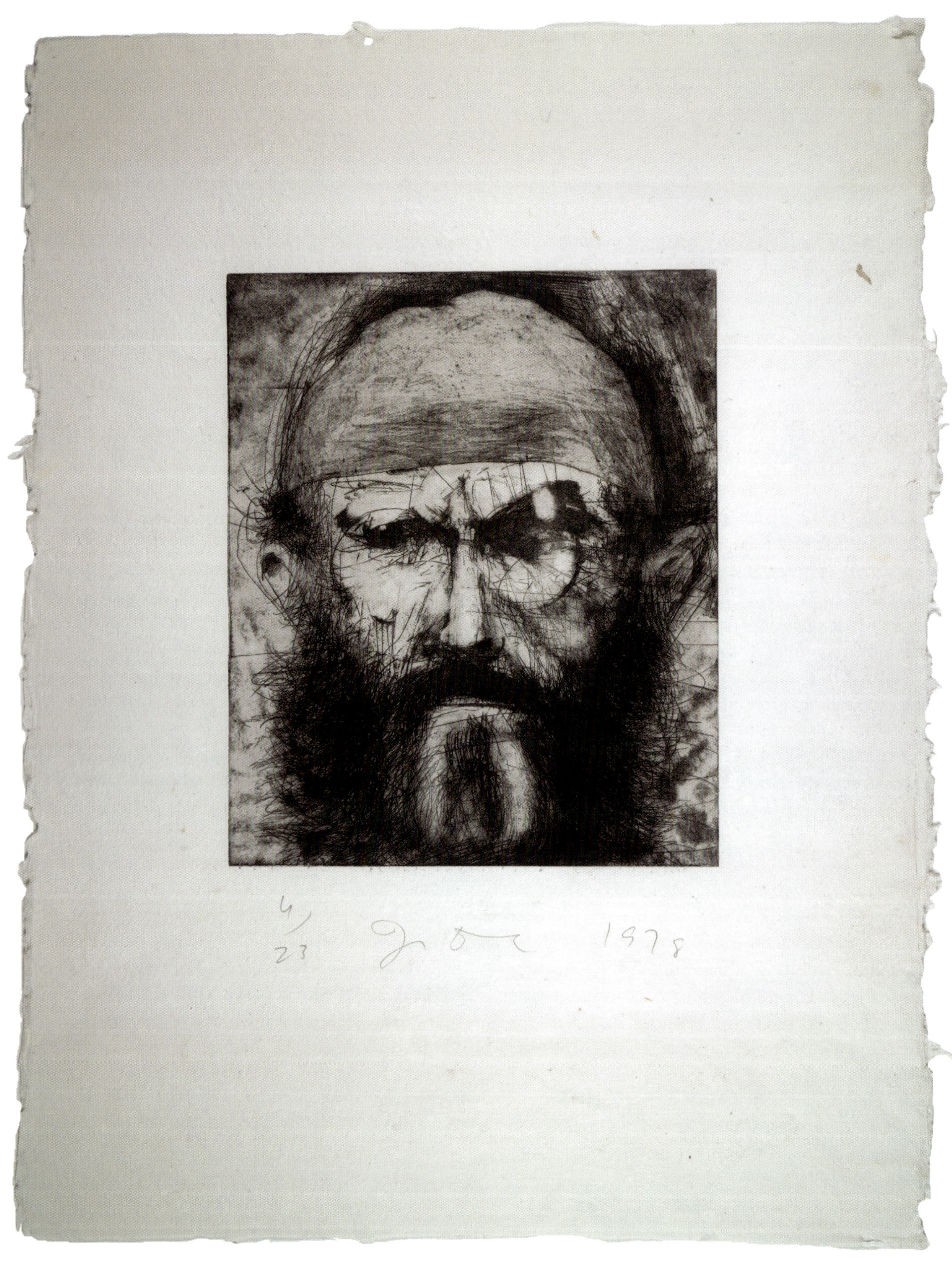
4/23
1978

40.

Jim Dine (born 1935)

Self-Portrait on J.D. Paper
Etching, 64.8 x 49.5 cm (25 1/2 x 19 1/2 in.), 1978
The Ruth Bowman and Harry Kahn Twentieth-Century American Self-Portrait Collection
NPG.2002.236

metaphorical significance. The underlying import of his self-expression, he insists, is not simply located in matters pictorial, but also physical. In addressing Dine's self-portrayal during a pivotal moment in the artist's career, the viewer must consistently attend not only to the power of the artist's symbolic and pictorial likenesses, but also to the very stuff of their making.

ACG

Notes

1 Dine's *Bathrobe* (1964), from *New York Ten* (1965), is included in *Jim Dine: Complete Graphics* (Berlin: Galerie Mikro, 1970), cat. 26; note that although this catalog gives a 1965 publication date for the portfolio, the print itself has an inscribed date of 1964. Jim Dine's *Self-Portrait on J.D. Paper* is included in Ellen D'Oench and Jean E. Fineberg, *Jim Dine Prints, 1977–1985* (New York: Harper and Row, 1986), 73, cat. no. 29.

2 "Poet of the Personal," *Time*, March 9, 1970, 50.

3 Dine grew up spending time in his grandfather's hardware store and his father's commercial paint and plumbing-supply store. According to Dine, the tools he figured "felt like relatives of mine, as though their last name was Dine" (quoted in Constance W. Glenn, *Jim Dine: Drawings* [New York: Harry N. Abrams, 1985], 15). Indeed, when the artist went to live in London, he found he could not use English objects in his work "because they're not mine" (quoted in "Dining with Jim: Robert Fraser Talks to Jim Dine about London and New York," *Art and Artists* 1 [September 1966]: 51; quoted by Marco Livingstone, *Jim Dine: The Alchemy of Images* [New York: Monacelli Press, 1998], 189).

4 "Poet of the Personal," 50. Emphasizing in later years the personal nature of his choice, Dine insisted: "Who's to say I wasn't searching for that robe? I was certainly searching for a means to make that self-portrait" (interview with Marco Livingstone, December 1, 1995; quoted in Livingstone, *Jim Dine*, 191). Dine describes his search for "a way to make a self-portrait besides just looking in the mirror" in "Walking Memory: A Conversation with Jim Dine, Clare Bell, and Germano Celant," in *Jim Dine: Walking Memory, 1959–1969*, ed. Germano Celant and Clare Bell (New York: Simon R. Guggenheim Foundation, distributed by Harry N. Abrams), 192. In 1979, Dine's use of the imagery of the bathrobe shifted. From that point forward, it was no longer based upon the advertisement, which he claimed to have lost, but instead upon a photograph of himself in one (Livingstone, *Jim Dine*, 198).

5 *Jim Dine* (New York: Sidney Janis Gallery, 1964).

6 Livingstone, *Jim Dine*, 193; on Dine's interest in etching, see Susie Hennessy, "A Conversation with Jim Dine," *Art Journal* 39 (Spring 1980): 169; and Ellen G. D'Oench, "Jim Dine: Portrait of a Printmaker," in D'Oench and Fineberg, *Jim Dine Prints*, 1–21. The choice of etching represented a departure for Dine, who, at the time, gravitated toward lithography, a method of printmaking he later discounted.

7 I thank Ann Wagner for sharing this observation with me (personal communication, April 4, 2008).

8 Dine interview with D'Oench and Feinberg, quoted in D'Oench, "Jim Dine: Portrait," 14.

9 Quoted in Hennessy, "A Conversation with Jim Dine," 169.

10 Quoted in Thomas Krens, "Conversations with Jim Dine," in *Jim Dine Prints: 1970–1977* (New York: Harper and Row, 1977), 32.

11 Dine addresses the transition in Hennessy, "A Conversation with Jim Dine," 174–75.

12 Unpublished interview with Clifford S. Ackley, quoted in D'Oench, "Jim Dine: Portrait," 6.

13 D'Oench and Feinstein point out that this print "is a greatly reduced second state of *Dark Blue Self-Portrait with White Crayon*, 1976." After extensively reworking the plate, Dine printed it on handmade linen paper bearing his initials. (Ellen G. D'Oench and Jean E. Feinberg, "Catalogue Raisonné," in *Jim Dine Prints*, 73, no. 29).

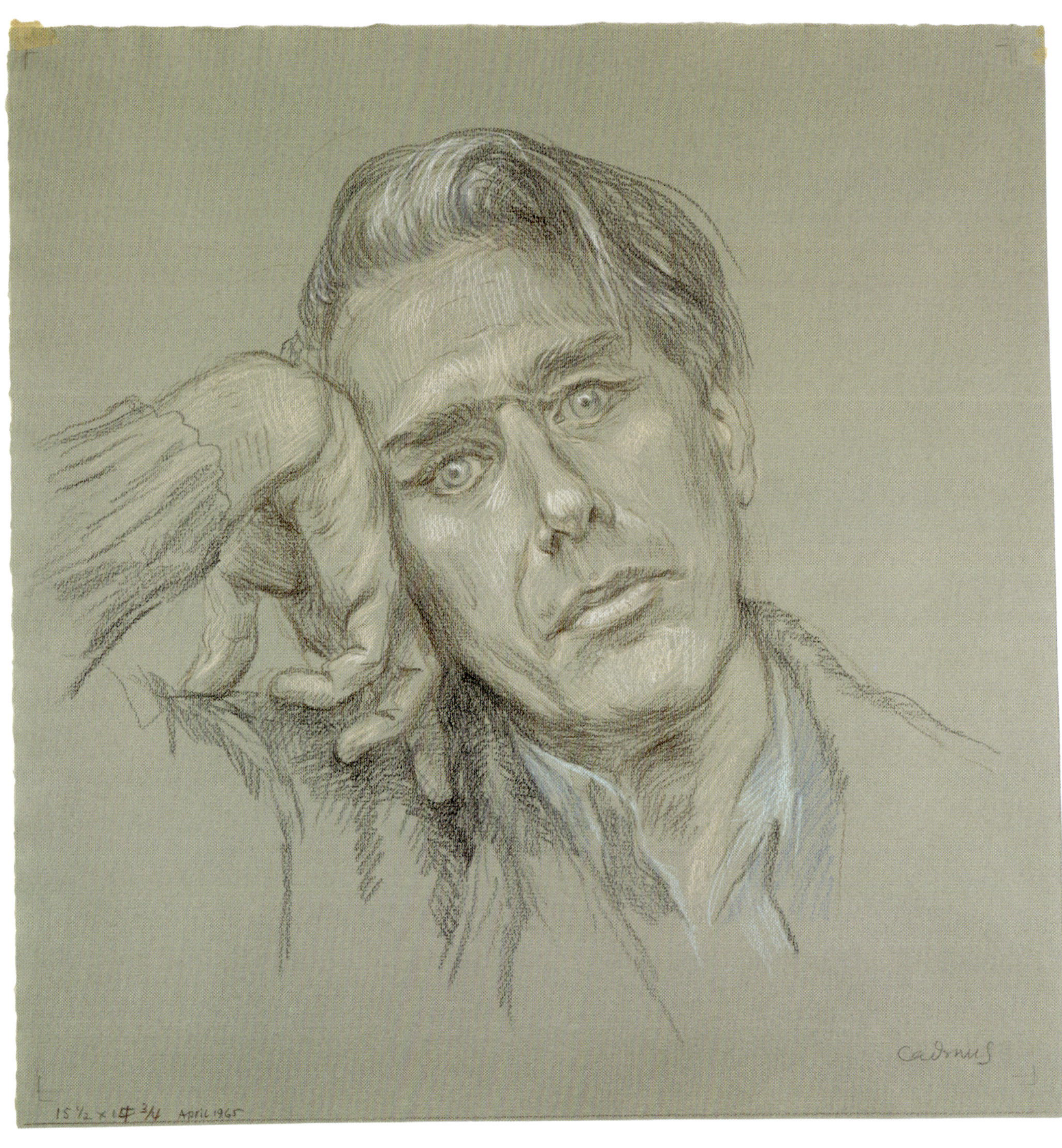
Cadmus

41.

Paul Cadmus (1904–1999)

Crayon on paper, 41.8 x 39.2 cm
(16 7/16 x 15 7/16 in.), 1965
The Ruth Bowman and Harry Kahn Twentieth-Century American Self-Portrait Collection
NPG.2002.219

SHORTLY BEFORE making his self-portrait, dated April 1965, Paul Cadmus met the young dancer Jon Anderson, who would become his lifelong partner and the model for the extensive series of nude male drawings that dominated his mature work. But throughout his life, when no one else was available, Cadmus posed himself. "I've done a great many just plain self portraits," he once noted, "being the most easily available model, and in between pictures . . . , there I am, ready to pose."[1] Although the angled hand, dark-toned paper, and subtle touches of color recall his meticulously rendered nudes,[2] his sharp, unrelenting gaze conveys a less admiring appraisal, as if he is comparing his aging face to his lover's youth.

From the beginning of his career, critics praised Cadmus for his ability to draw the human figure. During his first one-man show at the Midtown Galleries in 1937, critic Edward Alden Jewell admired his "splendid draftsmanship . . . so lusty and firm yet so full of unforced subtlety."[3] In the exhibition brochure's "Credo," Cadmus outlined his belief that "art is not only more true but also more living and vital if it derives its immediate inspiration and its outward form from contemporary life."[4] Fame followed notoriety in the 1930s, when his satiric paintings of drunken sailors soliciting favors from male and female civilians caused controversies.[5] Although his career started to fade in the 1940s with the rise of abstract expressionism, interest in his work revived in the 1980s and 1990s.[6] Cadmus continued to concentrate on figurative subject matter, often choosing the medium of highly finished drawings, inspired by Renaissance and Baroque masters and the French artist Jean-Auguste Dominique Ingres. A good drawing, in his view, was "less an act of exploration than a fully resolved work, which, like a poem or musical composition, was worth consideration only in its final, perfected form.[7]

WWR

Notes

1 Lincoln Kirstein, *Paul Cadmus* (New York: Rizzoli, 1986), 55.
2 See, for example, Justin Spring, *Paul Cadmus: The Male Nude* (New York: Universe Publishing, 2002), 111.
3 Edward Alden Jewell, "Cadmus Canvases Hung at Midtown," *New York Times*, March 27, 1937.
4 Paul Cadmus, "Credo" (New York: Midtown Payson Galleries, 1937); reprinted in Philip Eliasoph, *Paul Cadmus: Yesterday and Today* (Oxford, Ohio: Miami University Art Museum, 1981), 31.
5 Richard Meyer, *Paul Cadmus: The Sailor Trilogy* (New York: Whitney Museum of American Art, 1996), unpaginated; Richard Meyer, *Outlaw Representation: Censorship and Homosexuality in Twentieth-Century American Art* (New York: Oxford University Press, 2002), 37–57.
6 See, for example, Eliasoph, *Paul Cadmus*; Guy Davenport, *The Drawings of Paul Cadmus* (New York: Rizzoli, 1989); Jonathan Weinberg, "Cruising with Paul Cadmus," *Art in America* 80 (November 1992): 102–8; Spring, *Paul Cadmus*.
7 Spring, *Paul Cadmus*, 39.

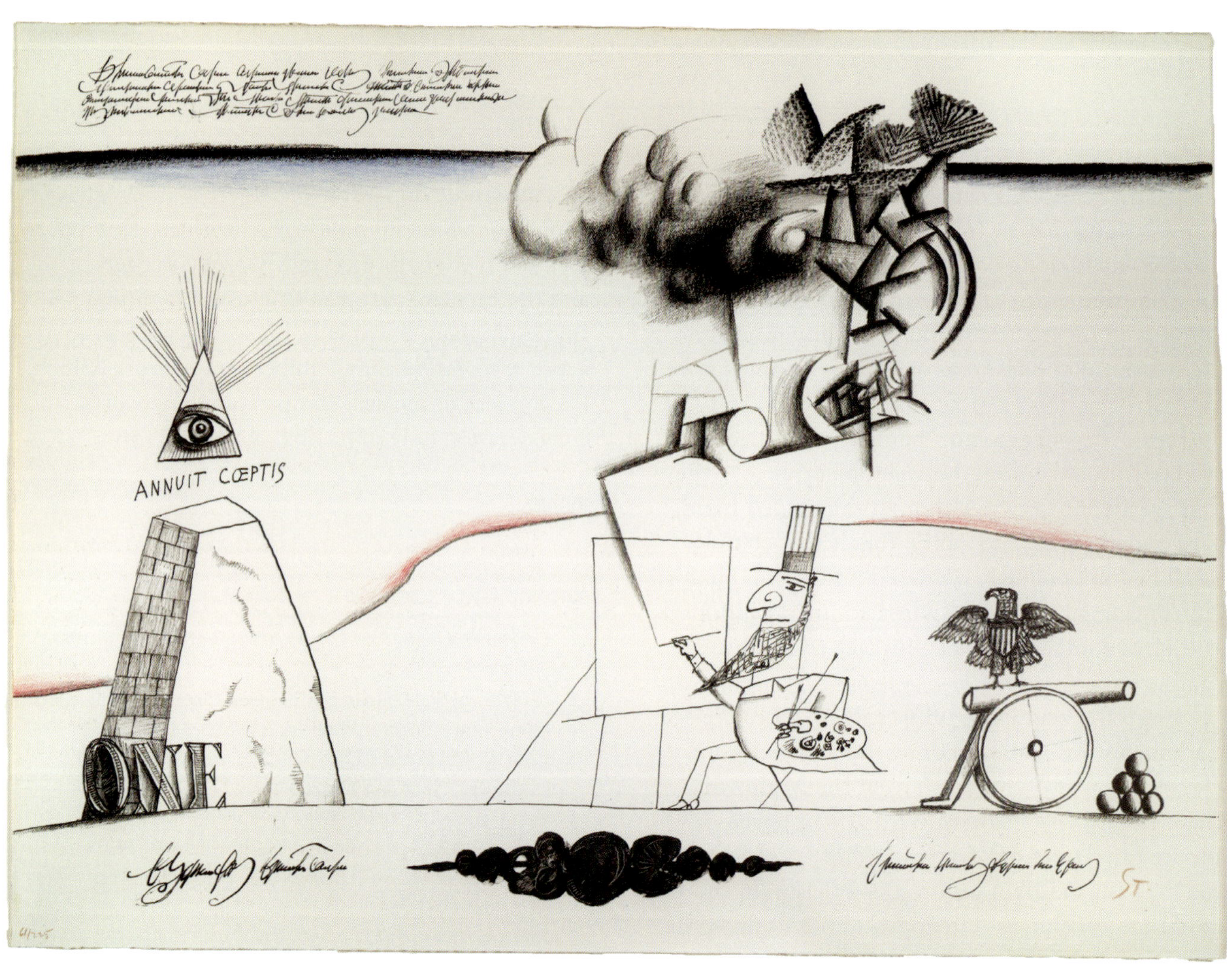
ANNUIT CŒPTIS
ONE

42.

Saul Steinberg (1914–1999)

Sam's Art
Lithograph, 43.2 x 55.7 cm (17 x 21 15/16 in.), 1965
The Ruth Bowman and Harry Kahn Twentieth-Century American Self-Portrait Collection
NPG.2002.343

THROUGHOUT nearly sixty years contributing cartoons and more than ninety covers to the *New Yorker*, Saul Steinberg blurred the boundaries between cartoons and fine art.[1] He published and exhibited his cartoons worldwide, and also had a retrospective at the Whitney Museum of American Art in 1978. The renowned critic Harold Rosenberg, who wrote the retrospective's catalog, celebrated Steinberg as an artistic anomaly, proclaiming, "He is a writer of pictures, an architect of speech and sounds, a draftsman of philosophical reflections."[2] In the lithograph *Sam's Art*, Steinberg portrayed himself in the guise of Uncle Sam, one of his favorite Americana motifs. Whereas he typically drew Uncle Sam with a straight nose, here he has given him a profile that matched his own, and depicted him self-referentially as an artist.

A Romanian-born Jew trained as an architect in Italy, Steinberg came to the United States during World War II. Fascinated that architectural draftsmanship could result in a building, he pursued drawing itself as a "way of reasoning on paper."[3] In his self-portrait, the thought process appears as a jumble above his head, not yet applied to the blank canvas. Official-looking pictorial forms, including formal (but illegible) script, bald eagles, and Masonic pyramids from the back of the dollar bill raise issues about governmental authority, immigrant identity, and assimilation. *Sam's Art* thus illustrates what Rosenberg called the "universe of accepted ideas that he suddenly strip[ped] of their acceptance."[4] Steinberg used such imagery in his art, he admitted, to "[play] with . . . the voyage between perception and understanding."[5]

Steinberg believed that being an immigrant empowered him. He honed his sensitivities by constantly traveling throughout the United States, and explained that displacement "is the tradition of the American. As a matter of fact, this is the tradition of the artist—to become somebody else. An artist who doesn't become somebody else remains the next-door girl or boy."[6]

ECR

Notes

1 These figures come from the Saul Steinberg Foundation's website. Another excellent resource is Joel Smith, *Saul Steinberg: Illuminations* (New Haven, CT: Yale University Press, 2006).

2 Harold Rosenberg, "Saul Steinberg," in *Saul Steinberg* (New York: Knopf, 1978), 10. Rosenberg also proclaimed him "a Duchamp who has transcended anti-art by exposing the power of form-making on every level of human experience," ibid., 36. Steinberg himself explained, "I never like to sell the object. . . . In that way I consider myself to be doing the work of a poet who prints the words but keeps the manuscript." Robert Hughes, "The World of Saul Steinberg," *Time*, April 17, 1978, 96.

3 Reflecting on architectural draftsmanship, Steinberg wrote, "The frightening thought that what you draw may become a building makes for reasoned lines." Saul Steinberg, "Chronology by Saul Steinberg" in *Saul Steinberg*, 235; Rosenberg, "Saul Steinberg," 30; and Steinberg interview conducted by Grace Glueck, 1971, Archives of American Art, Smithsonian Institution, Washington, DC.

4 Rosenberg, "Saul Steinberg," 12.

5 Quoted in Smith, *Saul Steinberg*, 156, from Jean Vanden Huevel, "Straight from the Hand and Mouth of Steinberg," *Life*, December 10, 1965, 66.

6 Glueck interview. For additional information on Steinberg's travels in the United States, see John Gruen, "Saul Steinberg, Master of Wit and Fantasy," *ARTnews* 77 (May 1978): 132–38.

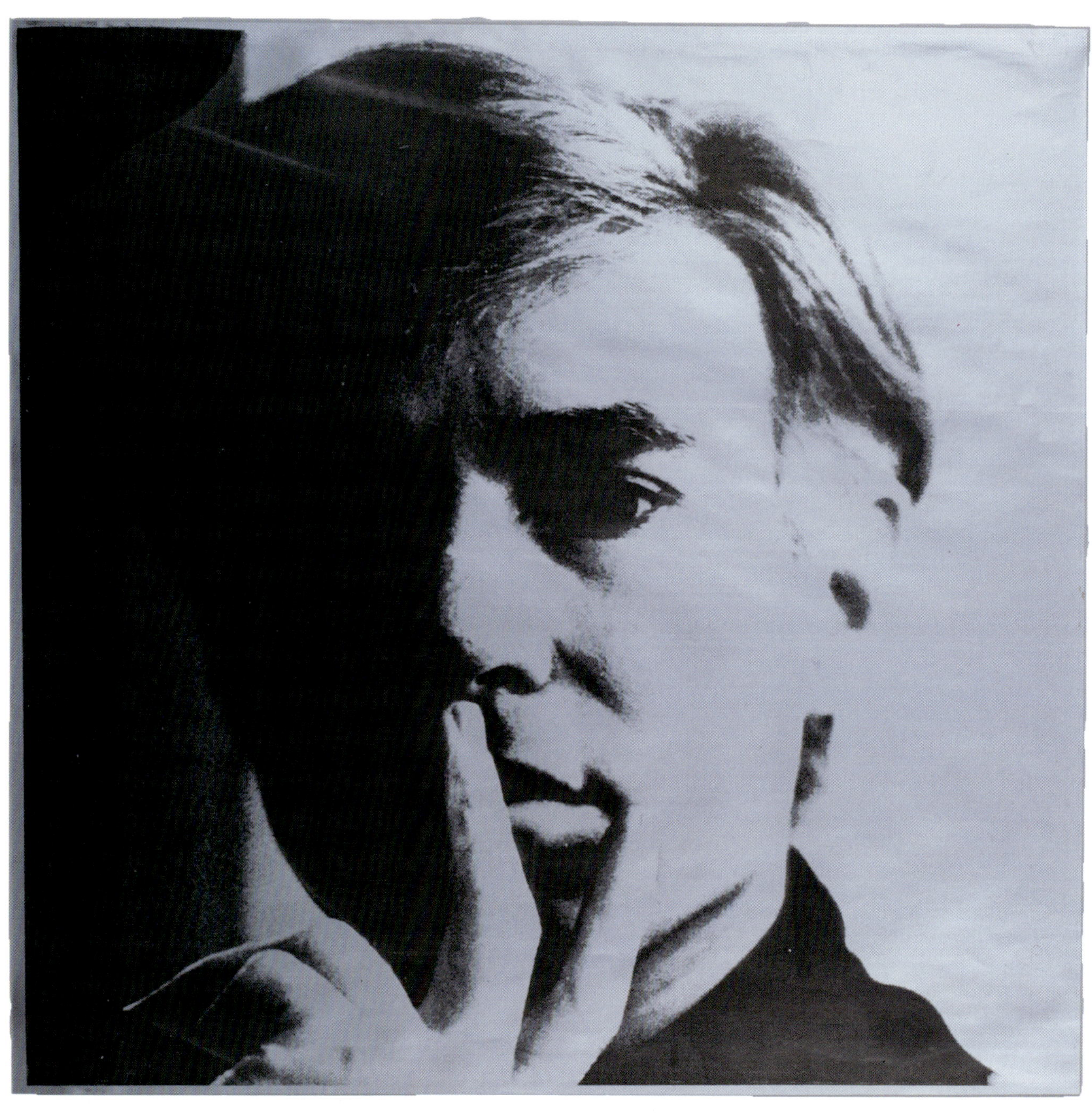

43.

Andy Warhol (1928–1987)

Offset lithograph on silver-coated posterboard, 58 x 57.7 cm (22 13/16 x 22 11/16 in.), 1966
The Ruth Bowman and Harry Kahn Twentieth-Century American Self-Portrait Collection
NPG.2002.357

KNOWN FOR HIS reinvention of portraiture during the 1960s, Andy Warhol raises important questions about the nature of self-representation with this 1966 self-portrait. Created for a 1966 exhibition at the Leo Castelli Gallery at which he announced his (supposed) retirement from painting, the offset lithograph, based on a photograph by an unknown maker, pictures the artist with his face cast deeply into shadow.[1] The print's mechanical appearance and manufacture further disguises evidence of Warhol's presence, rather than boasting of it. The artist has even relegated his signature to the work's back, rendering it invisible to most viewers.

Warhol's choice of a silver background distances the artist from the viewer, while resonating with aspects of his public persona. Embedded in the metallic background, which recalls Warhol's famous pronouncement, "I want to be a machine," one reads references to his studio—called the Factory—the cinema (appropriate given Warhol's experimentation with filmmaking), religious icons (Warhol had recently been dubbed "Saint Andrew" in the press), and, more darkly, to the "silvering over" of Warhol's *13 Most Wanted Men* at the 1964 World's Fair in New York.[2]

Conceptually overturning the perception of access suggested by much self-portraiture, Warhol's self-representation serves as a form of protective armor, even as Warhol used the mechanism to enhance his professional reputation. Ironically, in the very deployment of multiples of this image, quickly executed as a series of silk-screen paintings, Warhol demonstrated the deceptive lure of false familiarity.[3] Shortly after exhibiting his self-portrait in an international venue, the artist permitted a double to replace him at lectures. Once discovered, the ruse drew the ire of the public, but made the artist's point: "If you want to know all about Andy Warhol, just look at the surface of my paintings and films and me, and there I am. There's nothing behind it."[4]

ACG

Notes

1 The work is often misidentified as a silk screen. However, close analysis demonstrates that the work is offset, as identified by Frayda Feldman and Claudia Defendi, *Andy Warhol Prints: A Catalogue Raisonné, 1962–1987,* 4th ed. (New York: D.A.P. Publishers, in association with Ronald Feldman Fine Arts, Edition Schellmann, The Andy Warhol Foundation for the Visual Arts, Inc., 2003), 65. The source image at the Warhol Foundation gives no photographer. However, the photograph has often been attributed to Rudy Burckhardt. During his lifetime, Warhol did nothing to refute this identification. However, before his death, Burckhardt denied taking any pictures of Warhol. See George Frei and Neil Printz, *The Andy Warhol Catalogue Raisonné,* vol. 2B: *Paintings and Sculptures, 1964–1969* (New York: Phaidon Press, 2004), p. 407, "Self-Portraits, 1966–67," n. 1.

2 Warhol declared "I want to be a machine" in an interview with Gene Swenson. "What Is Pop Art? Interviews with Eight Painters" (part 1), *ARTnews* 62 (November 1963): 26. On Warhol's "canonization," See "Saint Andrew," *Newsweek,* December 7, 1964, 100–103A. On the "silvering over" of Warhol's murals, see Richard Meyer, *Outlaw Representation: Censorship and Homosexuality in Twentieth-Century American Art* (Oxford: Oxford University Press, 2002), esp. 128–53.

3 The first group appeared only months later at a popular exhibition of the artist's work, organized by the Boston Institute of Contemporary Art. The same image would go on to represent Warhol at the 1967 World's Fair in Montreal.

4 Quoted by Dietmar Elger, "The Best American Invention—To Be Able to Disappear," in *Andy Warhol: Self-Portraits* (Ostfildern-Ruit: Hatje Cantz Verlag, 2004), 127.

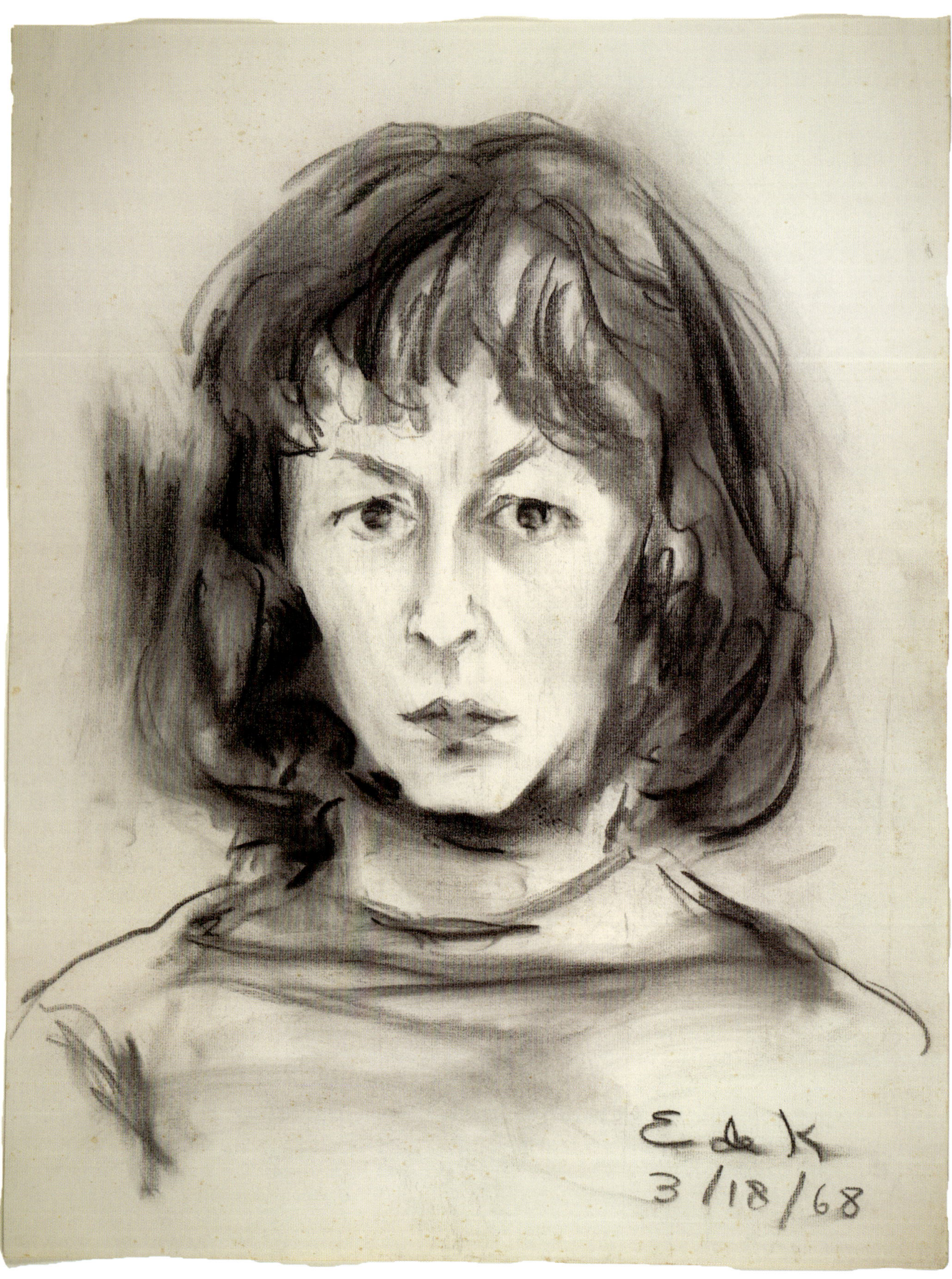
E de K
3/18/68

44.

Elaine de Kooning (1918–1989)

Charcoal on paper, 60.2 x 46 cm
(23 11/16 x 18 1/8 in.), 1968
The Ruth Bowman and Harry Kahn Twentieth-Century American Self-Portrait Collection
NPG.2002.285

IN HER larger-than-life self-portrait head of 1968, Elaine de Kooning evinces the determination and assurance that put her on the map of mid-twentieth-century American art. As an artist and as a critic, de Kooning spanned the seemingly unbridgeable gap between abstraction and representation. A confirmed portraitist—doing portraits were an "addiction," she told one critic[1]—she nonetheless infused her paintings with the energetic, gestural brushstrokes renowned in the work of her husband, Willem de Kooning. As critic Valerie Petersen noted in 1962, de Kooning's portraits, exhibiting "a bold synthesis of abstract excitement and the simplicity of gesture peculiar to her subjects," were as much a part of the New York School of painting as the "housepainter's brush and oversized canvases."[2]

In her groundbreaking 1955 *ARTnews* essay, "Subject: What, How or Who?" de Kooning maintained that the battle for legitimizing abstract art was over; it was the artist introducing representational elements who was put on the defensive. For committed abstractionists, she commented with emphatic italics, the battle cry is "*Enter nature, exit art.*" She countered critic Clement Greenberg's notion that representational forms can be returned to art "only by pastiche or parody" by arguing that abstract art had been so thoroughly explored, the "image and object can be *left out* only by pastiche and parody."[3]

"The portraits that excite me personally," de Kooning claimed, "are portraits that penetrate, that expose."[4] She was never more penetrating than in her self-portraiture.

Her charcoal self-portrait, so different from her more gestural and abstract oils, nonetheless exudes a similar energy. It also reveals her unparalleled skills as a draftsman. Drawings, she claimed, were "more austere and grander than color because drawing seemed to be the mind grasping."[5] In this image she has dispensed with abstract backgrounds and honed in on the expression of her own face with rigorous discipline and skill.

WWR

Notes

1 Gerrit Henry, "Ten Portraitists—Interviews/Statements," *Art in America* 63 (January–February 1975): 35.
2 Valerie Petersen, "U.S. Figure Painting: Continuity and Cliché," *ARTnews* 61 (Summer 1962): 51.
3 Elaine de Kooning, "Subject: What, How or Who?" *ARTnews* 54 (April 1955): 26–28.
4 Lawrence Campbell, "Elaine de Kooning: Portraits in a New York Scene," *ARTnews* 62 (April 1963): 34.
5 Ibid., 63.

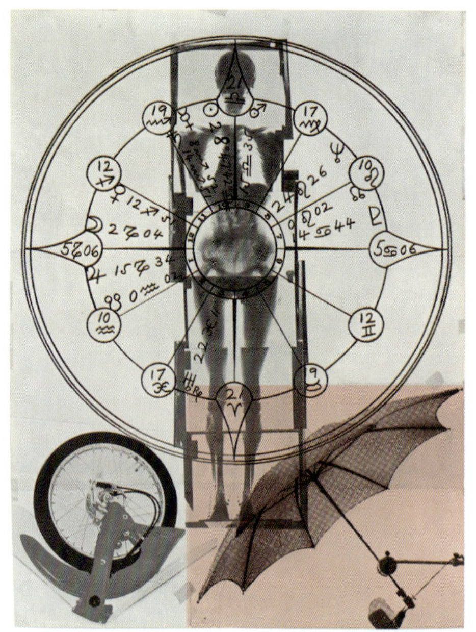

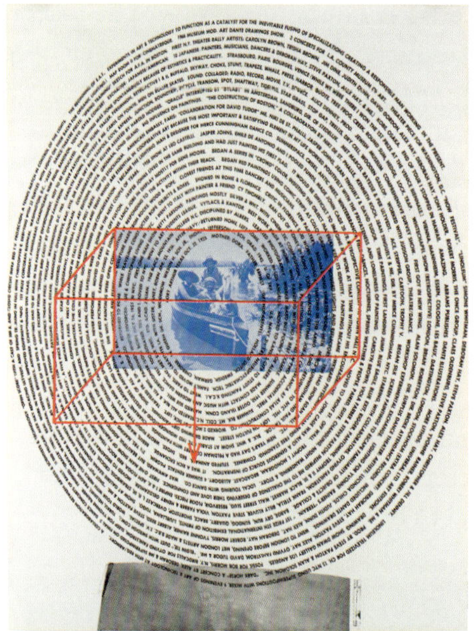

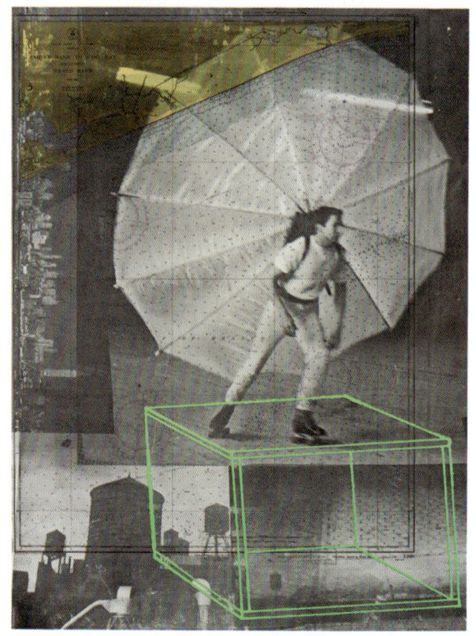

45.

Robert Rauschenberg (1925–2008)

Autobiography
Color offset lithograph on three sheets of paper, each approximately 168 x 123.8 cm (66 1/8 x 48 3/4 in.), 1968
The Ruth Bowman and Harry Kahn Twentieth-Century American Self-Portrait Collection
NPG.2002.313

CREATED IN 1968, four years after Robert Rauschenberg became the first American to win the international painting prize at the Venice Biennale, *Autobiography* demonstrates through its combination of text, images, size, and medium the extraordinary ambition and innovation of its subject. The artist appears in each of the three panels, at top through an X-ray, in the center as a child in a boat with his parents, and at bottom in a still photograph of his performance-piece *Pelican*.[1] In addition to photographic imagery, Rauschenberg has layered other signifiers of his identity into the work: the first panel includes an astrological chart (Libra); the middle contains a detailed autobiographical narrative of his life and career; the third panel combines a navigational chart and a picture of oil tanks—which document his hometown of Port Arthur, Texas—with a vertically oriented image of the New York skyline—which refers to his later residence in Manhattan.[2] The concentric spiral at the center of the composition is suggestive of the tread of a fingerprint, providing yet another marker of personal identity.

As the work's imagery and scale suggest, Rauschenberg consistently worked across traditional disciplinary boundaries. His commitment to artistic experimentation becomes abundantly clear in the narrative embedded in the print. Rauschenberg describes his heritage and lists important artworks and accolades. He repeatedly makes reference to his ongoing efforts to work outside of his comfort zone and create deliberately "awkward" situations for himself, working in theater, experimenting with lithography, or exploring new technologies. The sort of destabilization that Rauschenberg repeatedly sought as an artist registers itself in this extremely large print, with a spiraling autobiographical narrative that can only be read with effort, and preferably in collaboration with other viewers. As is frequently the case with Rauschenberg's work, the participation of the viewer in the "completion" of the work, in this case through the act of reading, is critical.[3] The medium of *Autobiography* further demonstrates the artist's desire to break down artificial barriers, using the traditionally commercial technique of offset lithography and pushing it into the realm of fine art.[4]

ACG

Notes

1 For further discussion of this imagery, see Carla Gottlieb, "Self-Portraiture in Postmodern Art," *Wallraf-Richartz Jahrbuch* 42 (1981), 284–86. *Pelican* debuted in 1963, but the photograph included here appears to be from a 1965 performance.

2 The text panel of *Autobiography* is transcribed in Calvin Tomkins, *Off the Wall: Robert Rauschenberg and the Art World of Our Time* (New York: Penguin Books, 1980), 303–6.

3 On Rauschenberg's tendency to involve "his viewers in the actual physical aspects of the creative process," see Ruth E. Fine, "Writing on Rocks, Rubbing on Silk, Layering on Paper," in Walter Hopps and Susan Davidson, eds., *Robert Rauschenberg: A Retrospective* (New York: Guggenheim Museum of Art, 1997), 382.

4 As Mary Lynn Kotz has observed, the large (more than sixteen and one-half feet tall) three-part print was the first fine art print to be made on a press designed for printing billboards. Mary Lynn Kotz, *Rauschenberg/Art and Life* (New York: Harry N. Abrams, 1990), 155.

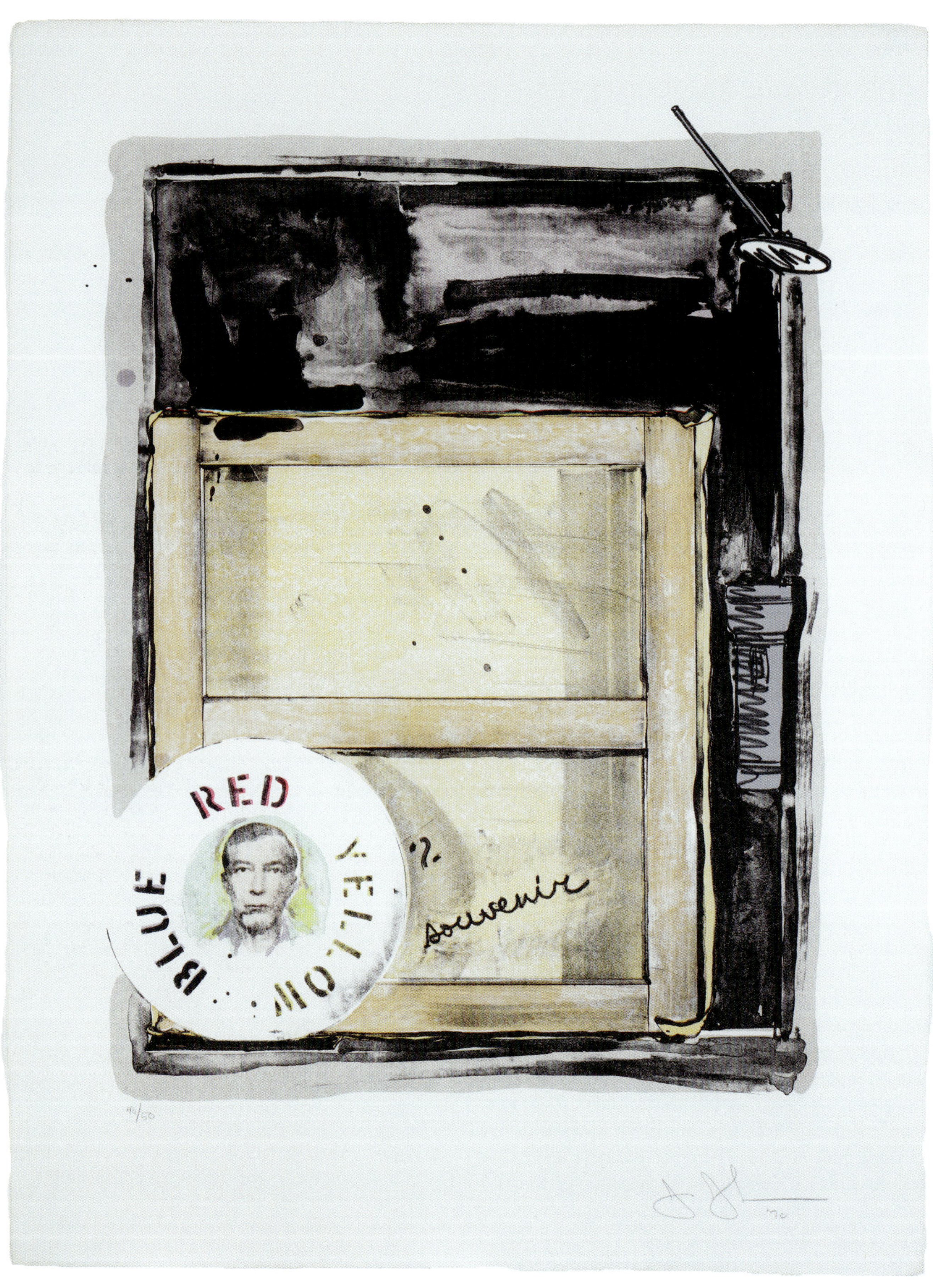
RED
YELLOW
BLUE
Souvenir

46.

Jasper Johns (born 1930)

Souvenir
Color lithograph, 78.1 x 56.8 cm
(30³/₄ x 22³/₈ in.), 1970
NPG.2002.383

BASED ON HIS 1964 assemblage, *Souvenir 2*, (see fig. 2-2), Johns's lithograph *Souvenir* was created in 1970 for the first retrospective exhibition of his prints.[1] "I like to repeat an image in another medium to observe the play between the two: the image and the medium," the artist has remarked.[2] As suggested by its title—which refers in part to the plate in the lower left—inspired by a souvenir Johns saw in Japan, the theme of memory and perception runs through the composition. It references not only multiple examples of Johns's work—including several versions of *Souvenir*, a series of flashlight sculptures, and compositions incorporating overturned canvases—but also the distortions and transformations introduced in the process of recollecting the past.

In light of the work's translation through time and process, it is notable that in both the original composition and the print, it is the plate, bearing his picture—a rarity in his art—around which the composition as a whole functions. In a 1964 note, Johns directed himself to "Determine the size of [the painting] from plate size."[3] In developing the lithograph six years later, Johns started with a photo silk screen of the plate.[4] His provocative inclusion of an image of himself in this "souvenir" invites inevitable scrutiny. Yet related drawings from 1964 describe only a "photo" to be installed in this spot, raising questions about the degree of emotional significance with which Johns endowed this conspicuously expressionless self-portrayal.[5]

Indeed, efforts to probe the likeness for psychological content are deflected by the artist, who playfully mused in 1966: "Thinking anything could be a souvenir of something else, not specifically a self-portrait. Ego was not clear. Maybe just another way of dishing up a Johns."[6]

ACG

Notes

1 This work is discussed in detail by Richard S. Field, "Watchman and Souvenir," *Jasper Johns: Prints, 1960–1970* (Philadelphia: Philadelphia Museum of Art, 1970), unpaginated. See too Michael Crichton, *Jasper Johns* (New York: Whitney Museum of American Art, 1977), 51. *Souvenir* has been widely discussed in the context of self-portraiture. See Anne Goodyear's essay in this volume.

2 Quoted in Christian Geelhaar, "Interview mit Jasper Johns/ Interview with Jasper Johns," in Geelhaar, ed. *Jasper Johns: Working Proofs* (Basel: Kunstmuseum Basel, 1979), 41–62, 63–72 (interview conducted October 16, 1978); reprinted in Kirk Varnedoe, ed., *Jasper Johns: Writings, Sketchbook Notes, Interviews* (New York: Museum of Modern Art, 1996), 191.

3 Jasper Johns, Sketchbook Notes, Book A, p. 53, 1964; reprinted in Varnedoe, *Jasper Johns*, 58.

4 Field, "Watchman and Souvenir."

5 Roberta Bernstein notes the similarity of Johns's depiction of himself in *Souvenir* and Marcel Duchamp's self-representation in *Wanted: $2,000 Reward*. See Bernstein, *Jasper Johns' Paintings and Sculptures, 1954–1974: "The Changing Focus of the Eye"* (1975; Ann Arbor: UMI Research Press, 1985), 115. See too Nan Rosenthal and Ruth E. Fine, *Drawings of Jasper Johns* (Washington, DC: National Gallery of Art, 1990), cat. 51, p. 192. On Johns's indication of the placement of a "photo" on the plate in his 1964 drawing *Souvenir*, see Rosenthal and Fine, *Drawings of Jasper Johns*, 192–93. A similar notation is also made in Johns's Sketchbook Notes, Book A, p. 53, 1964, reprinted in Varnedoe, *Jasper Johns*, 35. Johns's creation of an artwork in which his likeness is "hidden" by the presence of other suggestive objects fits in with the discourse of the Watchman and the Spy raised in Johns's Sketchbook notes in 1964. See Johns, Sketchbook Notes, Book A, p. 55 (1964), reprinted in Varnedoe, *Jasper Johns*, 59. See also Field, "Watchman and Souvenir"; Crichton, *Jasper Johns*, 51; Bernstein, *Jasper Johns' Paintings and Sculptures*, 114; and Rosenthal and Fine, *Drawings of Jasper Johns*, 192.

6 Quoted by Charlotte Willard, "Eye to Eye," *Art in America* 54 (March–April 1966): 57.

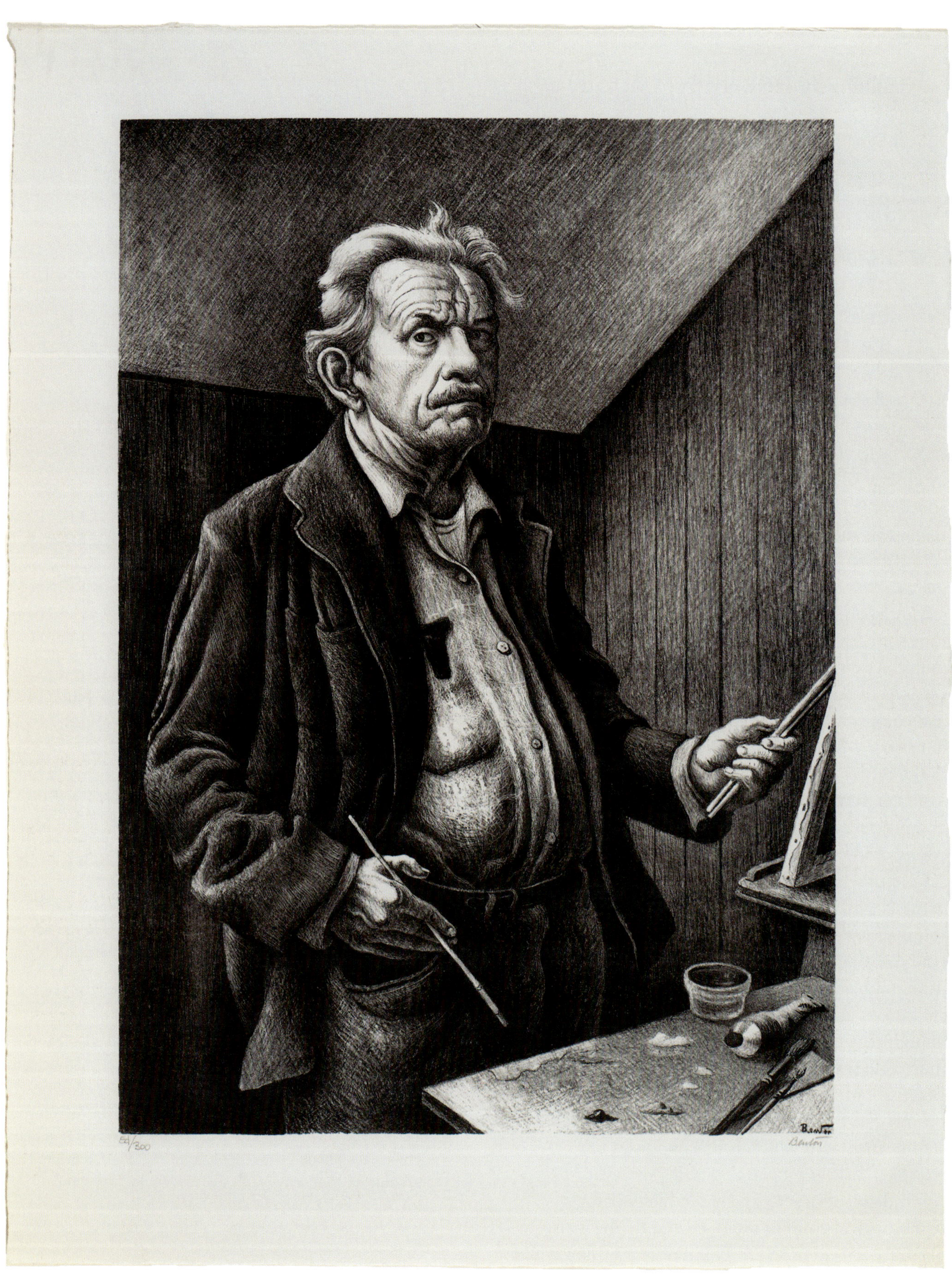

47.

Thomas Hart Benton (1889–1975)

Lithograph, 61 x 46.4 cm (24 x 18¼ in.), 1972
The Ruth Bowman and Harry Kahn Twentieth-Century American Self-Portrait Collection
NPG.2002.205

WITH THIS monumental lithograph and the painting on which he based it, leading regionalist artist Thomas Hart Benton added another memorable character to the American panorama he had created over the decades.[1] Here he appeared as "Grandaddy Benton."[2] With his upright stance and defiant glare, the aging artist took his place alongside the colorful fellow midwesterners who populated his murals and easel paintings of American history and culture.

For the feisty painter of the American scene who fearlessly traveled back roads to find subjects for his works, it was not easy to admit that he was aging. Yet realism was Benton's credo—he had to be honest in describing his gray hair and furrowed brow. He took evident delight in such visual play as likening the wrinkles of his neck to the folds of the jacket that hung loosely over his skinny arms.[3] He vigorously scratched on the lithographic stone to highlight the bulging belly that strained his belt.

As a man, however, Benton steadfastly refused to surrender to mortality a moment before his final breath. After he suffered a stroke and heart attack in 1966, Benton only momentarily cut back on his activities when he cancelled a trip on the Buffalo River.[4] He soon returned to painting mural after mural and gradually took up his accustomed strenuous life. He proudly boasted that after making this print, he lost his potbelly through the exercise he got building a stone retaining wall.[5] The artist professed not to care if such work put him at risk. In a 1973 interview with Mike Wallace, Benton boasted that he still drank and was still painting. In fact, he said, "I think I paint better than ever."[6] In this proud old-age self-portrait with brushes firmly in hand, Benton asserted the truth of that statement.

APW

Notes

1 The 1970 painting on which this print is based is held by Lyman Field and United Missouri Bank of Kansas City, N.A., trustees of Thomas Hart and Rita P. Benton Testamentary Trusts. The painting is illustrated in Matthew Baigell, *Thomas Hart Benton* (New York: Harry N. Abrams, 1974), 18.

2 Quoted in Creekmore Fath, comp. and ed., *The Lithographs of Thomas Hart Benton* (Austin: University of Texas Press, 1979), 188.

3 Benton admitted that after an episode when he exhausted himself dangerously swimming in the Hudson River, he "quit bothering much about my physical self. . . . I soon began to get a little flabby around the middle and in a short time saw my shoulder muscles go down and my arms and legs get stringy." Thomas Hart Benton, *An Artist in America*, 4th rev. ed. (Columbia: University of Missouri Press, 1983), 305.

4 Ibid., 367–68.

5 Quoted in Fath, *Lithographs of Thomas Hart Benton*, 188.

6 Quoted in Henry Adams, *Thomas Hart Benton: An American Original* (New York: Alfred A. Knopf, 1989), 338–39.

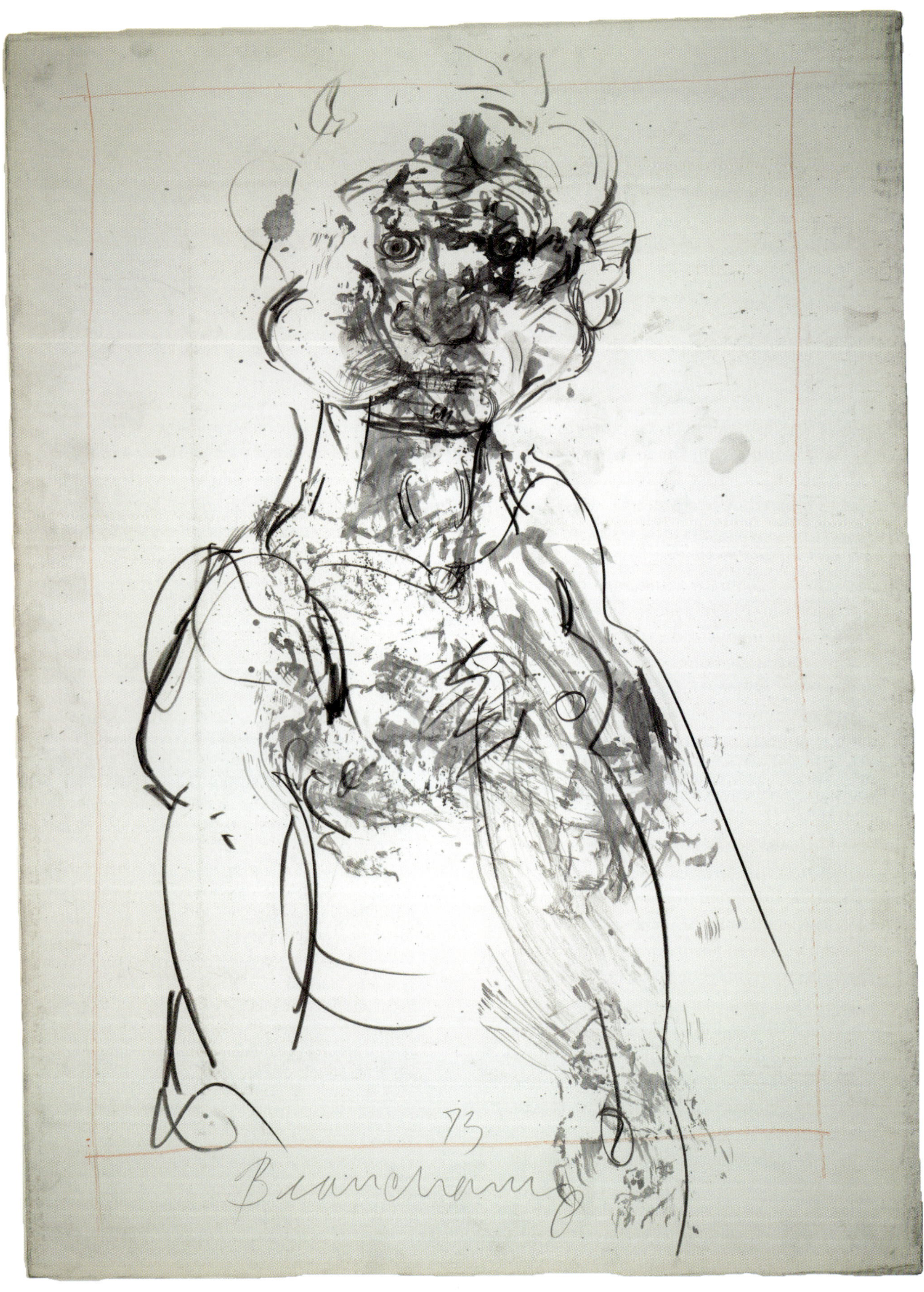

48.

Robert Beauchamp (1923–1995)

Graphite and wash on paper, 70.9 x 50.4 cm (27 15/16 x 19 13/16 in.), 1973
The Ruth Bowman and Harry Kahn Twentieth-Century American Self-Portrait Collection
S/NPG.2002.199

SEVERAL YEARS after completing this image, Robert Beauchamp remarked that a self-portrait, to his mind, should "look a certain way . . . reveal your emotions or capture what you think your character is."[1] His comment gives us some insight into this piece, portraying his handsome, angular body as grotesque, almost demonic. Similar self-depictions, numbering more than 100,[2] that he rendered in drawings, paintings, and sculptures throughout the 1970s led art historian April Kingsley to proclaim that "through this purgative action, this flaying open of his raw interior, and through the self-mockery it entails, we have been given access to a level of psychological reality not often reached in painting."[3]

Beauchamp's self-portraiture was but one aspect of his intense focus on the human figure during the 1970s.[4] He also repeatedly painted his brothers, one an alcoholic, another wheelchair-bound by polio. It was a reorientation for Beauchamp, who was known for the prior two decades as a painter of "wild phantasmagoria," ranging from, in Beauchamp's own words "pregnant women" to "floating feathers" to "skin tone."[5]

Although this self-portrait marks the beginning of Beauchamp's shift toward portraiture, it evinces his career-long concerns. Beauchamp trained with the abstract expressionist Hans Hofmann, but immediately thereafter, he took up figurative work because he felt he "was going through life with blinders on."[6] With his decidedly abstract figuration, he "tr[ied] to . . . lose reality, to make life more exciting, to enlarge experience, to expand."[7] This self-portrait's confluence of exuberant splatters, brushstrokes, and graphite outlines evinces how deeply he delved into the artistic process itself; Kingsley asserted, in 1984, the "freedom of his paint handling, the lightning speed of his line, the cut of his brush can be awe-inspiring."[8] Despite this accolade, Beauchamp insisted that the "search is constant, the struggle never lets up."[9] In this self-portrait, we sense some of the tension between that searching and virtuosity.

ECR

Notes

1 Robert Beauchamp oral history interview by Paul Cummings, January 16, 1975, Archives of American Art, Smithsonian Institution, Washington, DC.

2 Joan Marter, "Robert Beauchamp: Haunting Images," *Arts Magazine* 53 (February 1979): 146.

3 April Kingsley, "The Floating World of Robert Beauchamp," in *Robert Beauchamp: An American Expressionist* (Syracuse, NY: Everson Museum of Art, 1984), 15.

4 The critic Gerrit Henry wrote that Beauchamp's portraits from the 1970s were "deeply moving emblems of the human condition." Henry, "Robert Beauchamp, an Appreciation," in *Robert Beauchamp: Paintings and Drawings* (New York: Monique Knowlton Gallery, 1996), 4.

5 Gerrit Henry, "Robert Beauchamp," *ARTnews* 80 (Summer/June 1981): 238–40; Robert Beauchamp, *Art Now*, October 1969, quoted in Kingsley, "Floating World," 11.

6 Beauchamp oral history interview.

7 Robert Beauchamp, "Self-Interview," in *Robert Beauchamp: An American Expressionist*, 19–20.

8 Kingsley, "Floating World," 12.

9 Beauchamp, "Self-Interview," 21. As Kingsley explains, "The artist's process . . . is as completely arbitrary as that of a child finding monsters in the ceiling cracks." Kingsley, "Robert Beauchamp," in *The Figurative Fifties: New York Figurative Expressionism* (New York: Rizzoli, 1988), 58.

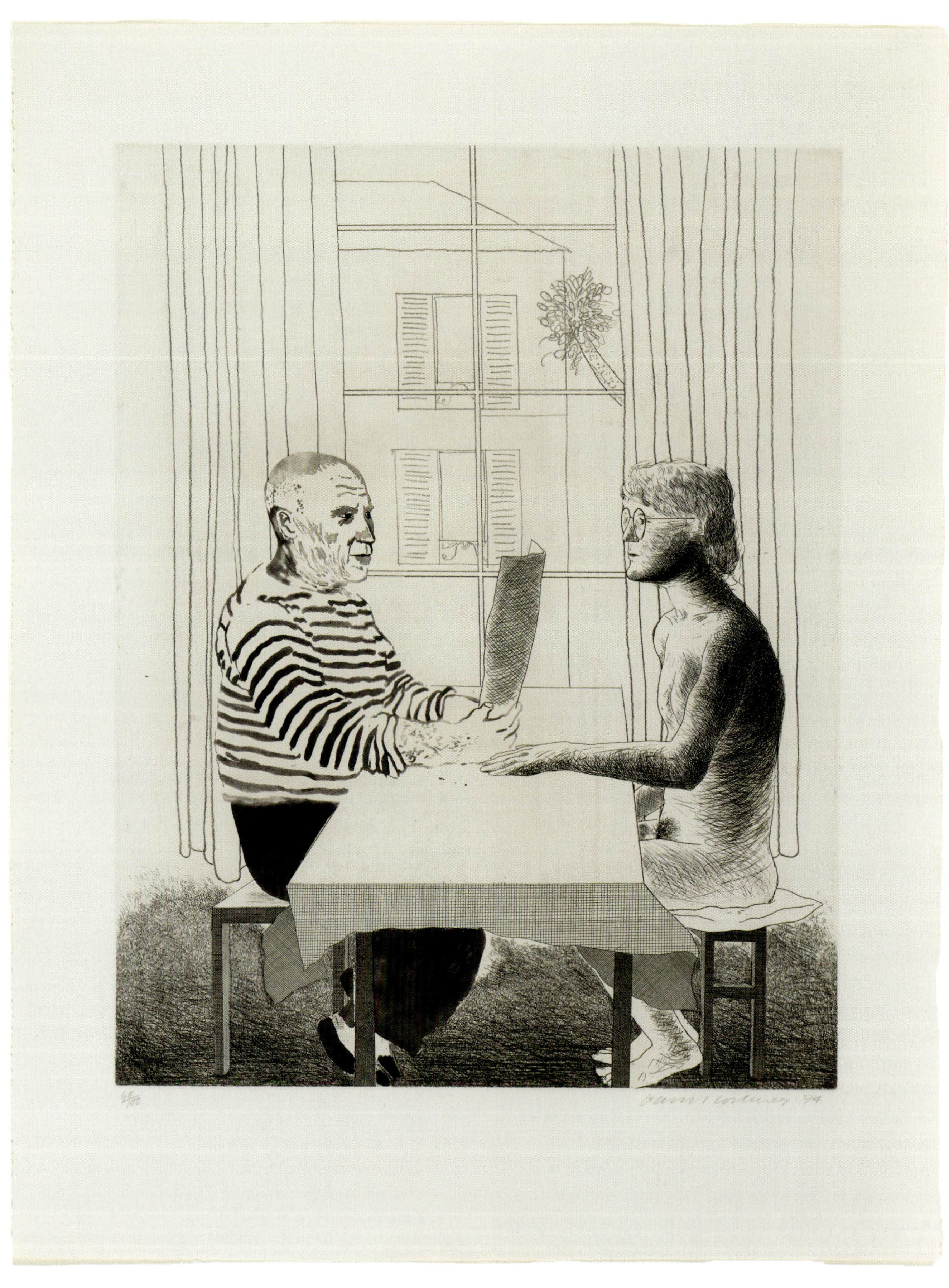

49.

David Hockney (born 1937)

Artist and Model
Etching and aquatint, 75.2 x 57 cm
(29⅝ x 22 7/16 in.), 1973–1974
The Ruth Bowman and Harry Kahn Twentieth-Century American Self-Portrait Collection
NPG.2002.272

"I'VE ALWAYS BEEN obsessed with seeing," noted David Hockney in a 1985 interview.[1] These portraits, each including representations of the artist himself, created roughly a decade apart at moments of artistic exploration, elegantly capture Hockney's commitment to exploring new ways of seeing and, particularly, to recording embodied perception as experienced over time. Critical to Hockney's effort has been the example of Pablo Picasso, specifically the lessons of cubism. "The only aspect of time one can grasp are the moments where we find ourselves in the company of others, moving among them," Hockney has asserted. "Only the cubists understood that."[2]

Hockney's intense interest in Picasso is evident in his 1973–1974 etching *Artist and Model*. The work grew out of an invitation to participate in a portfolio dedicated to Picasso, who died in 1973.[3] Although not personally acquainted with the older artist, Hockney had long felt his influence.[4] Probably using a photograph of Picasso by Robert Doisneau published on the cover of *Life* to create his counterpart's likeness, Hockney cast himself in an intimate tête à tête with his hero.[5] Although a historical fiction, the scenario captured an important intersection between the two artists, for Hockney created the print with the assistance of Aldo Crommelynck, who had for two decades produced prints with Picasso, introducing many technical innovations.[6] Hockney's careful observation of Picasso's methods suggests that the work's title might be interpreted in flexible terms.[7] Although Hockney, given his nudity and even his position on the page—which corresponds to a series of "artist and model" compositions by Picasso in the final decade of his career—has generally been interpreted by art historians as occupying the position of "model," it would seem that, in fact, it is the elder artist who serves as a subject and "muse" for the younger.[8]

The lessons of cubism that Hockney identified with Picasso would retain their importance for him, as became apparent in the early 1980s with his development of a series of photographic collages.[9] Deliberately conceived as a challenge to the monocular vantage point and short duration characteristic of photography, Hockney saw what he was doing as analogous to cubism: a mating of form and content intended to capture the world as physically experienced. As Hockney explains: "Nobody stands still, the head looks around at the world and even if the head stays still, the eyes move around. . . . But it does relate to yourself of course; because it's telling you where you are, and I would assume therefore, it has a great deal to do with who you are."[10]

One of Hockney's most poignant images is a nonconventional double-portrait in which the artist pictures himself—through the intentional inclusion of the tips of his feet—with his mother.[11] Using snapshots taken at Bolton Abbey, where Hockney's parents courted, the portrait takes as its subject both the passage of time and human relationships, and brings to mind Hockney's assertion that "cubism led to what I think is the greatest psychological portraiture ever done."[12] Studying the image, one steps into Hockney's shoes, visible at bottom center, and watches him observing his mother, absorbing the space in which they find themselves after his father's death.[13] One of the most prominent features of the portrait is an empty space that hovers above his mother's head. While perhaps referring to the privacy of thought and personal reflection that can never be fully accessed by others, another interpretation

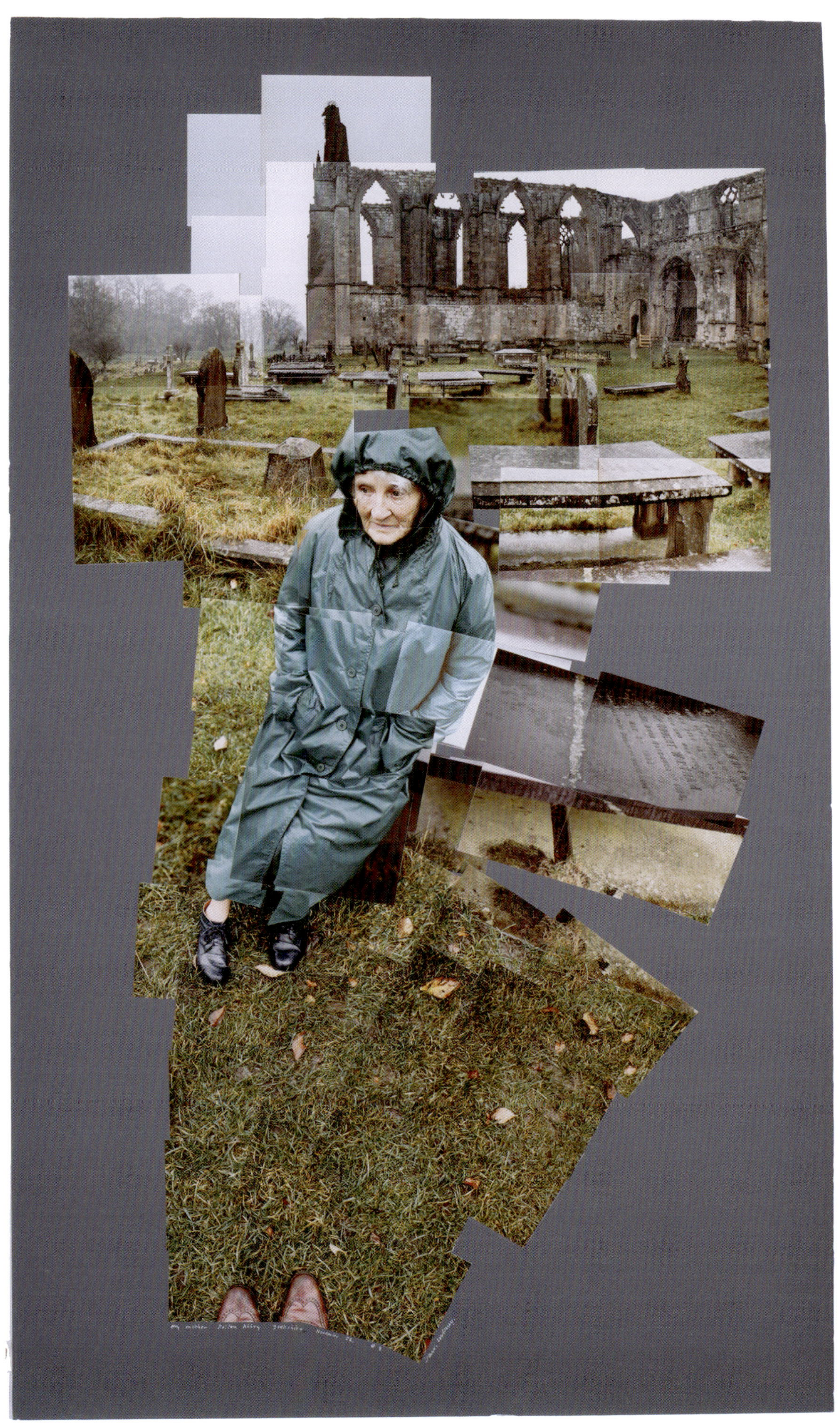
my mother Bolton Abbey Yorkshire November 82 #1 David Hockney

50.

David Hockney (born 1937)

My Mother Bolton Abbey, Yorkshire, Nov. 82 #3
Photographic collage (chromogenic prints) on paper, 120.5 x 70 cm (47 7/16 x 27 9/16 in.), 1982
The Ruth Bowman and Harry Kahn Twentieth-Century American Self-Portrait Collection
NPG.2002.273

is possible.[14] As Hockney has suggested, it may deliberately invoke the artist himself: "In a sense, *you are* a void," he has declared. "The world begins outside of you, and it's why, in the end, I've come to believe that this space very close to us is mysterious."[15]

ACG

Notes

1 Quoted in Pierre Saint-Jean, "David Hockney: An Interview," *Gazette des Beaux-Arts* 106 (December 1985): 231.

2 Jill Spalding, "Entretien: David Hockney," *Beaux Arts Magazine*, 7 (November 1983): 28 (translation mine).

3 Marco Livingstone explains that the Berlin publisher Propyläen Verlag asked Hockney to take part in the portfolio *Homage to Picasso*; *Artist and Model* was undertaken in 1973 with this in mind, but was set aside and completed in 1974 and published by Petersburg Press; see Marco Livingstone, *David Hockney*, rev. ed. (London: Thames and Hudson, 1996), 163–64.

4 Hockney recounts his reaction to Picasso's death in Lawrence Wechsler, "True to Life," in David Hockney, *Cameraworks* (New York: Alfred A. Knopf, 1984), 18; and in Milton Esterow, "David Hockney's 'Different Ways of Looking,'" *ARTnews* 82 (January 1983): 54.

5 Picasso appears wearing a sailor's shirt with the right sleeve rolled back, as in Hockney's etching, on the cover of a special double issue of *Life* dedicated to Picasso (December 27, 1968). Picasso's orientation is shifted slightly in Hockney's etching, where he appears from the side rather than from the front. Although Hockney does not specify the source, he does acknowledge that his rendition of Picasso was based on a photograph; see David Hockney, *That's the Way I See It*, ed. Nikos Stangos (London: Thames and Hudson, 1993), 20.

6 Livingstone, *David Hockney*, 163.

7 Livingstone notes that Hockney's print may in part have been inspired by Michel Leiris, "The Artist and His Model," in *Picasso 1881/1973*, ed. Roland Penrose and John Golding (London: Paul Elek, 1973), 243–63; see Livingstone, *David Hockney*, 164. On Hockney's admiration of Picasso, see Gert Schiff, "A Moving Focus: Hockney's Dialogue with Picasso," in *David Hockney: A Retrospective*, ed. Maurice Tuchman and Stephanie Barron (Los Angeles: Los Angeles County Museum of Art; and New York: Harry N. Abrams, 1988), 47. On Hockney's Picasso painting, *Reclining Nude and Man in Profile*, 1965, see also Esterow, "David Hockney's 'Different Ways of Looking,'" 54.

8 On the interpretation of Hockney as Picasso's model see Wechsler, "True to Life," 18; and Livingstone, *David Hockney*, 166; Schiff suggests that Hockney portrayed himself nude to suggest his own baptism in the presence of his "model," Picasso (Schiff, "A Moving Focus," 42).

9 Hockney's engagement with Picasso during the 1980s included delivering lectures on his paintings of the 1960s and purchasing one of his paintings from this period (Schiff, "A Moving Focus," 47).

10 Quoted in Saint-Jean, "David Hockney," 227.

11 Hockney has created many portraits of his parents, both as a pair and individually. In one interesting pair, *My Parents and Myself* (1975) and *My Parents* (1977) Hockney first includes himself in a mirror (in the 1975 painting) and then leaves himself conspicuously absent (in the 1977 version). For interesting remarks on these works and Hockney's depiction of his family, see Henry Geldzahler, "Hockney: Young and Older," in *David Hockney: A Retrospective*, 16.

12 Hockney's quotation is included in Esterow, "David Hockney's 'Different Ways of Looking,'" 55. On the personal significance of the site for Hockney's parents, see Wechsler, "True to Life," 25.

13 According to Henry Geldzahler, Picasso's death and that of his father were intertwined in Hockney's mind (Geldzahler, "Hockney," 15); Wechsler notes that beginning in the fall of 1982, Hockney began including photographs of his feet in his photographic montages, signaling his own embodied presence as a viewer (Wechsler, "True to Life," 23).

14 Wechsler speculates that this empty area may allude to Hockney's mother's consciousness of her own mortality (Wechsler, "True to Life," 25).

15 Quoted in Saint-Jean, "David Hockney," 227; the emphasis is Hockney's.

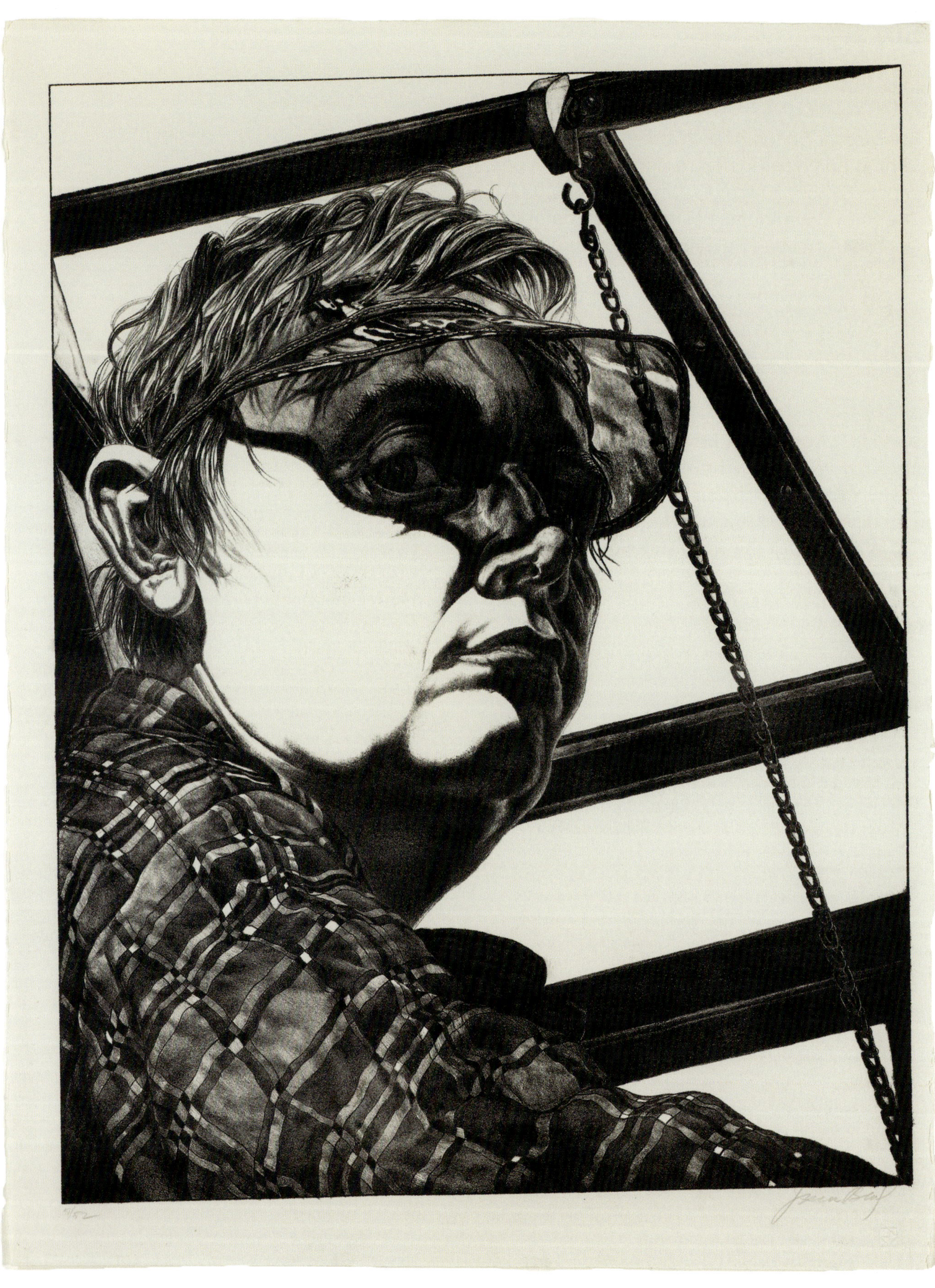

51.

Jack Beal (born 1931)

Lithograph, 76.5 x 56.8 cm (30 1/8 x 22 3/8 in.), 1974
The Ruth Bowman and Harry Kahn Twentieth-Century American Self-Portrait Collection
NPG.2002.198

THE IMPACT OF Jack Beal's piercing gaze in this monumental self-image is daunting. This, the artist explains, is why he feels more comfortable portraying himself: "In other people's portraits I have often felt like a headhunter, robbing the soul and spirit of the sitter. In order to get the intensity I need, I peer relentlessly at the sitters."[1] Beal has obsessively studied the world around him ever since 1962, when, disenchanted by the dominant style of abstract expressionism, he turned to painting from nature.[2] He became one of the few realist artists of the time to paint from life rather than from photographs.[3]

When Beal's realist style won him a commission to paint murals for the United States Department of Labor in 1974, he built a new studio to accommodate the four enormous panels and the many assistants and models required.[4] Apparently he was working in this new space when he noticed the bold geometry of the skylights that would appear in this 1974 lithograph; the portrait, however, records more than a casual glance.

Beal, a master of pictorial composition, sketched himself for this print in a view from below, with the skylights and a hanging chain dramatically framing his head.[5] He noted that in such self-portraits he posed to create "*precise* placement of the light and shade."[6] Thus he shaped the fall of the light so that his visor's shadow visually cut his face diagonally in half and left his eyes intriguingly obscured. In the lithograph, Beal replaced the short-sleeved shirt of the sketch with a long-sleeved plaid whose grid of lines let him model the fabric's surface while compositionally balancing the diagonals of the skylights. As in all his art, his realism was not simple observation of existing reality. As the viewer feels, looking up at the dominating artist, Beal marshaled every element in the image to achieve complete visual control.

APW

Notes

1 Quoted in Eric Shanes, *Jack Beal* (New York: Hudson Hills Press, 1993), 63.
2 Mark Strand, ed., *Art of the Real: Nine American Figurative Painters* (New York: Clarkson N. Potter, 1983), 44–45.
3 On realists of this period, including Jack Beal, see Frank H. Goodyear Jr., *Contemporary American Realism Since 1960* (Boston: New York Graphic Society, in association with the Pennsylvania Academy of the Fine Arts, 1981).
4 Shanes, *Jack Beal*, 50.
5 The sketch, in the collection of Emily S. Alexander, is reproduced as drawing #6 in Joseph Wilfer, *Jack Beal: Prints and Related Drawings* (Madison, WI: Madison Art Center, 1977). Beal observes, "I'm interested in composition—pictorial composition—which is something that I feel has not been stressed in teaching." Quoted in Strand, *Art of the Real*, 48.
6 Quoted in Shanes, *Jack Beal*, 63.

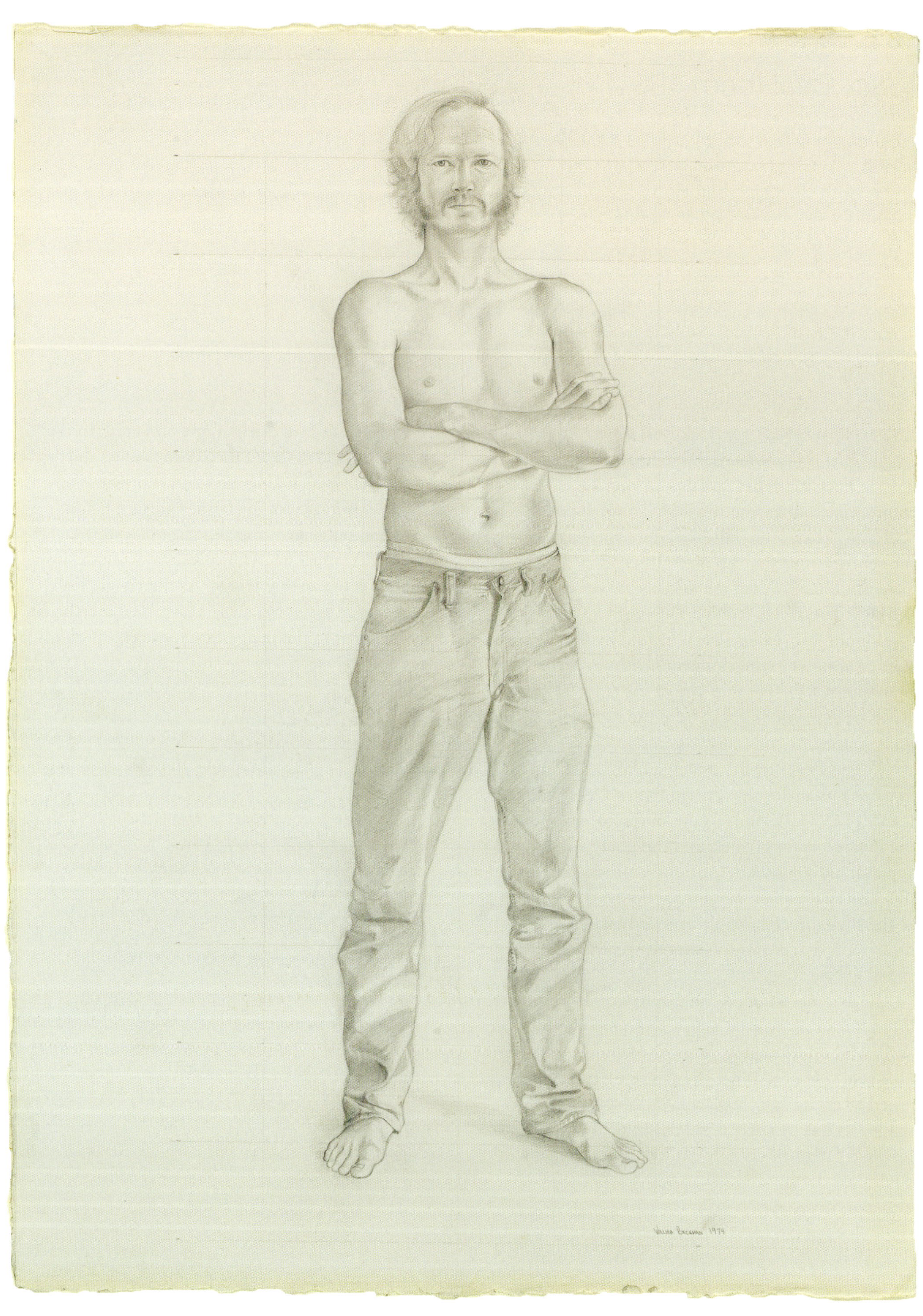
1974

52.

William Beckman (born 1942)

Study for a Self-Portrait
Graphite on paper, 57.2 x 40.9 cm
(22½ x 16⅛ in.), 1974
The Ruth Bowman and Harry Kahn Twentieth-Century American Self-Portrait Collection
S/NPG.2002.201

"I AM NOT A traditional portrait painter," William Beckman insists. "I am not interested in likeness. I am more interested in what feels right to me."[1] The meticulous care that Beckman lavishes upon these dual self-portrait drawings, created twenty-three years apart, may seem startling in light of the artist's pronouncement. But there is no inconsistency. Beckman does not approach portraiture as a tool of flattery. Nor does he care to portray sitters he does not know well. Undaunted by wrinkles, veins, stubble, Beckman turns an exacting eye upon his subjects, directing his gaze beneath the skin to tease out portrayals that project far more than mere physical appearance.[2]

Each of these drawings represents a study for a finished painting. Yet drawing is an act Beckman embraces, noting that from the earliest moments of his career "drawing came naturally to me." While each of the final works places these figures in a distinct setting—one an interior, the other a landscape—the drawings testify to the central importance of the figure for Beckman. The confrontational stance the artist adopts in each work is deliberate, demanding an active response from the viewer. The pose is reinforced by the composition, which provides no space into which the figure of the artist might visually recede. The powerful presence of the figures created by Beckman is accentuated still further by monumental physical scale, particularly in the case of *Overcoats #1* of 1997. This larger-than-life charcoal is nearly the same size as the finished work. The earlier drawing, by contrast, is a good deal smaller than the finished six-foot-tall painting it anticipated. But although the size of the work changes, the sense of scale does not.

In each self-portrait, the artist adopts a posture that creates a tension between distance and intimacy. Reflecting on his interest in portraiture, the artist observes, "I love being all alone. My way of being with someone I like is by painting that person. It gives me company." This dynamic between absence and presence, between imagination and experience extends into his depiction of self. In the 1974 self-portrait, Beckman bares his chest and allows the waist of his jeans to droop, exposing the elastic band of his briefs. Yet his stance, with arms crossed, and intense expression, offers no hint of warmth and imposes psychological distance between this figure and the viewer. In similar fashion, in Beckman's later self-portrait, the artist allows his overcoat to open up, and yet closes himself off by placing his hands in his pocket and a wary expression on his face. The gestures and use of clothing are not arbitrary. As the artist explains, "I tend to include in my paintings [items of] autobiographical significance." Yet the artist does not regard himself as a storyteller and does not intend for all items to be easily deciphered. In the case of the overcoats, however, Beckman, who grew up in the cold climate of Minnesota, provides some insight. He explains that the work "makes reference to Nikolai Gogol's short story of 1842 'The Overcoat,' which I read when I was about nineteen or twenty. . . . Here, the overcoats have to do with exposure to society. A closed coat is about protection and hands in pocket convey a similar message."

Beckman's repeated willingness to return to himself as subject represents not only a formal exercise, but also an act of self-examination. Undeterred by the aging process, Beckman captures his changing countenance with unflagging courage.

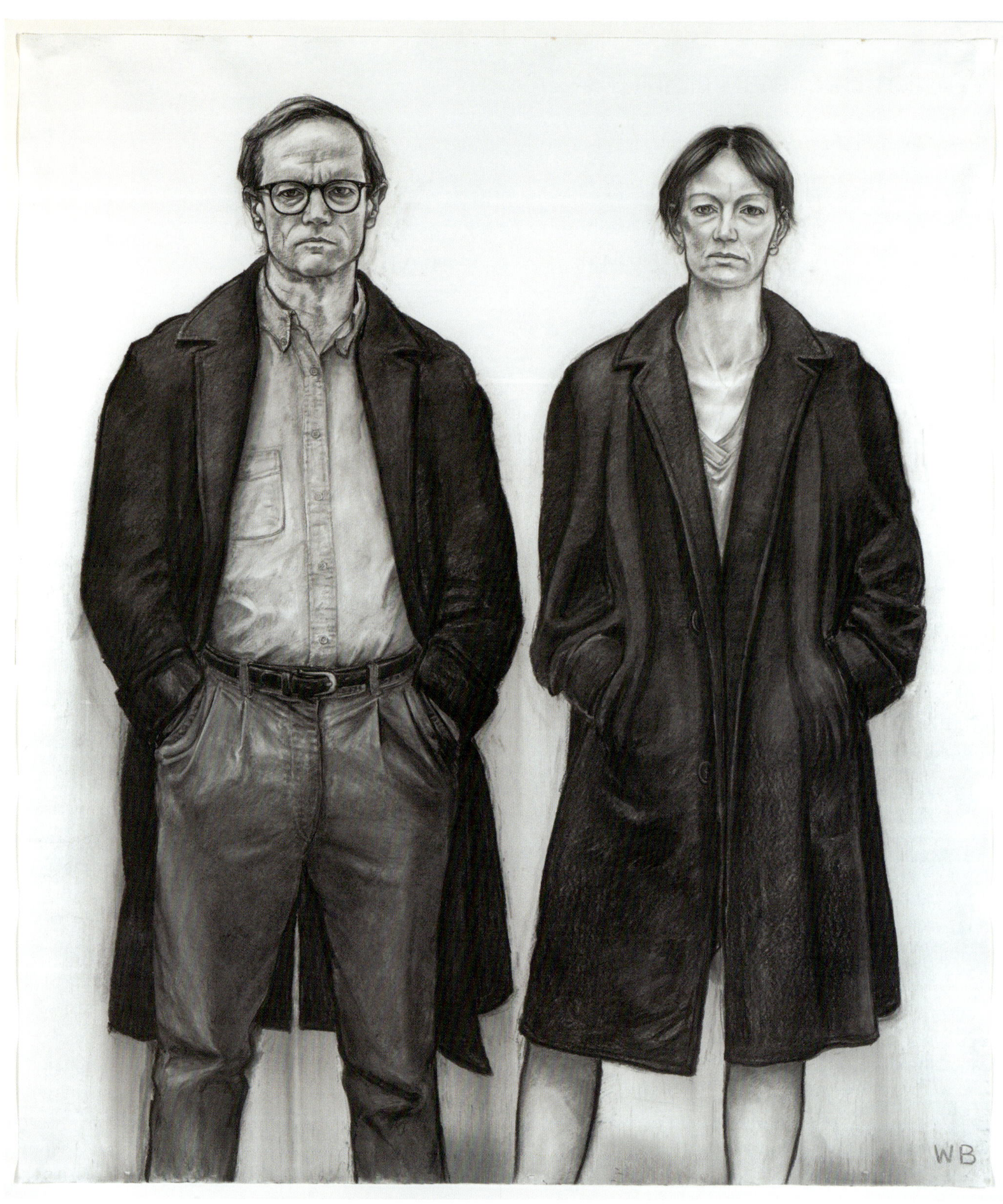
WB

53.

William Beckman (born 1942)

Overcoats #1
Charcoal on paper, 228.6 x 193.7 cm (90 x 76 1/4 in.), 1997
Partial gift of Dr. Thomas Huerter
NPG.2005.162

"This is about survival," the artist says of his use of overcoats. The statement might even apply to the act of self-portrayal.

ACG

Notes

1 All quotations from Beckman included here come from his telephone conversation with the author and Carolyn Kinder Carr, February 21, 2006. For a valuable overview of Beckman's career, see Carl Belz, *William Beckman* (Seattle: Frye Art Museum, 2002; distributed by University of Washington Press, Seattle).

2 Frank H. Goodyear Jr. makes a similar observation regarding Beckman's desire to go beyond likeness in his portraiture; see Goodyear, "William Beckman," in *Seven on the Figure* (Philadelphia: Pennsylvania Academy of the Fine Arts, 1979), 25.

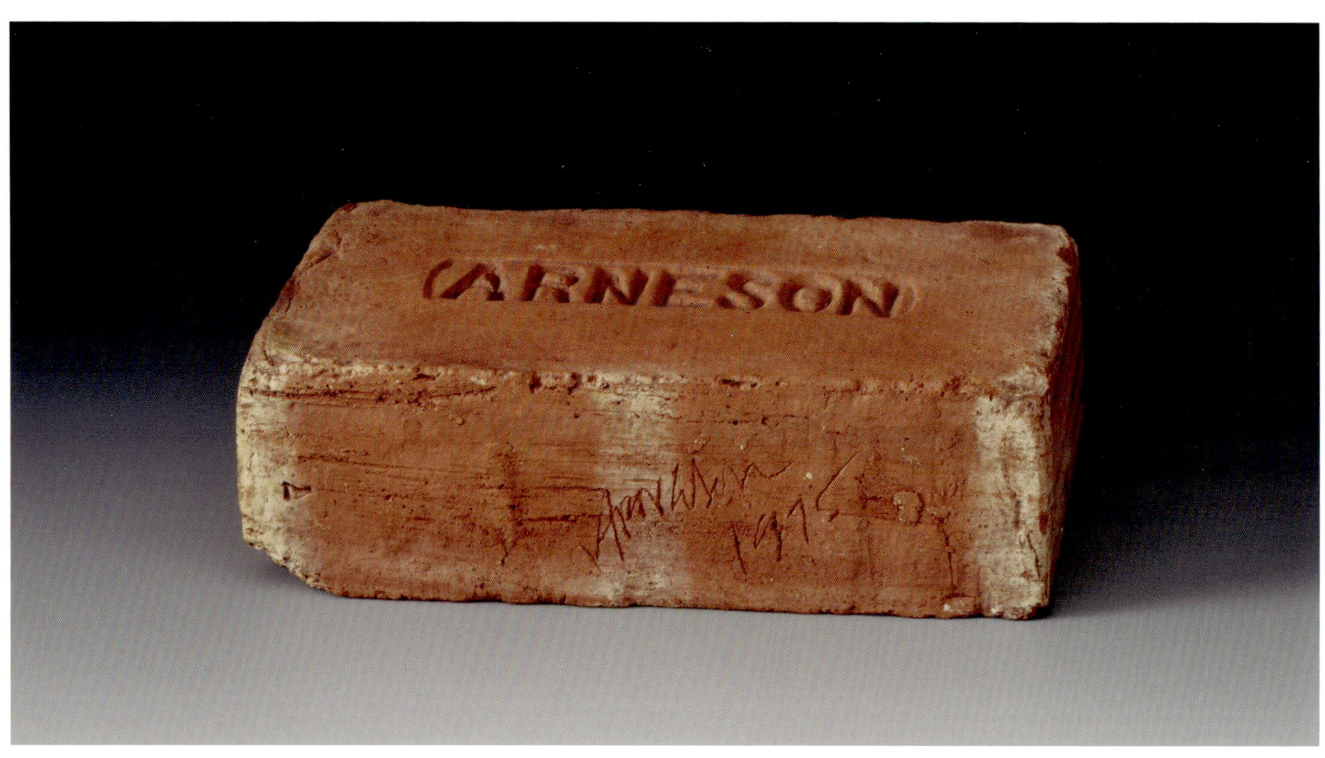
ARNESON

54.

Robert Arneson (1930–1992)

Brick
Terra-cotta, 7 x 22 x 10.8 cm
(2 3/4 x 8 11/16 x 4 1/4 in.), 1975
The Ruth Bowman and Harry Kahn Twentieth-Century American Self-Portrait Collection
NPG.2002.191

WELL KNOWN FOR his ceramic sculptures and his numerous self-portraits, Robert Arneson tests the boundaries of self-representation, and even those of art itself, with his 1975 *Brick* and *California Brick*, which pare down identification to an elemental unit. As though responding to this reductiveness, Jack Lemon of Landfall Press—where Robert Arneson executed the works as part of his *Brick Suite*, consisting of five prints and the terra-cotta brick—remarked: "The reason we did the brick project was that the brick has been a part of [Robert] Arneson's work. . . . Actually, the three-dimensional brick is the main object in the suite and the prints are portraits of the brick."[1]

As Lemon suggests, the brick itself invites identification with Arneson, who employed the device in several self-portraits.[2] Indeed, here the brick functions as a self-representation in its own right. In this case, the nature of Arneson's self-portrayal is not iconic, but metonymic and indexical, reflecting his touch. In other words, the brick does not picture the artist, but instead refers to him symbolically: associatively through his use of it in other artworks (including, as noted above, self-depictions) and physically through the act of stamping his name on its top and inscribing his signature on its side. Yet should this act of transforming what might be read as an ordinarily utilitarian object into a self-portrait seem pretentious, Arneson cuts the brick down to size in the accompanying etching.

California Brick, the title of which bears a clear reference to Arneson's West Coast roots, expresses a poignant tension.[3] Broken into two parts and seemingly torn away from the wall behind it, the brick seems the victim of a recent and sudden apocalyptic force that has also left a fragmented cigar, still smoking, in its wake. The fissure dividing the brick might refer to the fault lines of Southern California and resulting earthquakes. But other interpretations are possible. Playfully irreverent, Arneson understood the freedom that comes from the breakdown of materials and their transformation into something else. In 1965, the splitting in the kiln of a traditional self-portrait bust inspired an unforeseen result: *Self-Portrait of the Artist Losing his Marbles*.[4] But in addition to the liberation that such accidents produce, the work may also have reflected darker concerns. In February 1975, after suddenly hemorrhaging, Arneson was diagnosed with bladder cancer, an illness that would plague him for the remainder of his career.[5]

Yet if Arneson's *California Brick* reflects the impact of an uncontrollable, and perhaps invisible, force, the fragments seem to survive, as does the intact brick that inspired it, stamped with the artist's name and inscribed with his signature. "I like to do portraits if they project an attitude," Arneson remarked.[6] Defiant in their posture, this pair of self-portraits launches a persistent challenge to the assaults of nature and the force of convention.

ACG

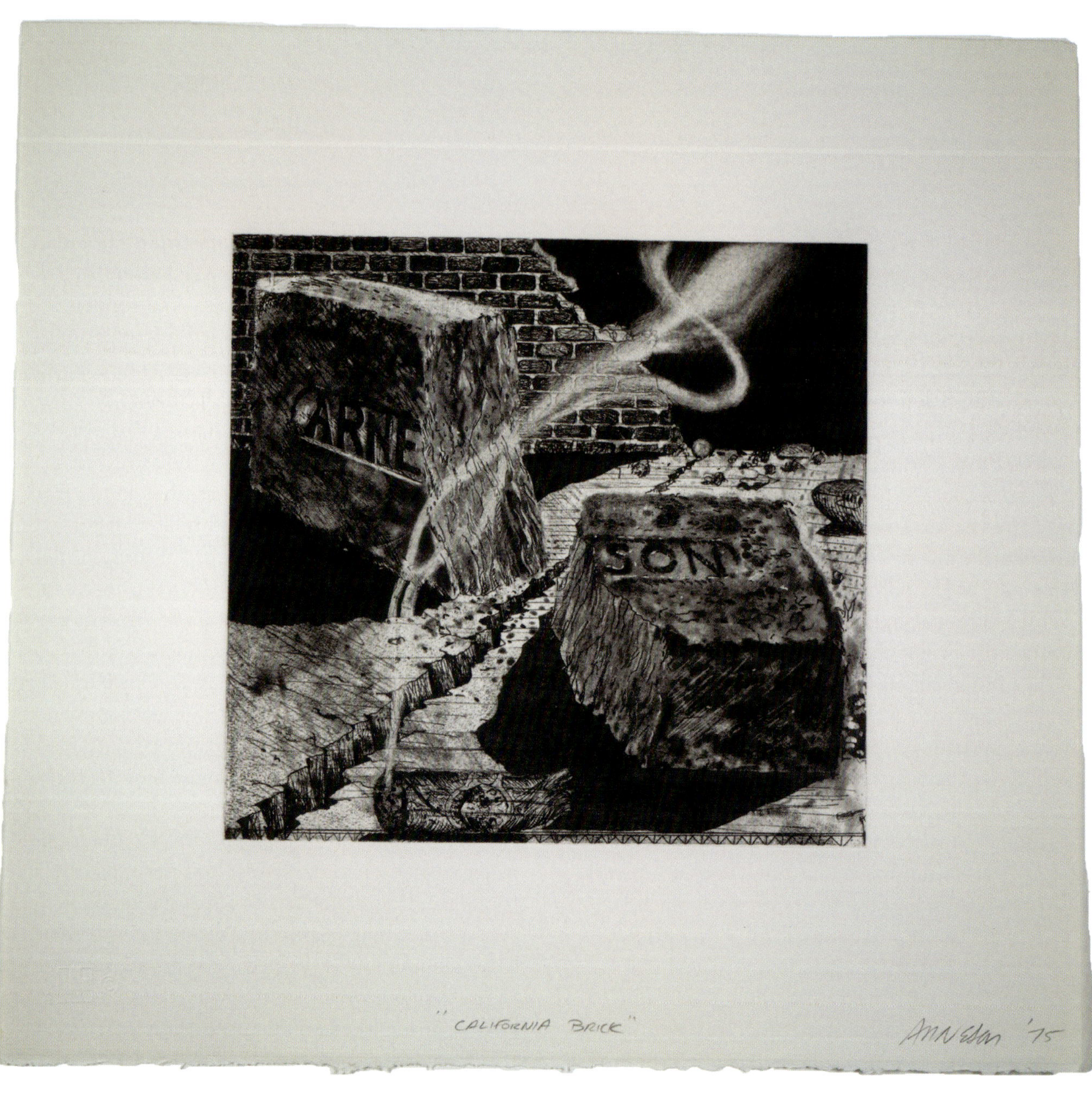
ARNE
SON
"CALIFORNIA BRICK"
'75

55.

Robert Arneson (1930–1992)

California Brick
Etching, 40.7 x 42 cm (16 x 16 9/16 in.), 1975
The Ruth Bowman and Harry Kahn Twentieth-Century American Self-Portrait Collection
NPG.2002.190

Notes

1 Quoted in Joseph Ruzicka, "Landfall Press: Twenty-Five Years," in *Landfall Press: Twenty-Five Years of Printmaking* (Milwaukee: Milwaukee Art Museum, 1996), 82 n. 44.

2 Examples of these include his *Kiln Man* (1971), *Fragment of Western Civilization* (1972), *Balancing Act* (1974), and *Temple of Fatal Laffs* (1989).

3 In 1982, Arneson would create a self-portrait entitled *California Artist.*

4 Jonathan Fineberg, "Humor at the Frontier of the Self," *Robert Arneson: Self-Reflections* (San Francisco: San Francisco Museum of Modern Art, 1997), 12.

5 Ibid., 16.

6 Quoted by Joanne Silver, "Visual Arts: A Head for Attitude, Sculptor Robert Arneson Stayed Acutely Insightful to the Very End," *Boston Herald*, August 27, 1999, S05.

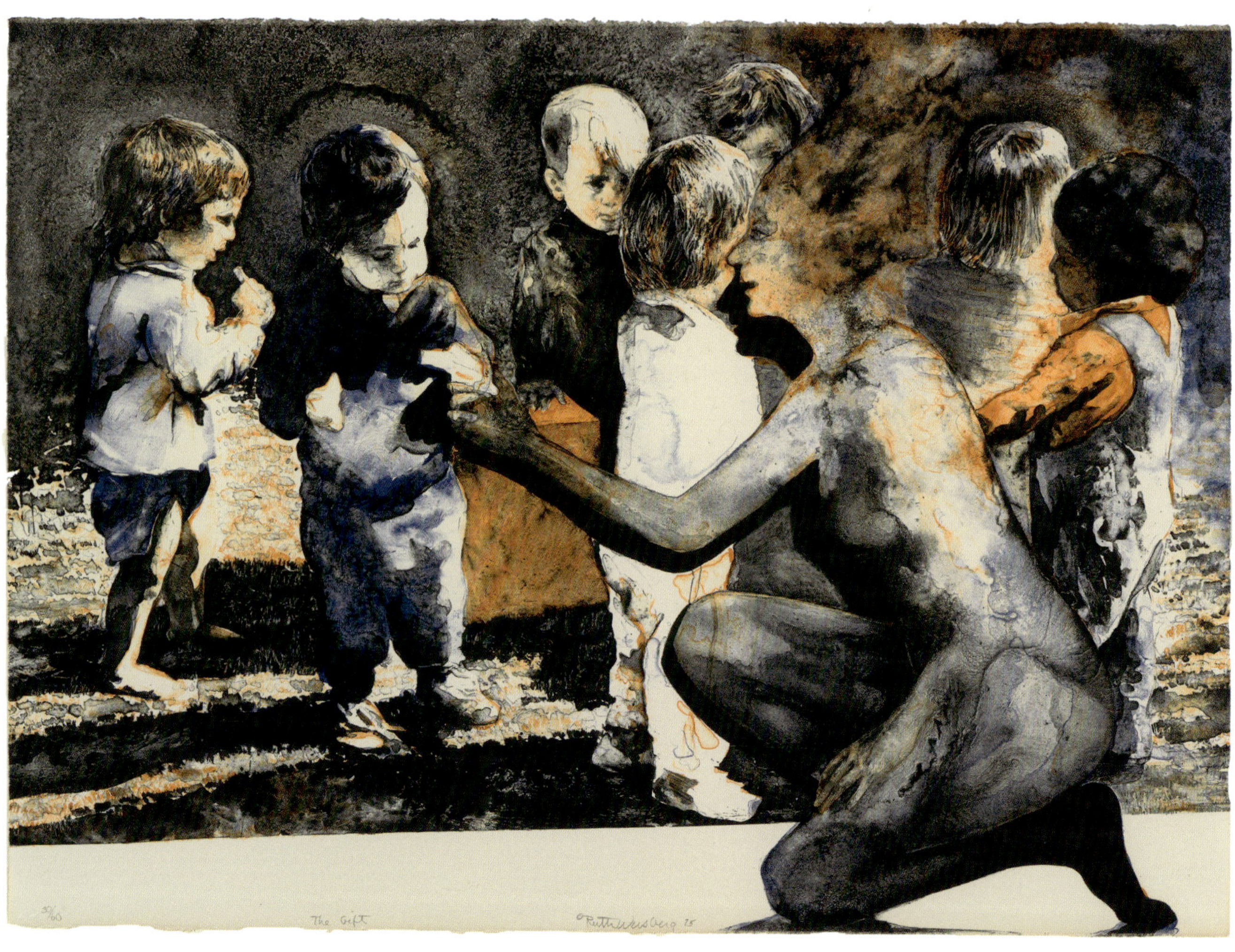
The Gift

56.

Ruth Weisberg (born 1942)

The Gift
Color lithograph, 57.2 x 76.4 cm
(22 1/2 x 30 1/16 in.), 1975
The Ruth Bowman and Harry Kahn Twentieth-Century American Self-Portrait Collection
S/NPG.2002.364

RUTH WEISBERG, a much-honored teacher and dean at the University of Southern California, infuses her paintings and prints with autobiographical reference. But as one colleague has pointed out, Weisberg also "functions as Everywoman, who plays the role of guide to our memories, dreams, fears and aspirations."[1]

Weisberg's concern for the human condition is implicit in this lithograph, derived from photographs and videos of a 1975 performance piece, also entitled *The Gift*. Dressed in a black leotard, she danced on a stage in front of a video of a toddler's birthday party, which included her own young daughter.[2] Women's roles and family relationships are consistent themes in Weisberg's work. The gift of the title is mutual: her gift of life to her child is returned with the many benefits of parenthood. But as she reaches out to the children, one senses the bittersweet implication that her attempt at affectionate connection is futile. The mother will never touch the child of the film who frolics behind her in such proximity.

In her translation of these themes into a lithograph, Weisberg uses the puddles, drips, and splashes of liquid lithographic tusche to convey a sense of layered, ambiguous space. Very intentional in her choice of medium, she claims that her inspiration is "often embedded in an idea of materiality." The articulation and sedimentation of the ink appealed to her: "tusche washes are not just veils of color," she notes. "They are texture and color merged into one." For this print, the flowing quality of the medium substituted for the motion of the dance. "I often think of my lithographs as arrested movements," Weisberg has said, "both in terms of the poses of the figures and how the medium is used."[3] Although the relationship between figure and background is ambiguous, the print still implies a haunting sense of generational disconnection.

WWR

Notes

1 Ann Sutherland Harris, "Preface," *Ruth Weisberg: A Circle of Life* (Los Angeles: Fisher Gallery, University of California, 1986), 8.

2 Interview between Aurora Stokowski and Ruth Weisberg, October 22, 2003, notes from National Portrait Gallery object file.

3 *Ruth Weisberg Prints: Mid-Life Catalogue Raisonné, 1961–1990* (Fresno, CA: Fresno Museum of Art, 1990), 9–10.

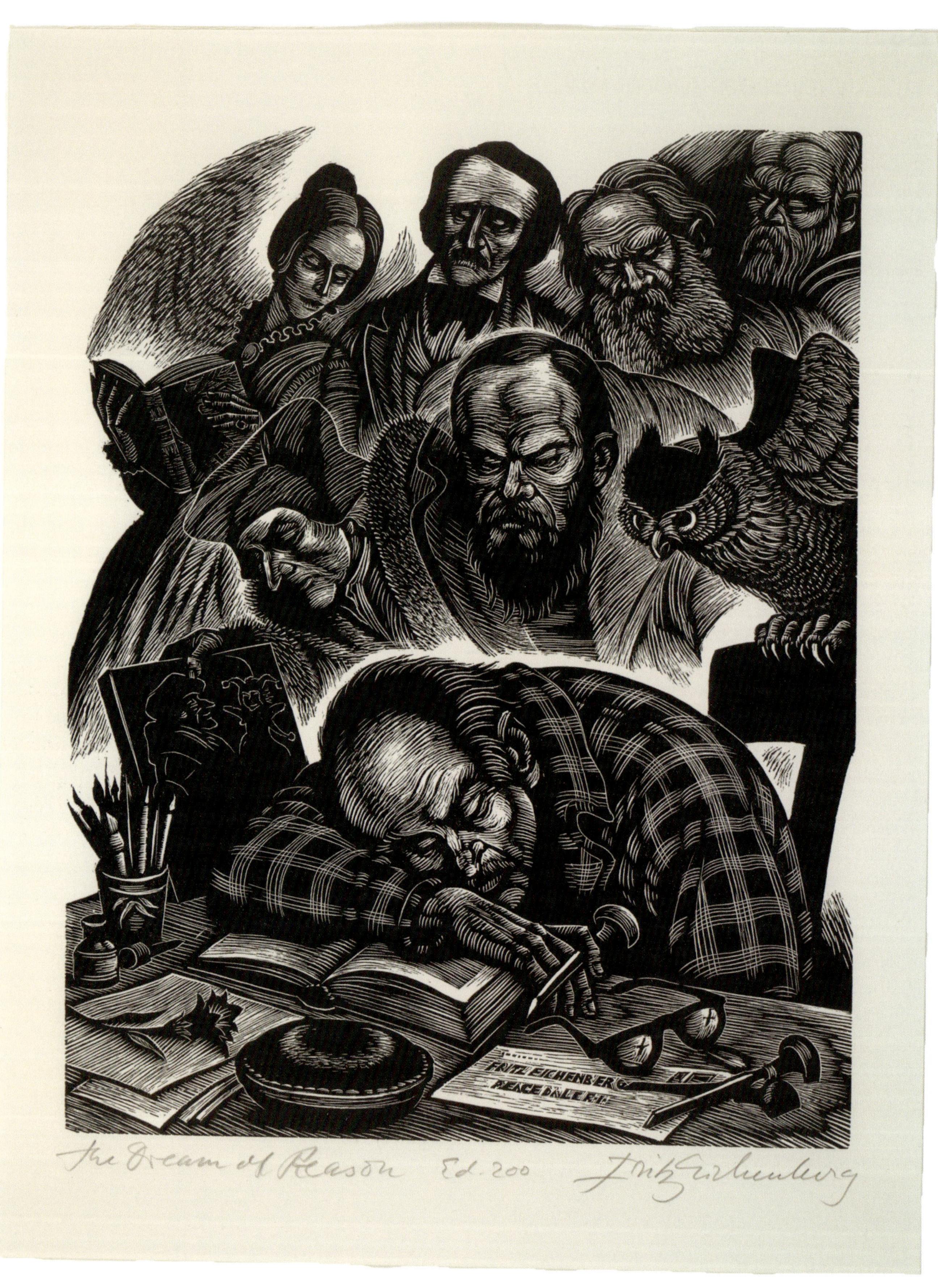
The Dream of Reason
Ed. 200
Fritz Eichenberg

57.

Fritz Eichenberg (1901–1990)

The Dream of Reason
Charlotte Brontë (1816–1855) or Emily Brontë (1818–1848), Edgar Allan Poe (1809–1849), Fëdor Dostoevski (1821–1881), Lao Tzu (c. 6th century BC), Leo Tolstoy (1828–1910), Desiderius Erasmus (c. 1466–1536), Fritz Eichenberg (1901–1990)
Wood engraving, 27.9 x 20.9 cm (11 x 8¼ in.), 1976
The Ruth Bowman and Harry Kahn Twentieth-Century American Self-Portrait Collection
NPG.2002.242

IN *THE DREAM OF REASON* Fritz Eichenberg cast his self-portrait as an allegory of the process of creating illustrations.[1] The artist began illustrating books when he was a student at the Academy of Graphic Arts in Leipzig, in his native Germany. After moving with his family to the United States in 1933, Eichenberg became a respected art teacher and illustrator. For more than fifty years he crafted insightful visual interpretations of immortal literary works from around the world, including many volumes by the authors pictured in this print.[2]

Eichenberg's *The Dream of Reason* makes a witty play on Spanish artist Francisco Goya's famous print *The Sleep of Reason Produces Monsters*.[3] Goya's image, featured in a portfolio decrying the abuses of Bourbon rule in eighteenth-century Spain, shows the sleeping artist haunted by the fearful night creatures that arise when the control of reason relaxes.[4] Eichenberg, in contrast, has closed his eyes to aid his creative enterprise. After steeping himself in the book he is illustrating, and performing his customary careful research, the artist puts aside his glasses—and thus his external vision.

Supported by the author's text, and keeping his burin and pens at hand, Eichenberg lets his imagination take over. The wisdom found in dreams appears as an owl, the same bird that in Goya's print embodies the terrors of the night. The figures of American, European, and Asian authors long dead appear above Eichenberg, their eyes closed as they lean toward the artist. The translucent Erasmus bridges the gap of centuries to pick up a wood block engraved with his own image.[5] Among the papers and tools, near the book and the sandbag that supports the block during engraving, a blossom appears. This detail may poetically suggest how the mind flowers when great illustration helps to connect reader to author.

APW

Notes

1 The artist identifies himself by including a letter addressed to himself at his home in Peace Dale, Rhode Island. *The Dream of Reason* appeared as the frontispiece to Fritz Eichenberg, *The Wood and the Graver: The Work of Fritz Eichenberg* (New York: Clarkson N. Potter, 1977).

2 Eichenberg taught at the University of Rhode Island and the Pratt Institute in Brooklyn. See Eichenberg, *The Wood and the Graver*, 199; Fritz Eichenberg oral history interview by Harlan Phillips, December 3, 1964, Archives of American Art, Smithsonian Institution, Washington, DC; and Fritz Eichenberg oral history interview by Robert Brown, May 14 and December 7, 1979, Archives of American Art. Eichenberg illustrated complete books by and/or created portfolios inspired by all of the authors shown in this print except Lao Tzu, of whom he created a single print in 1966. For a complete list of illustrations by Eichenberg, see Curt Visel, *Fritz Eichenberg: Werkkatalog der illustrierten Bücher, 1922–1987* (Memmingen, Germany: Edition C. Visel, 1987).

3 Eichenberg called Francisco Goya (1846–1828) "a colossus whose genius seized upon the issues of violent change, of revolution, war, and barbarity to create memorable prints that still speak powerfully to our time." Fritz Eichenberg, *The Art of the Print* (New York: Harry N. Abrams, 1976), 219, 222.

4 Goya's etching and aquatint, titled in the original Spanish *El sueño de la razon produce monstruos*, appeared as plate 43 in the portfolio *Los Caprichos*, first published in 1799. Alfonso E. Pérez Sánchez and Eleanor A. Sayre, *Goya and the Spirit of Enlightenment* (Boston, Madrid, and New York: Museum of Fine Arts, Boston, 1989), 110–17.

5 The image shown on the block is based upon the print *Dame Folly Speaks* from Eichenberg's portfolio, *In Praise of Folly by Desiderius Erasmus* (Baltimore: Aquarius Press, 1972), inspired by Erasmus's book of the same title.

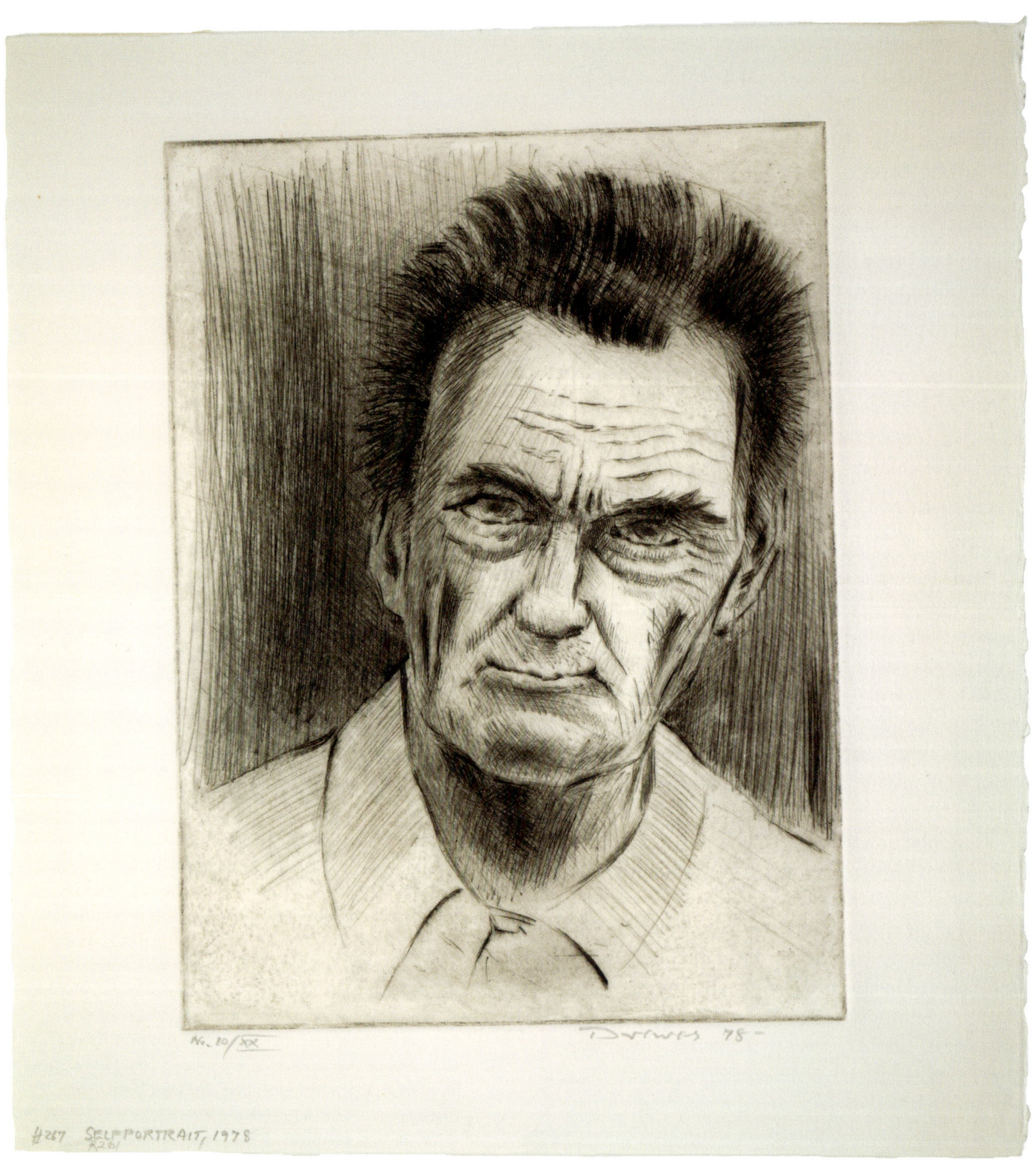

58.

Werner Drewes (1899–1985)

Drypoint, 38 x 34.4 cm (14 15/16 x 13 9/16 in.), 1978
The Ruth Bowman and Harry Kahn Twentieth-Century American Self-Portrait Collection
S/NPG.2002.238

THE VIGOROUS strokes Werner Drewes scratched into a copper plate to make this print reveal a man full of creative energy. In 1965 he had retired after teaching for nineteen years at the School of Fine Arts at Washington University in St. Louis, but his art-making did not slacken. In 1978, the year he made this portrait, Drewes made prints, painted, and toured Germany. His fellow artist Arthur Osver wrote admiringly to Drewes, "All that industry and drive—that zest for work, travel and painting. . . . Bravo!"[1]

Drewes thrived on art and travel. In 1921 and 1922 the German-born artist studied at the Bauhaus in Weimar. Longing to study the old masters and to paint, he "ran away and went across the Alps to Italy."[2] Drewes made prints as he traveled around Spain, South America, and the United States, before his 1927 return to the Bauhaus. After settling in the United States in 1930, Drewes taught art in New York, Chicago, and St. Louis, often leaving to visit Europe, Mexico, and distant parts of the United States.

When Drewes made this drypoint in 1978, he lived in Reston, Virginia, near Washington, D.C. There he devoted himself to colorful abstract paintings and woodcuts. He also depicted landscapes and made portraits of friends. Self-portraits were rare in his early and mid-career work, but beginning in 1969 he thoughtfully portrayed his wrinkled face in intaglio or woodcut about once a year.[3] He may have intended to study the aging process, or perhaps he was merely fascinated by his own rugged features. Despite the undiminished strength of this 1978 image with its networks of lively drypoint lines, it was the artist's last self-portrait print. Problems with his hands and arms slowed his art in 1979,[4] but Drewes continued working until days before his death in 1985.[5]

APW

Notes

1. Letter from Arthur and Ernestine Osver to Werner and Maria Drewes, March 27, 1978, Werner Drewes Papers, 1924–1984, Archives of American Art, Smithsonian Institution, Washington, DC. For details of Drewes's graphic works and his life, see Ingrid Rose, *Werner Drewes: A Catalogue Raisonné of His Prints*, ed. Ralph Jentsch (Munich and New York: Verlag Kunstgalerie Esslingen, 1984).
2. Quoted in Martina Roudabush Norelli, "A Conversation with Werner Drewes," *Werner Drewes: Sixty-Five Years of Printmaking* (Washington, DC: Smithsonian Institution Press for the National Museum of American Art, 1984), 14.
3. Rose, *Werner Drewes Catalogue Raisonné.*
4. Letters from Arthur and Ernestine Osver to Werner and Maria Drewes, January 17 and April 4, 1979, Werner Drewes Papers, 1924–1984, Archives of American Art.
5. Exhibition announcement, *Werner Drewes: Paintings and Works on Paper, 1930s through 1980s* (Los Angeles: Tobey C. Moss Gallery, 2006).

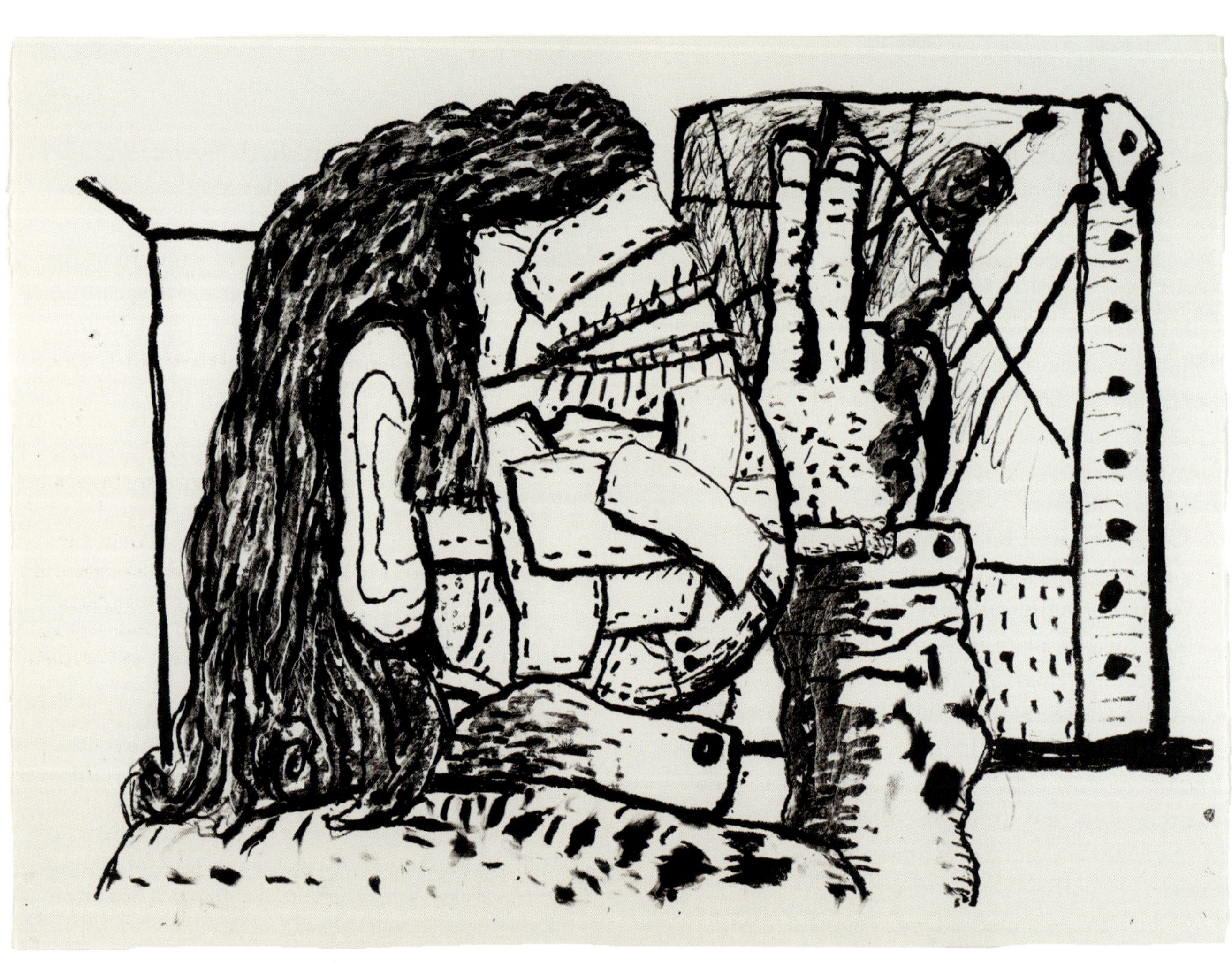

59.

Philip Guston (1913–1980)

Painter
Lithograph, 81.4 x 108.3 cm (32 1/16 x 42 5/8 in.), 1979
The Ruth Bowman and Harry Kahn Twentieth-Century American Self-Portrait Collection
NPG.2002.261

PHILIP GUSTON created his lithographic self-portrait, *Painter*, in the final year of his life. He had suffered a heart attack in 1979, and would be killed by another in 1980. By that time, he had been producing haunting self-portraits for years. Their cartoonish appearance hearkened back to Guston's youth, when, in the aftermath of his father's suicide, his mother bought him a correspondence course in cartooning.[1] He started his career as a figurative painter, producing murals in the United States and Mexico in the 1930s, and easel painting in the 1940s.[2] In the 1950s Guston rose to prominence as one of the foremost abstract expressionist painters,[3] but returned to figuration in the 1960s, when "[t]he war, what was happening to America, the brutality of the world" made him "sick and tired of all that Purity!" that abstract painting implied.[4]

In the year of this self-portrait, illness affected Guston's works, and these late pieces often confronted mortality.[5] *Painter* seems to illustrate a reference he made, the previous year, to his work as a "battle . . . with dozens of brushes as weapons."[6] Here, his battle-scarred and bandaged face with its Cyclopean eye (a common self-depiction of the 1970s) stares out at his right hand.[7] The multivalent pose could suggest his cigarette smoking, a benediction, or the artist's meditation on his future ability to produce art. Such arduous self-reflection characterized Guston's career, which author Nicole Krauss called "an unflinching journey towards the most unflinching expression of self."[8]

Guston once said, "The canvas you are working on modifies all previous ones in an unending baffling chain which never seems to finish. For me the most relevant question and perhaps the only one is, 'When are you finished?' When do you stop? Or rather why stop at all?'"[9] *Painter* attests to that determination, even in the face of Guston's physical decline.

ECR

Notes

1 Janis Ekdahl, "Chronology," in Robert Storr, *Philip Guston* (New York: Abbeville Press, 1986), 115–17.
2 In the 1940s Guston began a lifelong career as a teacher in colleges and universities. See Ross Feld, "Philip Guston," in *Philip Guston* (San Francisco: San Francisco Museum of Modern Art, 1980), 13.
3 Michael Kimmelman writes, "After de Kooning, he had been, during the 1950s and 60s, probably the most imitated Abstract Expressionist for his tremulous, watery fields of small, brightly colored brushstrokes." Kimmelman, "Anxious Liberator of an Era's Demons," *New York Times*, October 31, 2003, E37.
4 William Berkson, "The New Gustons," *ARTnews* 69 (October 1970): 44; quoted in Storr, *Philip Guston,* 52–53. See also John Yau, "The Phoenix of the Self," *Artforum* 27 (April 1989): 149.
5 Storr, *Philip Guston,* 91. For additional information on the later years of Guston's life, see Kim Sichel and Mary Drach McInnes, *Philip Guston, 1975–1980: Private and Public Battles* (Boston: Boston University Art Gallery; Seattle: University of Washington Press, 1994).
6 Ross Feld, "Guston in Time," *Arts Magazine* 63 (November 1988): 43.
7 *Painting* is one of a series of prints the artist produced in collaboration with Gemini Graphic Editions Limited (G.E.L.) in Los Angeles during the final year of his life. Gemini G.E.L. ultimately published a catalog with text by John Coplans.
8 Nicole Krauss, "The First Painter after the Last," *Modern Painters* 16 (Winter 2003): 86. Guston remarked, "People, you know, complain that it's horrifying. . . . But what's the alternative? I'm trying to see how much I can stand." Feld, "Philip Guston," 29.
9 Philip Guston, "Faith, Hope and Impossibility," *XXXI ARTnews Annual 1966* (October 1965): 101; quoted in Storr, *Philip Guston,* 99.

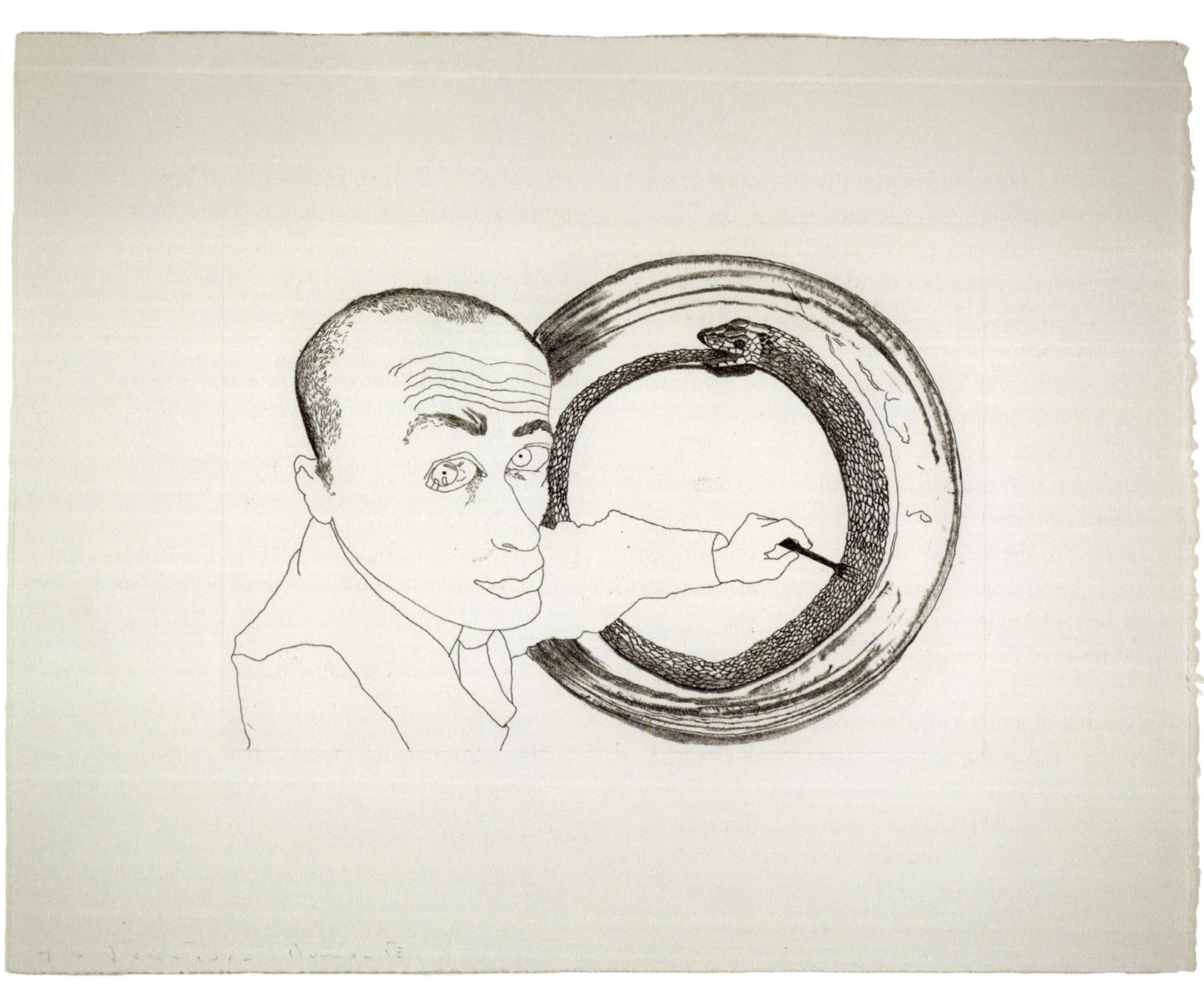

60.

Francesco Clemente (born 1952)

Self-Portrait #4 (Snake)
Etching, 41.1 x 51.6 cm (16³/₁₆ x 20⁵/₁₆ in.), 1981
The Ruth Bowman and Harry Kahn Twentieth-Century American Self-Portrait Collection
S/NPG.2002.229

INTENSELY MYSTICAL, Francesco Clemente's 1981 self-portrait etching invites us to meditate on the work's provocative serpentine imagery. As is common with the work of this Italian-born artist, who divides his time between Rome, Madras, and New York, the viewer encounters not a literal truth, but instead a symbolic order. As Clemente has explained,

> That was one of the earliest strategies of the work, to give the same weight to what's interior and what's exterior, and to consider the body as the line dividing the exterior from the interior. The line of the drawing is a continuation of the line of the body, and what's inside you overflows to the outside, and what's outside flows inside. What is outside of you has an emotional valency [*sic*], and what's inside you has objective valency also.[1]

The artist seems to address himself quite directly to his audience, looking intently at the spectator and presenting himself, formally dressed, with a tie at his neck. As Clemente engages the viewer, he simultaneously probes, with a fork, an image of the Ouroboros, or the snake biting its own tail. Replete with symbolic significance across many cultures, the form conveys notions of infinity and spiritual rebirth that are consistent with Clemente's own view of the risks and challenges of self-portraiture, providing a powerful metaphor for the very act of self-representation:

> If the face is a mask—no, a persona—that means the face reminds you of what is constant in your consciousness, but also reminds you of what is not constant. It reminds you of the fact that you keep dying and being born, again and again and again. The consciousness of the self is not always there. It comes up in flashes. To meditate on your face means to meditate on this continuous transition we all go through, which we are not aware of, or we dislike being aware of, because it's frightening.[2]

ACG

Notes

1 Vincent Katz, "Interview with Francesco Clemente," in Vincent Katz, *Life Is Paradise: The Portraits of Francesco Clemente* (New York: PowerHouse Books, 1999), 174.

2 Ibid.

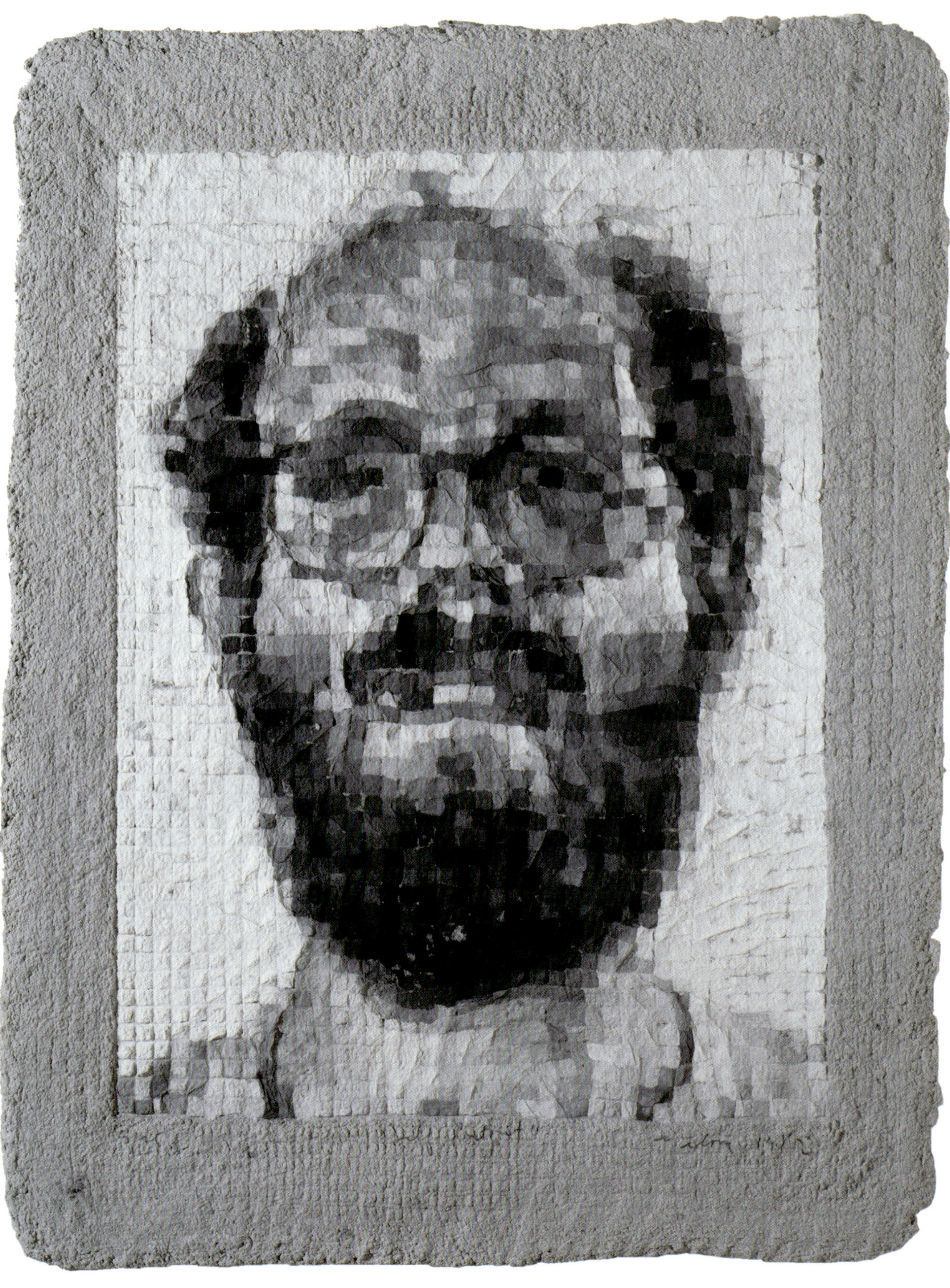

61.

Chuck Close (born 1940)

Self-Portrait/Manipulated
Handmade toned-paper pulp cast on grid,
97.8 x 73 cm (38½ x 28¼ in.), 1982
The Ruth Bowman and Harry Kahn Twentieth-Century American Self-Portrait Collection
NPG.2002.230

SINCE THE LATE 1960s, Chuck Close's monumental heads, dissolving into separate patches and then coalescing into Brobdingnagian mug shots, have been transforming notions of portraiture, and he has returned to self-portraiture regularly. *Self-Portrait/Manipulated* is part of a series of handmade paper multiples he started in the early 1980s, in collaboration with master printer Joseph Wilfer. Following Close's color-coded drawing, Wilfer squeezed liquefied rag pulp in twenty-two different shades of black, gray, and white into the sections of a plastic grid. After the grid was removed, the liquid pulp dried, bonding to the thick handmade background paper.[1] This piece, like much of Close's grid-inspired art, creates a perceptual tension between individual units and the unified whole.

Different approaches to drying and finishing the handmade multiples changed their effect. In *Self-Portrait/Manipulated*, the pulp was still wet when the grid was removed. By pushing through the pulp with his fingers, Close softened the rigidity of the grid structure. And instead of flattening the paper under weights, he let it air-dry naturally, creating a rough, almost organic, three-dimensional texture. The result is a highly animated surface that seems to move before one's eyes. Although he based the picture on the same 1975 photograph that has been the source for other portraits, Close has personalized it with hands-on mark-making and literal fingerprints.

"I was just trying to paint anonymous people," Close has said about his portraits of himself and his friends.[2] But a self-portrait can never seem anonymous to the viewer, no matter how bland the expression. Close, restlessly innovative and experimental, tells us something new in each self-portrait. The exuberant, handcrafted surface of this picture contributes more to our understanding of the artist than the blurred features of his face.

WWR

Notes

1 Richard Solomon, introduction to *Chuck Close Handmade Paper Editions* (New York: Pace Editions, 1982), unpaginated; Lisa Lyons and Robert Storr, *Chuck Close* (New York: Rizzoli, 1987), 35; *Chuck Close Editions: A Catalogue Raisonné and Exhibition* (Youngstown, OH: Butler Institute of American Art, 1989), unpaginated, no. 31; Siri Engberg and Madeleine Grynsztejn, eds., *Chuck Close: Self-Portraits, 1967–2005* (San Francisco and Minneapolis: San Francisco Museum of Modern Art and Walker Art Center, 2005), 124–25.

2 "Close Encounters," *Artforum* 36 (April 1998): 92.

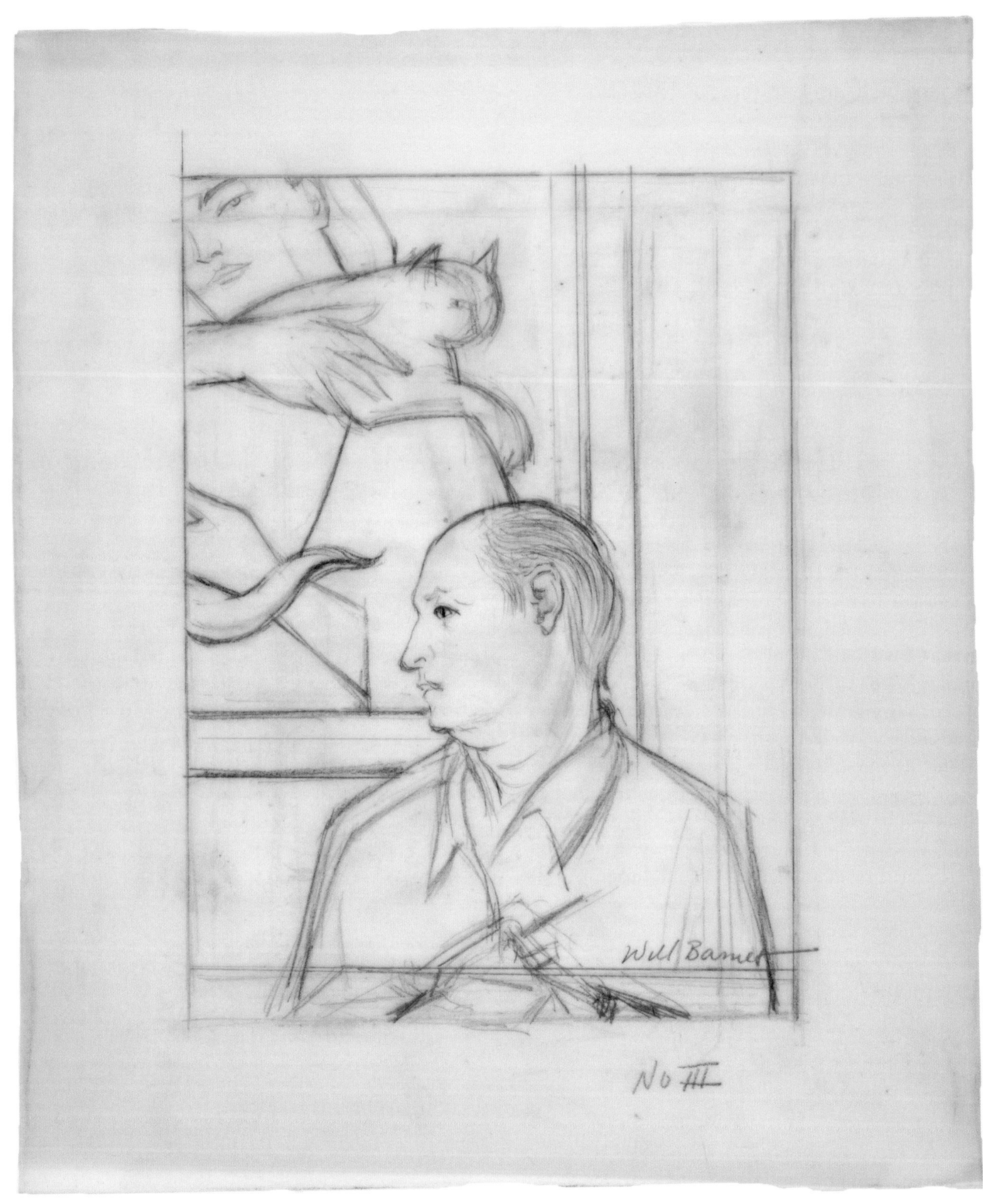
Will Barnet
No III

62.

Will Barnet (born 1911)

Self-Portrait with Elena and Cat
Graphite on paper, 30 x 24.6 cm
(11 13/16 x 9 11/16 in.), c. 1982–83
The Ruth Bowman and Harry Kahn Twentieth-Century American Self-Portrait Collection
NPG.2002.196

WILL BARNET'S family and the quiet scenes of his domestic life proved an inspiration throughout his career. "If Vermeer can take the corner of a room and make a work of art out of it," he once commented about his apolitical subjects, "why bother to run around painting lynching scenes and coal miners?"[1] Here he sketches himself in front of a painting of his wife Elena. Barnet had been working in an abstract style for more than a decade when he returned in the early 1960s to out-of-fashion figurative art. His 1966 image of Elena, titled *Woman and White Cat*, was one such subject. The family cat frequently appeared in his work as an echo of the female form.[2]

"Portrait painting," Grace Glueck reported in a 1968 *New York Times* review, "not exactly today's most swinging genre, is cleverly practiced by Mr. Barnet, whose big, flat posterish forms evoke his earlier work as a hard-edge abstractionist."[3] The artist admitted that the same considerations that impelled him to work abstractly were still present, "so that a portrait, while remaining a portrait, becomes . . . an abstraction: the *idea* of a person in its most intense and essential aspect."[4]

In this drawing, one can see Barnet refining the abstract qualities that he brought to portraiture. He posed his frontal torso and profiled head on a plane as flat as the two-dimensional painting behind him and, with a characteristic spareness, established a compositional structure enlivened by what he called "deeply felt, life-affirming horizontal and vertical forces."[5] In a large charcoal and in the finished painting of this same image,[6] he made the hand and brush horizontal and straightened the head, which here seems tilted back. Despite his emotionless expression, which becomes even more remote in the painting, Barnet implies through the compositional structure of the image his deep connection to his wife.

WWR

Notes

1 Paul Cummings, interview with Will Barnet, January 15, 1968, Archives of American Art, Smithsonian Institution, 31; quoted in Gail Stavitsky, *Will Barnet: A Timeless World* (Montclair, NJ: Montclair Art Museum; distributed by Rutgers University Press, 2000), 15.
2 Robert Doty, *Will Barnet* (New York: Harry N. Abrams, 1984), 9, 101.
3 Grace Glueck, "New Portraits by Will Barnet," *New York Times*, February 10, 1968, 28.
4 "Will Barnet's Abstract Portraits," *Arts Magazine* 40 (April 1966): 48.
5 Stavitsky, *Will Barnet*, 19.
6 For drawing, see Johanna Garfield, "Will Barnet and the Family," *American Art* 9 (Spring 1995): 112; for painting see *Will Barnet at Kennedy Galleries* (New York: Kennedy Galleries, 1984), unpaginated (fig. 5).

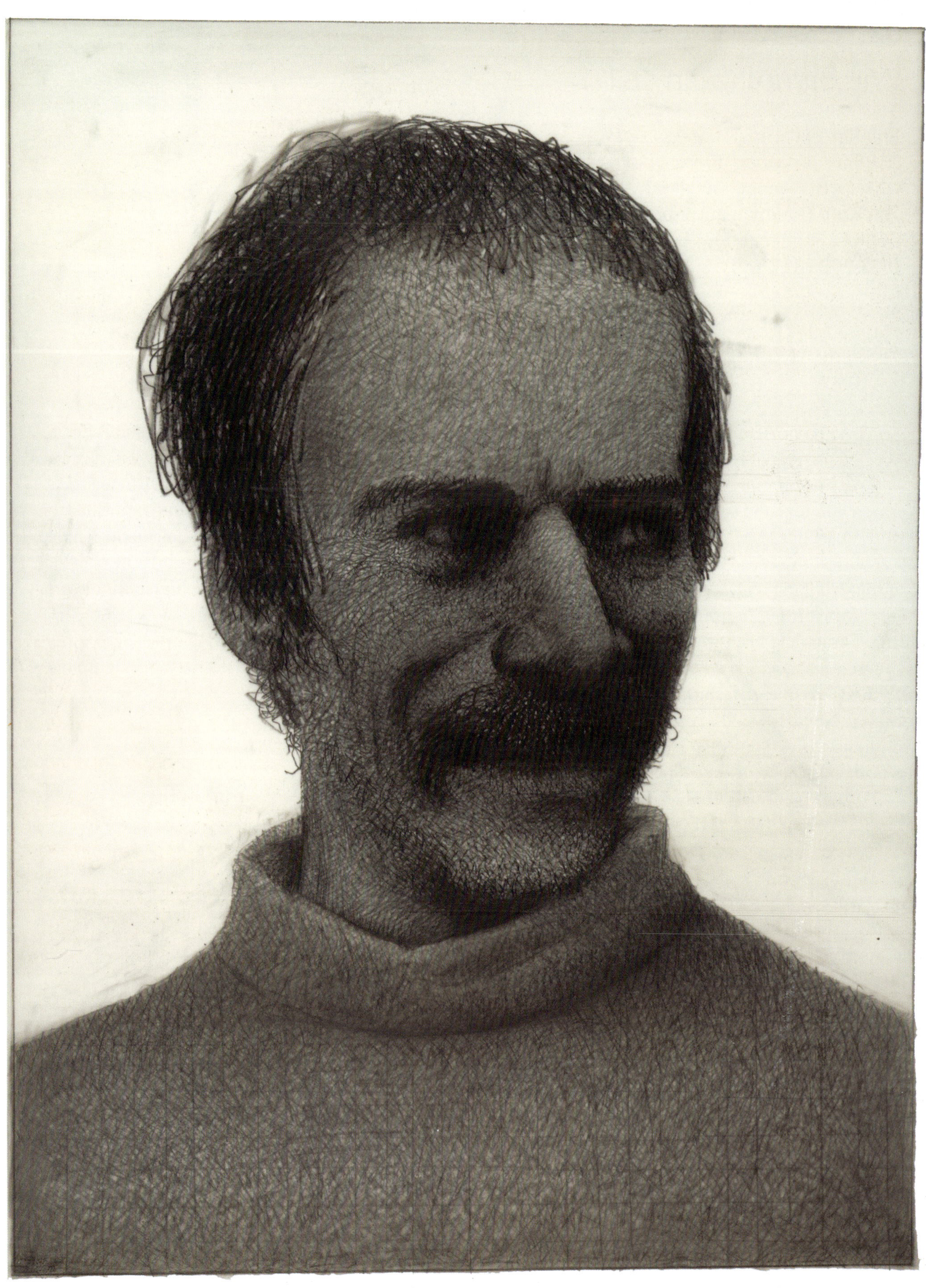

63.

Gregory Gillespie (1936–2000)

Graphite on frosted Mylar, 43.1 x 31.6 cm (16 15/16 x 12 7/16 in.), 1983–1984
The Ruth Bowman and Harry Kahn Twentieth-Century American Self-Portrait Collection
S/NPG.2002.252

"I AM MY OWN greatest model," Gillespie claimed. "I'm always available, I do exactly what I need to do—it's perfect."[1] Indeed, self-portraiture played a critical role in Gillespie's career. Gillespie's turn to the self, however, was not merely motivated by the artist's desire to hone his skills. Instead, through self-portraiture Gillespie provided himself with an opportunity to carry on an internal dialogue, to address the hopes, fears, and contradictions that shaped his outlook and his art: "That's how I see life. A crazy mixture of the astoundingly beautiful, the hilarious, and the horrifying—and every nuance in between."[2]

Raised in a Roman-Catholic household shaped by the mental illness of his mother and his father's alcoholism, Gillespie found in self-portraiture an arena in which he could come to terms with the aspirations and painful fears that assaulted him. Gillespie's translucent self-portrait, executed in graphite on Mylar, and intended to be exhibited with light passing through it, seems to invite a comparison to the stained-glass windows of Catholic churches. Gazing off to the side at an unseen source, Gillespie's expression radiates satisfaction.[3] The light that filters through the image intensifies the sense of spiritual fulfillment. The challenge of maintaining such harmony is conveyed by the work's very materiality: the heavily worked graphite in which he has executed the work is inherently fragile, perpetually threatening to disturb the artist's crisp marks. It is, indeed, this very tension that Gillespie courts through his self-portraits, which seek both to come to terms with and to transcend the human struggles and aspirations that inform them. As the artist explained: "It's almost as if, since there was so much chaos in my childhood, my job as an artist is to make it beautiful, to give back some order and stability, and to make a living from it. So my job is to turn the chaos and pain into art."[4]

ACG

Notes

1 Gerrit Henry, "Gregory Gillespie's Manic Masterpieces," *ARTnews* 85 (December 1986): 118.

2 Quoted in "An Interview with Gregory Gillespie: Questions from the Lenders to This Exhibition," in Forum Gallery, *Gregory Gillespie: Self-Portraits, 1969–1991: A Comprehensive Survey* (New York: Forum Gallery, 1992), unpaginated.

3 The work is related to *Smiling Self-Portrait*, 1983–1984, oil and alkyd on canvas on board, private collection, illustrated in Forum Gallery, *Gregory Gillespie.*

4 Quoted in Donald D. Keyes, "Interview with Gregory Gillespie," Belchertown, Massachusetts, January 9, 1999, in Keyes, *A Unique American Vision: Paintings by Gregory Gillespie* (Athens, GA: Georgia Museum of Art, University of Georgia, 1999), 54.

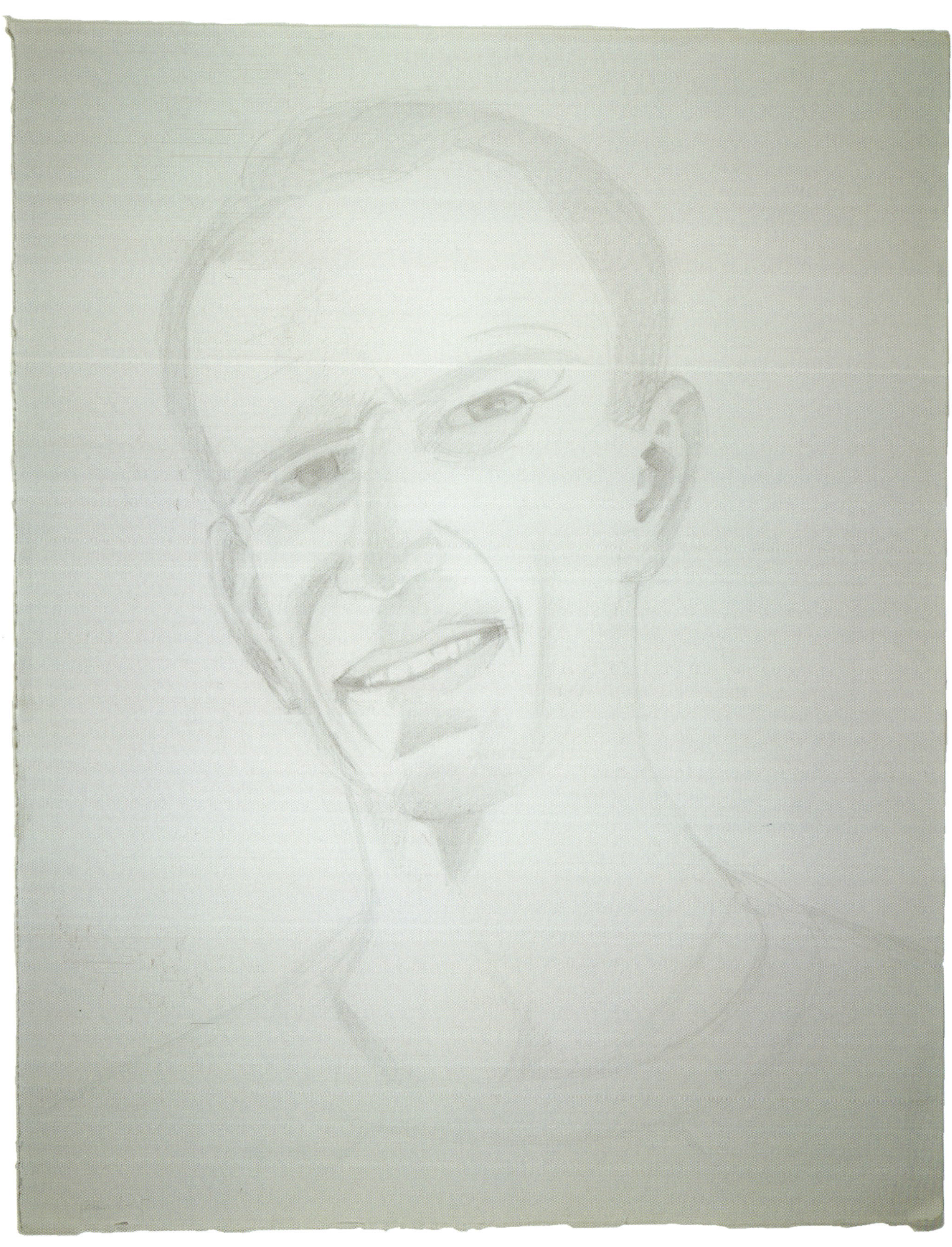

64.

Alex Katz (born 1927)

Graphite on paper, 62.8 x 49 cm
(24 3/4 x 19 5/16 in.), c. 1987
The Ruth Bowman and Harry Kahn Twentieth-Century American Self-Portrait Collection
NPG.2002.279

ALEX KATZ'S large but delicate graphite drawing is a sketch for a 1987 triple self-portrait in oil, *Sweatshirt III*. The grinning face of the drawing corresponds to the central bust of the painting, which is flanked by two similar but unsmiling images, all sporting the same red and gray sweatshirt.[1] Despite the smile, which normally reveals mood or emotion, Katz maintains the enigmatic detachment that has become a hallmark of his approach to portraiture.

Drawing, Katz told Mark Strand, was an important step toward making his large paintings. He made his drawings slowly, taking the time "to move a line that way, make a shadow darker, change my proportions, move the gesture around a little bit." He considers his drawings rehearsals that precede the faster "performance" of the painting.[2] The graphite drawing reveals the complex compositional planning behind his art. Here the tilt and turn of the head is carefully calculated, in contrast to the confrontational frontal images that flank it in the final painting. "Every line is questioned," he has said about his drawings, "and moved and altered and stuff like that."[3]

Katz had decided early in his career to concentrate on figurative work, despite being advised by older artists that traditional portraiture was obsolete. But he distanced himself from approaches that incorporated emotional, psychological, or biographical narrative. In his self-portrait, little is revealed by that guarded, enigmatic smile. The large scale and smooth, flattened style reveal his debt to billboard advertising, the movie close-up, and the media-obsessed culture of the era. "The look," he has insisted, "belongs to the time, it doesn't belong that much to the person."[4] Nonetheless, his faces, critic John Russell noted, "are never less than taut, and in his observation of human beings, he is the equal of Hercule Poirot."[5]

WWR

Notes

1 John W. Coffey, *Making Faces: Self-Portraits by Alex Katz* (Raleigh: North Carolina Museum of Art, 1990), 30–31.
2 Mark Strand, ed., *Art of the Real, Nine American Figurative Painters* (New York: Clarkson N. Potter, 1983), 129.
3 Alex Katz oral history interview by Paul Cummings, October 20, 1969, Archives of American Art.
4 Robert Enright, "The Years of Figuring Restlessly: An Interview with Alex Katz," *Border Crossings* 21 (August 2002): 60.
5 John Russell, "Art: Alex Katz's Works, Ever Nice, Never Empty," *New York Times*, March 11, 1983.

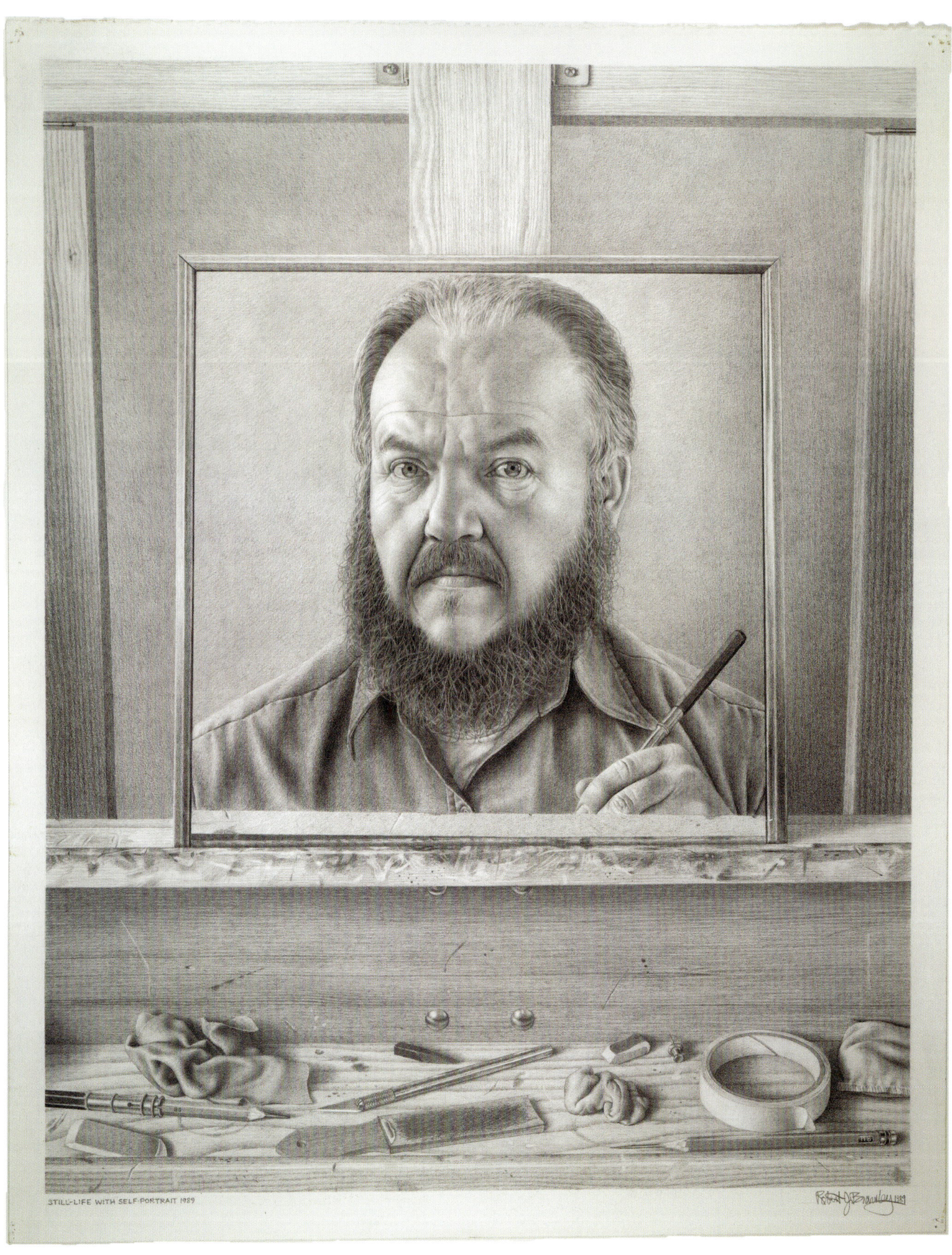
STILL-LIFE WITH SELF-PORTRAIT 1989

65.

Robert Julius Brawley (1937–2006)

Still-Life with Self-Portrait
Graphite on paper, 65.4 x 50.8 cm
(25¾ x 20 in.), 1989
The Ruth Bowman and Harry Kahn Twentieth-Century American Self-Portrait Collection
S/NPG.2002.370

ROBERT BRAWLEY'S intently focused eyes reflected in a mirror relentlessly attract the viewer's gaze, even while one remains keenly aware of the artist's hand at work. Eye and hand, vision and creation are the twin poles of this drawing.

Brawley placed the tools of his trade prominently in the foreground: a pencil, sandpaper for sharpening, erasers, and a knife. The tools evoke the weeks of labor Brawley put into such a drawing. The artist saw a "biographical" aspect in the image, "in the utilization of the tools and instruments of drawing."[1]

After his initial training in drawing from life, Brawley began his career as an abstract expressionist painter who rarely drew. By the time he began teaching at San Francisco's Lone Mountain College in 1971, Brawley was a realist who painted from photographs. When the school closed suddenly in 1978, the artist and his wife sold their belongings and traveled to Mexico, where Brawley began sketching local plants. This return to drawing from life led him to the close visual study seen in mature works like this drawing.[2]

While this drawing at first appears to be a simple record of the artist's reflection, easel, and tools, Brawley wrote that the work "was drawn from a mirror, but it was also 'composed' or organized around a formal idea . . . of forms . . . in a symmetrical arrangement."[3] He positioned every element, from the diagonal knife to the apparently random scratches on the easel, to bring attention to his hand and eyes.[4]

The work reveals the dichotomy between physical and mental processes. But ultimately Brawley felt that craft and comprehension merged, stating: " My own understanding of the image is developed and meshed with its creation. . . . I do not understand the image until it has evolved through . . . hands-on work."[5]

APW

Notes

1 Robert Julius Brawley letter to James M. Goode, May 26, 1990. A copy of the letter is in the Robert Julius Brawley vertical file in the National Portrait Gallery/Smithsonian American Art Museum library, Smithsonian Institution, Washington, D.C. This drawing, apparently once in Goode's collection, is probably the one discussed in this drawing.

2 "Robert Julius Brawley," *American Artist* 47 (August 1983): 42–43, 92–93. Brawley grew up in Moses Lake, Washington. His early art training at the University of Washington and Emma Frye Museum School in Seattle concentrated on drawing the figure from life. Later he moved to Los Angeles and attended the Otis Art Institute in the evenings. Finally he studied abstract art at the San Francisco Art Institute, receiving his BFA and MFA simultaneously in 1965. "Brawley," *American Artist*, 42.

3 Brawley letter to Goode, May 26, 1990.

4 The Smithsonian American Art Museum is one of the collections that owns a 1990 lithograph very similar to this drawing. In the later lithograph, the composition is more compressed and the objects on the easel are differently arranged.

5 Robert Julius Brawley artist's statement, website of the Manhattan art gallery OK Harris, okharris.com.

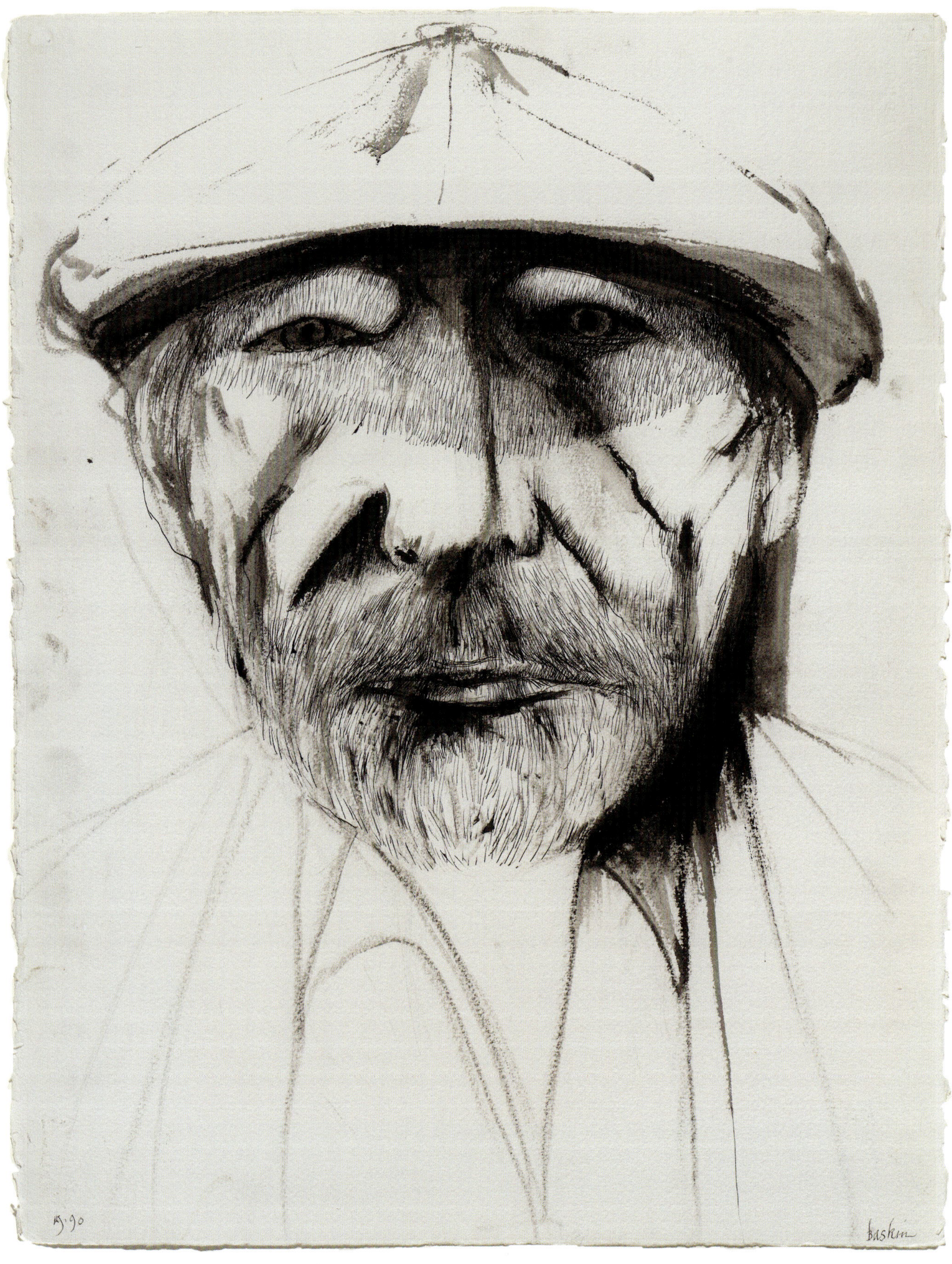

66.

Leonard Baskin (1922–2000)

Ink and ink wash on paper, 76.6 x 58.4 cm (30 3/16 x 23 in.), 1990
The Ruth Bowman and Harry Kahn Twentieth-Century American Self-Portrait Collection
NPG.2002.197

"MY EYES ARE my best feature," Leonard Baskin once commented. "They're hooded, like a cobra's. I tell people I've been pulling on the lids for years to make them look that way."[1] Cobra eyes, cast into shadow by the cap so frequently found in his self-portraits, feature prominently in Baskin's 1990 ink drawing. But the looming face does not match the tone of his humorous self-description.[2] The startlingly large scale and distortions of nose and cheeks obviate easy identification with the subject. Depicting a face or figure meant more to Baskin than likeness or self-appraisal. The study of humanity, including its cruelty, suffering, and heroic endurance, was Baskin's lifelong commitment. "Our human frame, our gutted mansion," he stated, ". . . is yet a glory. Glorious in defining our universal sodality and glorious in defining our utter uniqueness. The human figure is the image of all men and of one man."[3]

Renowned for his full-length figurative sculpture,[4] Baskin's accomplishments in the graphic arts were equally remarkable. As a draftsman, printmaker, illustrator, printer, and founder of the Gehenna Press, he celebrated the expression of ink on paper. Admitting his attraction to the "immediacy of purpose" that he found in the long tradition of popular printmaking, he described "seeing in its quintessential black and whiteness, the savagery of Goya, the melancholy of Dürer and the gentleness of Rembrandt."[5] His drawings reflect the same sensibility, and, as one art historian has argued, cannot be "disentangled" from his sculpture and printmaking.[6]

The powerful, unsettling effect of this self-portrait pervades Baskin's work. A brutal sort of beauty characterized many of his anguished figures (and the creatures that impersonate them).[7] Norman Geske, who included his work in a 1968 Venice Biennale exhibition on new approaches to figurative art, noted, "There is more than a touch of the prophet's thunder about Baskin."[8]

WWR

Notes

1 Leonard Baskin, *Life*, January 24, 1964, 42.
2 "Our age touts gigantism," Baskin states, "as though the colossal is axiomatic for the great: and I too draw on an immense scale. Leonard Baskin, *Baskin: Sculpture Drawings and Prints* (New York: George Braziller, 1970), 10.
3 Peter Selz, *New Images of Man* (New York: Museum of Modern Art, 1959), 35.
4 See Irma Jaffe, *The Sculptures of Leonard Baskin* (New York: Viking Press, 1980).
5 William S. Lieberman, "One Classic, One Newcomer: Feininger, Baskin," *ARTnews* 54 (May 1955): 31.
6 Winslow Ames, "Drawings," *Leonard Baskin* (Brunswick, ME: Bowdoin College Museum of Art, 1962), unpaginated.
7 The poet Ted Hughes described this quality as a "startling, sinister beauty . . . created so openly and directly out of pain." Alan Fern and Judith O'Sullivan, *The Complete Prints of Leonard Baskin: A Catalogue Raisonné, 1948–1983* (Boston: Little Brown, 1984), 14.
8 Norman Geske, *The Figurative Tradition in Recent American Art* (Washington, DC: Smithsonian Institution Press, 1968), 17.

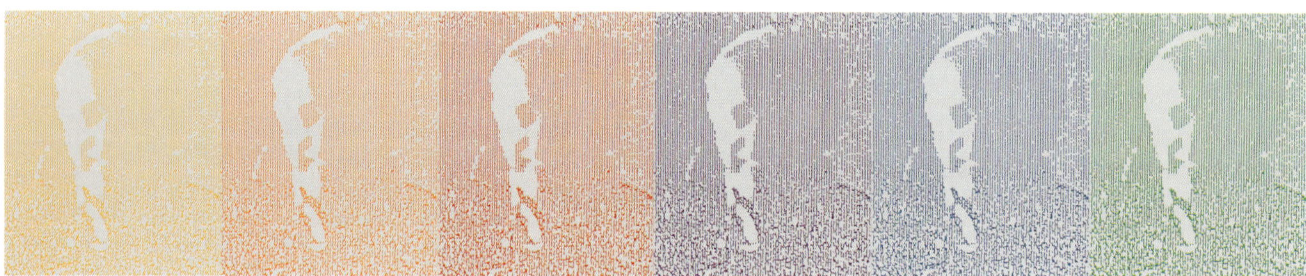

67.

Ellsworth Kelly (born 1923)

EK/Spectrum III
Color lithograph, 37.3 x 102 cm
($14^{11}/_{16}$ x $40^{3}/_{16}$ in.), 1990
The Ruth Bowman and Harry Kahn Twentieth-Century American Self-Portrait Collection
NPG.2002.280

KNOWN FOR HIS bold abstract compositions that often incorporate areas of pure color, Ellsworth Kelly might not immediately come to mind as an avid self-portraitist. Yet self-representation has played an important role in his career. The artist's early self-portraits reveal him experimenting with various artistic styles and grappling with the influence of such giants as Michelangelo, Picasso, and Matisse.[1] More mature self-depictions have enabled Kelly to hone his formidable skills as a draftsman and to negotiate the relationship between two- and three-dimensional form.[2]

Just as many of Kelly's color compositions carry within them echoes of forms observed in the natural world, so too does this self-portrait merge abstraction with representation. Indeed, the tension between these two poles is expressed through the work's title, *EK/Spectrum III*, which transforms a study of the self into a formal enterprise. Part of a series of similar works, the image of Kelly's face was captured with a Polaroid and then duplicated with a photocopier.[3] This process of flattening and further abstracting the artist's visage is enhanced by its systematic replication in primary and secondary colors, bringing to mind the artist's use of the spectrum in prints and paintings to explore optical effects. Along these lines, Kelly's description of his 1951 *Colors for a Large Wall* also applies to this self-representation: "There is neither form nor ground in the painting. The painting is the form and the wall is the ground . . . a work midway between painting and sculpture."[4] Here, likeness emerges through the structural application of pigment on paper. Rather than filling a decorative function, color becomes shape, a formal element that both literally and metaphorically represents the artist who is pictured, testifying not only to his appearance, but, even more important, to the concerns that have informed his work.

ACG

Notes

1 See Harry Cooper, "Kelly's Selvage," in *Ellsworth Kelly: Self-Portrait Drawings* (New York: Matthew Marks Gallery, 2003), unpaginated.

2 Discussing an early self-portrait by Kelly, Diane Waldman observes: "It is clear that Kelly's fundamental interest was not only in depiction but in restructuring or redefining the figure in relationship to the space that surrounds it." See Waldman, "Ellsworth Kelly" in Waldman, ed., *Ellsworth Kelly: A Retrospective* (New York: Guggenheim Museum, 1996), 15. Kelly has also noted that the experience of drawing from a model (or portrait subject) versus from one's reflection in a mirror is fundamentally different in terms of one's experience of space: a mirror reflection transforms three dimensions into two, and one views the reflected image of the self from a much closer distance than one views another person (see Cooper, "Kelly's Selvage"). The importance of portraiture as source of inspiration for Kelly is suggested by a recent view of the artist's studio that reveals a wide range of portraits and self-portraits pinned up on his wall (see Walman, *Ellsworth Kelly: A Retrospective*, divider page).

3 *EK/Spectrum III*, in Gemini G.E.L. Online Catalogue Raisonné, National Gallery of Art, Washington, DC, 2008.

4 Quoted in Nathalie Brunet, "Chronology, 1943–1954," in Yve-Alain Bois, Jack Cowart, and Alfred Pacquement, *Ellsworth Kelly: The Years in France, 1948–1954* (Washington, DC: National Gallery of Art, 1992), 192.

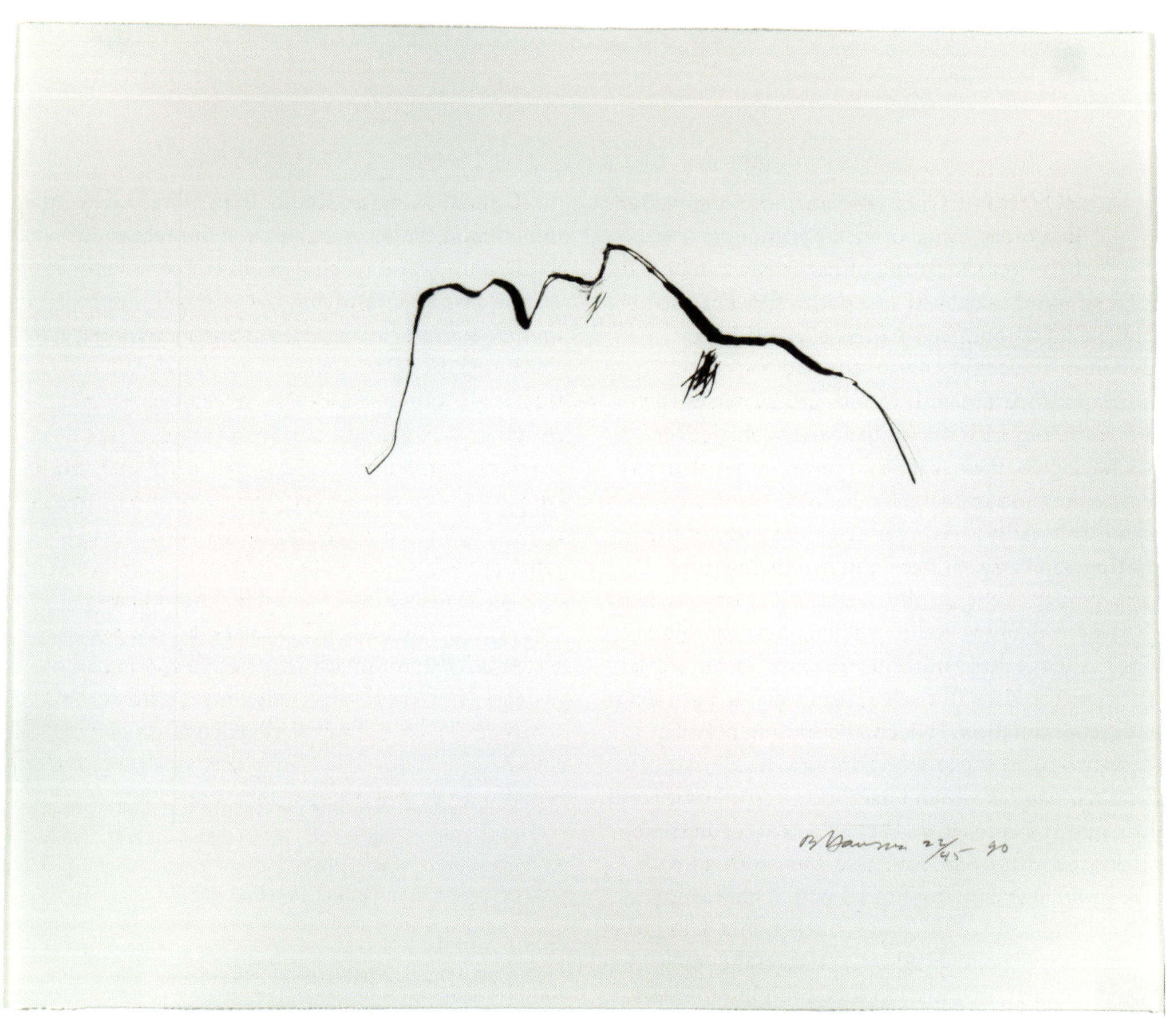

68.

Bruce Nauman (born 1941)

Drypoint, 42.7 x 49.3 cm (16 13/16 x 19 7/16 in.), 1990
The Ruth Bowman and Harry Kahn Twentieth-Century American Self-Portrait Collection
NPG.2002.306

A SOPHISTICATED ARTIST who has worked in a broad range of media, Bruce Nauman has, over the course of his career, consistently returned to his own body as a site of experimentation. Nauman's self-reflexive turn finds expression in this self-portrait of 1990. As is often the case with Nauman's work, this untitled self-portrayal subverts traditional expectations for the genre, functioning to distance the artist from the viewer rather than to foster a sense of comfortable engagement. Nauman's drypoint etching reflects the artist's interest in the front-back reversals inherent in printmaking, an effect similar to that of the molds with which he has worked to make sculpture. Yet here, it is not only a mirror reversal with which Nauman works, but also a shift of orientation. Rotated ninety degrees, the artist's profile hovers between a recognizable image and a fluctuating line—alternately thick and thin—that marks the page. Such vulnerability fits tightly with Nauman's vision of what art can do: "Art is interesting to me when it ceases to function as art—when what we know as painting stops being painting, or when printmaking ceases to be printmaking—whenever art doesn't read the way we are used to. In this manner, a good piece of art continues to function, revealing new meaning and remaining exciting for a long time, even though our vision of what art is supposed to be keeps changing."[1]

Operating, quite literally, at the boundaries of portrayal, Nauman creates a perceptual game of presence and absence reminiscent of Marcel Duchamp's 1957 *Self-Portrait in Profile*, an image that exploits negative rather than positive space. With this suggestive yet elusive outline of his features, Nauman teases the viewer. Whether sleeping, unconscious, or daydreaming, whether speaking or merely breathing, the artist, through his likeness, resists personal contact, even as he exposes himself. Ultimately, this may be the artist's most provocative gesture: that of deliberate withdrawal, even as he makes himself visible: "Not knowing what you're supposed to look at keeps you at a distance from the art while the art keeps you at a distance from me," reflects Nauman. "I think that's a very strong part of my work—giving you some information about myself by giving you a piece of art, but also not letting you get any closer to me."[2]

ACG

Notes

1 Christopher Cordes, "Talking with Bruce Nauman," in *Bruce Nauman Prints, 1970–89* (New York: Castelli Graphics and the Lorence-Monk Gallery; Chicago: Donald Young Gallery, 1989), 25.

2 Ibid., 24.

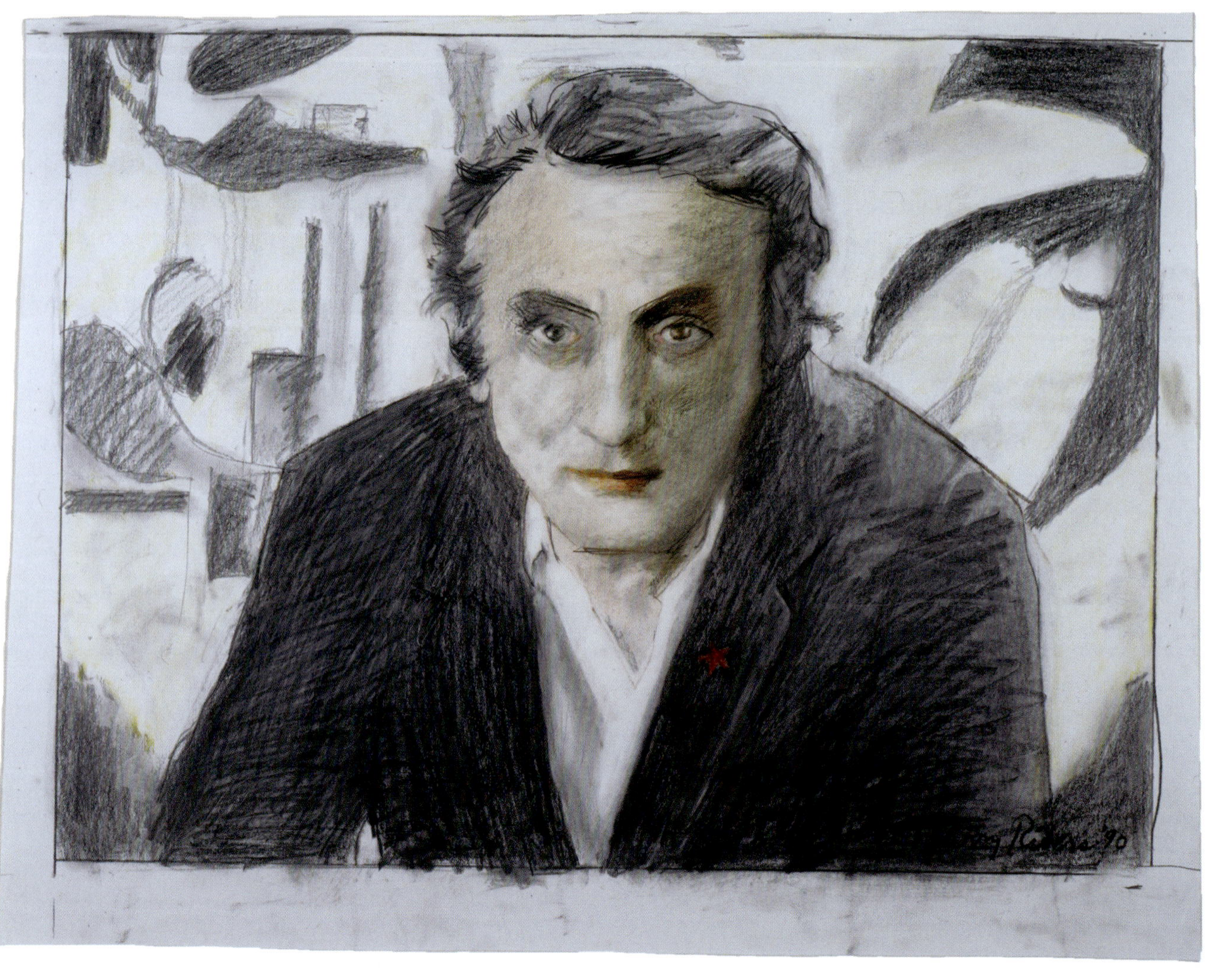

69.

Larry Rivers (1923–2002)

Self-Portrait with Star
Graphite and colored pencil on paper,
53.4 x 69.7 cm (21 x 27 7/16 in.), 1990
The Ruth Bowman and Harry Kahn Twentieth-Century American Self-Portrait Collection
NPG.2002.316

IN THE 1950s, when Larry Rivers realized he was "frantic to draw the figure,"[1] most of the avant-garde art world considered representation obsolete. But Rivers, as he later explained, was "cocky and angry enough to do something no one in the New York art world doubted was *disgusting*, *dead*, and *absurd*."[2] Trained as a jazz musician—a profession he never entirely abandoned—he took up painting with the encouragement of artist friends. Studying with Hans Hofmann, he learned abstract expressionist principals of composition but soon started to incorporate figures into his work in a provocative mix of gestural abstraction, blurred representation, words, and fragmented borrowings from other artists. Ever the nonconformist, Rivers frequently outraged his audience with his subject matter, variously referencing colonial, Jewish, or African American history, old master paintings, erotica, popular culture, and his personal life. While some suspected that he courted provocation for its own sake, scholars now understand his rebellious moves as truly innovative, profoundly influencing those returning to figurative styles.[3]

Rivers's subjects often came from his own orbit: friends, wives, lovers, children, and, not infrequently, himself. "The distance between his life and his art is minimal," one critic wrote, "each is a spectacle, something to see. . . . Performance is Rivers's true calling."[4] His 1990 *Self-Portrait with Star*, as Jacquelyn Serwer has recently discovered, was inspired by a photograph.[5] The photographer was peering at the artist through foreground plants whose leaves, silhouetted against the white canvas in the background, surrounded the head with abstract shapes and cast shadows around the studio. Rivers, assumedly intrigued with the pairing of straightforward representation and enigmatic abstraction, flattened the space and made the leaves and shadows unreadable. Odd touches of color, including a red lapel star implying leftist leanings, disquieting tones of yellow, and excessive redness in the eyes and lips, lend an intriguing, unsettling tone.

WWR

Notes

1 Frank O'Hara, "Larry Rivers: Why I Paint as I Do," *Art Chronicles, 1954–1966* (New York: Braziller, 1975), 110, quoted in Judith Stein, "Figuring Out the Fifties, *The Figurative Fifties: New York Figurative Expressionism* (Newport Beach, CA: Newport Harbor Art Museum, 1988), 41.

2 O'Hara, "Larry Rivers," 111–12.

3 Jacquelyn Days Serwer, "Larry Rivers and His 'Smorgasbord of the Recognizable'" in Barbara Rose and Jacquelyn Days Serwer, *Larry Rivers: Art and the Artist* (Boston: Little, Brown, 2002), 58.

4 Barbara A. MacAdam, "Still Raging Rivers," *ARTnews* 93 (November 1994): 148–50.

5 Serwer found the photographic image in an Italian exhibition catalog and generously shared her discovery; see Achille Bonito Oliva and Furio Colombo, *Larry Rivers, Mostra Personale* (Rome: Galleria D'arte Il Gabbiano, 1992), 51.

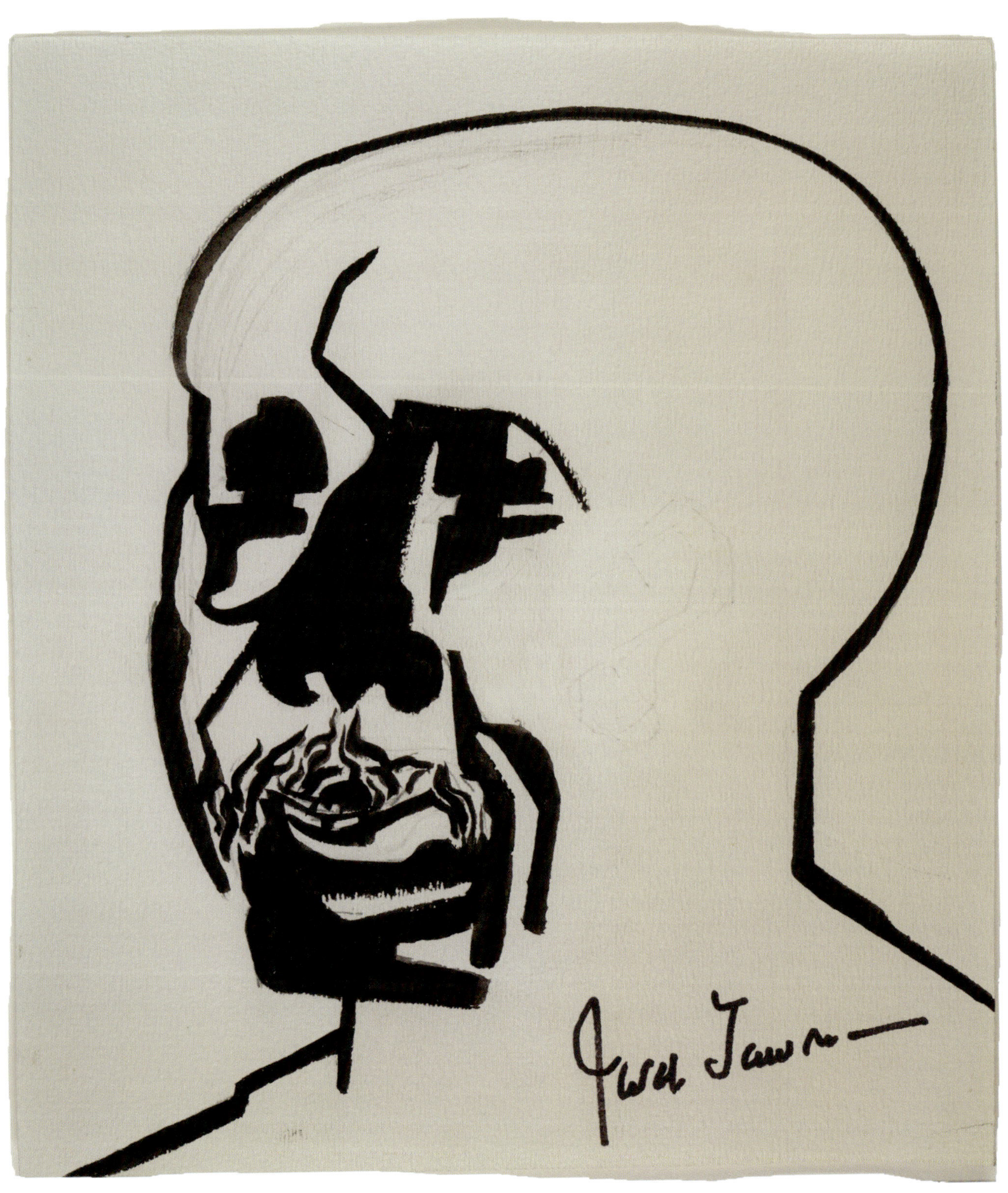

70.

Jacob Lawrence (1917–2000)

Ink over graphite on paper, 28.6 x 24.8 cm (11 1/4 x 9 3/4 in.), 1993
The Ruth Bowman and Harry Kahn Twentieth-Century American Self-Portrait Collection
NPG.2002.292

AS A CHILD in Harlem in the 1930s, Jacob Lawrence first encountered art at Utopia Children's House. At this settlement house he modeled fantastical papier-mâché masks based on African masks he saw in museums, and painted abstractions inspired by the colorful throw rugs in local homes.[1] This masklike self-portrait, like Lawrence's acclaimed paintings depicting African American life and history, maintains his early interest in creating dynamic patterns grounded in the visual life around him.

Lawrence treated his own face like any other subject—as the basis for the expressive abstract shapes on which he built his art. Lawrence concentrated his appearance into a few essential lines and shapes. A black arc describes the shape of his skull only thinly covered by hair. His shaggy mustache is a complex of wavy lines flanked by heavier curves evoking folds of aging flesh. Lawrence left most of his face white to set off the abstracted black shapes of his nose, eyes, mouth, and mustache. Faint pencil lines show the angular ear he considered including, but deleted to avoid visual confusion. Lawrence's observation was keen, but the reflection of the artist in this work is even clearer in his characteristic approach to art as pattern than it is in the record of physical features.

Lawrence used a geometric grid of black and white to signify his eyes and eyelids. For decades he had experimented with ways to indicate eyes; they often appeared as wide, frightened circles in Harlem scenes of the thirties and as anxious downward-pointing triangles in the fifties. In his paintings of Hiroshima bombing victims, Lawrence dramatized death with gaping eyeholes in bloody skulls. The black squares of the eyes in this drawing are more complex, restrained, and cryptic than his earlier visual formulas. Here he forces the viewer to confront his sophisticated abstract vision.[2]

APW

Notes

1 Lawrence's teacher at Utopia Children's House was Charles Alston. See Charles Alston oral history interview by Harlan Phillips, September 28, 1965, Archives of American Art, 5. For the masks and pattern sheets Lawrence made as a child, see Ellen Harkins Wheat, *Jacob Lawrence: American Painter* (Seattle: University of Washington Press, in association with the Seattle Art Museum, 1986), 29. For further details about Lawrence's life and art see Peter T. Nesbett and Michelle DuBois, eds., *Over the Line: The Art and Life of Jacob Lawrence* (Seattle and New York: University of Washington Press, in association with Jacob and Gwendolyn Lawrence Foundation, 2000).

2 This drawing first appeared in the *New Yorker*, where its strong black shapes make it stand out from columns of text. The magazine commissioned it to accompany a review of Lawrence's work at Midtown Payson Gallery. Peter T. Nesbett, Michelle DuBois, with assistance from Stephanie Ellis-Smith, *Jacob Lawrence: Paintings, Drawings, and Murals (1935–1999): A Catalogue Raisonné* (Seattle: University of Washington Press, in association with Jacob Lawrence Catalogue Raisonné Project, 2000), 274; *New Yorker*, December 27, 1993, 30.

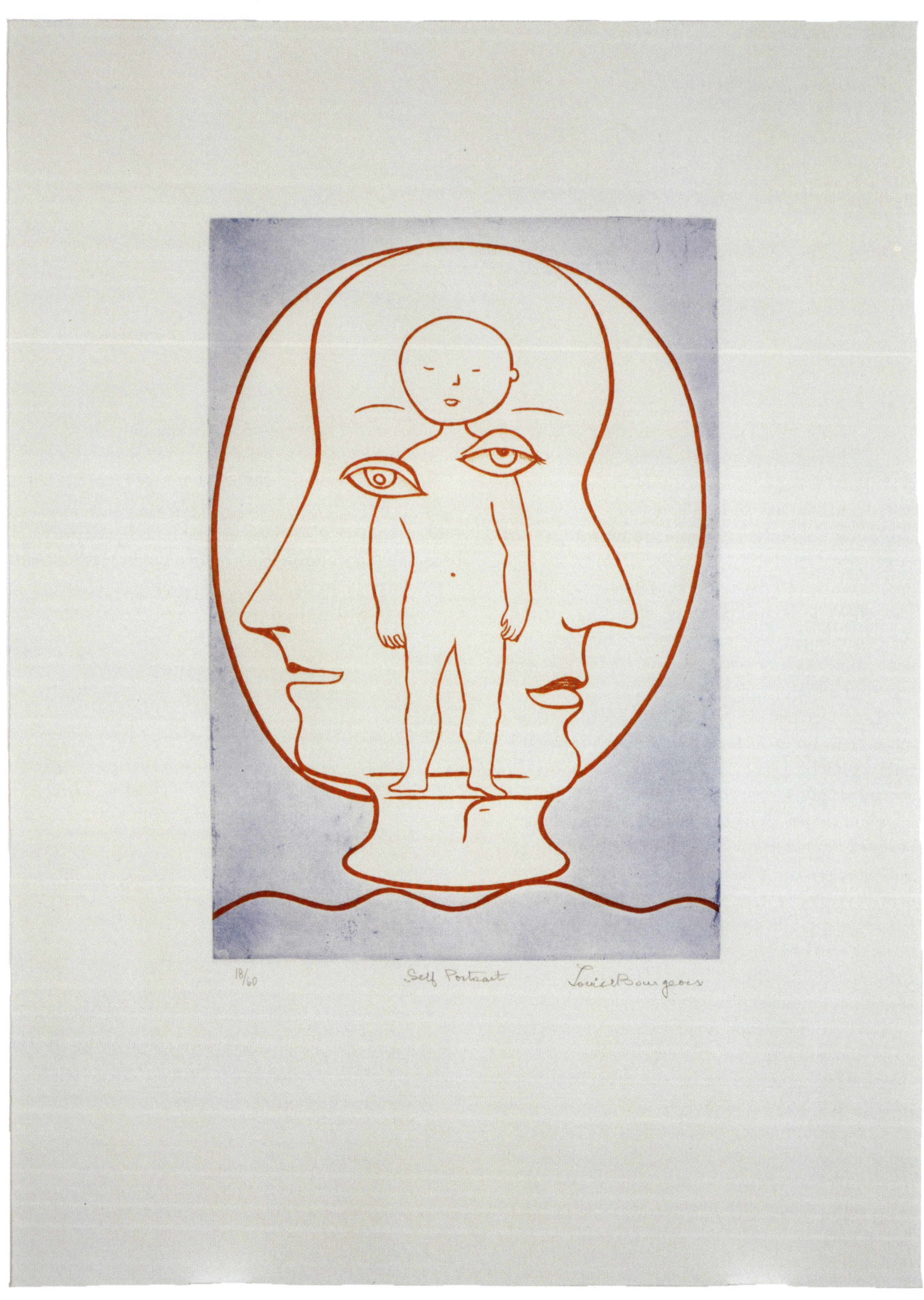
18/60
Self Portrait
Louise Bourgeois

71.

Louise Bourgeois (born 1911)

Drypoint and soft ground etching,
68.5 x 48.9 cm (26 15/16 x 19 1/4 in.), 1994
The Ruth Bowman and Harry Kahn Twentieth-Century American Self-Portrait Collection
NPG.2002.215

LOUISE BOURGEOIS'S etched self-portrait of 1994 expresses personal identity in terms that transcend the self.[1] Basing her composition on an untitled drawing of 1940, Bourgeois explains: "The strong figure on the right is the father, and the softer figure on the left is the mother. And there, in between, this creature appears. It is simply a self-portrait." Yet although Bourgeois's work often reflects the emotional toll of her childhood, this familial group generates a sense of well-being: "[My parents] seem to endorse me, for better or for worse."[2] While noting the work's autobiographical roots, Bourgeois enhanced its broader symbolic implications in transforming it into a print, inspired by the birth of a friend's daughter.[3]

Avoiding mimetic likeness, Bourgeois uses composition to describe the disparate forces that have shaped her. Fusion of the parental forms into a protective womblike vessel has special significance: "We are all vulnerable in some way, and we are all male-female," Bourgeois has commented.[4] Even more suggestive is Bourgeois's use of a Janus-style arrangement to convey "the . . . polarity we represent [between] violence and revolt . . . and a need for peace."[5] Color amplifies this dynamic. Describing blue as "my color," Bourgeois associates it with "freedom."[6] Red, by contrast, signifies "energy" that can verge into "pain . . . violence . . . danger."[7] Even the activity of etching reflects these competing tendencies. Directing a sharp tool across a plate, asserts Bourgeois, "[converts] something aggressive into something acceptable."[8]

Noteworthy, then, is the incision of a wave into this self-portrait. This line, absent from the original drawing, produces a suggestive analogy with Sandro Botticelli's *Birth of Venus*. As if inviting the comparison, Bourgeois observes: "You don't know if the little figure is a boy or a girl, but it is a little god, regardless."[9] Signifying the power of love to channel force productively, Bourgeois's self-portrait functions as a metaphor for creation itself.

ACG

Notes

1 This print, state VII of Louise Bourgeois's self-portrait, was published to benefit the Museum of Modern Art. See Deborah Wye, *The Prints of Louise Bourgeois* (New York: Museum of Modern Art, 1994), 186.

2 Louise Bourgeois with Lawrence Rinder, *Louise Bourgeois: Drawings and Observations* (Berkeley: University Art Museum and Pacific Film Archive, University of California, Berkeley; Boston: Bulfinch, 1996), 29.

3 Wye, *Prints of Louise Bourgeois*, 186.

4 Louise Bourgeois, "A Merging of Male and Female," first published in *New York*, February 11, 1974; republished in *Louise Bourgeois: Destruction of the Father/Reconstruction of the Father, Writings and Interviews, 1923–1997* (Cambridge, MA: MIT Press, in association with Violette Editions, London, 1998), 101.

5 Quoted in Wye, *Prints of Louise Bourgeois*, 75.

6 Bourgeois and Rinder, *Louise Bourgeois*, 48.

7 On red as "energy," see quotation in Wye, *Prints of Louise Bourgeois*, 186. On red as "pain . . . violence . . . danger," see quotation in Larry Qualls, "Louise Bourgeois: The Art of Memory," *Performing Arts Journal* 16, no. 3 (1994): 39.

8 Quoted in Wye, *Prints of Louise Bourgeois*, 23.

9 Quoted in ibid., 186.

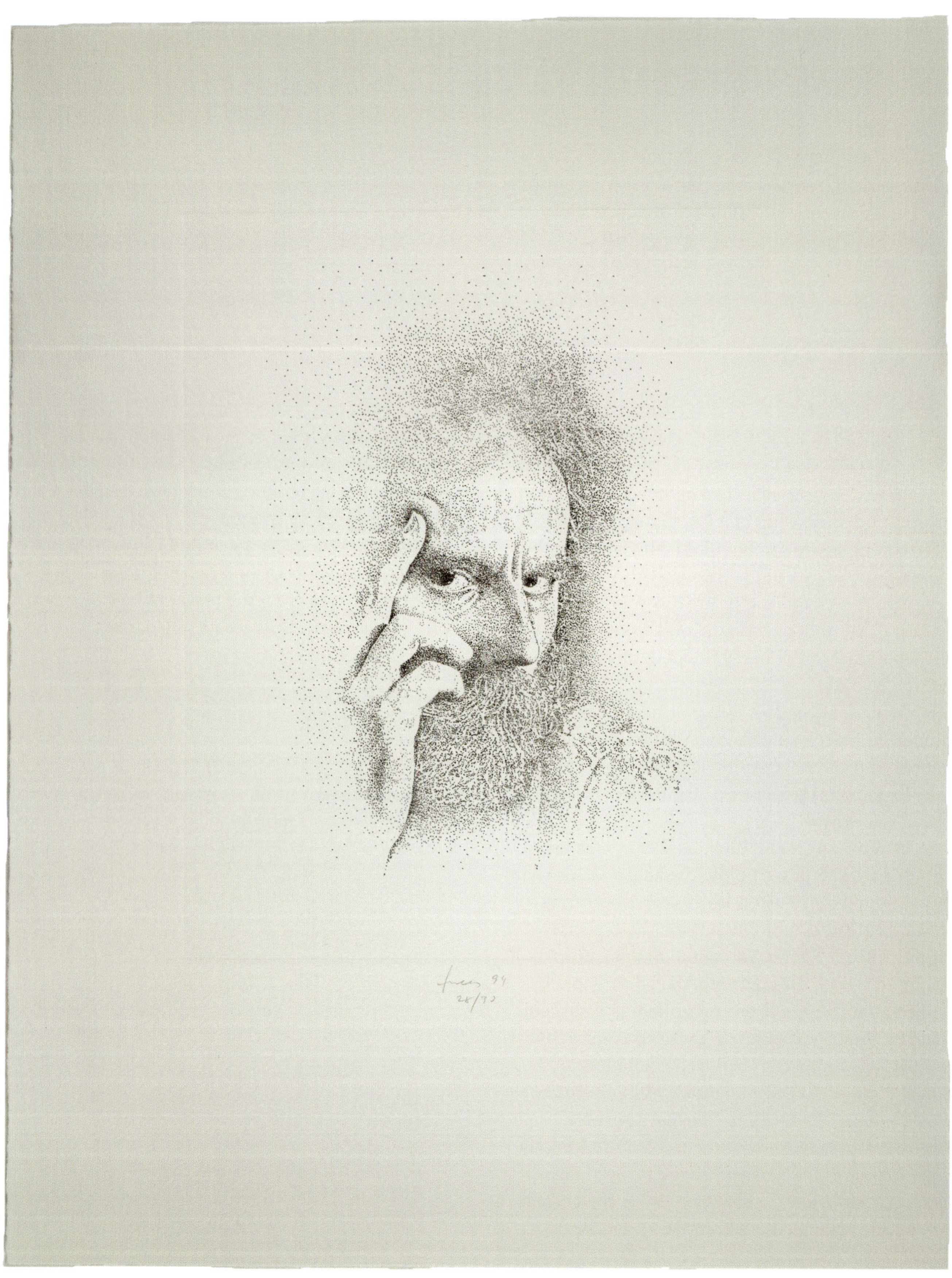

72.

Lucas Samaras (born 1936)

Published in *Self Portraits*, a portfolio of seven relief engravings
Relief engraving, 50.7 x 38.2 cm
(19 15/16 x 15 1/16 in.), 1994
The Ruth Bowman and Harry Kahn Twentieth-Century American Self-Portrait Collection
S/NPG.2002.319

"I HAVE FOUND for myself an uncultivated field, that uncultivated field is the self," Lucas Samaras has remarked. "For me, looking in the mirror produces a sense of wonder. I say, 'Who is that?' I look at my hand or rear-end and say, 'What is that?"[1] Well-known for his diverse and long-standing explorations of the field of self-portrayal, Samaras has arguably built a career around his depiction of the self, working in a diverse range of media including theater, writing, photography, film, sculpture, drawing, and printmaking. This 1994 relief engraving is part of a portfolio of seven images, based on drawings, depicting the artist in various guises and assuming different poses.[2]

Self-portraiture, while a rich realm of formal experimentation for Samaras, serves, even more importantly, as an arena for self-assertion and realization: "your work gives you life. . . . [I]t prevents you from being dead in a way," Samaras has remarked. Before turning in earnest to a career in visual art, Samaras explored theater, remarking in 1973: "Secretly I wanted to become a movie actor. I wanted to speak only with my body."[3] Intriguingly, in this self-portrait print, the artist uses his eyes to form an intense connection with his audience, while his mouth, covered by a thick beard, is rendered invisible. Language becomes emphatically pictorial.[4] Following this metaphor, one must attend to the portrait's strange composition. A host of small dots coalesce to form a likeness, but seem, simultaneously, to be on the point of dissolution. These picture elements—or pixels—promise yet another transformation and reformulation of the self—a self, perhaps, that is not only personal but also communal: "And so this body is my body and it is also my ancestors' body," notes Samaras. "It takes pictures and it is pictures. It has prettiness, ugliness and temporality and through it I exist in a heightened state among others."[5]

ACG

Notes

1 Quoted in John Greun, "The Apocalyptic Disguises of Lucas Samaras," *ARTnews* 75 (April 1976): 32. Quoted in Donald Kuspit, "The Aesthetics of Trauma," in Marla Prather, *Unrepentant Ego: The Self-Portraits of Lucas Samaras* (New York: Whitney Museum of American Art, 2003), 58 n. 2.

2 A group of related drawings, including that directly related to this print, is reproduced in Prather, *Unrepentant Ego*, 264–72; see esp. 267.

3 Lucas Samaras, "On the Film 'Self,'" *Opus International* 43 (April 1973): 27; quoted by Prather in chronology to *Unrepentant Ego*, 28.

4 Along these lines, it may be relevant that Samaras immigrated to the United States in 1948 at the age of eleven, knowing no English. As Prather points out, he immediately gravitated to art classes in school, where his lack of English was not a barrier (*Unrepentant Ego*, 16).

5 Lucas Samaras, "The Art of Portraiture, in the Words of Four New York Artists," *New York Times*, October 31, 1976, D29; quoted in Prather, *Unrepentant Ego*, 32.

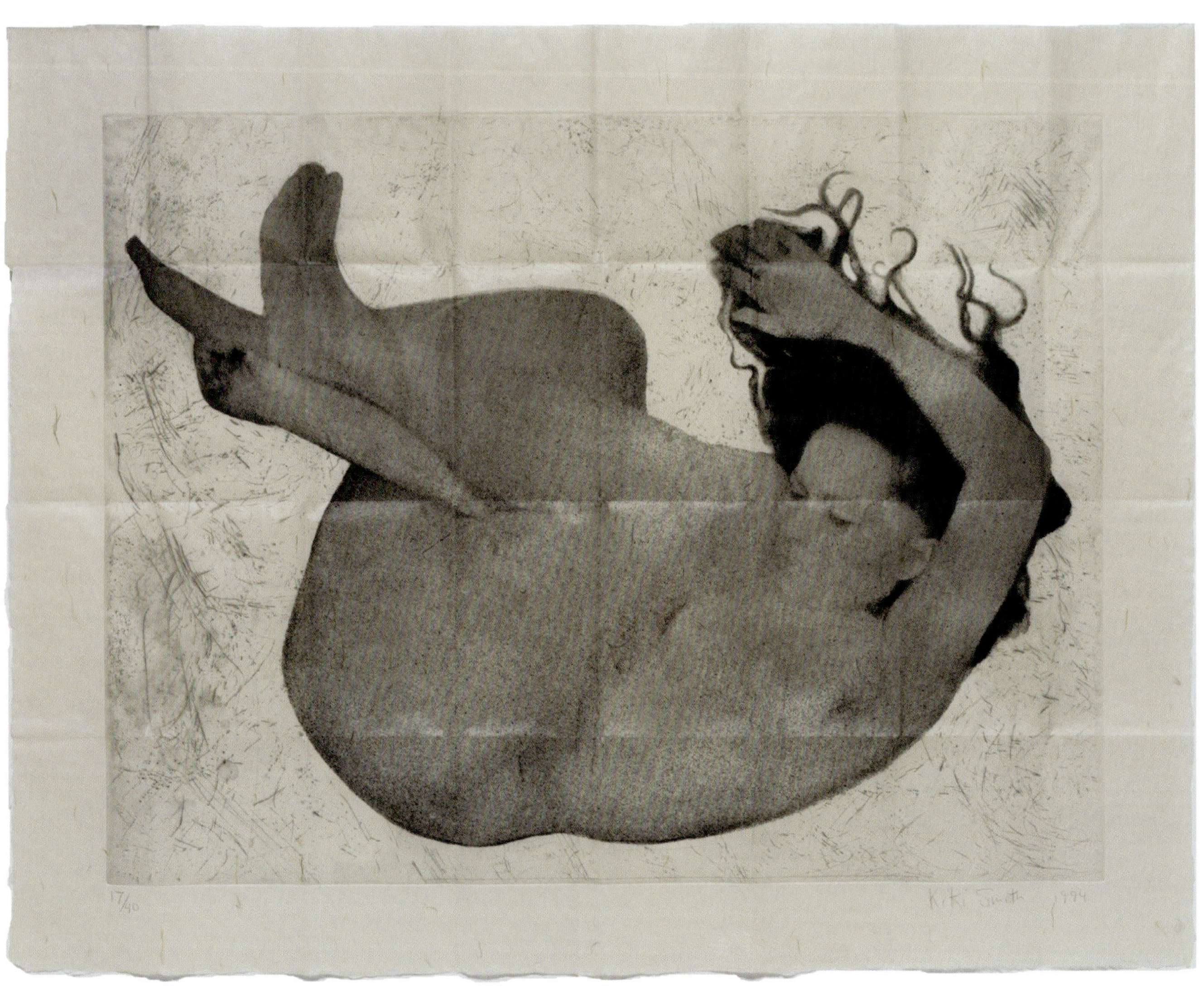

73.

Kiki Smith (born 1954)

Free Fall
Photogravure, etching, and drypoint,
84.5 x 106 cm (33¼ x 41¾ in.), 1994
The Ruth Bowman and Harry Kahn Twentieth-Century American Self-Portrait Collection
S/NPG.2002.334

CREATED IN 1994, Kiki Smith's *Free Fall* pictures the artist's own body. A gifted sculptor and printmaker, Smith has long focused on the human form, both as object and process. Extremely sensitive to her use of materials, she gives the medium of paper a sculptural quality, and the physicality of this object plays a key role in reinforcing its imagery. "Printmaking technique really changed the world," notes Smith. "I'm thinking in terms of deconstruction: so much contemporary art comes from what it means to put things together in a process, putting elements together to make a whole. Other kinds of art are not made in that layering way, where you can look at each layer separately."[1]

As is typical of Smith's work, process and form are interlinked in *Free Fall*. Based on a photograph, the image, a photogravure, delicately captures visual impressions of the artist's limbs, face, and hair. The texture of these surfaces, enhanced by the infrared film used by the photographer, was further accentuated by the artist's use of sandpaper to mark the plate.[2] As Wendy Weitman has pointed out, the print, which folds into and out of a small cardboard enclosure, similar to a book cover, seems to mimic the falling implied by the title.[3] Another metaphor seems to be operative as well: that of birth, a theme that the artist has approached on several occasions. In this sense, the cardboard housing functions as a sort of womb, nurturing and protecting the fetal-like image it contains. Pursuing this metaphor of nascent development and birth, the work evokes the "unfolding" of the creative process itself. As the artist remarks: "My career has stopped being linear. A couple of years ago, the story line or narrative fell apart. I had always said that I'd want to be in free fall; . . . I am in a kind of free fall now."[4]

ACG

Notes

1 Quoted in Christopher Lyon, "Free Fall: Kiki Smith on Her Art" (from an interview conducted April 4, 2005) in Helaine Posner, *Kiki Smith* (New York: Monacelli Press, 2005), 40.
2 Wendy Weitman, "Experiences with Printmaking," in *Kiki Smith: Prints, Books, and Things* (New York: Museum of Modern Art, 2003), 26.
3 Ibid., 26.
4 Quoted in Lyon, "Free Fall," 40. At the time the photograph on which *Free Fall* is based was made, Smith noted that the pose made reference to her experience as an artist. (Weitman, "Experiences with Printmaking," 26).

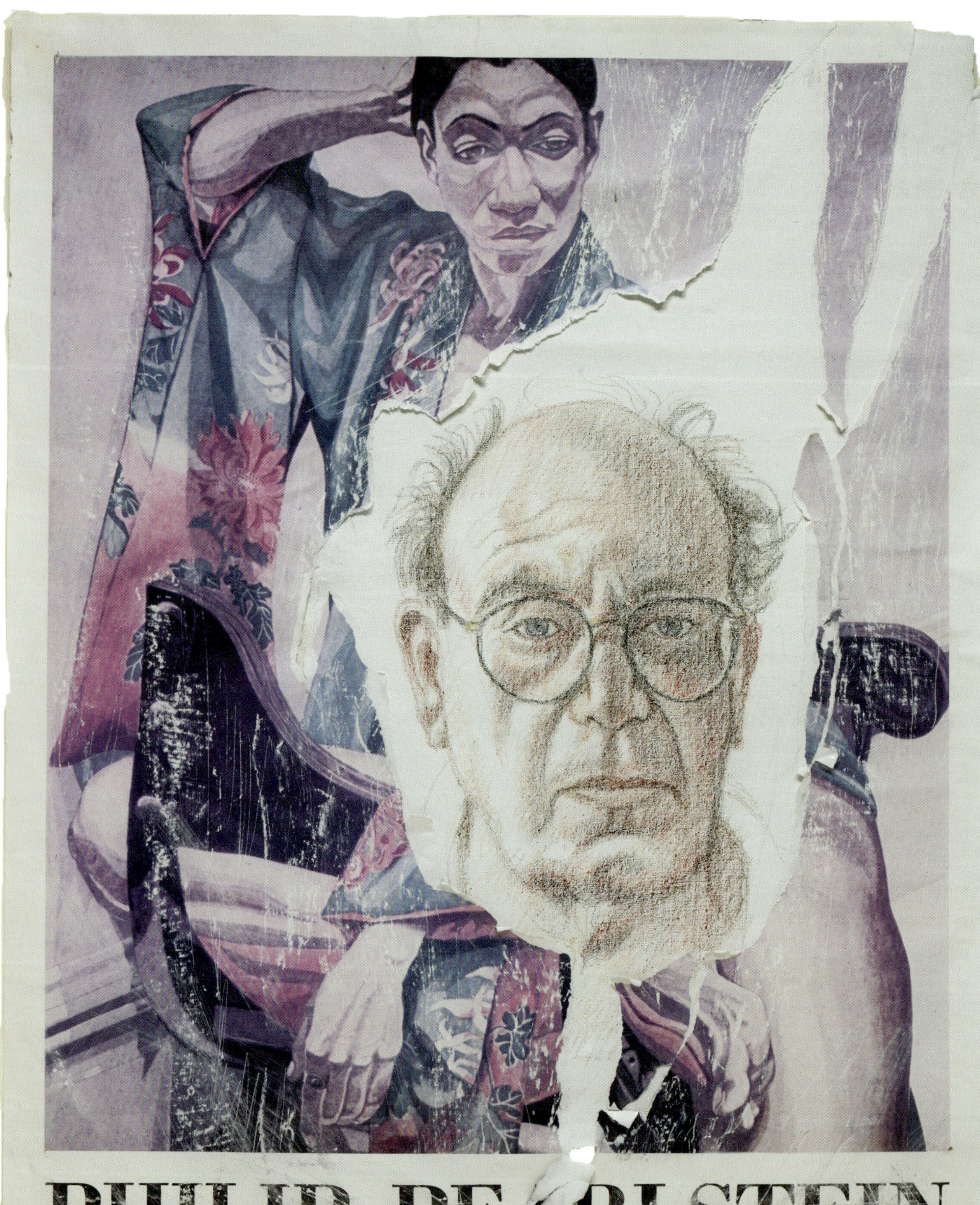

PHILIP PEARLSTEIN

ACQUARELLI - STAMPE 6 APRILE 1983

IL PONTE

Via S. Ignazio 6
Roma - 679.6114

74.

Philip Pearlstein (born 1924)

Collage with torn color poster and crayon on canvas, 100.3 x 70.4 cm (39 1/2 x 27 11/16 in.), 1996
The Ruth Bowman and Harry Kahn Twentieth-Century American Self-Portrait Collection
NPG.2002.311

IN HIS 1996 self-portrait, which layers a torn poster from a 1983 exhibition over a piece of canvas, Philip Pearlstein confronts us with issues of technique and representation that he has addressed over the course of his career. Fascinated by the tension between figuration and surface abstraction, Pearlstein, known primarily for his unconventional depictions of models from life, disrupts our expectations by juxtaposing a poster reproducing his aquatint *Model in Green Kimono on Savonarola Chair* (1979) with an image of his aging face.[1]

The work came about unexpectedly, as the artist was in the midst of preparing for an exhibition, when the poster "suffered the accident that gave it its character as a frame."[2] Playing with the torn paper, Pearlstein layered canvas behind it and rendered his likeness using Crayola crayons that he had recently received at a convention of elementary and high school art teachers.

Pearlstein's self-portrait differs from other self-representations in his artwork in offering an uninterrupted, nondistorted view of his face. As the artist has explained, several other works offer "partial" views of the artist—incidental glimpses of the top of his head or feet with the express intention "to show that my paintings are of models in my studio, without further meaning than that of artistic enterprise."[3] Resisting psychological interpretations of his artwork, Pearlstein portrays himself with an expression that echoes that of the model, whose image appears on the poster in the background. The poster's inscription, advertising an exhibition of Pearlstein's watercolors and prints in Rome, playfully provides a label identifying the likeness.

In a 1981 interview, Pearlstein observed that "my work has been getting more and more involved in dealing with the implied space between surfaces."[4] Eager to create work that is non-photographic in nature, he has spoken of his desire to "break the picture plane, to get the forms to look as though they exist with measurable distances from each other, and with a sense of air around them." In this work, such relationships are explored both literally and metaphorically, as work from the past recycles to the present, revealing the artist behind the art.

ACG

Notes

1 The aquatint was based on a watercolor of the same title in the collection of the Santa Barbara Museum of Art; it is reproduced in John Perreault, *Philip Pearlstein: Drawings and Watercolors* (New York: Harry N. Abrams, 1988), fig. 113. The creation of the print is discussed in Judith Goldman, "The Proof Is in the Process: Painters as Printmakers," *ARTnews* 80 (September 1981): 150, and in Richard S. Field, *Philip Pearlstein Prints, Drawings, Painting* (Middletown, CT: Davison Art Center, Center for the Arts Galleries, Wesleyan University, 1979), 27.

2 Unless otherwise noted, quotations come from Philip Pearlstein, "Self and Other Portraits: Painting Noses or Demons," talk delivered at the first Edgar P. Richardson symposium, National Portrait Gallery, Smithsonian Institution, November 19, 2003.

3 Most of these portrayals seem to be relatively recent. See, for example, Pearlstein, *Models with Two Mirrors and Fish* (1990) and *Two Models with Fan in Front* (2000). Both works are reproduced in Robert Storr, *Philip Pearlstein Since 1983* (New York: Harry N. Abrams, in association with Robert Miller Gallery, 2002); see 64–65 and 103, respectively.

4 Quoted in Sanford Sivitz Shaman, "An Interview with Philip Pearlstein," in *Art in America* 69 (September 1981): 124.

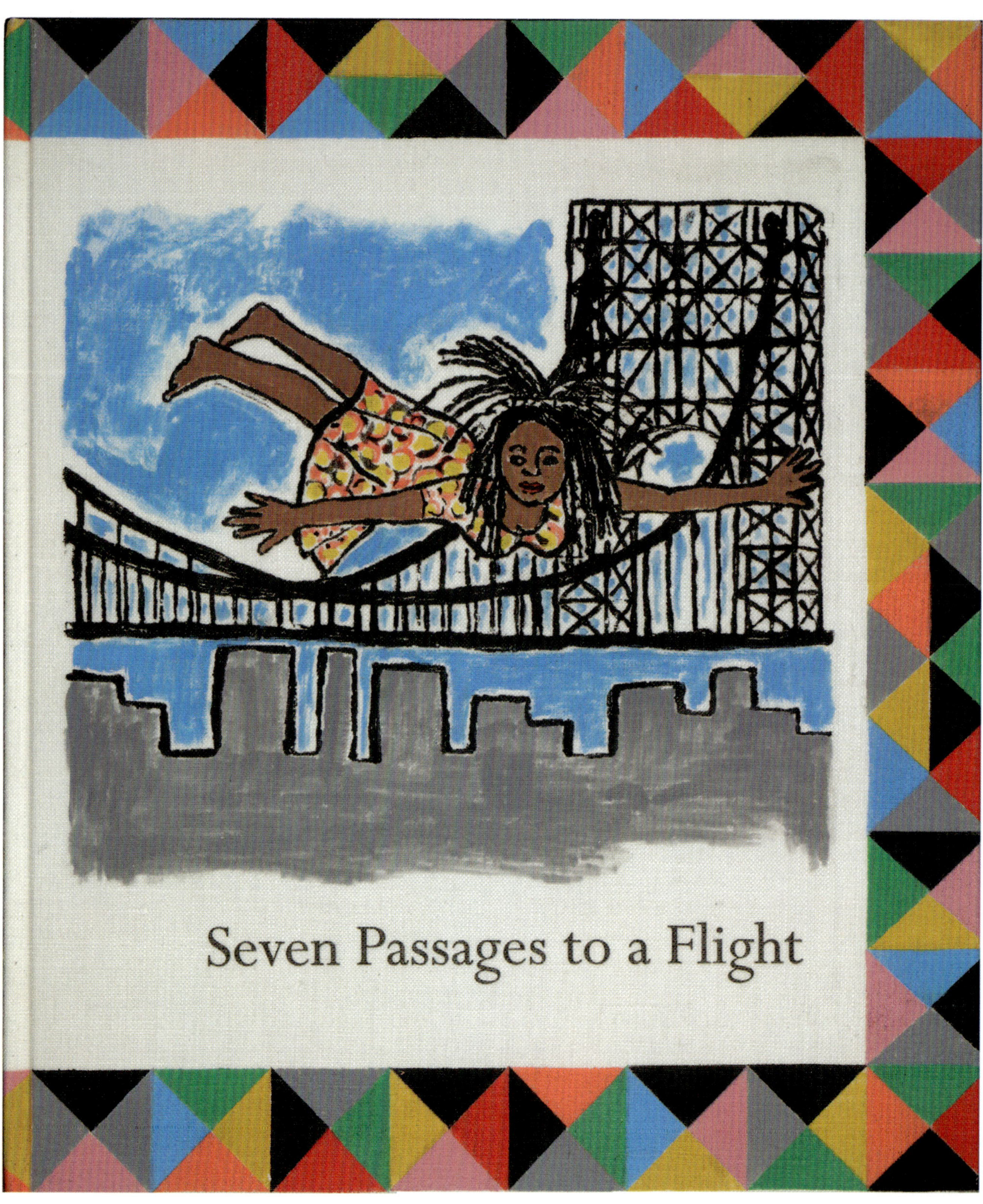
Seven Passages to a Flight

75.

Faith Ringgold (born 1930)

Seven Passages to a Flight
Book of hand-painted etchings and pochoir borders on linen, 24.2 x 39.4 x 2.1 cm (9½ x 15½ x 13/16 in.), 1998
NPG.2004.24

FAITH RINGGOLD based her artist's book, *Seven Passages to a Flight*, on memories of her Harlem childhood. A lifelong activist for racial and gender equality, Ringgold has received numerous honorary degrees for her advocacy, teaching, children's books, performance art, and innovative work with textiles and soft sculpture. This copy of *Seven Passages to a Flight* is one of a deluxe edition of ten that came with an accompanying quilt incorporating each of the images. Flight, for Ringgold, serves as a metaphor for overcoming the challenges that she encountered as a black woman. "Anyone can fly," she wrote in her award-winning children's book, *Tar Beach*, "all you need is somewhere to go you can't get to any other way."[1] From her own Harlem "tar beach" rooftop as a child, Ringgold could see the George Washington Bridge, which became for her a symbol of liberation and opportunity. Here, she depicts herself as a child flying over the bridge in one image; in another she is accompanied by her husband Burdette ("Birdie"). The imagery of flying, she has written, "is about achieving a seemingly impossible goal with no more guarantee of success than an avowed commitment to do it."[2]

Ringgold began her work with textiles in the 1970s, taking cues from "tankas," Tibetan paintings with fabric borders. For many years she collaborated with her mother, a fashion designer and talented seamstress, to produce dolls, masks, costumes, and soft sculptures. By the early 1980s, she was making her innovative story quilts, which were also inspired by African piecework and black American quilting traditions. A great-great grandmother had made quilts as a slave, and Ringgold's use of fabric reflects strongly felt feminist convictions and an appreciation for the legacy of "women's work." In discussing the "battle" against a white male-dominated art world, Ringgold has noted: "After I decided to be an artist, the first thing I had to believe was that I, a Black woman, could penetrate the art scene, and that, further, I could do so without sacrificing one iota of my blackness or my femaleness or my humanity."[3]

Ringgold's *Seven Passages to a Flight* explores the African American experience by incorporating historical faces and autobiographical memories in a process that combines fact, fantasy, and history. Some images merge her own childhood experiences into those of her two daughters. Another scene depicts the figures of Marian Anderson and Paul Robeson from the mosaic murals that Ringgold had made for the subway station at 125th Street in New York City. Entitled *Flying Home: Harlem Heroes and Heroines*, the murals were inspired by a song by Lionel Hampton. Although she has had to breach many

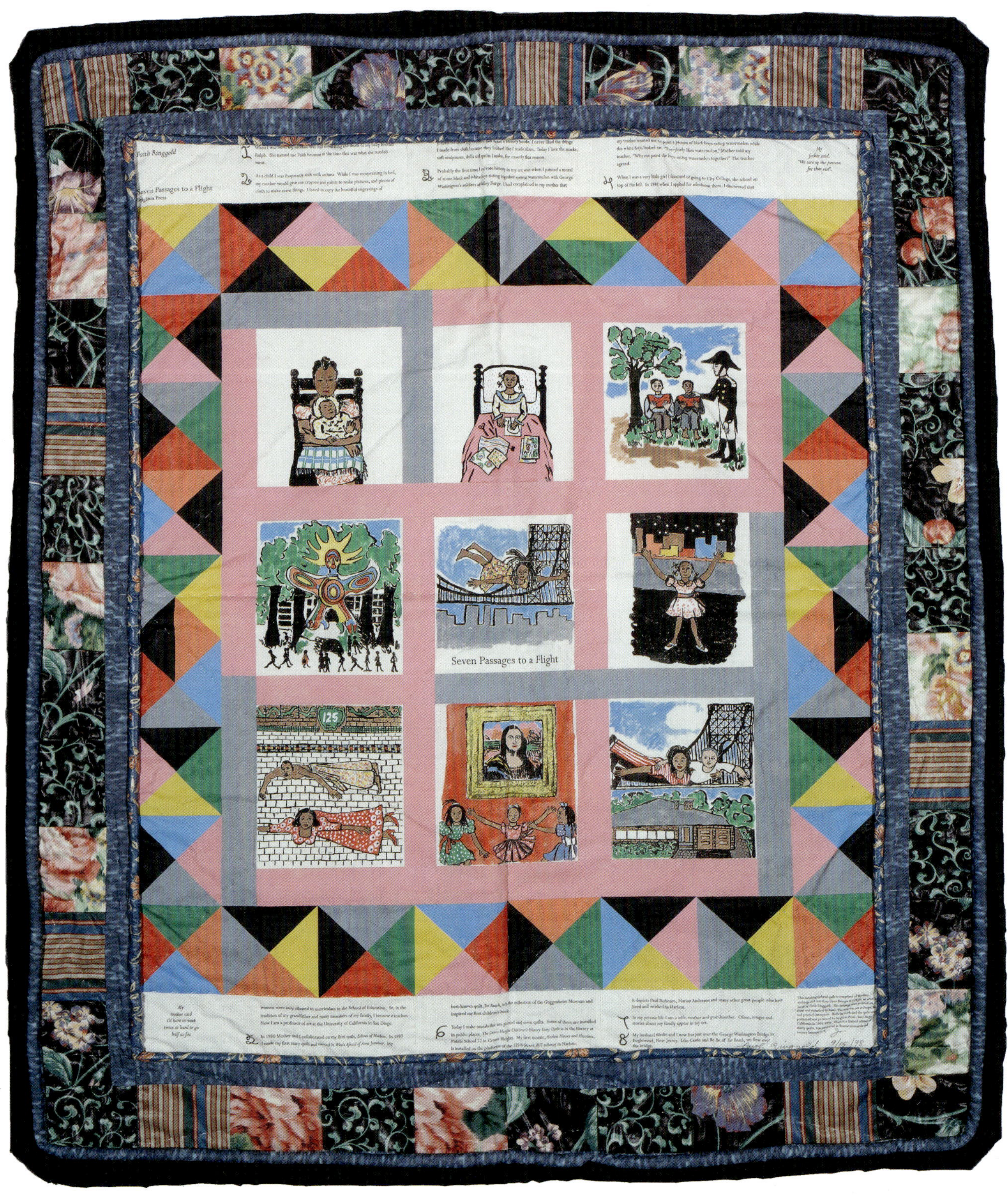
Faith Ringgold
Seven Passages to a Flight
125
Seven Passages to a Flight

76.
Faith Ringgold (born 1930)

Seven Passages to a Flight
Quilt with hand-painted etching and pochoir borders on linen, 128.4 x 109.3 cm
(50 9/16 x 43 1/16 in.), 1998
NPG.2004.25

barriers along the way, Ringgold insists that her career and her work are not about racism. The story of her life, she notes, is "about attainment, love of family, art, helping others, courage, values, dreams coming true."[4]

WWR

Notes

1 Faith Ringgold, *Tar Beach* (New York: Crown, 1991), unpaginated.
2 Faith Ringgold, *We Flew over the Bridge: Memoirs of Faith Ringgold* (New York: Bulfinch, 1995), 261.
3 Freida High Tesfagiorgis, "Afrofemcentrism and Its Fruition in the Art of Elizabeth Catlett and Faith Ringgold," *Sage* 4 (Spring 1987): 27.
4 Ringgold, *We Flew over the Bridge*, 270.

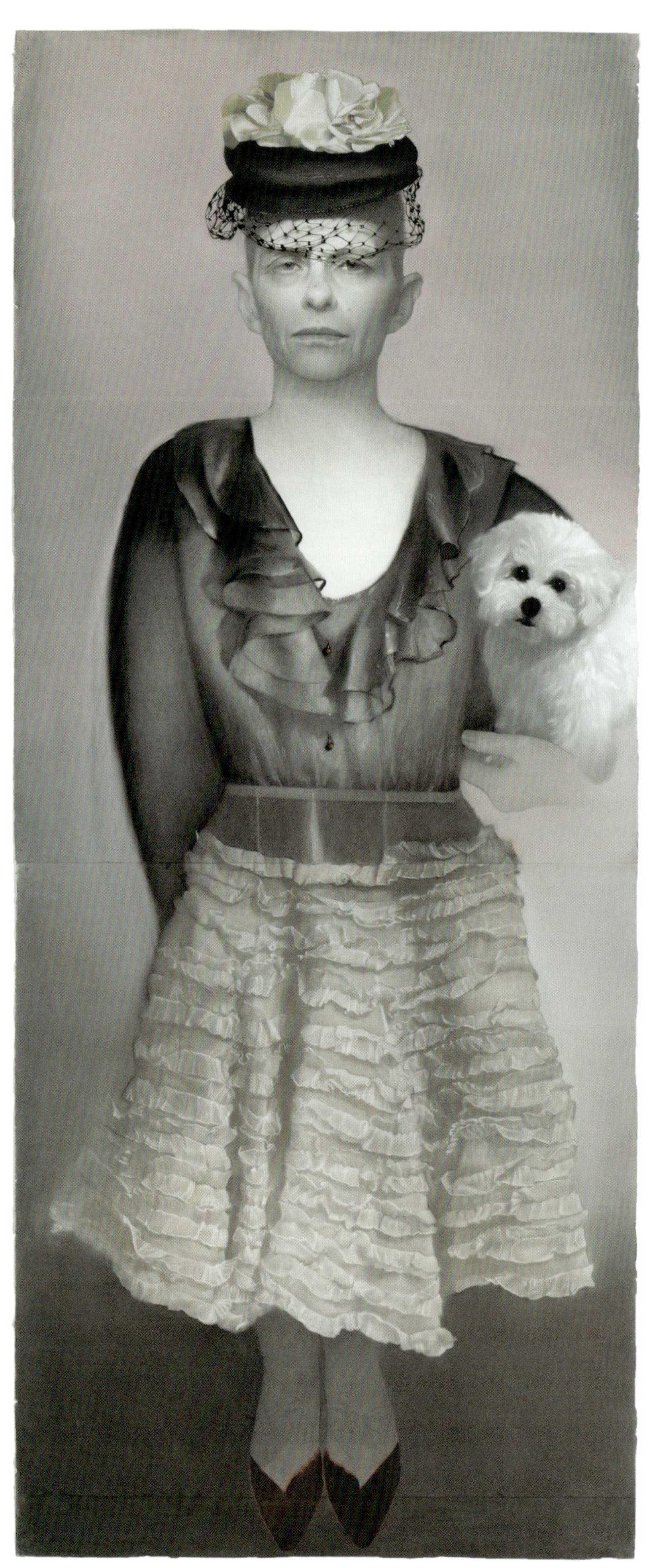

77.

Susan Hauptman (born 1947)

Copper Self-Portrait with Dog
Pastel with copper leaf on paper, 250.8 x 103.8 cm ($98^{3}/_{4}$ x $40^{7}/_{8}$ in.), 2001
Gift of an anonymous donor
S/NPG.2006.108

LIKE SO MANY of Susan Hauptman's self-portrayals, *Copper Self-Portrait with Dog* appears purposefully disjointed. The hyperrealism of the ruffled skirt and the dog contrasts bizarrely with the folk-naive rendering of the feet and the mismatched proportions. Juxtaposing the ultra-feminine ruffles and flowers with a masculine, nearly hairless head creates a disturbing disparity. The whimsical costume, with its canine "accessory," appears comical at first glance, but the confrontational pose and serious expression deny laughter. Even Hauptman's beautiful, meticulous technique stands in stark contrast to rougher, seemingly unfinished portions of the drawing.

All of this disjunction forces us to look and think more deeply about Hauptman's concerns, a process that parallels the artist's own "quest," as writer Jamake Highwater, a former studio neighbor, called it. According to Highwater, Hauptman "stared into a brilliantly lighted, oblong mirror. She stood for hours in the glare of the spotlights. Sometimes she wore a funny, old-fashioned evening gown. Sometimes she was naked. In that mirror-image she went in search of herself."[1]

Hauptman's search for the self has been a constant in her work. This drawing was one of eight self-portraits and three still lifes prepared as a collective narrative for the Forum Gallery's second solo exhibition of her work in 2002.[2] Most of the portraits pair her unsmiling masculine face with flouncy-feminine costumes from the mid-twentieth century. Frequently, a dog, rendered with lifelike realism, serves as a sentient foil to the costume, which appears to take on an artificial life of its own at center stage. Hauptman draws upon self-portrait traditions of dressing up and masquerading, but she does not do so to impersonate others or to reinvent the self. The constant pairing and contrasting seems instead to be an exploration of dualities within herself that coexist with creative tension.

WWR

Notes

1 Jamake Highwater, "Artists Who Work All Night Long," *Christian Science Monitor*, September 14, 1988, 26.

2 Suzaan Boettger, *Susan Hauptman: Drawn from the Heart* (New York: Forum Gallery, 2002), unpaginated.

SELECTED BIBLIOGRAPHY

Bond, Anthony, and Joanna Woodall. *Self Portrait: Renaissance to Contemporary*. London: National Portrait Gallery, 2005.

Borzello, Frances. *Seeing Ourselves: Women's Self-Portraits*. New York: Harry N. Abrams, 1998.

Brilliant, Richard. *Portraiture*. Cambridge, MA: Harvard University Press, 1991.

Chadwick, Whitney, ed. *Mirror Images: Women, Surrealism, and Self-Representation*. Cambridge, MA: MIT Press, 1998.

Cohen, Joyce Tenneson, and Patricia Meyer Spacks. *In/Sights: Self-Portraits by Women*. Boston: David Godine, 1978.

Cox, Richard. *American Self-Portraits: An Exhibition of Original Prints*. New Orleans, LA: Tahir Gallery, 1981.

DeSalvo, Donna. *Face Value: American Portraits*. Southampton, NY: Parrish Art Museum, 1995.

Dreishpoon, Douglas. *Artists Look at Themselves: The Collection of Dr. and Mrs. August L. Freundlich*. Tampa, FL: Tampa Museum of Art, 1996.

Elger, Dietmar. *Andy Warhol: Self-Portraits*. Ostfildern-Ruit: Hatje Cantz Verlag, 2004.

Engberg, Siri, and Madeleine Grynsztejn, eds. *Chuck Close: Self-Portraits, 1967–2005*. San Francisco and Minneapolis: San Francisco Museum of Modern Art and Walker Art Center, 2005.

Galligan, Gregory. "The Self-Portrait: Manet, the Mirror, and the Occupation of Realist Painting." *Art Bulletin* 80 (March 1998): 139–71.

Gamwell, Lynn, and Victoria Kogan. *Inside Out: Self Beyond Likeness*. Newport Beach, CA: Newport Harbor Art Museum, 1981.

Goldin, Amy. "The Post-Perceptual Portrait." *Art in America* 63 (January–February 1975): 79–82.

Goode, James. *Contemporary Self-Portraits from the James Goode Collection*. Washington, DC: National Portrait Gallery, 1993.

Gottlieb, Carla. "Self-Portraiture in Postmodern Art." *Sonderdruck aus dem Wallraf-Richartz-Jahrbuck*. Koln, Germany: Dumont Buchverlag, 1981.

Kelly, Sean, and Edward Lucie-Smith. *The Self-Portrait: A Modern View*. London: Sarema Press, 1987.

Koortbojian, Michael. *Themes in Art: Self-Portraits*. New York: Scala Books, 1991.

Kozloff, Max. *The Theatre of the Face: Portrait Photography Since 1900*. New York: Phaidon, 2007.

Lochridge, Katherine. *As We See Ourselves: Artists Self Portraits*. Huntington, NY: Heckscher Museum, 1979.

Lomas, David. "Inscribing Alterity: Transactions of Self and Other in Miro Self-Portraits." In *Portraiture*, Joanna Woodall, ed. Manchester: Manchester University Press, 1997, 167–86.

Maxwell, Douglas, et al. *Inside Out: Psychological Self-Portraiture*. Ridgefield, CT: Aldrich Museum of Contemporary Art, 1995.

McKinnon, E. Luanne. "Notes on the Gaze." In *Eye to Eye*. Winter Park, FL: The George D. and Harriet W. Cornell Fine Arts Museum, Rollins College, 2006.

Meskimmon, Marsha. *The Art of Reflection: Women Artists' Self-Portraiture in the Twentieth Century*. New York: Columbia University Press, 1996.

Moser, Joann. *Face to Face: Self-Portraits in the Museum Collection*. Iowa City: University of Iowa Museum of Art, 1979.

O'Conner, Francis V. "The Psychodynamics of the Frontal Self-Portrait." In *Psychoanalytic Perspectives on Art*, vol. 1. Mary Mathews Gedo, ed. Hillsdale, NJ: The Analytic Press, 1985, 169–221.

Quick, Michael, et al., *Artists by Themselves: Artists' Portraits from the National Gallery of Design*. New York: National Academy of Design, 1983.

Rebel, Ernst, and Norbert Wolf. *Self-Portraits*. Los Angeles: Taschen, 2008.

Rideal, Liz. *National Portrait Gallery Insights: Self-Portraits*. London: National Portrait Gallery, 2005.

Rideal, Liz, et al. *Mirror, Mirror: Self-Portraits by Women Artists*. London: National Portrait Gallery, 2001.

Rose, Barbara. "Self-Portraiture: Theme with a Thousand Faces." *Art in America* 63 (January–February 1975): 66–73.

Self-Evidence: Identity in Contemporary Art. Lincoln, MA: DeCordova Museum and Sculpture Park, 2004.

Smalls, James. "The African-American Self-Portrait: A Crisis in Identity and Modernity." *Art Criticism* 15 (2000): 21–45.

Sobel, Dean. *Identity Crisis: Self-Portraiture at the End of the Century*. Milwaukee, WI: Milwaukee Art Museum, 1997.

Sullivan, Terry. "Multiple Personalities: Self-Portraits in Series by Four Masters." *American Artist* 61 (September 1997): 31–41.

Sundell, Nina, et al. *The Sense of Self: From Self-Portraiture to Autobiography*. Washington, DC, and New York: Independent Curators, 1978.

Symmes, Marilyn. "Silent Scrutiny: Self-Portrait Prints." In *American Identities: Twentieth-Century Prints from the Nancy Gray Sherrill, Class of 1954, Collection*. Wellesley, MA: Davis Museum and Cultural Center, 2004.

Van Devanter, Ann, and Alfred V. Frankenstein. *American Self-Portraits, 1670–1973*. Washington, DC: International Exhibitions Foundation, 1974.

Varnedoe, Kirk. "Introduction." In *Modern Portraits: The Self and Others*. New York: Wildenstein Gallery, 1976.

Ward, David C. "An Artist's Self-Fashioning: The Forging of Charles Willson Peale." *Word and Image* 15 (April–June 1999): 107–27.

Weingrod, Carmi. "Up Close and Personal: Artists and Their Self-Portraits." *American Artist* 59 (February 1995): 14–17.

West, Shearer. "Self-Portraiture." In *Portraiture*. Oxford: Oxford University Press, 2004.

Wurster, Lisa. "Portraits of the Artist." *The Artist's Magazine* 23 (April 2006): 38–44.

Yaari, Monique. "Who/What Is the Subject? Representations of Self in Late Twentieth-Century French Art." *Word and Image* 16 (October–December 2000): 363–77.

Yablonsky, Linda. "To Thine Own Self Be True." *ARTnews* 102 (November 2003): 138–43.

Yard, Sally. *Images of the Self*. Amherst, MA: Hampshire College, 1979.

Yau, John. "The Phoenix of the Self." *Artforum* 27 (April 1989): 145–51.

IMAGE CREDITS

© 2009 The Josef and Anni Albers Foundation/Artists Rights Society (ARS), NY: cat. 7

© Ivan Albright: cat. 33

Art © Robert Arneson/Licensed by VAGA, New York, NY: fig. 3-7; cats. 54, 55

© 2008 Artists Rights Society (ARS), New York/ADAGP, Paris/Succession Marcel Duchamp: fig. 3-1

© 2009 Milton Avery Trust/Artists Rights Society (ARS), NY: cat. 24

Art © Will Barnet/Licensed by VAGA, New York, NY: fig. 1-1; cat. 62

© Leonard Baskin: cat. 66

© Jack Beal: cat. 51

© William Beckman, courtesy of Forum Gallery: cats. 52, 53

Art © Thomas Hart Benton/Licensed by VAGA/New York, NY: cat. 47

© Isabel Bishop Estate, courtesy DC Moore Gallery: cats. 14, 15

Art © Louise Bourgeois/Licensed by VAGA, New York, NY: cat. 71

© Paul Cadmus Estate: cat. 41

© 2009 Calder Foundation/Artists Rights Society (ARS), New York/ADAGP, Paris: cat. 38

© Vincent Canadè: cat. 13

Art © Minna Wright Citron/Licensed by VAGA, New York, NY: cat. 22

© Chuck Close, courtesy PaceWildenstein, NYC: figs. 2-6, 3–6; cat. 61

© Elaine de Kooning Trust: fig. 2-1; cat. 44

© Pele de Lappe: cats. 26, 27

Photograph © 1994 The Detroit Institute of Arts: fig. 3-4

© 2009 Jim Dine/Artists Rights Society (ARS), NY: cats. 39, 40

© Werner Drewes: cat. 58

Art © Fritz Eichenberg/Licensed by VAGA, New York, NY: cat. 57

Art © Antonio Frasconi/Licensed by VAGA, New York, NY: cat. 35

© Gregory Gillespie, courtesy of Forum Gallery: cat. 63

Art © George Grosz/Licensed by VAGA, New York, NY: cat. 8

© Philip Guston Estate: cat. 59

© Susan Hauptman, courtesy of Forum Gallery: cat. 77

© David Hockney: cats. 49, 50

© 2009 Renate, Hans, and Maria Hofmann Trust/Artists Rights Society (ARS), NY: cat. 30

Art © Jasper Johns/Licensed by VAGA, New York, NY: figs. 3-2, 3-3; cat. 46

Art © Alex Katz/Licensed by VAGA, New York, NY: cat. 64

© 2009 Jacob and Gwendolyn Lawrence Foundation, Seattle/ Artists Rights Society (ARS), NY: cat. 70

© Ellsworth Kelly: cat. 67

© Estate of Roy Lichtenstein: fig. 3-5

Image © The Metropolitan Museum of Art, New York City: fig. 1-1

Image courtesy of the Museum of Modern Art, New York, Kate Keller: fig. 3-8

© 2009 Bruce Nauman/Artists Rights Society (ARS), NY: cat. 68

© Estate of Alice Neel, 1980: fig. 2-7

© 2009 Estate of Louise Nevelson/Artists Rights Society (ARS), New York/ADAGP Paris: cat. 28

© Brian O'Doherty: fig. 2-3

© Philip Pearlstein: cat. 74

Art © Robert Rauschenberg/Licensed by VAGA, New York, NY: cat. 45

© Faith Ringgold 1998: cats. 75, 76

Art © Larry Rivers/Licensed by VAGA, New York, NY: cat. 69

Art © Estate of Theodore Roszak/Licensed by VAGA, New York, NY: cat. 19

© Lucas Samaras: cat. 72

© Kiki Smith, courtesy PaceWildenstein, New York: cat. 73

© Estate of Raphael Soyer, courtesy of Forum Gallery, New York: cats. 9, 10

© 2009 The Saul Steinberg Foundation/Artists Rights Society (ARS), NY: cat. 42

© Estate of John H. B. Storrs: cat. 6

© 2009 The Andy Warhol Foundation for the Visual Arts/ ARS, New York: fig. 3-4; cat. 43

Art © June Wayne/Licensed by VAGA, New York, NY: cat. 37

© Ruth Weisberg: cat. 56

Art © John Wilson/Licensed by VAGA, New York, NY: cats. 31, 32

Art © Grant Wood/Licensed by VAGA, New York, NY: cat. 29

All images from the National Portrait Gallery were taken by Mark Gulezian.

INDEX

Italicized page numbers refer to illustrations.